Philosophy and Religious Belief

GEORGE F. *inger* THOMAS

CHARLES SCRIBNER'S SONS, NEW YORK

To
My Colleagues
and
Graduate Students
at
Princeton University

Library of Congress Catalog Card Number 76-106534

Contents

Philosophy and Religious Belief

Introduction: *The Crisis of Belief*

This book is a sequel to my *Religious Philosophies of the West*. In that volume my approach to the philosophy of religion was historical and critical, and my aim was to show how the major problems and concepts arose and developed in philosophical thought beginning with Plato. In this book my purpose is not historical but *constructive*. I do not attempt to deal with the whole range of problems but discuss systematically some of the most fundamental ones, such as the nature and validity of religious experience, the existence and character of God, the problem of evil, the nature of man, and the relation of man's freedom to God's grace.

I have formulated my own views in *dialogue* with some of the thinkers who have stimulated my thinking. Their views are usually presented and examined at the beginning of each chapter, in order that I may make use of them, either to agree or to disagree, in developing my own. The consideration of what others have had to say about a problem may help the reader not only to understand better my own view but also to correct or supplement it by the insights of others. For philosophical thinking is dialectical, critically examining different views in the hope of arriving at a conclusion which will include the elements of truth in all of them.

My general point of view may be briefly suggested by referring to a few crucial issues. With respect to *method*, I believe that the philosopher of religion should not restrict himself to the analysis of religious language and concepts, but should also attempt to evaluate the truth and value of fundamental religious beliefs and to draw out their implications for a world view. This means that his purpose should be constructive as well as critical and therefore that he must take a stand on relevant metaphysical issues. To some contemporary philosophers this may condemn the book. But others may welcome an attempt,

vii

however imperfect, to arrive at conclusions on perennial issues concerning God, man, and their relation to one another.

With respect to religious *knowledge*, I believe that religious beliefs have arisen from the religious experience of mankind and that the function of reason is not to originate religious beliefs of its own but to clarify, critically examine, and evaluate the actual beliefs of religious men. In this sense, I am an empiricist rather than a rationalist. But I am also convinced that religious knowledge can be attained only by broadening the view of experience that has been held by most British and American empiricists and taking seriously the whole range of experience, including religious and moral experience. At the same time, I maintain that a philosophy of religion cannot be based exclusively on religious experience, as Schleiermacher and others attempted to do. For a critical examination by reason of beliefs that have arisen from religious experience is necessary to separate the truth from the error in them. Hence, rational argument has an indispensable role in the philosophy of religion, although it should never pretend to take the place of religious experience or to substitute a "religion of reason" for the actual religions of mankind.

One of the main purposes of the book is to analyze the nature and basis of *Western theism* which originated from the religious and moral experience of the ancient Hebrews and early Christians and has been formulated in conceptual terms by many philosophers down to our own time. I have also sought to examine critically the claim that Western theism provides the basis for a philosophy which is more nearly adequate than rival religious philosophies such as Western pantheism and Hindu monism as well as modern naturalism. However, I have tried to show that some traditional formulations of theistic conceptions of God, man, and their relation to one another are inconsistent with religious experience in its highest form and unacceptable to reason. For this reason, I have taken into account recent criticisms of these formulations and have attempted to restate the basic theistic beliefs in terms more consistent with modern experience and thought. There are also, of course, other theistic religions such as Islam, Bhakti Hinduism, and Amida Buddhism. I have discussed Bhakti Hinduism briefly in chapter 11, and it deserves more careful consideration than I am competent to give it. But I have preferred to concentrate on the fundamental beliefs of Western theism which are shared, I believe, by Jews and Christians despite the differences between them.

What is the *religious situation* to which this book attempts to speak?

Throughout the Western world contemporary men face a *crisis* of religious belief, a crisis which involves not only belief in God but also belief in man and in the meaning of life. There are many social as well as intellectual causes of this crisis. Among the latter the most obvious is the effect of *science,* especially the scientific method, on modern thought. Although new scientific theories such as the Darwinian theory of evolution have in the past led to a "conflict" of religion with science, a more important source of tension between them in our time is to be found in philosophical conclusions drawn from such theories by naturalistic thinkers, e.g., the view that man is only a complex animal whose mind is reducible to physiological processes.

But the major threat from science to religious belief today is the claim that the scientific method is the only dependable method of attaining truth in every field and that all other methods produce mere opinions which cannot be verified by others and hence are worthless. Since religious beliefs have not been developed and cannot be verified by the scientific method, this claim has led natural scientists such as Julian Huxley and philosophers such as John Dewey to reject belief in God as a survival of prescientific thinking. Many sociologists and psychologists also have made exclusive claims for the scientific method in their zeal to defend the scientific character of the modern study of social and psychological phenomena. Even in the humanities, scholarship and criticism have been deeply affected by scientism of this kind. As a result, the scientific method has been dominant in many of the major academic disciplines and a powerful force in others, and the thinking of educated men has been conditioned by it from their first years in school until the completion of their formal education. It is not surprising, therefore, that many in our scientific age find it difficult to accept religious beliefs and that some find the religious language used in church and synagogue completely meaningless. This causes them to dismiss men's religious experience as merely "subjective" and the beliefs that have arisen from it as only "projections" of the imagination reflecting the childish beliefs of a prescientific age.

Again, the tempo of technological change since the Second World War has been breathtaking and it has transformed not only our civilization but also our mental and spiritual attitudes. As a result, many persons in our society are almost exclusively interested in the acquisition of *technical knowledge and skills* and have little or no concern for humanistic studies and spiritual values. They are more interested in means than in ends, in technical know-how than in the purposes it should serve. Preoccupation with technology has also encouraged the tendency to master and exploit nature for human ends rather than wonder at its mystery and order, and this impersonal attitude has often been extended to man's relations with other persons. Moreover, a primary concern for technology has fostered the idea that all problems which confront men can be solved by the application of the right method and that there are no mysteries which cannot be solved but must simply be accepted. Whereas the solution of technical problems gives man a sense of power over his natural environment and tends to enhance his pride in his achievements, his confrontation of the mystery of love or God can awaken feelings of awe in him and make him aware of his dependence on forces beyond his control. But if he denies the reality of the mystery because he cannot fully comprehend it or bend it to his purposes, if he narrows his vision to the finite things he can understand and master, he loses his ability to believe in an infinite, spiritual reality which transcends the world of nature.

The dominance of the scientific method, the preoccupation with technology, and the enhancement of man's power by the application of both were major causes of the growth of religious skepticism in the nineteenth century. Their influence, along with other causes, has culminated in the twentieth century in a frank and often militant *atheism*. The success of the Communist revolution in Russia made atheism a part of the official ideology of a great European nation. Although atheism has probably not been as common in Western Europe and America as religious skepticism and indifference, there is no doubt that it is more widespread than it has ever been before. Moreover, the atheism of contemporary existentialists such as Sartre is more radical than that of atheists of the nineteenth century, many of whom sought to preserve a religious attitude of devotion by directing it towards human values and ethical ideals that were originally derived from Judaeo-Christian morality. Atheism is also to be found even among radical theologians who have spoken of the "absence of God," the "eclipse of God," or the "death of God." Although these phrases are sometimes used merely descriptively to refer to the fading out of the sense of God's presence and reality in our time, some of those who speak of the "death of God" really mean that He has ceased to exist for themselves as well as for others or at least that they can no longer believe in the God of theism.

The contemporary crisis of belief involves not only man's belief in God but also his belief in *man* himself. In the nineteenth century men were inspired by a vision of unlimited progress and had supreme confidence in their capacity to overcome all the evils from which mankind has suffered. In contrast, many in our time have lost their belief that man is truly rational and can be trusted to use the immense power he has acquired through science and technology for the good of humanity. Through their experience of two world wars, totalitarian dictatorships, and the threat of nuclear war, they have discovered the depths of folly and cruelty of which man is capable. Although most men continue to affirm an optimistic attitude towards man's possibilities, they are often assailed, at least subconsciously, by cynicism about human nature and dread of the future.

Man's loss of belief in himself also has intellectual sources. The last hundred years have produced a series of challenges to the traditional view of man as a rational and spiritual being. The naturalistic interpretation of the Darwinian theory of evolution seemed to deny the uniqueness of man and to affirm that he is merely more complex than his animal ancestors. Marxism subordinated the individual to his class. Anthropology showed how his beliefs and values are relative to his culture. Psychoanalysis emphasized the power of subconscious forces in determining his thinking and conduct. And behaviorism identified his mind with his publicly observable behavior and pictured his acts and attitudes as determined by social conditioning. As a result of these and other ideas, many have come to think of man as only one animal species among others and the ancient picture of him as made in the image of God no longer has meaning for them.

Finally, many men of today have lost their belief in the *meaning of life*. They have ceased to believe that the world is good, that they are under the care of a wise Providence, and that they can attain meaning in their lives by devotion to objective values and obedience to moral principles which have their source in the will of God. Rather, they have come to believe that values are merely subjective, objects of human desire or feeling, and that moral ideals are products of a particular culture and completely relative to it. Having lost their faith in a wider and deeper purpose, they can find no meaning in life beyond the satisfaction of their own desires and the achievement of success in the eyes of others. With no goal before them to which they give unconditional loyalty, they cannot rise above a narrow and self-centered existence and an uncritical conformity to the values of their group. Since man is a spiritual being who cannot find meaning in his life unless he can devote himself to some object of ultimate concern, it is not strange that so many in our time find their lives empty and meaningless and suffer such deep anxiety that they are plunged into despair.

Acknowledgments

I wish to express my gratitude to my former teachers in the Department of Philosophy at Yale and Harvard Universities, my former colleagues in the Department of Philosophy at Swarthmore and Dartmouth Colleges, and my colleagues of many years in the Department of Religion at Princeton University for the help they have given me in my thinking about the problems of religion. I am also indebted to many of my undergraduate and graduate students at Princeton University for helping me to deepen and clarify my understanding of the basic issues through discussion with them.

I wish to thank especially a number of friends who have read one or more chapters of the book and have made criticisms and suggestions which have assisted me in revising them: Philip Ashby, Malcolm Diamond, Gene Outka, John Reeder, and R. B. Y. Scott of the Department of Religion at Princeton University; Fred Berthold of the Department of Religion at Dartmouth College; Diogenes Allen of Princeton Theological Seminary; and Basil Mitchell of Oxford University.

Several of the chapters in an earlier form were originally offered as Haskell Lectures at Oberlin College and others at the Philadelphia Divinity School.

I am deeply indebted to Princeton University for several leaves of absence during which a large part of the book was written. The excellent libraries at Princeton University, Princeton Theological Seminary, and Dartmouth College have generously made their library facilities available to me. Mrs. Joel Nystrom and Mrs. Gerald Landry, the secretaries of the Department of Religion, have kindly typed most of the chapters for me, some of them more than once. My wife has helped me in ways too numerous to mention, reading the chapters and suggesting changes in style and substance, making the index, and, above all, bearing with me during the long and often painful process of writing.

1

The Philosophical Approach to Religion

Religion and Philosophy

Can philosophical reflection help us as we confront the contemporary crisis of belief? Many religious people, including some recent theologians, would deny that it can. They assert that religion does not depend upon philosophy either for its origins or for its justification. Indeed, some of them think that philosophical reflection is antithetical to religious faith and has a withering effect upon the religious life. Others, including some philosophers as well as theologians, believe that the philosophy of the recent past has made such a radical break with traditional philosophy that it can no longer contribute anything constructive to religious thought. What are we to think of these two views of the relation of religion and philosophy?

As to the first of them, the history of religion makes it clear that religion did not originate from philosophical speculation. Men experienced and responded to the holy or the sacred long before they attempted to conceive its nature clearly or felt the need to justify belief in it by rational argument. But the question raised by the present crisis of belief is whether, since scientific and philosophical criticisms have produced widespread skepticism and atheism, men can continue to believe or recover belief unless they are convinced that belief is justified. Although there have been other sources of unbelief such as modern preoccupation with technology, there can be no doubt that scientific and philosophical tendencies have greatly contributed to the crisis. Therefore, those who cannot accept or live by a blind faith have a right to inquire of the philosophy of religion what their attitude towards these tendencies should be.

1

The second view is primarily the result of the recent "revolution in philosophy" in Great Britain and the United States which is known as "analytical philosophy." Analytical philosophy has usually confined itself during the last generation to problems of language; most of the analysts have been indifferent to theological problems, and they have shown no interest in "transcendental" metaphysics. Also, the existentialism of continental Europe has been either atheistic or opposed to objective thinking as a ground of religious faith. Because of this divorce of recent Western philosophy from theology and metaphysics, our time is not favorable to the sort of alliance between philosophy and theology, reason and faith, which existed in the Middle Ages. But is it certain that Anglo-Saxon analytical philosophers will continue to neglect the perennial problems of theology and metaphysics, or that continental religious existentialists will never again seek to ground their religious commitment in metaphysics? The question can be answered only by the next generation of philosophers. But "revolutions" have occurred many times in the history of philosophy, and there is little reason to suppose that the recent "revolution in philosophy" has fixed the future course of Western philosophy for all time. Indeed, there are indications that the sharp divisions between analytical, existentialist, and more traditional philosophers are breaking down. If so, the time may be ripe for philosophical reflection, without apology, on the fundamental problems of religion.

At first sight, however, it may seem that religion and philosophy are so different in their nature and purpose that philosophy is bound to be exclusively critical in its attitude towards religion. Religion is primarily a *commitment of faith* and a *way of life* based upon it. In the opinion of many, it has nothing to do with the rational demand for an explanation of the world, and its sole purpose is to respond by worship and obedience to the revelation man has received from God. Thus, it is wholly practical, consisting of a descending movement of God to man followed by an ascending movement of man to God and the consequences of this double movement for man's life. As such, it has no interest in the theoretical questions about nature and man with which science and philosophy have always been concerned. In contrast, it is said, philosophy is solely a process of *critical inquiry* which accepts nothing on the authority of others, is critical of all claims to truth based upon revelation, and affirms nothing without subjecting it to close scrutiny by reason. It is aware of the human tendency to accept uncritically the opinions of others and the gulf there is between opinion and knowledge. Consequently, it demands the suspension of judgment until an opinion has been thoroughly investigated, and it insists upon a critical examination of even well- and long-established opinions. Thus, while religion is primarily an affirmation of faith in the Divine as it is encountered in experience and a commitment to it in worship and obedience, philosophy is a continuous process of critical inquiry into opinions which involves a suspension of judgment with respect to the truth of any and all of them.

Clearly, there is some truth in this view. For there is a basic difference in *aim* or *purpose* between religion and philosophy. The primary aim of philosophy is the attainment of knowledge for its own sake, while the primary aim of religion is a living relationship with that which is regarded as the ultimate source of meaning and value in life. In other terms, the primary aim of philosophy is theoretical, truth, while the primary aim of religion is fullness of life. Of course, the philosopher also has a secondary aim that is practical, the attainment of the good insofar as it depends upon knowledge of the truth; and the religious man has a secondary aim that is theoretical, knowledge of the truth in order that he may worship the true God rather than an idol. But clearly, the primary aim of the one is truth, of the other, life.

This difference between the aims of religion and philosophy accounts for the *tension* between them and for the difficulties which have often prevented fruitful dialogue between them. Philosophy demands that the mind engaged in critical inquiry keep itself open to new evidence and avoid premature commitment; religion insists that the mind affirm as real the Divine which has been experienced and that the self enter at once into a personal relationship with It or Him. William Temple has expressed the difference in a striking sentence: "The primary assurances of religion are the ultimate questions of philosophy." [1] For religion requires a confident affirmation of faith in the Divine if it is to attain the fullness of life it seeks, while philosophy requires a critical attitude towards every belief that is proposed to it in order to determine whether it is true or a mere opinion.

However, it is possible to exaggerate this difference. Religion at its best is deeply interested in the truth. It is not content to worship and serve any being who is less than the true God or to approve any conduct which falls short of what He truly demands. For example, the eighth-century Hebrew prophets denounced the Baals of the Canaanite fertility cults and the popular view that the way to please God was through animal sacrifice rather than justice and mercy. Similarly, the author of the Book of Job, confronted by the suffering of the righteous, rejected uncompromisingly the traditional theory that suffering was a punishment for wickedness. As a result of this kind of internal criticism

[1] Temple, William: *Nature, Man and God*, London, Macmillan, 1951, p. 35.

by honest and courageous men, the fundamental beliefs of Biblical theism were continually reformulated in the light of new understanding derived from experience. For a religious affirmation of faith does not require one to close one's mind to new truth nor is it necessarily opposed to critical examination of itself to determine how far it is confirmed by experience and reflection. On its side, philosophy does not require a permanent suspension of judgment. It employs the method of critical inquiry not to evade commitment to definite conclusions but only to prevent hasty and premature commitment.

It is true that in certain periods philosophy has been almost exclusively critical in its attitude and has neglected its constructive function, just as in certain periods religion has been too authoritarian to permit critical inquiry. Indeed, we have been living in a period in which many theologians have distrusted the appeal to experience and reflection and many philosophers have been so imbued with the skeptical spirit that they have seemed unable to affirm anything important, suspending judgment on ultimate issues to the point of paralyzing the capacity for commitment. However, this is not essential to the method and purpose of either religion or philosophy. The greatest theologians of the past have in different ways made use of philosophy and the greatest philosophers have developed constructive philosophies, although some of them have had, like Descartes, to pass through a period of radical doubt before doing so.

If this is the correct view of the relation between religion and philosophy, their differences warrant constant tension but not radical opposition between them. Moreover, the tension can be and often has been fruitful for both, since their differences in nature and purpose make it possible for them to complement one another. For example, philosophy can contribute to the health and development of religion by its clarification of religious concepts, its criticism of unworthy and irrational beliefs, its elimination of contradictions between beliefs, and its development of the implications of beliefs for conduct.[2] In addition, a highly developed religion such as Biblical theism makes affirmations concerning the nature of God, man's nature and destiny, the material world, and the meaning of history. Philosophical analysis is necessary to formulate these affirmations in conceptual terms and to show their implications for a world view, if they are to be clearly understood and are to provide a perspective upon experience as a whole. For religion in its most developed forms is similar to philosophy in that it is interested in the truth about the whole of reality.

[2] Thomas, G. F.: *Religious Philosophies of the West*, New York, Charles Scribner's Sons, 1965, pp. xiv–xvi.

Philosophy of Religion:
Its Nature and Conditions

We have spoken of the need for philosophy of religion and have shown how the interaction between philosophy and religion can be beneficial to religion. This brings us to the crucial question, what is the *nature* of the philosophy of religion? It must be confessed that there is in our time no agreement on the answer to this question. This is due in part to the fact that there are at present several radically different views as to the nature of philosophy, e.g. the views of traditional, analytical, and existentialist philosophers; in part to the fact that philosophy of religion is a hybrid discipline which combines two different forms of human activity and derives its method from the one, philosophy, and its data and problems from the other, religion. However, it is possible to say certain things about its nature and conditions.

(1) The first and most obvious is that philosophy of religion is a *branch of philosophy*. This implies that its purpose is to discover the truth about religion and that it is not to be identified with or subordinated to the defense of a particular religion. For philosophy of religion must be approached in an independent spirit if it is to be philosophy at all. This means that it should be based upon a critical examination of the relevant data rather than upon authority. Also, it requires that anyone who is to deal with the subject seriously must be prepared to submit himself to the discipline of philosophy. Ideally, he should have made a thorough study of the history of philosophy and be familiar with the major philosophical theories. It is not sufficient for him to know what Plato, Aquinas, Kant, and other philosophers thought about religion. Since their ideas concerning religion were deeply affected by their views on other subjects, it is necessary that he should know the philosophy of each as a whole, especially his metaphysical position and his theory of knowledge. He should also have acquired the habit of philosophical thinking, so that he may be able to think independently about the problems and not merely echo the opinions of philosophers he has read. Thus, he must not only have acquired sufficient knowledge of the major philosophical theories of the past and present; he must also be a philosopher himself.

(2) The second thing that may be said is that the philosophy of religion presupposes a knowledge of the *history of religions* and *religious thought*. The philosopher of religion cannot think broadly and critically about religion unless he has studied the major forms of religious experience and belief which have developed in the history of religions. The indifference of most philosophers and theologians to

the objective study of the history of religions, which has been developed by many patient and conscientious scholars in the nineteenth and twentieth centuries, was one of the causes of superficial thinking about religion in the last few generations. Reductionistic theories of religion such as that developed by Freud have been taken seriously by many readers because they have been too ignorant of the history of religions, including their own, to recognize the errors in such theories.

The Western philosopher of religion should have a special knowledge of the thought of the religions which have most deeply influenced Europe and America, i.e. Judaism and Christianity. If he has little understanding of the religions which have affected his own culture, he is not likely to understand religions of other cultures. Moreover, if he is to make a contribution to the religious thought of his own people, he must pay special attention to the beliefs and problems which have arisen in their major religious traditions. The use he should make of these beliefs and problems and the way he should deal with them we shall consider later.

(3) We come now to a third point which is more controversial. What should be the *attitude* of the philosopher of religion towards religion? Is it sufficient that he know *about* religious phenomena "from the outside," or should he have a *personal concern* for religion? In other words, should he approach religion as a detached spectator or should he be "existentially involved" in the questions with which he deals?

One's answer to these questions will depend, at least in part, upon his conception of the purpose of the philosophy of religion. If its purpose is merely to make a comprehensive investigation of the phenomena studied by the history of religion and to arrive at descriptive generalizations about the nature and forms of religion, a detached and objective method may be adequate. For this is essentially a scientific task for which the objective attitude of the spectator is appropriate, although one should also have "empathy" if he is to penetrate beneath the externals of a religion to its essence and spirit. But if the purpose of the philosophy of religion is not only to *describe* religious phenomena but also to *evaluate* the claims of religion to truth, the objective or detached attitude is quite inadequate. In other words, it can produce a science of, but never a philosophy of, religion.

To assume that the method by which religious truth is attained must be identical with the method by which scientific truth concerning natural phenomena is established would be justified only if the object of religious knowledge were of the same kind as the objects of scientific knowledge and the thinker's relation to it were the same. But the object of religious knowledge, as we shall see later, is not a finite thing or process in space and time. The universal testimony of the religious consciousness, as Otto has shown, is that the "Divine" or "Holy" is in some sense transcendent and other than the finite things and events of the natural world.[3] The method of determining the truth about the "Holy," therefore, must differ substantially from that of determining scientific truth. To deny this is to deny the distinctive character of the object of religion and to accept the view of naturalism that there is no transcendent reality and that "nature is all the reality there is." Furthermore, religion has always affirmed that the relation of a person to God must be more than intellectual if he is to attain knowledge of Him. It is recognized by all the higher religions that the sensuous, the worldly, and the cold-hearted cut themselves off from the presence of God. In contrast, the spiritual, the sensitive, the humble, the "pure in heart" are able to "see" God. Moreover, in religion willingness to acknowledge and respond to the truth one sees is a precondition for the discovery of new truth. In short, religious truth can be recognized only if the whole self is involved, feeling and will as well as reason.

If this is the case, creative work in the philosophy of religion requires not only a knowledge of philosophy and of the history of religions but also an *existential concern*. This does not mean that the philosopher of religion must be an adherent of a particular religion such as Judaism or Christianity. Significant contributions to the philosophy of religion have been made by "believers," "unbelievers," and others who would have regarded themselves simply as "inquirers" committed neither to belief nor to unbelief. But the philosopher of religion must at least take religious questions seriously in the sense of regarding the answers he gives to them as profoundly important for his own personal existence and not merely as a matter of theoretical interest.

The fact that many persons in intellectual circles maintain that the philosopher of religion needs to have only an "academic" interest in religion indicates the extent to which the scientific demand for objectivity is dominant in these circles. Such persons are firmly convinced that religious beliefs are always held merely on the basis of blind trust in authority and that it is impossible for a religious believer or even for one with an "ultimate concern" for religion to think critically about religious beliefs. They believe that an existential concern with religion, especially on the part of a religious believer, inevitably distorts the vision of the philosopher of religion and prevents him from approaching religious problems with an open mind. Curiously enough, the logic of this view is not applied to philosophical thinking in other fields such as art or politics. It is taken for granted that a philosopher

[3] Otto, Rudolf: *The Idea of the Holy*, tr. by J. W. Harvey, Oxford, Oxford University Press, 1923, Ch. V.

interested in aesthetics will have a personal concern with art and may have strong preferences among works of art, but it is not supposed that this will disqualify him from making aesthetic judgments about works of art or natural beauty. Similarly, the political philosopher is assumed to be personally interested in government and to have political convictions of his own, but it is not believed that this will prevent him from making sound political judgments. Indeed, personal concern or interest is normally assumed to be a necessary condition of significant aesthetic and political judgments.

Of course, everyone knows that a commitment to a particular theory of art or political ideology, if held in a dogmatic and fanatical manner, will blind one to the truth and value in rival theories. But this is usually attributed to the rigid way in which the commitment is maintained by the individual or to the incompatibility of a certain kind of commitment, e.g. to the Communist party, with independent thinking. Distortions of truth which result from either of these factors can best be overcome not by avoiding all commitment—even if that were possible—but by depending upon other thinkers with different commitments to correct them. However, this should warn us that there are religious commitments such as fundamentalism which do not admit that religious beliefs are open to question by reason and which are consequently incompatible with critical inquiry. This implies that the commitment of a philosopher of religion to a particular set of religious beliefs must be of such a kind as to permit and even encourage him to examine them critically and if necessary to revise them. For the philosopher of religion, whatever his personal views may be, must be prepared to open his mind to new truth and to follow wherever it leads him.

It must be admitted that this requirement creates a tension in the mind of a philosopher of religion who is committed to a particular set of religious beliefs, e.g. a Jew or a Christian. How can he maintain his faith and at the same time examine it critically? How can he continue to accept the "primary assurances" to which he has committed himself and yet treat them as "ultimate questions" and subject them to critical inquiry? Of course, a similar problem also exists in other fields, since loyalty to old truth and value must be held in tension with openness to new. This is the only way in which the demand of practical life for decision can be reconciled with the demand of the theoretical reason for further inquiry.

In the case of religion the tension is particularly acute and hard to maintain. That it is not impossible to maintain it, however, is shown by the fact that from the time of Socrates and Plato deeply religious men have also been philosophers. It is psychologically impossible, of course, for a man committed to a religious faith to engage continuously in a critical examination of his faith. But it is quite possible for him to make a critical examination of his faith from time to time without abandoning it. Indeed, that is what the religious believer must do whenever his faith is challenged by criticisms from others or by doubts in himself. Of course, if he finds no answer to the criticisms or is overwhelmed by the doubts, he may feel that he must abandon his faith. But so long as his faith maintains itself in the face of them, it may be strengthened rather than weakened in the process of dealing with them. However, it would be a mistake to suppose that religious beliefs are subjected to critical examination only when they are threatened by criticisms and doubts. The religion of theism, at least, demands that men worship God "in spirit and in truth" and that they love God with the "mind" as well as the "heart." But whether critical inquiry is forced upon one by external criticism and doubt or voluntarily undertaken in response to a demand of faith itself, it is compatible with faith if it leads back again to commitment and worship. As there is an *alternation* in life between work and rest, action and thought, there is an alternation in religion between worship rising from faith and inquiry seeking to know.

(4) In the fourth place, the philosopher of religion inevitably approaches the problems with which he deals from a particular *point of view* or what is sometimes called a "stance." His mind is not a "tabula rasa" on which no knowledge of or attitude toward religion has been written by his past experience. Whether his point of view or attitude is that of a believer, an unbeliever, or an inquirer, there are always presuppositions in his mind which are bound to affect his thinking. In the first decades of the twentieth century some philosophers who had been influenced by the scientific method sought to develop a purely empirical philosophy of religion. They assumed that one could approach the study of religious phenomena entirely without presuppositions and with the cool objectivity of a geologist studying rock formations. After a thorough examination of the data furnished by the sciences of religion, the philosopher was to draw empirical generalizations concerning the nature and forms of religion and its relation to other aspects of human experience. In the same spirit of objectivity, he was to arrive at conclusions concerning the truth and value of religion in general and the various forms of religion in particular. This dream of a presuppositionless approach to religion has faded away. It is now recognized that the mind comes to any and every subject with presuppositions and that the unbeliever starts with presuppositions no less than the believer.

If so, it is essential that the philosopher of religion should openly acknowledge his point of view or "stance" at the time he is speaking or writing. Only in this way can his presuppositions be made clear to those who hear or read what he has to say. Failure to do this in the past has often had unfortunate consequences for rational theology. When a theist presented arguments for the existence of God, for example, he sometimes left the impression that he himself was starting without belief and was arriving at belief solely on the basis of the argument. Almost inevitably he was regarded by others as merely "rationalizing" a belief he already possessed, pretending to draw a rabbit out of his hat which he had previously put there himself. Of course, the fact that he already possessed a belief in God was irrelevant to the validity of the argument. But human reason is a function of the personality as a whole and is bound to be affected in some measure by what a person already believes. This is as true of the unbeliever as it is of the believer. In considering the argument from design, a skeptic like Hume is obviously affected by his unbelief just as a believer like Aquinas is affected by his belief. Whether an antecedent belief in God makes the theist more sensitive to the evidence for God and thus enables him to appreciate such an argument more clearly or whether it blinds him to defects in the evidence and flaws in the reasoning is a debatable question. But that in their thinking the believer is affected by his belief and the unbeliever by his unbelief is beyond question. If so, both should make their point of view and presuppositions clear.

Purpose and Method

The *purpose* of the philosophy of religion is threefold: the examination of religious phenomena to determine the nature and forms of religion and its relation to other aspects of human experience; the clarification of religious concepts and statements; and the evaluation of the truth or falsity of religious beliefs. We shall consider briefly each part of this purpose and the method appropriate for the attainment of it.

(1) Obviously, the philosopher must determine the *nature* of religion and define its *relation* to morality, science, and other aspects of human experience. One of the greatest contributions of nineteenth-century philosophers of religion such as Schleiermacher and Hegel was their serious attempt to attain this purpose. Before that time interest in religion had been largely confined to Judaism and Christianity, the dominant religions of the West. The development of interest in other religions, however, led Hegel and others to concern themselves with the evolution of the religious consciousness which the new science of the history of religions was beginning to describe.

The method most appropriate for this purpose is clearly the *phenomenological* method. Since the philosopher is not a historian of religions, he must depend to a large extent upon the work of historians of religion who have used the phenomenological method in analyzing the nature and manifestations of religion in the course of its history. Although this method was used by Hegel in his early work *Phenomenology of Spirit,* it has been refined and perfected only in the twentieth century.

One of the best descriptions of it has been offered by a distinguished historian of religions, Gerardus Van der Leeuw. "Phenomenology," he says, "is the systematic discussion of what appears." [4] In order to restrict itself to "what appears," it uses the method of "intellectual suspense," *epoche,* employed by Husserl and other phenomenologists. "It implies that no judgment is expressed concerning the objective world, which is thus placed 'between brackets,' as it were. All phenomena, therefore, are considered solely as they are presented to the mind, without any further aspects such as their real existence, or their value, being taken into account; in this way the observer restricts himself to pure description systematically pursued, himself adopting the attitude of complete intellectual suspense, or of abstention from all judgment, regarding these controversial topics," i.e. the "real existence" and "value" of the phenomena.[5]

Van der Leeuw recognizes that it is impossible to contemplate in an attitude of such pure intellectual detachment an event which is "an ultimate experience" and which "manifests itself in profound emotional agitation." [6] Therefore, although it is advisable and expedient to presuppose this "intellectual restraint" in order to avoid the distortion of vision that results from prejudice, it is necessary that it be accompanied by "self-surrendering love." As Van der Leeuw puts it, "this [intellectual restraint] is never the attitude of the cold-blooded spectator: it is, on the contrary, the loving gaze of the lover on the beloved object . . . since to him who does not love, nothing whatever is manifested; this is the Platonic, as well as the Christian experience." [7] Parenthetically, it should be noted that some phenomenologists of religion would prefer to speak of "empathy" with the religious phenomenon rather than "self-surrendering love," but only those who are wedded to an interpretation of objectivity as complete detachment would deny that feeling is involved as well as intellectual restraint.

[4] Van der Leeuw, G.: *Religion in Essence and Manifestation,* New York, Harper Torchbook, 1963, Vol. II, p. 683.

[5] *Ibid.,* p. 646, note 1.

[6] *Ibid.,* p. 683.

[7] *Ibid.,* p. 684. Brackets added.

Van der Leeuw completes his description of the phenomenology of religion by contrasting it with other disciplines. The historian of religion must use the phenomenological method and the phenomenologist of religion must work with historical material; and in most cases the same investigator is both a historian and a phenomenologist. However, the historian's first task is simply to establish what has actually happened and he must describe what he has found even if he does not understand it. In contrast, "when the phenomenologist ceases to comprehend, he can have no more to say," [8] for his distinctive task is to "understand" or "comprehend" the meaning of the historical facts. The phenomenology of religion also differs from theology. Theology speaks about God Himself, but, since God "does not appear" in such a way that we can comprehend Him, phenomenology cannot speak of Him. It is only "at home on earth, although it is at the same time sustained by love of the beyond." [9]

How is the phenomenology of religion related to the philosophy of religion? Although it is not philosophy of religion, says Van der Leeuw, it is a "preparation" for the latter, because it "constitutes the bridge between the special sciences concerned with the history of religion and philosophical contemplation." [10] Hence, philosophy of religion cannot dispense with it, as it tended to do when it started from the deism of the eighteenth century or from the European Christianity of the nineteenth century. But the purpose of the philosopher of religion differs from that of the phenomenologist. As Van der Leeuw expresses it, "the philosopher wishes to move what he has discovered by means of the dialectical motion of Spirit," to "stir the world in his inner life." [11] Perhaps he attributes here an ambition too grandiose to the philosopher of religion, one which might have motivated idealistic philosophers like Hegel but hardly the more sober and critical philosophers of our time. But his point is clear: the philosopher of religion must use the phenomenology of religion as a "preparation" for—or, as we would prefer to say, the first stage of—his distinctive task of clarifying the concepts and principles necessary for the interpretation of religion, on the one hand, and determining the truth or falsity of religious beliefs, on the other.

That the phenomenology of religion cannot be sharply separated from the philosophy of religion and can lead directly into it is illustrated by the fact that one of the greatest phenomenologists of religion of this century, Rudolf Otto, was also a philosopher of religion. We shall have

[8] *Ibid.*, p. 686.
[9] *Ibid.*, p. 688.
[10] *Ibid.*, p. 687.
[11] *Ibid.*, p. 687.

occasion later to refer to his best known work in the philosophy of religion, *The Idea of the Holy,* which based its conclusions on phenomenological analysis of the religious experience. Although it is only the rare thinker who combines the capacity for phenomenological description with the very different capacity for philosophical analysis and construction, it is natural that a phenomenologist who has an existential interest in religious truth should see his work as pointing towards the philosophy of religion. Thus, an historian and phenomenologist of religion of the last generation, Joachim Wach, pointed out that "we do not any longer believe that history *as such* can supply us with norms by which to regulate our lives. And with norms we have again become desperately concerned. . . . What we wish to know is, what is *true?*" [12] "The nineteenth century, living in outward security could afford lovingly to investigate the minutest details of phenomena," he wrote, but it is necessary in our time to concentrate on "a concern with meanings, rather than with facts for the sake of collecting them, and a striving for the achievement of a unified outlook on life." [13] Since the philosophy of religion seeks to achieve such a "unified outlook," the phenomenology of religion obviously contributes to it and in this sense is a part of it.

However, phenomenological description is only the beginning of the task of the philosopher of religion. For his ultimate purpose is to analyze the concepts and principles which are necessary for the interpretation of religion and to arrive at conclusions about the truth and value of religious beliefs.

(2) In developing the concepts and principles necessary for the interpretation of religion he must employ the *analytical* method. Plato's use of dialectic to analyze such concepts as "piety" or "holiness" was one of the earliest and most important contributions of analysis to the philosophy of religion. He showed, among other things, that "piety" should not be defined as doing "what is pleasing to the gods." Rather, he suggested that an act is not right from the mere fact that it is commanded by the gods but is commanded because it is intrinsically right.[14] He also argued that one of the principles of theology is that the gods are good and should never be regarded, as they had been by poets like Homer, as causes of evil.[15] Thus, he clarified the meaning of the concept "piety" and established the fundamental principle that the "divine" is essentially good.

[12] Wach, J.: *Types of Religious Experience.* Chicago, Univ. of Chicago Press, 1951, pp. xi, xii.
[13] *Ibid.,* p. xiii.
[14] Plato: *Euthyphro,* 8b–10a.
[15] *Republic,* Bk. II, 378.

It should be noted that in this process of dialectical analysis Plato starts with what is now called "linguistic analysis" and usually deals with words used in the "ordinary language" of the religion of his time. But he seeks to go beyond the words in which a concept is expressed in order to grasp the meaning of the concept itself; and he does not assume that ordinary language adequately expresses all concepts with which the philosopher must deal. Thus, he regards analysis of language as only one part, although an important part, of the analytical task of the philosopher in clarifying concepts and statements. In contrast, a number of analytical philosophers in Great Britain and America have recently sought to identify the method of philosophy with linguistic analysis. They maintain that such analysis helps philosophers to avoid errors due to the misuse of language, e.g. what Ryle calls "category-mistakes," and to eliminate "pseudo-problems" arising from the grammatical form of words, e.g. the tendency to infer from the importance of common nouns and adjectives in speech that universals have an independent reality.

Although there is truth in this view, it does not warrant the conclusion that linguistic analysis is the *whole* of philosophical analysis. For one thing, some philosophical problems cannot be resolved by linguistic analysis because they are not due to linguistic mistakes but to conflicts between different points of view. As H. A. Hodges has said, these problems arise from "a disorder of intellectual perspectives" and what is required to solve them is "a way of judging the relative worth of different standpoints" which are expressed in language; and the analysis of language itself cannot meet this need.[16] It can be met only by an analysis and evaluation of the "standpoints" or "perspectives" or "conceptual systems" themselves. Ultimately, the philosopher must look beyond language to the facts which are expressed, often very inadequately, in it. A. J. Ayer has recently pointed out that this is what linguistic analysts like Gilbert Ryle are constantly doing themselves. Thus, when Ryle analyzes the language in which we speak about the mind, "he tries to make us fix our attention on the actual phenomena of what is supposed to be our mental life." [17] As we have said, this has always been the method used in the analysis of concepts since the time of Plato. The ultimate appeal is to the facts as disclosed in experience and grasped by reason.

(3) In addition to the phenomenological description of religious phenomena and the analysis of religious language and concepts, the

[16] Hodges, H. A.: *Languages, Standpoints, and Attitudes*, Oxford, Oxford University Press, 1953, pp. 21–23.

[17] Ayer, A. J.: *Philosophy and Language*, Inaugural Lecture at Oxford University, Oxford, Clarendon Press, 1960, p. 24.

philosopher of religion must undertake an *evaluation* of religion, in general and in its major forms, with respect to the *truth* of its beliefs and its *value* for human life. In order to perform this third task, he must use another method, that of *metaphysical thinking*. He must critically examine experience, in its various aspects and in their relations to one another, in order to determine whether it supports the claim of religious belief to truth, and, if so, which of the various forms of religious belief is most consistent with religious experience and with established beliefs derived from other sources. A religious belief is not self-validating; its truth and value cannot be judged solely from within itself. It must be judged not only as an expression of the religious experience which originally gave rise to it, but also by its capacity to interpret man's experience as a whole.

Some philosophers have held that metaphysical thinking is futile and can give us no help in determining the truth and value of religious beliefs. This view, which developed in the nineteenth century under the influence of Hume's skepticism and Kant's rejection of metaphysics, resulted in Protestant circles in a substitution of religious experience (Schleiermacher) or of a special revelation appropriated by faith (Kierkegaard) for the appeal to reason in determining the truth of religious beliefs. It had the great merit of warning against the tendency of some rationalistic philosophers (Hegel) to make religious beliefs depend for their validity upon the ability of man's reason to demonstrate them with certainty and fit them into a metaphysical system. But the assumption that religious experience by itself is sufficient easily leads into religious subjectivism and invites the criticism that religious experience cannot be shown to correspond to an objective reality. It is essential, therefore, for the philosopher of religion to evaluate the truth and value of religious beliefs by considering whether they are compatible with and supported by a world view which does justice not only to religious experience but also to other aspects of experience.

There have been several different conceptions of the way a philosopher of religion should perform this metaphysical part of his task.

Some philosophers of religion have simply accepted the *dominant* metaphysical system of their own time and made it the framework of their philosophical thinking. This procedure, which was adopted by the Christian Platonists in the early Church and by many Protestant idealists in the nineteenth century, has a great advantage for the purposes of religious apologetics: it makes use of the metaphysical point of view which is most familiar and acceptable to educated persons in a particular age. But the danger of accommodation to the reigning philosophy of a particular period is great. It leads to the virtual identification of religious belief with that philosophy and consequently to a distortion of it, as in the case of Hegelian idealism.[18] Moreover, when that philosophy ceases to dominate the intellectual scene, the interpretation of religious beliefs in terms of it loses its appeal. Of course, it is impossible for a philosopher of religion not to be affected, even deeply affected, by the philosophical movements of his own time and to make more use of one philosophy than of others in dealing with a particular problem. But he should maintain his independence and avoid becoming an uncritical adherent of a particular metaphysical system.

Another way in which the philosopher of religion may perform his metaphysical task is to accept a metaphysical theory developed in the *past* as authoritative and to use it as the basis of his interpretation of religion. The most striking example of this is the adoption of Aristotle's metaphysics by Aquinas and his use of its concepts and presuppositions in his rational theology, a policy which is also followed by Thomistic philosophers of our time. The advantage of this policy is that it enables the philosopher to base his thinking upon the principles of a philosophy which has shown itself to possess enduring value and which may seem to be more suitable for his purposes and closer to the truth than any contemporary philosophy. Unfortunately, there has never been full agreement at any time, even in the time of Aquinas, as to which of the metaphysical systems of the past is most adequate. Moreover, to adopt a past philosophy as authoritative is to assume that a further advance in metaphysical thinking is impossible or at least improbable. For it permits the philosopher to accept new insights only insofar as they are consistent with the metaphysical system which he has adopted. In consequence, it seems to most philosophers to involve a virtual abandonment of the philosophical task by closing the mind to insights which conflict with views accepted on authority from the past.

There is a third method of dealing with the metaphysical task which is both more realistic and more creative than the two methods we have described. It is based upon a frank recognition that no metaphysical system has ever been able to establish itself as the final truth and the conviction that no such system is likely to do so in the future. The nature of philosophy involves constant criticism of past theories and development of new ones. Its task is a never-ending one. From time to time, a philosopher of genius constructs a metaphysical theory which flourishes for a time because it embodies a fresh and creative vision of reality and seems to be in harmony with many of the intellectual tendencies of the time. But the metaphysical outlook will inevitably change with the further development of science and the enlargement of experience in every field.

[18] See the criticism of Hegel in Thomas, *op. cit.*, ch. 10.

Therefore, the philosopher of religion should carefully consider the various metaphysical theories available on each issue he faces and adopt the theory which seems to him most adequate. This will require him to have a thorough knowledge of the history of philosophy and an ability critically to evaluate the major metaphysical theories of the past and present. Therefore, he will have to enter the arena of philosophical conflict as an active participant. Although he may not have the creative ability to construct a metaphysical system of his own, he must take the responsibility for making decisions between different metaphysical theories on the major issues with which he deals. There is risk involved in this policy, but the only alternative is for him to evade the last and most important task of the philosopher of religion, the determination of the truth and value of religious beliefs.

Metaphysics: Its Nature and Method

Since this view that the philosopher of religion must concern himself with basic metaphysical issues runs counter to the antimetaphysical attitude of many contemporary philosophers, it is necessary to discuss at some length the nature of metaphysics and the possibility of a religious metaphysic. We shall begin by rejecting two modern attitudes towards metaphysics, that of rationalism and that of logical positivism. Since the decline of absolute idealism, most philosophers have abandoned the rationalistic conception of metaphysics maintained by Spinoza and Leibniz, attacked by Kant, and revived in a different form by Hegel. The primary reason for the abandonment of this conception has been its incompatibility with modern man's understanding of the sources and limitations of knowledge. Rationalists claimed that their systems consisted of necessary and certain truths and provided a complete account of every aspect of reality. It has become impossible for modern thinkers to accept such a claim for any system. They know that knowledge of reality must be based, at least in part, upon experience and must be modified with changes in experience. This does not mean that metaphysical systems will no longer be constructed, but it does mean that no particular system is likely to be accepted as containing the final and complete truth about reality. Moreover, the historical fact that no metaphysical system has ever been able to win acceptance from all philosophers is evidence that final knowledge in metaphysics is unattainable. Therefore, Kant's criticisms of rationalistic metaphysics must be regarded as conclusive.

But the dismissal by logical positivism of all metaphysical assertions as "nonsensical" is even more unacceptable.[19] According to A. J. Ayer,

[19] Ayer, A. J.: *Language, Truth and Logic*, London, Victor Gollancz, 1936, p. 34.

Kant regarded the impossibility of metaphysics as only a "matter of fact," whereas it is really a "matter of logic." [20] There are only two kinds of significant statements: analytic statements which are true but give us no information about the world, and statements of fact which are meaningful only insofar as they can be verified in principle by sense experience. Metaphysical statements are obviously not analytic, since they claim to tell us something about the world. But they are also not statements of fact, since they are incapable of being verified. Therefore, although they may be "emotionally" significant, they have no meaning but are "literally senseless" or "nonsensical." [21] This positivistic view has been subjected to severe criticism and has few adherents today. Urmson and others have pointed out that the status of the verification principle itself is dubious. It cannot be an empirical statement and was not proposed as a generalization based upon an exhaustive study of metaphysical statements.[22] On the other hand, if it is viewed as an analytic statement, it is an arbitrary rule concerning the use of the word "meaningful" and those who are not positivists are not bound to accept it.[23] Nor is this rule for the use of "meaningful" implicit in ordinary discourse, because it requires the rejection of ethical and theological statements that have ordinarily been regarded as meaningful.[24] Such a restriction of meaning would limit it in an intolerable way and would prohibit discourse concerning many matters which are highly important for human life.

A third conception of metaphysics has been emerging in recent years, although it has taken different forms. Against logical positivism, it asserts the possibility and the importance of metaphysics; against rationalism, it makes no claim that a metaphysical system containing a complete and final account of reality is attainable.

(1) According to this view, the *need* for metaphysical thinking arises in part from the fact that different sciences offer conflicting explanations of the same phenomenon and it is necessary to adjudicate their opposing views. For example, the physiologist may explain human acts as effects of physical causes, the psychologist as due to the influence of nonrational mental processes, and the moralist as determined by a free choice of the will.[25] These different explanations can be reconciled only by assessing the validity of each type of explanation from a broader

[20] *Ibid.*

[21] *Ibid.*, p. 35.

[22] Urmson, J. O.: *Philosophical Analysis*, Oxford, The Clarendon Press, 1956, p. 168.

[23] *Ibid.*, p. 169.

[24] *Ibid.*, p. 171.

[25] Walsh, W. H.: *Reason and Experience*, Oxford, The Clarendon Press, 1947, p. 236.

point of view than that of the specialized scientist.[26] Moreover, a science concerned with a particular field of experience tends to extend itself to other fields and to offer an interpretation of all reality, e.g., physics may lead to the philosophy of materialism,[27] and metaphysics is necessary to check pretensions of this kind. Hence, the philosopher cannot confine himself to analysis but must also undertake the task of synthesis, seeking to develop a unitary interpretation of experience. In developing this more comprehensive view, he must take account not only of the scientific description of phenomena but also of other approaches to reality, e.g., moral, aesthetic, and religious.

Metaphysics not only attempts to reconcile the conflicting views of the different sciences and to provide a more comprehensive view of things than any or all of them can offer; it also seeks to bring about a change from the ordinary view of things to a profounder view. A group of analytical philosophers has recently described metaphysics as "an attempt to re-order or to reorganize the set of ideas with which we think about the world," "a kind of conceptual revision." [28] This "conceptual revision" may be undertaken in order to establish the special sciences on the firm foundation of a general theory of being or to provide an ultimate authority for morality. Whatever the motive may be, the "conceptual revision" is achieved by reorganizing our ideas about the world, "promoting some ideas to key positions, downgrading or dismissing others," until the metaphysician re-draws the whole map of our thought,[29] so that things are seen to be in reality different from what they appear to be. For example, from the perspective of Plato's idealism the changing things of sense are seen to be less real than the unchanging Ideas or Forms.

(2) How does a metaphysician develop a single scheme of explanation which will comprehend all aspects of reality and provide a perspective from which the world may be seen in a more profound way? The *origin* of such a metaphysical scheme is an insight which is taken to be a clue to reality. W. H. Walsh calls this insight an "imaginative picture" from which the metaphysician starts and to which he constantly returns.[30] For example, the origin of materialism is a picture or vision of reality as a vast and mindless machine, while the basis of idealism is a vision of the world as the manifestation of mind and its ideas and purposes. Of course, this insight or vision is only the beginning, because the metaphysician must develop its implications by

[26] *Ibid.*, p. 237.
[27] *Ibid.*, p. 237.
[28] Pears, D. F., ed.: *The Nature of Metaphysics*, London, Macmillan, 1960, p. 21.
[29] *Ibid.*, pp. 21, 22.
[30] Walsh, W. H.: *Metaphysics*, London, Hutchinson University Library, 1963, p. 81.

means of a coherent pattern of concepts and principles and present arguments to show that these provide the most adequate account of experience. But a metaphysical scheme is always inspired by an original insight and should never be viewed as a product of the dialectical ingenuity of a logical but unimaginative mind. Argument is essential for its construction, but it builds upon the foundation of a vision.

This vision gives rise to what Dorothy Emmett calls a "judgment of importance" on a particular type of experience. The metaphysician takes this type of experience as a *key* to the interpretation of the totality of experience, capable of coordinating the whole range of diverse experiences.[31] The "key-idea" or "model" is extended by analogy to the whole of experience. As Walsh expresses it, metaphysicians "have an eye for likenesses of structure more acute than that of most of us and a tendency to extrapolate readily from partially discerned to overall patterns." [32] For example, the "key-idea" of Plato's idealism was the superior reality of unchanging Forms to changing material things. Of course, the metaphysician must do justice to the diversity of experience as well as to its unity. He must take account of different patterns within the wider pattern of reality and not distort the character of these patterns in order to fit them into the wider pattern.[33] Thus, a metaphysician takes a particular type of experience or aspect of reality which seems most important to him as the key to his interpretation of the whole of reality and extends it to other types of experience by analogy in order to unify all experience by means of a single pattern of concepts and principles.

(3) Whitehead pictures the *method* of the "speculative philosopher" as like the flight of an aeroplane. "It starts," he says, "from the ground of particular observation; it makes a flight in the thin air of imaginative generalization; and it again lands for renewed observation rendered acute by rational interpretation." [34]

Thus, metaphysics combines the method of rationalism and that of empiricism, starting from experience, using reason to construct a scheme of concepts and principles, and returning to experience to test their applicability to the facts. This is a different conception of the method of metaphysical thinking than that of the continental rationalists who believed that metaphysical propositions could be demonstrated with certainty like the conclusions of geometry and consequently used a basically deductive method of reasoning. Thus, Spinoza in his *Ethics*

---

[31] Emmett, D.: *The Nature of Metaphysical Thinking*, London, Macmillan, 1946, p. 196.
[32] Walsh, W. H.: *Metaphysics*, p. 170.
[33] Emmett, *op. cit.* pp. 201, 202.
[34] Whitehead, A. N.: *Process and Reality*, New York, Macmillan, 1929, p. 7.

began with a series of "definitions" and "axioms" he regarded as self-evident to reason and demonstrated in order the "propositions" of his metaphysics and ethics. One of the difficulties with this deductive method is that it is impossible to establish the premises upon which the conclusions are based, since this requires criteria by which acceptable intuitions of reason can be distinguished from unacceptable ones.[35] Furthermore, any attempt to deduce metaphysical propositions from first principles without appealing to experience fails to do justice to all the facts and results in conclusions contrary to some of them, as in Spinoza's reduction of the many things of nature to mere "modes" of one Substance. However, the inductive method is equally unsatisfactory. Although experience suggests the starting point for the development of a metaphysical theory, and a return to it is necessary to test the adequacy of its propositions, it cannot establish the truth of the latter. For metaphysical propositions differ from the general laws of the empirical sciences, since they are not descriptions of limited fields of experience but principles of the widest generality for the interpretation of the whole range of experience.

(4) But the fact that metaphysical conclusions cannot be demonstrated by the deductive method of mathematics or the inductive method of the empirical sciences does not mean that they are merely an expression of a particular philosopher's subjective experience and hence have no claim to objective validity. There are *criteria* which can be used to evaluate the truth or falsity of a metaphysical theory. In addition to *coherence* of the propositions of a theory with each other, the most important criteria are *comprehensiveness,* i.e., ability to cover all the major fields of experience, and *adequacy,* i.e., ability to cover them in such a way as to satisfy those who know best the facts in each particular field.[36] It is difficult, of course, to apply these criteria in practice, since every coherent metaphysical theory is capable of giving some account of all the major types of fact and opinions will differ about the adequacy of the account given by any particular theory.[37] Nevertheless, the criteria are useful and we do apply them in trying to determine the truth or falsity of a metaphysical theory. For example, we ask whether materialism can give an adequate account of the distinctive nature of living organisms, of human minds, and of moral obligation, or whether idealism offers an adequate account of the otherness of the material world and its recalcitrance to mind and its purposes.

Thus, although universal agreement on the answers to metaphysical questions cannot be expected, metaphysical conclusions are not arbi-

[35] Walsh, *op. cit.,* p. 168.
[36] *Ibid.,* p. 177.
[37] *Ibid.,* p. 178.

trary and unfounded. Since they cannot be demonstrated, metaphysics cannot be a science like mathematics or physics, a common possession of all mankind.[38] This was why Whitehead warned against the claims of metaphysical systems to finality. "Metaphysical categories are not dogmatic statements of the obvious; they are tentative formulations of the ultimate generalities." [39] But Whitehead also pointed out that, despite the tentative character of its conclusions, metaphysics has great value, negative and positive. Negatively, it is an effective "critic of abstractions" such as the Newtonian conception of "simple location" and protects men thereby from narrow views of the world based upon them. Positively, it enables them to correlate the conclusions of the special sciences with knowledge derived from other sources and thereby to attain a synoptic vision of the world and of man's place in it. Persons with a positivistic outlook hold that such a synoptic vision is useless and that we should limit our generalizations to the laws describing detailed facts. But, as Whitehead says, no matter of fact can be understood apart from interpretation, since the understanding of it "leads us beyond itself, to its contemporaries, to its past, to its future, and to the universals in terms of which its definiteness is exhibited." [40]

Religious Metaphysics

Up to this point we have been concerned with the nature, method, and value of metaphysical thinking in general. We must now face a question which is most crucial for the philosopher of religion: even if the necessity and value of metaphysics are granted, is a religious metaphysics possible? Kant criticized the theistic metaphysics of his time on the ground that man does not possess an "intellectual intuition" capable of presenting supersensible entities such as God and the soul to the understanding, so that the understanding cannot attain knowledge of them by applying its categories to them. From this he drew the conclusion that the only kind of metaphysics within the capacity of reason is one which analyzes the principles required for the interpretation of experience in different fields, e.g., science, ethics, and aesthetics. Although the practical reason must "postulate" the reality of God, freedom, and immortality as presuppositions of morality, reason cannot "know" but can only "think" these transcendent realities.

Some recent philosophers who have been favorably disposed towards a "metaphysics of experience" have rejected the possibility of "transcendent metaphysics" for reasons similar to those of Kant. As we have

[38] *Ibid.*, p. 183.
[39] Whitehead, *op. cit.*, p. 12.
[40] *Ibid.*, p. 21.

seen, W. H. Walsh defends metaphysics insofar as it consists of "absolute presuppositions" which make possible a coherent account of experience as a whole.[41] However, he maintains that metaphysics which claims to give us knowledge of transcendent realities cannot be justified. The arguments employed by metaphysics of this kind, he says, are "fundamentally faulty." The appeal to intuition to prove the existence of God (theism), or Forms (Platonism), or pure Spirit (idealism) is unconvincing because some individuals do not seem to have an intellectual intuition of this kind, and it cannot be shown that this is due to their preoccupation with things of the sensible world.[42] Nor can the existence of such supersensible realities be inferred from what we know in experience. "The difficulty here is that the things in question are supposed to be totally different in kind from anything we have met in common life . . . . You can argue from what falls within experience to what might fall within experience, but not to that which transcends experience altogether." [43]

These objections seem to be based upon misconceptions. The first assumes that *religious intuitions* have no cognitive value because they are not shared by everyone. But it cannot be denied that many persons throughout history have had what they have believed to be intuitions of the reality of a transcendent Being. The fact that others have not had them, or have refused to recognize them as intuitions of such a Being, may raise a question about their claims to truth, but it can hardly eliminate them from consideration as data by the philosopher of religion. The objection also assumes that metaphysicians who have taken seriously religious intuitions have attempted to pass directly from them to affirmations about God's existence and nature without taking account of other kinds of experience. It is true that mystics such as Eckhart and a few philosophers influenced by them have thought that the mystical experience itself authenticates the reality of God and that no arguments are necessary. But most theistic philosophers do not depend solely upon mystical or ordinary religious intuitions for their belief in God. Rather, they maintain that, while belief in Him may originally arise from such intuitions, it could not be sustained if it were not confirmed by reflection on experience as a whole. As we shall argue in a later chapter,[44] intuitions arising in religious experience must be submitted to rational thought to test their validity and also to interpret their meaning.

Walsh's second objection is that *transcendental realities* are "totally

[41] Walsh, *op. cit.*, p. 164.
[42] *Ibid.*, p. 186.
[43] *Ibid.*, p. 186.
[44] Chapter 3.

different" from those we experience, so that inference from the facts
of experience to them is impossible. There is some truth in this objection if it is directed against attempts of traditional rational theology to
infer God's existence from nature without any reference to an awareness of Him in experience. We shall criticize attempts of this kind later.
But theistic metaphysics need not assert, and usually has not asserted,
that God is "totally different in kind" from everything we know in experience, although the negative theology of some Christian thinkers
sometimes seems to assert this. For Western theism affirms that God is
in some sense the Creator of the world, that His wisdom and goodness
are manifested in His creatures, and that man has been created in His
image. If so, certain qualities or "perfections" of His creatures may be
attributed to Him by analogy. To say that He is "totally different" in
all respects from His creatures is to deny this and assert His transcendence at the cost of denying His immanence in the world and man.
Insofar as the objection rests on philosophical grounds, it seems to be
based upon the Kantian dualistic view that "things-in-themselves"
cannot be known because our categories are applicable only to "phenomena." This view assumes that the former cannot be known in and
through the latter, an assumption we have criticized elsewhere.[45]

A third objection to transcendental metaphysics on *linguistic*
grounds has been made by Stuart Hampshire. There is a "deeper
grammar" of language, he thinks, which "reflects the universal features
of human experience." [46] "All we can do, as philosophers, is to penetrate to this deeper grammar, which reflects the presuppositions of all
our thought and experience; and then we shall realize why it is that our
knowledge can never be complete, and why we can never have unconditional explanations of the nature of things, as they are apart from
the conditions of our experience of them." [47] Referring to the later
Wittgenstein's theory of language, Hampshire asserts that "we fall into
nonsense, mere idle words, if we consider questions or statements apart
from the actual context of human life in which the questions would
ordinarily be asked or the statements made. . . . At this point we
should stop and remain silent; that was Wittgenstein's advice." [48]

Now it is obvious that religious metaphysics must speak of supersensible realities in ordinary language. But does this imply that all
affirmations about such realities are necessarily "nonsense" and "idle"?
To assert that it does is to deny the possibility of using ordinary words
in an analogical sense to express the nature of anything which

[45] Thomas, *op. cit.*, Chapter 9.
[46] Hampshire, S.: essay on "Metaphysical Systems" in Pears, *op. cit.*, pp. 24, 25.
[47] *Ibid.*, p. 25.
[48] *Ibid.*, pp. 27, 28.

transcends the world of space and time. This is to impose an intolerable restriction upon our use of language. In effect, it assumes that language should be confined to the ordinary uses of earthbound men in a secular society which has lost its sense of the transcendent. This is convincing only to men who have already accepted some version of naturalism, which denies the reality of everything that transcends the natural order in space and time. Moreover, to affirm the reality of the transcendent is not to speak of that which is "outside all possible experience," as Hampshire asserts, for it is not true that "all conceivable experience is experience of a sequence of events in time." Mystical experience is not only "conceivable," it has been an actual experience of many persons; and it is an experience of a reality which is not "a sequence of events in time." Is it not clear from all of this that the modern dismissal of "transcendent metaphysics" is due not to the requirements of language as it is actually used but to the denial of everything transcendent by naturalism?

We conclude that attempts to eliminate "transcendent metaphysics" by arguments based upon Kant's metaphysical agnosticism and Wittgenstein's theory of language are not convincing. There is no valid reason why a metaphysical theory should not be developed which would do full justice to the religious experience of transcendent or supersensible realities as well as to experience of realities of the world of space and time. Indeed, if metaphysics is to give a complete and adequate account of all sides of experience, it must do so.

However, there is a special danger to be avoided and a special difficulty to be overcome in the development of a religious metaphysics. The danger is that a metaphysician who derives his "key idea" from a religious intuition of God and His relation to the world may be tempted to interpret physical, moral, and other aspects of experience in such a way as not to do full justice to their distinctive character. It is easy for a person whose primary concern is religion to distort the nature of other aspects of experience in order to make them fit smoothly into a religious pattern of interpretation. Hindu monism has often been accused of denying the plain evidence of the senses for the independent existence of the physical world since it affirms the sole reality of the Brahman as "One without a second"; and this may have partly caused the neglect of physical science which has had serious consequences in India. Theism, on its side, has often interpreted obedience to God's will as inconsistent with even a relative autonomy of practical reason in moral decisions.

A metaphysic can be adequate only if it is faithful to the facts and values in every area of experience. For example, the structure of the physical world must be accepted by the religious metaphysician as it is, even when a new scientific discovery seems to be difficult to reconcile with his faith. There is no such thing as a "religious" version of the *facts* of physics or biology, although their *meaning* will be different for the religious person than it is for the atheist or skeptic. The only way for the religious metaphysician to avoid the danger of distorting "secular" areas of experience such as morality and science in order to fit them into a religious world view is to respect the knowledge of these areas which has been accepted by those most competent to describe them. This implies, of course, that while he will take the "key idea" for his metaphysical interpretation from religion, he will also make full use of knowledge derived from all possible sources.

The special difficulty that faces the religious metaphysician is that he cannot attain a clear and precise knowledge of transcendent realities because of the limitations of human reason and experience. For this reason Kant's criticism of rationalistic metaphysics is useful as a warning to the religious philosopher that he should not make exaggerated claims for his metaphysical conclusions. Similarly, Hampshire's strictures against the use of ordinary words in a context where "ordinary experience is lacking" are a salutary corrective of dogmatic claims to comprehend fully the attributes and actions of God and to be able to express them in "clear and distinct" ideas. If the metaphysician is to use categories such as substance and causality when he speaks of God, he must realize that he is using them in an analogical sense. For example, if he speaks of Him as a "Being," he must not think of Him as one object among other objects, superior to but limited by them and by the conditions under which they exist. Perhaps the permanent value of Kant's insistence that we can "think" but cannot "know" God and the soul is that it reminds us of the difference between supersensible and sensible objects of knowledge and prevents us from claiming that we have more than a very partial knowledge of the former.

C. B. Daly has recently pointed out that the theistic metaphysician does not claim to attain a complete understanding which dispels mystery. "The theistic metaphysician does not pretend that the existence of God 'makes everything clear' and explains away all problems. He does not make a 'postulate of universal intelligibility' in the sense of demanding that reality shall be positively and exhaustively comprehended by us. He postulates intelligibility only in the minimal sense that being shall not be self-contradictory, or absurd." [49] Daly illustrates this point by reference to two of the major doctrines of theism. "The theist will not claim to understand Creation; but just that, without it, the existence of the world is impossible. He will not claim to compre-

[49] Daly, C. B.: essay "Metaphysics and the Limits of Language" in Ramsey, Ian (ed.): *Prospect for Metaphysics*, London, George Allen and Unwin, 1961, p. 204.

hend God; but just to know that he is real and that his reality 'exceeds by its immensity every concept that our minds can form' . . . But the humility of his little knowledge is of vast importance for man. Aquinas said: 'The least knowledge that can be had about the highest things is more desirable than the most exact knowledge about lesser things.' " [50] There are also other major doctrines of theism which cannot be "positively and exhaustively comprehended by us," as we shall indicate in later chapters. What theistic metaphysician would pretend to comprehend the nature of God's relation to the world, e.g., the way He is immanent in it without ceasing to transcend it? Or the precise manner in which His grace acts in the soul? Or the presence and power of evil in life?

This is one of the main reasons for the fact that religious thinkers have arisen again and again who have been hostile to metaphysics and natural theology. In the modern world Kierkegaard attacked "the System" of Hegel as an enemy of faith. His religiously motivated attack on metaphysical systems has been almost as effective as Kant's philosophical one. "Such closed systems are now out of fashion," says Howard Root.[51] "If we continue to say that there are reasons for accepting one set of beliefs rather than another, we are that far committed to something which I should call metaphysics. But it will have to be a metaphysics which can somehow do justice not only to our *desire* for a Natural Theology but also to our religiously inspired *distrust* of Natural Theology." [52]

The philosopher of religion cannot avoid wrestling with metaphysical issues, because he cannot evaluate the claim of religious beliefs to be true without relating them to the whole pattern of his beliefs about the world. But this does not require him to construct a complete metaphysical system which will answer all questions; and, as we have seen, he is well advised if he does not adopt the metaphysical system of another, whether of the past or of the present. Indeed, the fact that no metaphysical system has ever been able to win universal assent should warn him that, while the ultimate goal of metaphysical thinking is a unified pattern of interpretation which will be coherent, comprehensive, and adequate for all areas of experience, that goal will never be finally attained. At any rate, we shall make no attempt in this book to develop a complete system of metaphysics. Instead, we shall limit ourselves to some fundamental metaphysical questions raised by religious beliefs: e.g., the existence and nature of God; His relation to the world; and the meaning of natural and moral evil.

[50] *Ibid.,* pp. 204, 205. Aquinas, Thomas: *Summa Theologica,* Q.I, a, 5.
[51] Root, Howard: essay "Metaphysics and Religious Belief" in Ramsey (ed.), *op. cit.,* p. 67.
[52] *Ibid.,* p. 79, italics mine.

2

The Nature of Religion

The first task of any philosophy of religion is to analyze the nature of religion as it has manifested itself in history. There has been such a diversity of religious phenomena that one may be tempted to abandon the effort to describe the essential characteristics of religion. What is there in common, one may ask, between primitive and advanced religions, or even between advanced religions such as Hindu monism and Christian monotheism? Or what similarity is there between the prayer of the ancient Hebrews for victory over their enemies, the Tibetan prayer wheel which automatically turns out prayers, the prayers of penitence and praise of the Psalmist, the Lord's Prayer of Jesus, and the ecstatic union of the mystic with God?

Definitions of religion are generally unsatisfactory, and perhaps it is impossible to formulate a completely adequate one. However, if one is to think clearly about religion and to relate it to other forms of human experience, one must have at least a general conception of what it is and how it differs from other human concerns. In the absence of such a conception, one may easily confuse aesthetic experience, ethical idealism, or nationalism, with religion. Or one may be led into error by superficial assertions about it which have just enough truth to make them seem plausible. A good example is Lucretius' famous assertion, "Fear made the gods." Fear has undoubtedly played a part in the history of religions, not only in the primitive religions and in polytheism but also in higher religions including Biblical monotheism. Even in the New Testament we read that "It is a fearful thing to fall into the hands of the living God." [1] But this is only one side of the religious attitude. In ancient polytheism men not only feared the displeasure of their gods; they also thanked them for the blessings they bestowed. And in the New Testament we read, "There is no fear in

[1] Hebrews 10:31.

28

love, but perfect love casts out fear." [2] Again, Feuerbach and Freud have regarded religion as a product of wish-fulfillment. This view also may seem plausible when one considers that religious men have always sought benefits and deliverance from evils from their gods. On the other hand, in the higher religions they have learned not to expect from God the satisfaction of all their natural desires but to accept His will for them, whatever self-denial and sacrifice it may require of them.

Thus, an analysis of the essential characteristics of religion is necessary to prevent the confusion of it with other forms of experience and the reduction of it to something that may be associated with it but does not belong to its essence. Such an analysis is also indispensable for an understanding of the relation of religion to other human concerns. We shall begin by considering the theories of some modern philosophers of religion and theologians.

Religion as Feeling and Intuition: Schleiermacher

Schleiermacher's conception of religion was developed in opposition to the attempts of Kant and other philosophers of the Age of Reason to interpret it in purely rational and ethical terms. Kant had argued in his *Critique of Practical Reason* that the practical reason must postulate freedom of the will, immortality, and the existence of God as presuppositions or necessary conditions of the attainment of man's highest good, i.e., moral virtue and happiness in proportion to it. These postulates constitute a "pure rational faith" and provide the basis for Kant's definition of religion as "the recognition of all duties as divine commands." [3] In accord with this conception, he maintained that the individual should strive for virtue by his own will without depending upon assistance from divine grace and that rites and ceremonies are not essential to rational religion.[4] Although there is a certain appeal in this austerely ethical conception of religion, it is intolerably narrow. There is no place for emotion or worship in it and men must earn their salvation by their own moral efforts and need God only to crown their virtue with happiness.

In contrast, Schleiermacher regards religion as a unique form of experience which cannot be reduced or subordinated to morality. It

---

[2] I John 4:18.

[3] *Kant's Critique of Practical Reason* and other writings, tr. by T. K. Abbott, London, Longmans, Green & Co. 1889, p. 226.

[4] Kant, Immanuel: *Religion within the Limits of Reason Alone*, tr. by T. M. Greene and Hoyt Hudson, 1960, Harper and Row.

has its seat or locus not in the will but in *feeling*. While the essence of morality is activity, piety has a passive side. As he expresses it in his early *Addresses on Religion,* it is "a surrender, a submission to be moved by the Whole that stands over against man." [5] Again, while the aim of science and philosophy is to know things as they are, piety is compatible with lack of knowledge. "Quantity of knowledge is not quantity of piety." [6] But if piety is neither morality nor knowledge, what is it? Schleiermacher defines it as a feeling of the presence of the Infinite and Eternal in every finite thing and temporal event. While it is quite distinct from both morality and knowledge, it is not separated from them. Everything of worth arises from true religion. It is "impossible to be moral or scientific without being religious," and "while man does nothing *from* religion, he should do everything *with* religion." [7] Clearly, in this analysis of religion Schleiermacher's emphasis is on the immanence of the divine in the finite things and events of nature and history and on the immediate experience of it in feeling.

Schleiermacher developed his conception of religion in a more precise and systematic way in his later work, *The Christian Faith.* Piety is "neither a Knowing nor a Doing, but a modification of Feeling, or of immanent self-consciousness." [8] Although it is distinct from knowing and doing, it is a mediating link between them and stimulates both. Making more precise the nature of this feeling, he describes it as "the consciousness of being absolutely dependent, or, which is the same thing, being in relation with God." [9] Insofar as the self in its receptivity is affected by its "Other," it experiences the feeling of dependence, whereas insofar as it is active it experiences the feeling of freedom.[10] In the relation of the self to the finite world, it is both active and receptive, so that its relation to the world is one of reciprocity, e.g., in its relation to parents, country, or nature it both influences and is influenced by them.[11] But in its relation to that toward which it is wholly receptive without being able to influence it, it feels absolutely dependent. The idea of God is an expression of this feeling of *absolute dependence.*[12] The opposition between this feeling, the highest state of self-consciousness, and lower sensible states of self-consciousness is the

[5] Schleiermacher, F.: *On Religion,* New York, Harper Torchbooks, 1958, p. 37.
[6] *Ibid.,* p. 35.
[7] *Ibid.,* pp. 38, 59.
[8] Schleiermacher, F.: *The Christian Faith,* tr. by H. R. Mackintosh and J. S. Stewart, Edinburgh, T. & T. Clark, 1948, p. 5.
[9] *Ibid.,* p. 12.
[10] *Ibid.,* pp. 13, 14.
[11] *Ibid.,* p. 15.
[12] *Ibid.,* p. 17.

source of the instability and at times suffering of the religious life.[13]

Schleiermacher's view of the relation of religious feeling to *reason* is indicated by his conception of theology. "Christian doctrines," he asserts, "are accounts of the Christian religious affections set forth in speech." [14] Even conceptions of divine attributes and modes of action and assertions about the constitution of the world must be based upon descriptions of religious feelings.[15] Since all doctrines are simply expressions of religious experience, theology should be completely separated from speculative philosophy.[16] However, Schleiermacher himself was not free from the influence of philosophy, especially Spinoza's pantheism. In opposition to dualistic supernaturalism, he affirmed that divine activity is immanent in the natural instead of operating upon it from above. Accordingly, he was critical of belief in miracles and asserted that every finite thing or event can be viewed as a miracle.

The basic presupposition behind Schleiermacher's theory is that religion is an *essential element* in human experience. Religious feeling is a natural expression of man's relation to God and its historical development has resulted from an immanent unfolding of his consciousness of this relation. This presupposition has been sharply attacked by Neo-orthodox theologians such as Karl Barth on the ground that it is too anthropocentric, emphasizing man's religious experience rather than God's revelation. As we shall have to deal with this criticism of religious experience later, we shall not consider it here.

Schleiermacher's theory has also been criticized as too subjective and too narrow in defining religion as a form of feeling. In evaluating this criticism, it should be noted that there is an ambiguity in the meaning he attaches to "feeling." In the first edition of the *Addresses on Religion* he linked "feeling" with "intuition" and spoke of religion as "intuition and feeling." However, in the second edition he eliminated many of the references to "intuition" and spoke simply of "feeling," and in *The Christian Faith* "intuition" almost disappeared. But this does not prove that he meant by "feeling" only a subjective state, since he seems to use the term in the later work in a broad sense to include both an immediate intuition and the feeling that accompanies it. Indeed, Richard Brandt has argued that intuition is the primary element in Schleiermacher's concept of religious experience.[17] Moreover, the fact that he developed one of the most impressive systematic the-

[13] *Ibid.*, p. 24.

[14] *Ibid.*, p. 76.

[15] *Ibid.*, p. 126.

[16] *Ibid.*, p. 82.

[17] Brandt, R.: *The Philosophy of Schleiermacher*, New York, Harper and Bros., 1941, p. 98.

ologies of the modern period is a sufficient indication that he did not regard religious feeling as merely subjective but believed that the reality of God was disclosed in and through it.

However, the definition of religion as a "feeling of absolute dependence" is, to say the least, misleading. Schleiermacher argues that the locus or seat of religion cannot be knowing or willing, since there is no concomitant variation of religion with either of these. Theologians are not necessarily the most religious persons, and the most moral men are not always the most religious. This is obviously true, but it does not prove that religion is essentially feeling *rather than* knowing or willing. These three functions of the mind are intimately related to each other, and religion involves the whole self. The fact that some religious men are less moral than some nonreligious ones does not mean that morality is not an element in the religious life but only that it is imperfectly developed in such men. All of the functions of the mind are interdependent and support each other in the mature religious person, but it is the rare religious person who has developed all of them fully. Moreover, Hegel has pointed out that contradictory elements are to be found in feeling, the most debased as well as the noblest, and that whether a feeling is good or bad depends on its content.[18] In addition, a feeling is a momentary and transient state and can become permanent only if it is stimulated by keeping before the mind ideas of the divine.[19]

However, this does not imply that feeling is an unimportant element in religion, as Hegel often seems to think. It has always been recognized that without feeling knowledge of the existence of God or moral obedience to His will is a hollow shell without life. For example, Jonathan Edwards in one of his greatest treatises maintained that the "religious affections" are essential to religion,[20] and John Wesley asserted that there should be a union of knowledge with "vital piety." And there can be no doubt that the feeling of absolute dependence is an important aspect of religious feeling, especially in the higher religions. In these religions man is conscious that while his dependence upon other finite things, natural and human, is relative, his dependence upon the divine ground of his being for his existence and good is absolute. However, we shall see that the feeling of absolute dependence is not the whole of religious feeling. For there is also a feeling of the transcendence and absolute worth of the divine, which invites an active response from men. One of the weaknesses of the definition of religion

---

[18] Hegel, G. W. F.: *Lectures in the Philosophy of Religion*, tr. by E. B. Speirs & J. B. Sanderson, New York, Humanities Press, 1962, Vol. I, p. 130.

[19] *Ibid.*, p. 134.

[20] Edwards, Jonathan: *Treatise on the Religious Affections*, New Haven, Conn., Yale University Press, 1957.

as a "feeling of absolute dependence" is that it seems to imply that men are wholly passive and completely determined by the divine, whereas in ethical monotheism they respond with moral activity, as Schleiermacher himself says.

Another defect of Schleiermacher's theory is his theological empiricism, i.e., his view that religious beliefs are simply expressions of the religious feelings of a community or church. This empiricism unduly limits the role of reason in the religious life. If a theological statement such as "God is merciful" is taken seriously, it asserts not merely that a certain feeling is experienced in a religious community but also—and primarily—that a certain property belongs to God. That Schleiermacher believed that such statements *do* refer to properties of God as an objective reality is shown by the fact that he regarded some as truer than others, e.g., those of monotheism than those of polytheism. But if this is the case, theology must be more than a description of religious feelings and its doctrines must be shown to be consistent with each other and with experience as a whole. Hence, Schleiermacher's attempt to separate theology from metaphysics and base its doctrines upon religious experience alone was a mistake. Indeed, he was unable to make such a separation himself, as we have seen.

Despite these weaknesses of his theory, Schleiermacher's insistence that religious beliefs are derived from intuitions which arise in religious experience has had a profound effect upon later religious thought. For example, it has been one of the main influences upon the thought of Paul Tillich. Indeed, Tillich's assertion that the source of faith is an intuitive awareness of the Unconditioned and Ultimate as present in and presupposed by the conditioned beings and relative values of the finite world corresponds to Schleiermacher's view that religion is a "feeling" of the union of the temporal with the Eternal, the finite with the Infinite, the part with the Whole.

Religion as Knowledge: Hegel

"We know," says Hegel, "that in religion we withdraw ourselves from what is temporal, and that religion is for our consciousness that region in which all the enigmas of the world are solved, all the contradictions of deeper-reaching thought have their meaning unveiled, and where the voice of the heart's pain is silenced—the region of eternal rest, of eternal peace . . . All that has worth and dignity for man, all wherein he seeks his happiness, his glory, and his pride, finds its ultimate center in religion, in the thought, the consciousness, and the feeling of God." [21] In this eloquent passage, Hegel epitomizes his conception of

[21] Hegel, *op. cit.*, Vol. I, pp. 1, 2.

the nature and worth of religion: it unites man with God, the absolute beginning and end of all life, and thereby enables him to resolve all the contradictions in his thought and to overcome all the pain and sorrow of his temporal existence.

This conception is fully intelligible only in the light of Hegel's philosophy of absolute idealism. He maintains that the ultimate reality is Absolute Mind or Spirit, *Geist,* which is eternal and infinite. Unlike Aristotle's self-sufficient Unmoved Mover, the Absolute Spirit goes out of itself into its Other, the world of nature and man, and by overcoming the opposition of its Other it comes to self-consciousness. Thus, natural objects and human spirits are manifestations in space and time of the one universal and eternal Spirit. Since the Absolute Spirit is essentially rational and is immanent in the human spirit, man's reason can come by a process of dialectical thinking to know the structure of its thought, as well as its manifestations in nature and human spirit. Thus, Hegel's philosophy is idealistic, since he regards ultimate reality as spiritual, and rationalistic, since he affirms that the Absolute Spirit and its finite manifestations are wholly intelligible to the reason of man.

Hegel defines religion in terms of this idealistic world view. On its human side, religion is the consciousness on the part of the finite spirit of its relation to the Absolute Spirit, a relation of dependence but also of unity. On its divine side, which is prior, religion is the process in which the Absolute Spirit relates itself to the finite spirit and thereby relates itself to itself, i.e., comes to self-consciousness. "Thus religion is the Divine Spirit's knowledge of itself through the mediation of finite spirit." [22]

What is the relation of this conception of religion to the "positive" religions of history? Like Schleiermacher, Hegel opposes the negative attitude of the Age of Reason to these religions. The Divine Spirit, he asserts, is not beyond the world but has always been active in it, awakening the spirits of men to consciousness of itself. "Religion," he says, "is a product of the Divine Spirit; it is not a discovery of man, but a work of divine operation and creation in him." [23] In consequence, the philosopher of religion should not disparage the religions of history as irrational and superstitious but view them as stages in the development of the religious consciousness which possess at least relative and partial truth. Christianity is the "absolute religion" in which the human spirit has come to a full consciousness of its true relation of unity with the Absolute Spirit. Hence, the philosopher of religion should make use of the insights of the religions of history instead of dismissing them as products of priestly cunning and human credulity.

[22] *Ibid.,* p. 206.
[23] *Ibid.,* p. 33.

But *how* is the philosopher to interpret these religions of history and especially Christianity? Hegel's answer to this question is based upon his view of the relation of religion to reason. We have seen that he was highly critical of Schleiermacher's view that religion is feeling. To Hegel, feeling is only the indeterminate first stage of religion and it must be given form and stability by knowledge. Although he does not deny that feeling is an element in worship, religion is primarily *knowledge* rather than feeling.

What *kind* of knowledge does it offer and how is its knowledge related to that of philosophy? It offers knowledge of the highest truth, that the human spirit is one with the Absolute Spirit. But it expresses this truth in the form of imaginative or pictorial representation, *Vorstellung*, rather than concept, *Begriff*. This is its great limitation, since its images and ideas are derived from the world of the senses and are therefore inadequate to grasp spiritual reality. For example, it expresses the dependence of nature and man on the Absolute Spirit in the mythical story of the Creation, which represents God as wholly transcendent to, rather than immanent in, the world and His creation of it as contingent rather than necessary to Him. Hence, it is easy for the "understanding," *Verstand,* to discover apparent contradictions between religious assertions when their pictorial language is taken literally, e.g., God is one but He is also three "Persons." In contrast, the philosophical "reason," *Vernunft,* interprets the imaginative language of religion in a constructive manner.[24] It grasps the essential meaning of religious assertions and formulates them more precisely in the conceptual language of philosophy. Unlike the "understanding," "reason" brings to light the unity underlying the apparent contradictions between these assertions and shows their relation to each other in a coherent pattern.

According to this view, religion and philosophy have the same *object* or *content,* God the Absolute Spirit and His relation to nature and to the finite spirit of man. "The object of religion as well as philosophy," says Hegel, "is eternal truth in its objectivity, God and nothing but God, and the explication of God." [25] In this respect, they are identical with one another. On the other hand, they differ in *form,* since religion expresses the truth about God and the world in imaginative form while philosophy expresses it in conceptual form. Hence, religion is inferior to philosophy in its form. Indeed, philosophy is the highest

[24] Kant had distinguished between "understanding" and "reason" in his first *Critique*: the former is able to give us knowledge of phenomena, but the latter fails in its attempt to know things-in-themselves. In contrast, Hegel affirms that "reason" *can* attain knowledge of ultimate reality and hence is superior to "understanding" which is incapable of synthesizing diverse aspects of spiritual reality.

[25] Hegel, *op. cit.,* Vol. I, p. 19.

activity of "Absolute Spirit," since it includes in itself but raises to a higher level the truths expressed by art in a sensuous form and the truths expressed by religion in imaginative language.[26] The concrete, pictorial language of religion is indispensable for the spiritual life, since it fosters the union of the human spirit with the Absolute Spirit in worship. But the truths it expresses are more clearly and coherently formulated in the abstract, conceptual language of philosophy. Thus, the truths of the Christian religion are identical with but are more adequately expressed by those of Hegel's idealistic philosophy.

One of the great contributions of Hegel is his clear recognition and repeated insistence that religion is concerned with *truth*. This is why he criticizes Schleiermacher's religion of feeling so sharply, although he misinterprets it as merely subjective. Another important contribution is his acknowledgment, in opposition to the unhistorical bias of the Age of Reason, that the religious experience of men as it has developed in the history of religions must be taken seriously by the philosopher as a primary source of religious knowledge.

Unfortunately, he is not content to affirm that religion must be true and religious beliefs must be consistent with each other and with experience as a whole. He goes further and asserts that it is in its essence knowledge and that it differs from philosophical knowledge only in its form. But the difference lies deeper. As we have said, philosophy and religion differ in their primary aims, philosophy seeking truth primarily for the sake of truth but religion for the sake of wholeness and fullness of life.[27]

Another basic weakness of Hegel's conception of religion has to do with his view of the relation of the finite to the Absolute Spirit, of the individual to God. Although he is well aware that in its worldly existence the finite spirit is self-centered and hence estranged from the Absolute Spirit, he attributes this condition to the contradiction between its existence as an individual self and its universal nature as spirit. Hence, he is confident that the estrangement can be overcome by the finite self's recognition of its essential unity with the Absolute Spirit. This confidence rests upon his monistic view of the relation of the finite spirit of man to the Absolute Spirit, i.e., the view that the individual is in his essence a manifestation of the Absolute Spirit and can become reunited with the latter by coming to know his unity with it. This view seems to deny the transcendence of the Absolute Spirit, on the one hand, and to exalt the human spirit too much by minimiz-

[26] Hegel, G. W. F.: *The Philosophy of Mind*, tr. by William Wallace, Oxford, Clarendon Press, 1894, p. 182.
[27] Ch. 1.

ing the radical difference that separates it from the Absolute Spirit or God, on the other.

Paradoxically, while the human spirit is unduly exalted by Hegel's assertion of its unity with the Absolute Spirit, his monism leads him to subordinate it to the Absolute Spirit so that it seems to be only a means to the attainment of self-consciousness by the latter. It was this subordination of the individual to the universal which led Kierkegaard to attack Hegel's "system" not only because of its rationalism but also because it minimized the freedom and responsibility of the individual self. This attack was justified in the light of the fact that in his *Philosophy of History* Hegel seems to view the individual as only an instrument of the universal purposes of the World Reason or Absolute Spirit.[28] For the individual is not a mere manifestation of an impersonal Universal Spirit; he is a distinct and self-determining being with a dignity and worth of his own. Although he is called upon to surrender himself to God's will and purpose, he must decide to make that surrender himself and he must do so freely.

Religion and the Holy: Rudolf Otto

Although there were important differences between Schleiermacher and Hegel, they were similar at one crucial point: their analysis of man's religious experience led both to emphasize the *immanence* of God in the human spirit. Against this emphasis much religious thought since the first World War has been in sharp reaction. This reaction has taken different forms. Among the theologians, Karl Barth has attacked the immanentism of nineteenth century Protestant theology and has stressed the transcendence of God and man's complete dependence upon His grace.[29] But the philosopher of religion who has emphasized the transcendence of the divine most effectively is Rudolf Otto.

In *The Idea of the Holy*, Otto makes a penetrating phenomenological analysis of "the Holy," *das Heilige*. Religious experience is for him much more than the feeling of absolute dependence; it is the "creature-feeling" of one who is overwhelmed by his own nothingness in contrast to the Holy. For the Holy is a *mysterium tremendum* before which the religious man feels awe or dread because of its majesty.[30] His "creature-feeling" when confronted by the Holy is a subjective reflection of this.

[28] Hegel, G. W. F.: *The Philosophy of History*, tr. by J. Sibree, New York, Willey Book Co., 1944, Introduction.

[29] Barth, Karl: *Protestant Thought from Rousseau to Ritschl*, New York, Harper, 1959.

[30] Otto, Rudolf: *The Idea of the Holy*, pp. 10–18.

In its presence man has a feeling of "being but 'dust and ashes' and nothingness," which is the source of religious humility.[31] Also, the Holy is experienced as "active, compelling, alive," a "living God" rather than a mere ideal or static being.[32] Hence, it is not to be treated lightly or in a familiar manner but to be approached with awe.

The substantive word *mysterium* expresses the mysterious, incomprehensible character of the Holy. It is "the 'wholly other,' that which is quite beyond the sphere of the usual, the intelligible, and the familiar, which therefore falls quite outside the limits of the 'canny' and is contrasted with it." [33] Although it is often *associated* with extraordinary things or events of inanimate nature, animals, or men, as in the cult of the heavenly bodies and animal worship, the Holy is not *identified* with these phenomena. For it is incommensurable with everything we know, "supernatural." [34] This is why the mystic contrasts it with everything finite and speaks of it in negative terms.[35]

Although the Holy is "daunting," it is also "fascinating." Even when the creature feels dread in its presence, he is also attracted by it and turns towards it.[36] He has always sought to possess and be possessed by it, whether by magical or shamanistic methods in primitive religion or by mystical discipline leading to union with it at a more advanced stage.[37] For he experiences it as a reality or power which can bestow "salvation" and "beatitude" upon him, as in Christian conversion or the Buddhist experience of Nirvana.[38]

Thus far we have confined ourselves to what Otto calls the "non-rational" aspects of the Holy.[39] Otto emphasizes these aspects in opposition to the modern tendency to reduce religion to beliefs which can be expressed in conceptual terms and moral conduct which can be carefully defined. The Holy cannot be adequately expressed in concepts. But there is "above and beyond our rational being" what the mystics call the "ground" of the soul, and through this man has the capacity to apprehend and respond to the Holy. In this sense, the Holy is an "a priori category," for the feelings we have described are not derived from sense experience or from reason but from this deeper source in the mind.[40]

---

[31] *Ibid.*, pp. 20–23.
[32] *Ibid.*, pp. 23–24.
[33] *Ibid.*, p. 26.
[34] *Ibid.*, p. 28.
[35] *Ibid.*, p. 38.
[36] *Ibid.*, p. 38.
[37] *Ibid.*, p. 33.
[38] *Ibid.*, pp. 34–38.
[39] *Ibid.*, pp. 2, 3.
[40] *Ibid.*, pp. 117, 118.

There is also *a priori* knowledge of the necessary connection between the nonrational elements of the Holy and rational ideas which "schematize" them. For example, the daunting aspect is schematized by the ideas of moral will and justice; the attractive aspect by the ideas of goodness, mercy and love; and the mysterious aspect by the idea of the absoluteness of the divine knowledge and other attributes.[41] These rational ideas cannot completely express the nonrational elements, and there is always a danger that an elaborate mythology or theology will weaken and deaden the experience.[42] Nevertheless, rational elements are indispensable if religion is to be prevented from falling into "fanaticism" or "mysticality," and a criterion of the relative rank of a religion is the degree in which rational and nonrational elements are united in a healthy and harmonious way.[43]

This is illustrated by the process in which the Holy becomes "charged" with ethical meaning. The connection between the Holy and the ethical is not a *logical* one. "How should it be logically inferred from the still 'crude', half-daemonic character of a moon-god or a sun-god or a numen attached to some locality, that he is a guardian and guarantor of the oath and of honourable dealing, of hospitality, of the sanctity of marriage, and of duties to tribe and clan?" [44] But there is an *essential* interdependence of the nonrational Holy with rational ideas such as justice and goodness, as we have seen. Hence, a process of rationalization and moralization takes place. Ethical meanings derived from social and individual ideals such as obligation become attached to the "will" of the Holy and it becomes their author and guardian.[45] "The greatest distinction of the religion of ancient Israel, at least from Amos onwards, is precisely the intimate coalescence of both elements." [46]

In evaluating Otto's analysis of the Holy, we note first that it constitutes both a continuation and a correction of Schleiermacher's analysis. It is continuous with the view of the latter insofar as it bases its description of the Holy upon religious feeling and subordinates rational ideas to feeling. Also, in his assertion that there is a "religious *a priori*" or superrational capacity of the human spirit to experience the Holy, Otto assumes a point of connection with the Holy in man's nature and thus is in the immanentist tradition of Schleiermacher and Hegel. On the other hand, he differs from both these nineteenth century thinkers

[41] *Ibid.*, pp. 144, 145.
[42] *Ibid.*, p. 27.
[43] *Ibid.*, p. 146.
[44] *Ibid.*, p. 140.
[45] *Ibid.*, p. 114.
[46] *Ibid.*, p. 115.

in emphasizing the transcendence of the Holy. Against the romantic tendency of the nineteenth century to view God as an immanent spiritual principle in nature and man, he insisted upon the otherness of God and the creatureliness of man in His presence. By doing so he has helped to restore to twentieth-century man the sense of awe and mystery before the divine which has been seriously threatened both by romanticism and by the preoccupation of science and technology with the world of nature.

However, Otto's view of the Holy as "wholly other" than everything natural and human affirms the transcendence of God in too extreme a form. If carried to a logical conclusion, this would lead to a complete agnosticism about God's nature. Otto is aware of the danger that an emphasis upon the inexpressible character of God will lead to an exclusively negative theology, and he recognizes the necessity of speaking affirmatively of God by means of a "schematism" of ideas. But his fear of the deadening effect of "rationalization" upon the experience of the Holy and his insistence that the Holy is "wholly other" than everything natural and human tends to make valid affirmative statements about it difficult if not impossible. For affirmations about it can have no validity if it is so "other," so transcendent, that there can be no analogy between it and any finite creature.

Otto's strong emphasis upon the transcendence of the Holy also tends to make God remote and inaccessible to men. If he is regarded as "wholly other," He will seem beyond the reach of ordinary men and they will view the experience of Him as rare and unusual for those who are not mystics or saints. Perhaps this is the reason Martin Buber, with Otto probably in mind, says that God is the "wholly Other" but also the "wholly Same." [47] For religion should not be confined to ecstatic experiences which take a man out of the ordinary world; he may meet the Holy in his everyday life and relations within the world. Although theism has always affirmed the transcendence of God as well as His immanence, a one-sided emphasis upon His "wholly-other" nature can easily lead to a dualistic supernaturalism which pictures Him as completely separated from the world.

Religion as Encounter: Martin Buber

While Schleiermacher was influenced in his conception of religion by pantheism, Hegel by idealism, and Otto by mysticism, Martin Buber has been conditioned in his religious thought above all by the personal and ethical perspective of Biblical theism and by the reaction of existentialism against impersonal objective thinking. In his best-known work,

[47] Buber, Martin: *I and Thou*, Edinburgh, T. and T. Clark, 1947, p. 79.

I and Thou, he contrasts the relation between an I and a Thou with the relation between an I and an It. The two "primary words" "I-Thou" and "I-It" describe radically different relations of the individual to other beings. A being is an "It" or object to me when I manipulate, control, use, or compare it with other beings. For example, a person is an "It" to me when he is only a means of satisfaction or an object of curiosity to me. In contrast, a person becomes a "Thou" to me when I become directly related to him, when I am aware of him as an individual, and when there is mutuality or reciprocity between us. Of course, I-It relations are necessary in many situations, since we must often treat others as objects in carrying out our purposes. But a person who knows only I-It and never enters into I-Thou relations is excluded from a fully human existence. "All real living is meeting." [48]

Now, one can know God only in an I-Thou relation, a personal "encounter" with Him. Normally, one's encounters with Him take place in and through one's encounters with finite Thous. "Every particular Thou is a glimpse through to the eternal Thou; by means of every particular Thou the primary word addresses the eternal Thou." [49] This does not mean that "God" is only a name for the sum of personal relationships, for He is also transcendent to all finite Thous. But it does mean that He is not only the "wholly Other," but is "nearer to me than my I." [50] Hence, Buber is critical of the mystical experience which lifts one in ecstasy out of everyday life into a life beyond. "I possess nothing but the everyday out of which I am never taken . . . I know no fulness but each mortal hour's fulness of claim and responsibility." [51] Moreover, devotion to God, the "eternal Thou," is not exclusive. It does not require us to renounce relations with finite Thous, as Kierkegaard renounced Regina Olsen. "God wants us to come to him by means of the Reginas he has created and not by renunciation of them." [52]

Buber affirms without equivocation that God is personal, "the absolute Person." What does this mean? "It only means that God loves as a personality and that He wishes to be loved like a personality. And if He was not a person in Himself, He, so to speak, became one in creating Man, in order to love man and be loved by him, in order to love me and be loved by me. For . . . persons are the only ones who love." [53] Of course, Buber was fully aware of the cultural phenomenon

[48] Buber, M.: *Between Man and Man,* tr. by R. G. Smith, New York, Macmillan, 1948, p. 22.
[49] *I and Thou,* p. 11.
[50] *Ibid.,* p. 79.
[51] *Between Man and Man,* p. 14.
[52] *Ibid.,* p. 52.
[53] *Eclipse of God,* New York, Harper and Bros., 1952, pp. 81, 82.

of our time described as the "absence" or "death" of God, i.e., t
many have ceased to have a living, personal relation to God. But
regarded this as only an "eclipse of God." "An eclipse of the sun is soi
thing that occurs between the sun and our eyes, not in the sun itself.'
The eclipse of God is due to the fact that men have allowed the
relation to dominate their lives and this "steps in between and shuts
from us the light of heaven." [55]

Although this condition is not bound to continue, human thou
cannot make it give way. Indeed, philosophical thought about
may be a hindrance rather than a help, since it substitutes an "o
fication" of God for a personal "meeting" with Him. Hence, the
of religion is an ever-recurring struggle of religion with metaphy
struggle for the protection of lived concreteness as the meeting-plac
between the human and the divine." [56] Philosophers who offer humanity their systems only remove themselves and others from God.
Indeed, although images and ideas have a relative value as pointing
towards God, "they swell themselves up and obstruct the way to
Him." [57]

Buber was one of the most appealing as well as impressive religious
philosophers of the last generation. In the first place, he emphasized
in a secular and impersonal age the fact that religious faith, at least of
the theistic kind, arises from a personal and direct, although not
necessarily an unmediated, relationship with God. Like Schleiermacher,
he stressed the concrete experience of God as the essence of vital religion and subordinated to it the dogmas and rites of organized religion.
In the second place, he insisted that God is immanent and accessible
to men in their everyday lives. The "I" need not escape from the world
and its responsibilities to find God but can meet Him as the "eternal
Thou" in every finite and temporal "Thou." Finally, he did not accept
the fatalistic view of some contemporary philosophers that the individual is completely at the mercy of the depersonalizing forces which
have caused the "eclipse" of God in our time. Man does not have to
wait passively for God to manifest Himself at some more propitious
time but can make himself ready to encounter the "eternal Thou" here
and now in every finite "Thou" he meets.

These are some of the reasons for the appeal of Buber to our skeptical age and they set him apart from religious existentialists such as
Kierkegaard. Faith to him is not a "leap" which has no ground in religious experience and insight; it is the result of a personal encounter

[54] *Ibid.*, p. 34.
[55] *Ibid.*, pp. 166, 167.
[56] *Ibid.*, p. 49.
[57] *Ibid.*, p. 63.

with God. It is not a way of escape from despair; it is a positive affirmation of the presence of God and of fullness of life in relation to Him.

Our criticism of Buber is directed not against what he affirmed but against what he denied. Like Kierkegaard, he reacted against the "objective thinking" of speculative philosophers and rejected metaphysics and natural theology altogether. Regarding philosophical speculation as opposed to personal involvement and concrete experience, he viewed metaphysics as an enemy rather than an ally of I-Thou relationships with God. As a result, he was forced to rely almost exclusively upon religious experience and intuition.

Now, it is true that religion originates from concrete experiences of God rather than from philosophical speculation. But Buber is wrong in assuming that concrete experiences of an I-Thou relationship are self-authenticating and need no support from reflection on experience as a whole. By making this assumption he lays himself open to the criticism of Ronald Hepburn and others that there is a possibility of error and illusion in the claim of a person to have met God in a personal "encounter." Even if such a person has in fact experienced an encounter of some kind, he may have misinterpreted his experience.[58] Buber's view is that philosophical thinking about God reduces Him to an object in an I-It relation. But it is not true that the philosopher necessarily reduces a Thou to an It when he makes it an object of thought. Of course, conceptual "knowledge about" man in general differs from concrete "acquaintance with" a person, but the effort to attain the former is not incompatible with enjoyment of the latter. Indeed, personal acquaintance with a Thou requires some objective knowledge about him, and it may be deepened by scientific and philosophical knowledge about man in general. Of course, generalizations about man may be substituted for personal relationships with individual men, but if they are used to enhance rather than replace such relationships they are an ally rather than an enemy of them. Similarly, art or literary criticism may stand in the way of a direct response to a painting or poem by imposing arbitrary standards of judgment, but it enables us to understand better and enjoy more fully what we see or read if we do not allow it to take the place of a direct response on our part.

Philosophical criticism and interpretation are necessary in religion also. Religious experience must be related to other forms of experience if we are to determine which of the rival interpretations of it is most adequate. Buber affirms without argument the Judaeo-Christian interpretation of God as personal. But in view of the fact that Spinoza's

[58] Hepburn, Ronald: *Christianity and Paradox*, London, C. A. Watts and Co., 1958, p. 30.

pantheism and Hegel's idealism have conceived of Him in more impersonal terms, the theist cannot evade the question whether his view is supported by other aspects of experience than I-Thou encounters or is being accepted uncritically on the authority of the Bible. Furthermore, if the theistic view of God is found to be in accord with experience as a whole, it is necessary to relate the belief in Him to beliefs derived from other sources, e.g., scientific knowledge of nature and moral knowledge of the good. Hence, the theist cannot evade the task of drawing out the metaphysical and ethical implications of relationship with the eternal Thou.

Religion as Ultimate Concern: Paul Tillich

Paul Tillich's conception of religion must be understood in the light of his ontology or doctrine of being, on the one hand, and his existentialist analysis of the condition of man, on the other. He offers his *ontology* as an alternative to both traditional "supranaturalism" and the naturalism of recent philosophy. Like Schleiermacher, he is opposed to supranaturalism on the ground that it stresses the transcendence of God to the point of separating him from the world and man; but he is also opposed to naturalism because it leads to a reductionistic view of the world which fails to do justice to man's spiritual nature and especially his experience of the Holy. Against these two extreme views, he affirms that God is immanent in the world as "being-itself," the ground and power of being, but that He is also transcendent to it. He includes finite beings in His own spiritual life so that they participate in Him, but at the same time He transcends them by His freedom over against them and they are free in relation to Him. This view of the relation of God to the world was deeply influenced by Schelling's idealistic vision of finite things and persons as separating themselves in their freedom from God the divine source of their being but seeking to become reunited with Him.

This world view seems to be derived, at least in part, from Tillich's mystical experience of the unity of finite beings with the infinite ground of their being. He is critical of mysticism on the ground that "it plunges directly into the ground of being and meaning, and leaves the concrete, the world of finite values and meanings, behind." [59] However, there was a mystical element in his own religious experience. Like Schleiermacher, he had an immediate awareness of the unity of the finite and temporal world with the infinite and eternal ground of being

[59] Tillich, Paul: *The Courage to Be*, New Haven, Conn., Yale University Press, 1952, p. 186.

immanent in it. Hence, he was a "belief-full realist" who saw finite beings and events as real but as pointing beyond themselves to their transcendent source so that they constitute a sacramental universe. On the other hand, he was keenly aware of the separation of finite beings from the ground of their being, the estrangement of their existence from their essence. Consequently, while every "segment" of the finite world can become a symbol for God, nothing finite should ever be identified with Him. For this reason, Tillich repeatedly emphasized the "Protestant principle" that the Church or any other finite being becomes "demonic" when it is absolutized and made into an idol.

Tillich's ontology and qualified mysticism largely determine his conception of *religion*. Although he agrees with Schleiermacher and Hegel that religion belongs to man's spiritual life, he denies that its locus or seat is in "one spiritual function," such as feeling (Schleiermacher) or reason (Hegel). "Religion is not a special function of man's spiritual life, but it is the dimension of depth in all of its functions." [60] The meaning of "dimension of depth" is that "the religious aspect points to that which is ultimate, infinite, unconditional in man's spiritual life." [61] Thus religion or faith is the "ultimate concern" which is present in all creative functions of the human spirit, e.g. the unconditional demands of morality and the passionate longing for knowledge of ultimate reality.[62]

Although this conception of religion as "the dimension of depth" or "ultimate concern" in all spiritual functions might be taken to imply that it is purely a human phenomenon which involves no relation to God, this subjective and humanistic view of it is not intended by Tillich. For there is a "content" or "object" of man's ultimate concern, "the Unconditional," which "demands total surrender" from him and "promises total fulfillment" to him.[63] While the object of a man's ultimate concern may be and often is idolatrous, e.g., science, success, or the nation, such an ultimate concern is demonic and cannot provide total fulfillment because its object is not ultimate. The only proper content or object of ultimate concern is "the Unconditional" or God, for only He is truly ultimate.[64]

This broad conception of religion differs radically from the ordinary view of it. Ordinarily religion is regarded as man's relation to divine beings or a divine being, whereas Tillich maintains that it is a relation

---

[60] Tillich, Paul: *Theology of Culture*, New York, Oxford University Press, 1959, pp. 5, 6.

[61] *Ibid.*, p. 7.

[62] *Ibid.*, p. 8.

[63] Tillich, Paul: *Dynamics of Faith*, New York, Harper Torchbook 1957, p. 1.

[64] *Theology of Culture*, p. 40.

not to "a being" but to "being itself," the ground and power of being. Also, it is usually viewed as "a special sphere among others, in myth, cult, devotion, and ecclesiastical institutions," [65] whereas Tillich regards a particular religion of this kind as quite secondary to religion in his sense of the term. Indeed, he is often critical of particular religions, including Christianity, and in one of his sermons he speaks of the "yoke of religion," the dogmas and laws imposed by religions upon their adherents, and says roundly that Jesus "frees us from religion." [66] Religion as a "special sphere" involves the separation of the religious from the secular, the sacred from the profane. As a result, it sets itself above "secular" activities such as the creation of art and the pursuit of truth and ceases to be the "dimension of depth" in these and other spiritual functions. Religion as a "special sphere" is necessary only because of the estrangement of man's spiritual life from its depth, and according to the Book of Revelation "there will be no temple in the heavenly Jerusalem, for God will be all in all." [67]

This view of religion implies that there is a close relation between *religion and culture*. "Religion as ultimate concern," says Tillich, "is the meaning-giving substance of culture, and culture is the totality of forms in which the basic concern of religion expresses itself. In abbreviation: religion is the substance of culture, culture is the form of religion." [68] For an ultimate concern is present in every cultural function, e.g., artistic intuition, scientific thought, and moral activity.[69] However, there are radical differences between cultures with respect to the manner in which the religious "substance" is related to the cultural "form" in which it is expressed. Tillich's distinction between "autonomous," "heteronomous," and "theonomous" cultures describes three very different kinds of cultures. An "autonomous" culture is one like our own, in which man claims to be self-sufficient and recognizes no connection between reality and the eternal.[70] A "heteronomous" culture is one in which religion imposes itself as an alien law upon cultural activities and fails to recognize the legitimate independence of the latter. A "theonomous" culture, in contrast to both of these, "expresses in its creations an ultimate concern . . . not as something strange but as its own spiritual ground." [71] Only in such a "theono-

[65] *Ibid.,* p. 8.
[66] Tillich, Paul: *The Shaking of the Foundations,* New York, Charles Scribner's Sons, 1955, p. 99.
[67] *Theology of Culture,* p. 8.
[68] *Ibid.,* p. 42.
[69] *Ibid.*
[70] *Ibid.,* p. 43.
[71] *The Protestant Era,* Chicago, University of Chicago Press, 1957, p. 57.

mous" culture is the ideal relation between religion as "substance of culture" and culture as "form of religion" realized.

Tillich's conception of religion as the "dimension of depth" or "ultimate concern" manifested in all of man's spiritual functions has the merit of emphasizing the fact that religion at its best seeks to permeate and transform all of man's activities and interests, personal and social. His view that it is the "substance of culture" is simply a corollary of this conception. However, Tillich does not do justice to religion as a "special sphere" with doctrines, forms of worship, and an organized community. Since organized religions have centered their interest too much upon their own internal life and have been tempted to evade the struggle to transform the social institutions and cultural activities of their adherents, his criticism of the separation of the religious from the secular or profane is fully justified. But without the stimulus of religion as a "special sphere," it is difficult to see how religion as "the dimension of depth" in all spiritual functions would be possible. For man's awareness of and commitment to the Unconditional or God must be awakened and nourished by worship on special occasions and he must pay special attention to its implications for belief and conduct, if his religion is to be deep and strong enough to express itself in a culture.

Also, Tillich's view of the relation of God to man raises serious questions. In sharp reaction against the "supranaturalism" of orthodox Christian theism because of its overemphasis upon the transcendence of God, he stressed the immanence of God in the world as the ground and power of being. This made it possible for him to find God in the "depth" of finite beings and hence to view the human spirit as participating in Him despite its estrangement from Him. This has been one of the sources of his appeal to contemporary men because of their repudiation of dualistic supernaturalism. But it also leads to difficulties. He is not a pantheist, for he insists that God is not only the "ground of being" but also the "abyss of being" in whom all finite beings are transcended. However, since he regards God not as "a being" but as "being-itself," many have felt that a personal encounter with Him would be impossible and that the logical consequence of his view of God would be mystical union with abstract and impersonal Being. We shall return to this question when we discuss Tillich's conception of God in a later chapter.[72]

[72] Ch. 7.

The Essence of Religion

One conclusion that seems to emerge from the preceding analysis of modern theories is that religious phenomena have been too diverse and complex to make a definition of religion in general very useful. With the help of these theories and of recent phenomenological analyses of religion, however, it is possible to describe some of its most important aspects or characteristics.

(1) Religion is a *unique* and *irreducible* form of human experience and every attempt to derive it from or subordinate it to some other human concern is bound to fail. Kant's definition of it as "the recognition of all duties as divine commands" overlooks most of what is distinctive of it and makes it only a bulwark of morality. Schleiermacher's conception of it as a kind of feeling divorces it from the intellectual and volitional activity of the self. Hegel's interpretation of it as a kind of knowledge whose form is inferior to that of philosophy subordinates unduly both the emotional and ethical aspects of it. We would add that recent attempts of some psychiatrists and ministers to make it a source of peace of mind or integration of the self distort and even corrupt it.

(2) The attempt to find the *seat* or *locus* of religion in one function or part of the human spirit is misconceived. We have shown, for example, that Schleiermacher's identification of religion with a kind of feeling led to an unrealistic effort to separate theology from philosophy. Religion involves the *whole self* and an exclusive identification of it with any one part of the self results in an impoverishment of it. For the self is a unity in which all the functions are interdependent. Belief determines feeling and stimulates action; feeling gives vitality to belief and dynamic for action; and action is an expression of belief and feeling. Each function is indispensable because it has a distinctive role, e.g., belief defines the object of devotion and the kind of response that is appropriate to it, and moral activity seeks to transform the life of the individual and society. As the Biblical commandment expresses it, "Thou shalt love the Lord thy God with all thy heart, and with all thy soul, and with all thy might." [73] The limitation of religion to one function of the self implies that other functions are not necessarily involved in the response to God, and this weakens the power of religion to transform life as a whole.

(3) Religion involves a relationship between man and that which he regards as holy or divine. Hence, it can be understood only if it is viewed from both its human and its divine side. As Van der Leeuw says, when we approach it from the *human side*, "from below-

[73] Deuteronomy 6:4; Mark 12:30.

upwards," we observe that man never simply accepts the life that is given him but seeks to enhance its value. Although he attains meaning through his cultural activities, he cannot find the ultimate meaning of his life in this way. His goal is *salvation,* a new and higher life. "But in any case religion is always directed towards salvation, never towards life as it is given; and in this respect all religion, with no exception, is the religion of deliverance." [74] For man is a spiritual being who stands out from and above the rest of nature by his self-awareness, and his capacity for self-transcendence will never permit him to be content with life as it is.

This quest of man for salvation, for wholeness and fullness of life, is the existential side of religion. There is always a danger, of course, that it will result in a self-centered and mercenary attitude and overshadow the divine side of religion. In ancient polytheism the attempt was often made to bribe the gods by sacrifices to secure rewards and avoid punishments; and even in modern monotheism religion is often little more than a source of personal comfort and a means of escape from anxiety. But these distortions should not lead us to disparage man's concern for salvation, provided he does not seek it by and for himself alone. As Tillich points out, man regards the divine object of his ultimate concern as the source of meaning in his life, since it not only makes unconditional demands upon him but also promises him total fulfillment.[75] Even mystics and saints who have renounced the world and its values have hoped for self-fulfillment through their renunciation.

While salvation always involves deliverance from evils into fullness of life, it has been conceived in very different ways. In some religions, the primary evils from which men have sought deliverance have been natural and social disasters, e.g., sickness, defeat in war, and death. In others, they have been moral and spiritual, e.g., sin, guilt, and estrangement from God. Conceptions of the state of salvation or fullness of life have been correspondingly different. Some religions have sought mainly natural and social goods such as health, victory over enemies, and long life. Others have been chiefly concerned to attain forgiveness, reconciliation with God, and communion with Him. These differences have arisen from different conceptions of man, his good, and the nature of the divine. For example, in primitive religions the distinction between body and spirit had not yet been clearly drawn, so that the evils to be overcome and the goods to be attained were conceived primarily in natural rather than spiritual terms. On the other hand, in higher religions such as Hindu monism, prophetic Judaism, and Christianity

[74] Van der Leeuw, *op. cit.,* Vol. II, pp. 681, 682.
[75] Tillich, Paul: *Dynamics of Faith,* p. 1.

men have been deeply conscious of moral and spiritual evils from which they have longed for deliverance, and the primary good they have sought has been moral and spiritual transformation: "Create in me a clean heart, O God, and put a new and right spirit within me." [76]

(4) When religion is viewed from the *divine side,* "from above downwards," a somewhat different account of its nature must be given. For it is not only a quest for salvation, it is also a *response* to a Power which seems to confront man in his experience. As Otto points out, the Holy is experienced not as a self-sufficient being like Aristotle's Prime Mover but as a Power which is living and active. Man experiences it as an objective reality standing over against him and often encounters it when he least expects to. The Old Testament describes many unexpected and surprising encounters of God with men, e.g., His appearance to Moses in the burning bush and to Isaiah in the temple. The New Testament speaks of the Spirit of God as like the wind which "blows where it wills" and men "do not know whence it comes or whither it goes." [77] While men may long for an encounter with the Holy and prepare themselves for it, they cannot command its presence or control it in any way.

Although there have been different conceptions of the Holy, there has been broad agreement among phenomenologists of religion such as Otto and Van der Leeuw that it is *transcendent* in the sense of distinct from and other than everything natural and human. It has been associated at different stages in the history of religion with inanimate things, animals, and human beings, but it has not been simply identified with any of these. For it has been felt to be beyond and above the finite things or persons which have mediated its presence to men and consequently has been approached with awe. This is why communism, nationalism, and other modern movements which have generated passionate loyalty but have denied the reality of the Holy as an objective and transcendent reality should be regarded not as religions but as substitutes for religion. The radical difference between those who believe that nature and man constitute the whole of reality and those who believe that men are dependent upon a transcendent reality is too crucial to gloss over.

Since the way men conceive the Holy or Divine has a profound effect upon their whole life and thought, prophets and theologians have always striven to understand its nature and relation to the world as clearly as possible. The differences between their interpretations of it have led to serious and often tragic struggles in the history of religious thought. Many modern men, brought up to believe in

[76] Psalm 51:10.
[77] John 3-8.

religious liberty and to tolerate wide differences of religious belief, find incomprehensible the intolerance of Hebrew prophets such as Hosea and Jeremiah towards those who abandoned Yahweh and worshipped Canaanite Baals of fertility or Assyrian gods. They overlook the fact that men's conception of the Holy determines the nature of their worship and conduct. Thus, the cult of the Canaanite Baals involved sacred prostitution while that of Yahweh prohibited it, and the Baals made no high moral demands while Yahweh required justice, mercy, and humility.[78] For this reason as well as for the sake of truth, therefore, the age-long effort of philosophers and theologians to attain a true and worthy conception of the nature of the Holy and its relation to the world has been necessary and inescapable.

(5) The Holy is also experienced as the *Sacred* and as such is approached with reverence. It is felt to be of absolute worth and therefore to claim *absolute devotion,* although the conceptions of its worth and of the devotion appropriate to it have varied widely in the history of religion. The Sacred alone is worthy of unconditional devotion, while finite ends deserve only a relative devotion and must be subordinated to it. Tillich expresses this attitude when he contrasts the object of "ultimate concern" with objects of "preliminary concern" and points out that the latter become "demonic" when they become the objects of ultimate concern. Only that which can be the source of "unconditional demand" and "total fulfillment" is an adequate object of ultimate concern and worthy of absolute devotion.[79]

This principle has been interpreted in very different ways. Those who have stressed the utter transcendence and otherness of God and have sought to serve Him with passionate intensity have sometimes thought that *absolute* is equivalent to *exclusive* devotion. Medieval monks who were seeking with single-mindedness to attain a perfect love of God tended to think that devotion to Him required indifference to or even renunciation of everything finite. Although Kierkegaard was a Protestant, he respected this monastic ideal and believed that an "absolute relationship to the absolute 'telos'" required a life of rigorous self-denial within the world. In contrast, Tillich maintained that God as the ground of being is immanent in all man's spiritual functions, so that all his cultural activities have religious significance, and Buber maintained that "I" can and should meet the "Eternal Thou" in finite "Thous." Most religious men of our time would agree with Tillich or Buber against Kierkegaard on this point. But there is always bound to be a tension between the absolute claims of the Sacred and the relative claims of finite things and persons, and

[78] Micah 6:8.
[79] Tillich, Paul: *Dynamics of Faith,* p. 1.

the passionate intensity and exclusiveness of Kierkegaard's devotion is a valuable protest against the worldly temptation to get lost in relative ends or "preliminary concerns." When religion ceases to be the controlling concern of a person or a community, it loses its power.

(6) What is the nature of man's *response* to the Holy? How does he express his absolute devotion to it as the Sacred? Clearly, his response includes but also goes beyond the "feeling of absolute dependence" described by Schleiermacher or the "creature-feeling" of awe before the *mysterium tremendum* described by Otto. For the religious man actively responds to the Holy by *worship*, on the one hand, and *moral conduct*, on the other. We shall consider the latter aspect of response at the end of the chapter. Here we shall confine ourselves to the response of worship.

Although worship is not the whole, it is the heart, of religion. Since it arises as a response to the Holy which is experienced as a transcendent Reality independent of man, the objective side of worship is primary. If the subjective or human side of it does not spring from experience of the Holy and does not presuppose belief in its objective reality, it is bound to be unreal and insincere. Much "religious" behavior that appears to the outside observer to be worship does not arise from such an experience and belief but from social and other motives. Consequently, it has little or nothing in common with genuine worship.

Worship is devotion to the Holy or Divine as the Sacred, i.e., as that which possesses absolute worth. In its highest and purest form it is *adoration,* disinterested devotion to the Holy for its own sake. "If man," says Douglas Steere, "is ever to rise to his full humanity, he must praise and adore that which is the highest that he knows and freely offer up to it the best that he has. . . . No one can deny that in primitive man (and in that considerable substratum of the primitive man that dwells in all of us) this longing to offer up the best that he has, to the highest that he knows, is often overlaid with fear and with the desire to propitiate or gain favors from the power or powers beyond his control. Yet even this cannot blind us to this basic longing in men to praise and adore and to pour out their best gifts. For this longing persists after these fears or cravings for favors have been almost wholly stripped away. . . . Man is a praising and adoring being." [80]

This implies that adoration differs from *petitionary prayer.* Evelyn Underhill emphasizes this point, although she disparages prayer too much. " 'I come to seek God because I need him,' may be an adequate formula for prayer. 'I come to adore His splendour, and fling myself and all that I have at His feet,' is the only possible formula for wor-

[80] Steere, Douglas: *Prayer and Worship,* New York, Association Press, 1938, pp. 43–45.

ship." [81] This statement seems to be based upon a comparison between the highest, most disinterested form of worship and the lowest, most self-centered form of prayer, e.g., prayer for comfort, security or success. But petitionary prayer is not always self-centered. Miss Underhill herself admits that, when a person prays that he may be enabled to do God's will more perfectly, or for other persons, or for good causes, his prayer may be an expression not only of dependence upon God but also of homage to Him. However, it is true that adoration is the purest form of worship because it involves devotion to the Holy for itself. "Religion is adoration," wrote Friedrich von Hügel. "The most fundamental need, duty, honour, and happiness of men is not petition, or even contrition, nor again even thanksgiving . . . these three kinds of prayer which indeed must never disappear out of our spiritual lives . . . but adoration." [82]

Although corporate worship is a spiritual act, it is usually embodied in *ritual actions*. There is always a danger that it will lose its purity and spontaneity when it assumes a definite form, and the tendency to a cold formalism, a preoccupation with ritual forms in and for themselves, is ever present. But since man is an embodied rather than a pure spirit, his worship is naturally expressed in words, gestures, and acts which belong to the world of sense. For it is the nature of ritual acts such as sacraments that they unite an external, visible action with an inner, spiritual reality, so that sense and spirit collaborate in them.[83] By this means they are able not only to express feelings but also to strengthen commitments by expressing the faith of the worshipper in action. Symbolic acts such as kneeling in prayer, symbolic objects such as the cross, and symbolic images such as ikons of the saints are also used to represent spiritual realities. In general terms, symbols are invaluable in worship because men can give concrete form in things that are seen to their intuitions of and devotion to the unseen. There is always a danger of idolatry, of course, i.e., of identifying the symbolic act, object, or image with the spiritual reality it represents. But this danger is unavoidable, if men are to have something concrete before them to stimulate their imagination and feeling and focus their attention upon the unseen.

The purpose of worship is to lead men into a deeper understanding of the Holy or Divine and a more perfect union with it. "Worship, then, is an avenue which leads the creature out from his inveterate self-preoccupation to a knowledge of God and ultimately to that

[81] Underhill, Evelyn: *Worship*, New York, Harper, 1937, p. 9.
[82] Von Hügel, Friedrich: quoted by Douglas Steere, *op. cit.*, p. 34.
[83] Underhill, *op. cit.*, p. 26.

union with Him which is the beatitude of the soul." [84] This involves self-giving or self-surrender, which has always been expressed throughout the history of religion by sacrifice. In a sacrifice something costly is offered to the Holy, e.g., a lamb or a sheaf of grain. At the highest level, it involves self-sacrifice of the most difficult and painful kind, e.g., the monk's life of poverty, chastity, and obedience or the martyr's sacrifice of his life. For absolute devotion to the divine requires the subordination and may even require the renunciation of all that the world holds most dear.

Public worship and private prayer are interdependent. Public worship is formal and cold unless those who share in it engage in prayer when they are alone; and the prayers of the individual are deeply affected by his participation in the public worship of his religious community. Moreover, private prayer and public worship have, in general, the same purpose and content. In ethical monotheism, both include adoration, thanksgiving, confession of sin, petition, dedication, and intercession for others. Also, both are offered in the spirit of submission to God and with the purpose of entering into communion with Him. Of course, private prayer is more concerned with the individual's personal needs and concerns than public worship, but the latter also seeks to express the thoughts, feelings, and desires of the individual worshippers who constitute the religious community. Prayer is the center of personal religion. Without it, man is separated from God and public worship becomes a mere formality.

(7) Religion is usually mediated to a person through the tradition of a particular *religious community* and its form is largely molded for him by that tradition. The modern idea that religion is purely a "personal matter" is highly misleading. Even Whitehead seems to support this idea when he says that "religion is what the individual does with his own solitariness." [85] In reality, religion is primarily a social activity which is maintained and transmitted by a religious community, although it would disappear if the individuals in the community ceased to give their allegiance to it. Of course, an individual may pass from one religious community to another for any one of a number of reasons. But even if he renounces membership in a religious community and thinks he has embraced a purely personal religion, he will continue to be influenced in his religion by the beliefs and practices of some religious community.

For man is a social being, and all aspects of his spiritual life are affected by the culture of his group. His aesthetic experience, his moral

---

[84] Underhill, *op. cit.*, p. 17.
[85] Whitehead, A. N.: *Religion in the Making*, New York, The World Publishing Co., 1961, p. 16.

conduct, and his knowledge are largely, if not exclusively, determined by his culture. As, Schleiermacher pointed out, religious communities are a natural result of the tendency of inner experiences to express themselves in outward acts and the sharing of similar religious experiences by a number of persons. The individuals of one generation embrace religious beliefs and attitudes which are transmitted to them from the past. Long before they begin to think for themselves, they have been deeply influenced by the ideas and practices of a religious community.

The religious community preserves and interprets a tradition which is embodied in its scriptures and its common life. It develops forms of common worship which it regards as appropriate responses to the Holy, and through the regular use of these forms it enables its members to renew frequently their devotion. It also inculcates suitable moral conduct by rules or examples. Thus, it preserves the spirit of a religion and enables it to function as an organized force in the lives of men. Even reformers of religions such as the Hebrew prophets and founders of new religions such as the Buddha and Jesus were dependent upon religious communities for their original beliefs and attitudes. Each of them was nourished and stimulated by a religious community before he challenged its established tradition and sought to purify, modify, or enlarge it by a new vision.

(8) What is the relation between the *authority* of a religious community and the religious *experience* of an individual member of it? There have been fundamental differences within religions such as Judaism and Christianity with respect to this question. For example, the differences between Orthodox and Reform Judaism or between Roman Catholicism and Protestantism as to the nature and extent of the authority of the community are well known. The basic question is not whether the religious community possesses authority but how its authority is related to the experience of its individual members. The answer of William Temple to this question is that there is a "mutual interdependence" of the tradition of the community and the religious experience of the individual. "The supposed conflict between authority and experience," he writes, "is really a tension between two indispensable elements. For the *individual* Authority, whether as tribal custom or as alleged Revelation, is prior to Experience; in the *race* as a whole, Experience is prior to Authority." [86] In other words, while the tradition of the religious community is prior in the sense that it largely determines the form and content of the individual's experience, the religious experience of individuals is prior in the sense

---

[86] Temple, *op. cit.*, p. 329, italics mine.

that it was the original source of the tradition. Also, the tradition of the religious community is continually undergoing change as a result of criticism and reinterpretation by its individual members in the light of their experience. For example, modern members of the Christian community, influenced by intellectual and other cultural movements such as Renaissance humanism, modern science, and philosophical idealism, have questioned the authority of the Christian tradition at many points and have substantially modified its character. However, the individual is usually able to challenge the authority of the community's tradition only by appealing to an authority regarded by it as more ultimate than itself. For example, St. Francis challenged the worldliness of the medieval Church by appealing in behalf of poverty and humility to the authority of Jesus, and Luther based his attack on the authority of the Catholic Church of his time largely upon the authority of St. Paul.

Since they are interdependent, there is no necessary opposition between the authority of the religious community and the religious experience of the individual, provided the authority of the community is exercised in a spiritual way, i.e., with respect for the freedom and experience of the individual. On the other hand, if it is exercised by force or fear of penalty rather than by an appeal to the inherent truth of the tradition, it is opposed to the freedom of the individual and leads to the suppression of new truth. This can be avoided by the community only by acknowledging that it is not infallible and that "Intelligence and responsible judgment is the privilege and burden of spirit and personality." [87] This implies that, although the authority and tradition of the community are necessary in religion, the religious experience and reflection of individuals are equally essential for its vitality and development.

Religion and Morality

We noted above that the response of man to the Sacred includes moral conduct as well as worship. Throughout history morality has been closely associated with religion and even today many persons can hardly conceive of morality that is not based upon religion. However, since the Renaissance modern men have increasingly insisted upon the autonomy of morality as well as other forms of human activity, and philosophers have asserted that moral principles should be derived from reason and experience rather than revelation. Moreover, there is obviously *no necessary correlation* between religion and morality in men. As Schleiermacher pointed out, religious men

[87] *Ibid.*, pp. 345–349, 353.

are not always more moral than others and many moral men are not religious. On the other hand, Otto maintained that there is an *essential relation* between religion and morality and that one of the criteria of an advanced religion is the degree of moralization it has attained. What, then, is the relation between religion and morality?

Although some philosophers such as Kant have virtually reduced religion to a mere bulwark of morality and some theologians such as Brunner have disparaged morality that does not spring from religious faith, the relation of morality to religion is more complex than either of these one-sided views recognizes.

(1) *Religion and morality, at least in their highest forms, have a common root or origin in human nature.* (The qualification is important, for there has been much mercenary religion in which men worshipped the gods only for the benefits they hoped to receive from them and much prudential morality in which men conformed to the rules imposed by society merely from desire for its approval and fear of its disapproval.) Religion and morality at their highest level are manifestations of the spiritual capacity of man to transcend himself as he actually is by relating himself, on the one hand, to the Divine, and, on the other, to the Good. Animals below the level of man are bound by sensation and appetite to the natural order. But man as a spiritual being is able to experience a higher order of being and value and to transform his life by relating himself to it.

The primary concern of religion is with the establishment and maintenance of man's relationship to the Holy or Divine and with the transformation of his life which results from that relationship. On the other hand, morality in its purest form arises from the pressure upon man's consciousness of objective values and unconditional imperatives, which the ethical theist believes to be grounded in God, the transcendent Reality.[88] Its primary concern is with man's realization of the values and fulfillment of the obligations by which he is confronted. But the common aim of religion and morality is fullness of life.

It may be objected that morality is not based on objective values and unconditional imperatives grounded in a transcendent Reality, but arises from the human desire for personal happiness and social cohesion. This objection will doubtless seem convincing to those who have accepted the modern naturalistic view of the world, since there is no room in such a world view for any Reality which transcends the natural order. This is not the place to deal with the naturalistic view of morality. We will only point out here that it is contradicted by the fact that spiritual values such as truth and love seem to spring from a source that

[88] Cf. The moral argument in ch. 6.

transcends the natural order and that the unconditional character of moral imperatives cannot be explained by reference to social conditioning since they often require men to oppose their society even at the cost of persecution.

However, the objection may be restated in terms which do not presuppose a naturalistic world view. If morality originates from man's relationship as a spiritual being to a transcendent Reality, why does it often take a completely secular form, especially in modern culture? In answer to this objection it must be admitted that morality has often cut itself off from religion and that the process of secularization has gone far in the modern period. But the close relationship of morality to religion throughout the history of religion indicates that, whenever religion has been a living force, it has had a concern for morality and morality has been affected by it. Even the fact that morality has often been a severe critic of popular religion, as in Plato's *Republic,* indicates that it shares a common concern with religion for the higher life of man, although it may disapprove the way a particular religion conceives of that life. This close relationship of morality with religion in history suggests that the explanation of its modern divorce from religion is partly a loss of religious faith and partly a reaction against narrow forms of religious morality. The result is that many persons who acknowledge the claims of morality have ceased to be aware that it has a common root with religion. This is not surprising. While the concrete acts in which morality manifests itself are clearly visible, its spiritual root is hidden from view and can easily be denied. This has occurred in the case of many who have been so deeply influenced by the materialistic and this-worldly spirit of our modern culture that they are aware only of things and values of the natural and social order. However, even such persons frequently indicate by their awe and reverence for an act of singular moral heroism or purity that they are aware of something transcendent and sacred in it, although they have been so alienated from traditional religion that they do not use religious language for it.

(2) We have spoken first of the common spiritual root of morality and religion because it helps to explain their close relationship and mutual influence in history. But we must emphasize a second point which qualifies the first: although morality and religion grow from a common root, *they diverge from each other and manifest a relative independence of each other like branches of the same tree.* This explains the tension between them, a tension which sometimes leads to conflict and even to separation. How are we to understand this divergence and relative independence?

In answering this question, it may be helpful to recall our analysis of the relation between religion and philosophy.[89] We pointed out that the relation in that case also was one of both unity and diversity, that their unity was due to their common concern for truth about reality, but that their diversity resulted from the difference between them in aim and spirit. Similarly, morality and religion have a common concern for the attainment of the highest good or fullness of life, but they have different methods of achieving their aim. Since *religion* recognizes God as the Source of life and the Fountain of good, it seeks to gain the most fruitful relationship with Him through faith and to strengthen it through worship, so that the primary interest of religion is in man's relationship, personal and corporate, with God and the enhancement of life which results from it. However, if this interest becomes exclusive, as it often does in intense and single-minded persons, it may lead to a neglect of moral activity, as in passive mysticism. In contrast, although *morality* may derive its original impulse to the good from the pressure of the divine will upon human conscience, its primary task is to give expression to this impulse in the concrete situations of human life, to objectify or embody the good will in acts which will be appropriate to these ever-changing situations. Thus, while religion constantly seeks to direct man's attention to the center of his existence, his relationship to God, morality drives him outward to his relationships with his fellows.

Along with this difference in the direction of attention, there is a difference in attitude. Schleiermacher expresses this difference by saying that religion involves an attitude of passivity and receptivity, morality an attitude of activity. It is easy to exaggerate this difference, because religion involves both receptivity to divine influence and active response to it. But a difference of emphasis remains.

These differences account for the *tension* between religion and morality. When the claims of either are pressed to an extreme, there is inevitably a reaction on the part of the other and a counter-assertion of its claims. If moral seriousness leads men to exaggerate the efficacy of their own unaided reason and will, it awakens fear in strongly religious persons that man is exalting his own power and denying his need for God's grace. On the other hand, if religious zeal emphasizes trust in God and dependence upon His grace at the cost of minimizing man's own responsibility, it arouses the resistance of morally earnest men and leads them to assert man's capacities as a rational and free being. Thus, the danger is ever present that religion will subordinate

[89] Ch. 1.

the claims of morality, or that morality will minimize the need for religion, or that, after a struggle in which each resists encroachments by the other, there will be a separation of one from the other.

(3) Despite their divergence from one another, the fact that religion and morality have a common spiritual root and a common ultimate aim, fullness of life, makes it clear that *they have an "essential connection" with one another, as Otto maintained. This implies that while each should grant the distinctive function and relative independence of the other, they should recognize one another as allies.* Both sides of this statement must be stressed and asserted together. On the one hand, religion and morality are relatively independent and each should acknowledge the importance of the other and not attempt to dictate to it, e.g., religious communities should recognize the right of their members to determine their duties by their own reason and conscience. On the other hand, religion and morality should treat one another as allies rather than rivals and each should seek to strengthen and purify the other.

The latter point is especially important. It can be shown that *moral criticism* has at certain times purified religion of unworthy elements. In Greece, Plato sought to purify the popular polytheism by affirming that the gods are good and must never be regarded as a source of evil in the lives of men.[90] In India, the compassion of the Buddha and his rejection of caste distinctions among his monks were a powerful force for reform in Indian religion before Buddhism lost out in its long struggle with Hinduism. Even more striking was the criticism of the religion of the ancient Hebrews by prophets such as Amos and Micah who affirmed that Yahweh demanded justice and mercy to the weak and poor rather than sacrifice and that He would punish His people if they did not meet these moral demands. Unfortunately, the purification of religion through such moral criticism has been checked or negated by the conservatism of religious and political leaders and the moral inertia of most men. For example, after the expulsion of Buddhism from India, Hindu morality continued to require conformity to the pattern of duties defined by the caste system and the gods of the popular religion were only imperfectly moralized. And the radicalism of the Hebrew prophets and of Jesus' ethic of love was weakened in later Judaism and Christianity by the development of a legalistic ethic. Thus, while moral criticism has raised the level of great religions, most religious believers have failed to live up to the lofty ethical ideals of their prophets and founders.

It can also be shown that *religion* in its highest form has *raised*

[90] Plato: *Republic*, Books 2 and 3.

morality to a higher level. For example, the "dynamic religion" of Western ethical monotheism has inspired men with the vision of a world community and awakened a desire to overcome the forces that separate different classes, races, and nations and set them in opposition to each other. Based upon the belief that all men have been created by God and should love one another as brothers, this vision has made men aware that they have obligations not only to those of their own society but also to all mankind. Hence, it has aroused the desire to serve human needs wherever they arise and has stimulated modern political movements such as that which led to democracy and social movements such as the struggle for economic justice and racial equality. Thus, while what Bergson called "static religion" has usually been content to provide a divine source and sanction for the conservative social morality of a "closed society," "dynamic religion" has been one of the most powerful forces behind the creative morality that leads towards an "open society" of all mankind.[91]

[91] Bergson, Henri: *The Two Sources of Morality and Religion*, New York, Henry Holt, 1935.

3

Religious Experience:
Its Nature and Validity

In our analysis of the nature of religion, we pointed out that the religious experience of individuals is ultimately prior to the authority of the religious community.[1] Religious beliefs and practices have *originated* when men have been confronted by the Holy in their experience. They have been *transmitted* in a religious community from generation to generation, as the religious experiences and the forms of worship and conduct of its founder or founders have been repeated, with variations, by their followers. This repetition has not been the result solely of blind and passive submission by individuals to the authority of the religious community, for the more creative members of the community have *reinterpreted* its beliefs and practices from time to time in the light of their own religious experience. Thus, the religious experience of individuals and their reflection upon it has been not only the origin of religious beliefs and practices but also a source of their continuation from age to age and of the transformations they have undergone in every religious community. If so, it may be said that religious experience, with the interpretations men have put upon it, is the primary source of religious beliefs. The philosopher of religion, therefore, must analyze its nature and evaluate its claim to truth.

The Nature of Religious Experience

Religious experience may be understood in either a narrow or a broad sense. It is understood in a narrow sense when it is identified with a special kind of experience, in a broad sense when it is regarded as an attitude toward or perspective on the whole of experience. In its

[1] Ch. 2.

narrow sense, it is viewed as one kind of experience among others, one which occurs from time to time and is quite different from other experiences. An example of this view is Schleiermacher's definition of religion as "a feeling of absolute dependence" which is quite distinct from knowing and doing although it affects both of them. In conceptions of this sort religious experience is usually regarded as an intuition or feeling of the Holy or Divine, and the theological interpretation of its meaning in beliefs is regarded as based upon but not an integral part of it. In contrast, religious experience in the broad sense is an attitude which permeates and conditions the whole of experience. It determines man's thinking not only about the Divine but also about the world, and it informs his conduct not only in worship but in every other phase of his activity.

There is much to be said for each of these views. On the one hand, certain kinds of experience have seemed to religious people to possess crucial importance and hence to stand out from the rest of their experience, e.g., conversion and mystical union. Even the ordinary religious experience of men when they engage in private prayer or public worship seems to them to be different in quality from their experience as they go about their daily work. On the other hand, the most deeply religious persons have insisted that religion must not be confined to occasional experiences which are enjoyed at special times and places, but must permeate and control the whole of life. It would seem, therefore, that both conceptions are true in different respects and that they complement one another. The narrow conception is true in that special kinds of experience have given rise to religious beliefs and practices and are necessary to sustain and strengthen them in the present. But it is also true that religion in its highest form requires that everything a man does should be done in the spirit of devotion, e.g., that his work no less than his worship should be offered to God. Indeed, some deeply religious men have asserted that through the practice of the presence of God their consciousness of Him has become continuous, accompanying the performance of even the most menial tasks. The saint, especially, seems to be one whose whole life and thought are dominated by God. Thus, if we equate religious experience with a special kind of experience and limit it to particular times and places, we disregard the fact that in its purest and most intense form it will not be confined in this way but extends its influence to every phase of experience. At the same time, religious people need the stimulus offered by special occasions to strengthen and deepen their religious life; and religion is more likely to extend its influence over the whole of their thought and activity if religious experiences on these occasions bring their relation to God to the center of attention and intensify it.

We would suggest, therefore, that the narrow view of religious experience is justified insofar as men experience God's presence more deeply and strongly at some times than at others and that this is a necessary condition for the extension of their consciousness of Him to the whole of their experience. At the same time, the broad view is justified insofar as the goal of religion in its purest form is to permeate all experience and transform all the thoughts and actions of men. Hence, a distinction between sacred and profane is unavoidable, because special occasions are necessary to sustain and strengthen the religious life; on the other hand, it is an indication of the weakness of men's religion that they cannot experience every thing and event, every place and time, as sacred.

There has been a tendency among psychologists of religion such as William James to equate religious experience with *inner states* alone, neglecting the *outer actions* which often accompany, express, and strengthen them. But Van der Leeuw has pointed out that in the religious response to the Holy "inward action" must not be separated from "outward action." [2] Outer action is both an expression and a condition of inner experience. For example, a rite of purification such as baptism gives expression to the inner experience of passing from an old to a new life and at the same time deepens that experience. Again, symbolic acts such as standing, kneeling, or prostrating oneself in prayer express the inner feeling of devotion and at the same time intensify it. As we indicated in our discussion of worship, the expression of religious ideas and feelings in visible form is necessary because men are flesh as well as spirit, and religion is often expressed most effectively in ritual acts and moral conduct. Thus, "outward action" no less than "inward action" belongs to religious experience. The religious experience of a community must be expressed periodically in acts such as singing, preaching, praying, and performing sacramental rites. The moral aspect of a religion must also express itself in outer acts, and it can be argued that the best test of the quality of a person's religious experience is to be found not in his inner feelings but in his conduct. On the other hand, "outward action" is religious only insofar as it is an embodiment of "inward action," e.g., kneeling has religious significance only if it expresses a real intention to pray. In the absence of the latter, it may be a social or an aesthetic, but it can hardly be a religious, experience. Thus, religious experience includes both inner states of consciousness and the outer manifestation of them in the most intimate relation to one another.

[2] Van der Leeuw, G.: *op. cit.*, Vol. II, A, B.

Philosophical and Theological Objections

Since the rejection by Kant of the "proofs" of rational theology, many philosophers of religion have taken the religious experience of men as their starting-point. In this sense, modern philosophy of religion has tended to be empirical rather than rationalistic. As we have seen, some philosophers have held that religious knowledge arises immediately from religious experience, e.g., Schleiermacher, Otto, and Buber, while others have argued that religious experience must be interpreted within a philosophical framework constructed by reason, e.g., Tillich. But all of these thinkers alike have begun in their reflection on religion with the religious experience of mankind as it has developed in the history of religion.

A contemporary philosopher of religion who starts from religious experience must face the fact that the theory of experience of many philosophers today is opposed to the appeal to religious experience as a source of knowledge. This theory gives a privileged position to sense experience and regards other forms of experience as subjective and without cognitive value. Under the influence of the scientific method, it demands that religious beliefs must be verified like scientific hypotheses by an appeal to sense experience. It also assumes that the contents of immediate experience are mental, i.e., that we have no direct experience of objects but only of our ideas. In Hume's words, "nothing is ever really present with the mind but its perceptions or impressions and ideas" and "external objects become known to us only by those perceptions they occasion." [3]

But a broader and more inclusive view of experience refuses to dismiss areas of experience other than sense experience as merely subjective. As John Smith has pointed out, there are different "dimensions of experience" or "frameworks of meaning" within which experience is interpreted.[4] These are standpoints from which different relations of things can be understood and different purposes of the self can be carried out. Art, morality, and religion are such "dimensions of experience" [5] no less than science and should not be expected to meet the same conditions as are required for scientific knowledge. Moreover, a realistic theory of knowledge rejects the view that we have direct experience only of ideas in our minds and never of objects themselves. Rather, experience is "a product of the intersection of something encountered and a being capable of having the encounter, apprehending

[3] Hume, David: *Selections,* New York, Charles Scribner's Sons, 1955, p. 21.
[4] Smith, John: *Experience and God,* New York, Oxford University Press, 1968, p. 37.
[5] *Ibid.,* pp. 38, 39.

it, and feeling itself in the encounter, and capable of interpreting the results." [6] The object which is encountered is independent of the subject who experiences it and demands that he do full justice to all of its aspects and relations, not merely those in which science is interested. At the same time, the subject who experiences an object has a nature of his own, a nature which enters into his interpretation of it because of the interest he brings to it and the questions he asks of it.

The assumption that experience is merely "subjective" except in the privileged case of sense experience is the result of an arbitrary abstraction from one side of it. Of course, knowledge of the object cannot be immediately "read off" the experience of it, since the object may be complex and both the theoretical and the practical interests of the subject are involved in knowing it. Hence, the subjective factor must be recognized as important. Also, since there is always a possibility of error in interpreting the object, the subject must distinguish between the contents of his experience which are merely private and those which can be encountered by anyone and hence should be regarded as objective. But this does not mean that the contents or objects of our experience are always private and hence "merely subjective." "There is no warrant whatever," as John Smith says, "for supposing that the individual self starts out *knowing* that all of its 'experience' is private, personal, and confined wholly to its own consciousness, and that it then must find a way of surmounting that subjectivity in order to reach the 'external world.' " [7]

We have argued that the religious dimension of experience involves an encounter with reality and therefore has as much right to be taken seriously as the scientific dimension, although there is always a possibility of error in interpreting it. There is no sound reason, therefore, why the philosopher of religion should not take religious experience as at least one of the main sources of religious beliefs and make it the starting-point of his quest for religious truth. However, the use he makes of it will depend upon whether he thinks that it gives man an immediate knowledge of the Holy or Divine, as mystics assert, or whether he regards its apprehension as *mediated* and requiring *interpretation*. Under the influence of mysticism, William James and others have taken the former position. But there are serious objections to this. It may be argued that there is no immediate experience that is meaningful in itself, that the experience of God is always at the same time an experience of something else, and therefore that it is a mediated experience that requires to be interpreted.[8] Moreover, religious expe-

[6] *Ibid.*, p. 24.
[7] *Ibid.*, p. 33.
[8] *Ibid.*, p. 52.

rience tends to become a dimension of experience as a whole, as we indicated in the preceding section. This requires that it be interpreted and that its implications be drawn out by reason.

We shall consider in the latter part of this chapter some specific criticisms which have been directed by recent empiricists against the claims of religious experience. But we must take account here of a criticism of a very different kind which has been raised by Neo-orthodox theologians such as Karl Barth. These theologians have attacked the appeal to religious experience by Schleiermacher and others on the ground that it presupposes the capacity of man to relate himself to God by means of his own experience, whereas God can be known only as He has revealed Himself in the Scriptures.[9] If men are convinced, they assert, that they can know God by means of their own religious experience, they will conclude that they need not seek Him in His Word. To support this argument they point to the historical development of Protestant theology after Schleiermacher which was characterized by an increasing tendency to emphasize the immanence of God in human experience. This led, they believe, to a tendency of Liberal Christians to substitute religious experience for faith in God as revealed in the Bible.

There is an element of truth in this view, for an excessive preoccupation of man with his own religious experience can easily lead to a neglect of the divine object of the experience. But whatever may be one's opinion of nineteenth century Protestant theology, there is no essential connection between an appeal to religious experience and a denial of revelation. Of course, the philosopher of religion is not called upon to determine whether a revelation actually occurred at a particular time, or, if it did occur, whether the interpretation of it by a particular religious community is true. He can and should make no judgment concerning the claims of any "special revelation" in history. He may take into account fundamental religious beliefs which have originated in what a religious community has regarded as revelation, but he must subject them to critical examination to determine whether all or some of them can be supported by experience as a whole or are at least compatible with it.

But the fact that the philosopher of religion must not accept a revelation on authority and without critical examination does not mean that he denies its truth and wishes to replace it by religious experience. For there is no incompatibility between revelation and religious experience, as if a denial of the one is implied in an appeal to the other. Revelation involves a relation between God who gives and man who

[9] Barth, Karl: *Church Dogmatics*, Edinburgh, T. and T. Clark, 1955, Vol. 1, Part 2, ¶17.

receives it, and man can receive it only through the medium of his experience. Moreover, it can become intelligible to him only if he interprets it by means of his thought and expresses it in terms of his language. But this by no means reduces divine revelation to the human religious experience which is the medium for its reception. For religious experience, as we have said, is an encounter between the Holy and a human subject, and an interpretation of it which denied its divine object would be a distortion of it.

That which characterizes a "special revelation" which is the basis of a religious community is not that it has been received through another medium than religious experience but that it has occurred in particular historical situations and has been interpreted by particular persons, e.g., the prophets and apostles of the Bible. This implies that a special revelation is mediated by the historical situations in which it occurs and the prophetic minds which interpret it to others. But the fact that special revelations have occurred only in certain historical situations does not imply that there is a complete discontinuity between these revelations and man's general religious experience, as Barth seems to think. A special revelation need not negate the fragmentary and imperfect insights that come to men through their general religious experience but may purify them of errors, affirm the partial truths contained in them, and thus fulfill them. Thus, the relation of religious experience to revelation is a two-sided one: there is no incompatibility or even discontinuity between them since revelation must occur through the medium of religious experience, but a special revelation claims a concrete and definite disclosure of the Holy in history and provides a basis for the faith of a religious community.

General Characteristics and Specific Forms

It is the task of the historian and psychologist of religion rather than the philosopher of religion to describe the "varieties" of religious experience. But the philosopher who regards religious experience not only as the primary *source* but also as one of the main *grounds* of religious belief must at least offer a general analysis of some of the major aspects of religious experience and the beliefs associated with them.

There has been a remarkable development in the character of religious experience and of the religious beliefs associated with it from the primitive to the most advanced religions, a development in which many superstitious beliefs and crude practices have been eliminated. The philosopher of religion is interested primarily in the religious experience distinctive of the most advanced religions, since it is only these which offer "vital options" to men of today. Although there is a risk that he will be arbitrary and prejudiced in his decision as to which religions are the most advanced and which aspects of religious experience are most significant, he can profit in making his decision on each of these points from the work of modern historians and phenomenologists of religion who have been carefully studying the development of religions for more than a century and a half.

In the last chapter we pointed out that religion arises when man in his quest for fullness and wholeness of life is confronted by the Holy, a superior Power which is mysterious and incomprehensible to him. His response to the Holy, as described by Otto, is a feeling of awe as he recognizes his own weakness in the presence of its overwhelming majesty. This awe is accompanied by dread and in some primitive religions the element of dread seems to be dominant and men seek above all to propitiate the invisible powers that surround them. But men are not only daunted, they are also fascinated by and attracted to the Holy and seek to establish a relationship with it.

We also noted that this feeling of awe combined with dread and fascination is accompanied by an attitude of absolute devotion to the Holy as possessing absolute worth. At this point, Otto's description of the Holy is inadequate because he emphasizes its uncanny otherness in primitive religion so strongly that it is difficult to see why primitive men paid absolute devotion to it. But John Oman points out that even in primitive religion the feeling of the Holy was accompanied by a valuation of it as the *Sacred*. This valuation was obviously not always a moral valuation, since it was often given to material things. Hence, Oman distinguishes between the "moral sacred" and the "material sacred" and concedes that the latter has sometimes included "the most weird and debased objects." [10] For men's primitive experiences of the Holy were often associated with natural forms such as animals and stones, and primitive man could not separate the Holy from the whole context in which he experienced it.[11] But the germ of the "moral sacred," as the Hebrew prophets were to conceive it, was present in primitive man's valuation of something, however material and crude, as possessing an absolute worth incommensurable with worldly values of pleasure, comfort, or even life.[12] For this valuation liberated him from his bondage to the relative values of the material world and required him to subordinate everything including life itself to his absolute devotion to a higher reality.[13]

[10] Oman, John: "The Sphere of Religion," in *Science, Religion and Reality*, ed. by J. Needham, New York, Macmillan, 1925, p. 290.

[11] *Ibid.*, p. 291.

[12] *Ibid.*, p. 289.

[13] *Ibid.*, pp. 292–293.

However, there is an *ambivalence* in the attitude of man towards the claim of the Sacred to absolute devotion. On the one hand, man desires to comply with the demands of the Sacred upon him and to reach out towards the possibility it opens up to him; on the other hand, he attempts to escape from it and hold on to his life as it is.[14] When he yields to the latter tendency, his "avoidance of God" may take any one of several forms. He may simply try to ignore the demand of the Sacred; or he may presumptuously seize power for himself with what the Greeks called *hubris* towards the gods; or he may rely upon the habitual use of established rites or correct behavior.[15] On the other hand, he can overcome his dread before God by faith in Him, and avoidance then gives way to love. In the words of the New Testament, "There is no fear in love; but perfect love casteth out fear." [16] Man can approach God with confidence, so that the daunting aspect which made Him an object of dread is overshadowed by His gracious aspect. Perhaps this is what Whitehead meant when he spoke of the last stage in the development of religion as a transition "from God the enemy to God the companion." [17]

When man does not seek to avoid the demands of the Holy and Sacred but yields himself to it in faith he enters into *communion* with it. Van der Leeuw describes some of the forms this relationship with the Holy and Sacred has taken in the history of religion. Sometimes it has assumed the form of absolute submission, man humbling himself before God and seeking to serve Him, as in Parsiism.[18] Sometimes it has been based upon a covenant with Him, in which both man and God have pledged themselves to a definite course of conduct. For example, in the Old Testament Israel pledged herself to obedience to Yahweh's commands and Yahweh pledged Himself to prosper her and give her victory over her enemies.[19] Sometimes the relationship with God has become so intimate that service of Him and obedience to His commands has given way to friendship with Him and love for Him. For example, the Book of Deuteronomy represents Israel's love for Yahweh as an answer to His love for her in the past, despite the fact that her love for Him has been so vacillating.[20] Similarly, in Bhakti Hinduism it is the love of a personal God for man which invokes man's love and devotion. In the *Bhagavad Gita*, God says, "Dear art thou to

[14] Van der Leeuw, *op. cit.*, Vol. II, p. 466.

[15] *Ibid.*, pp. 468–470.

[16] I John 4:18.

[17] Whitehead, A. N.: *Religion in the Making*, New York, Meridian Books, 1961, p. 16.

[18] Van der Leeuw, *op. cit.*, Vol. II, pp. 472, 473.

[19] *Ibid.*, p. 474.

[20] *Deut.*, chs. 1–4; 8.

me most surely; therefore I will speak what is for thy good. Have thy mind on me, be devoted to me, sacrifice to me, do reverence to me. To me thou shalt come; what is true I promise; dear art thou to me." [21] And in Christianity God is love, and man's love for Him is a response to His antecedent love for man. "We love because He first loved us." [22]

Thus, *awe* in the presence of God as the Holy and *devotion* to Him as Sacred leads in theistic religions such as Judaism and Christianity to *communion* with Him which in its purest form is reciprocal love. But man's actual existence is imperfect, and he does not attain an ideal relationship with God easily and without effort. There is something in the human condition which prevents him from entering into such a relationship or disrupts it after he has attained it. This obstacle which stands in the way and must be overcome is not the same in all religions because the conceptions of man's condition and of God's nature are radically different. This may be illustrated by a comparison of the theism of Judaism and Christianity with the monism of Hinduism.

In Western theism, the relationship between man and God is distorted by man's *sin* and *guilt*. Jews and Christians are fully aware of other evils from which men suffer, e.g., natural evils such as pain and death, but the evil with which they are primarily concerned is sin. Sin is not the same as moral transgression or failure; it is the opposition of the human to the divine will. Its essence is not moral wrongdoing, although it leads to injustice and other forms of immorality; rather, it is estrangement or separation from God. Hence, it cannot be overcome by moral reformation but only by reconciliation with God. It is primarily an inner condition of the self and it affects every part of the self. Therefore, it should never be identified with particular "sins," although it manifests itself in sinful acts. Thus, it is essentially a religious rather than a moral state, for it is a disruption of the proper relationship between the self and God which destroys the harmony of man with God. He is "lost" like a sheep which has gone astray or a "prodigal" son who has left his father's house and wanders without purpose in the world.[23] He is alienated not only from God but also from his fellows and from his true self.

Deliverance from this state of estrangement can come only through *conversion* or *rebirth*, gradual or sudden. It begins with repentance, which is not mere sorrow over transgressions committed by the self but contrition for its alienation from God by sin and a turning away from sin towards Him. Repentance leads through faith to a radical trans-

[21] Quoted in Van der Leeuw, *op. cit.*, Vol. II, pp. 510, 511.
[22] I John 4:19.
[23] Luke 15.

formation of the self, a reorientation of it around a new center. The self is "born again," is reconciled to God, and enters upon a new life of peace and joy.

Rebirth has been a phenomenon of many religions. The *rites de passage*, rites which are performed at times of transition in life, e.g., at birth, puberty, marriage, and death, are of great importance in both primitive and advanced religions. The rite of initiation is especially interesting, since it marks the entrance of a youth into a new life as a responsible member of the group.[24] In the mystery religions of ancient Greece initiation into the mysteries of the god meant a renewal of life and the hope of life after death. Conversion in Jewish and Christian theism should be understood in somewhat similar but also different terms. The Psalmist cries out, "Create in me a clean heart, O God, and put a new and right spirit within me." [25] In the Gospel of John, Jesus says to Nicodemus, "Truly, truly, I say to you, unless one is born anew, he cannot see the Kingdom of God." [26] St. Augustine's conversion in the garden at Milan also involved a new birth, although it had been prepared for by years of restless searching.[27] Pascal's conversion, which was centered in the "God of Abraham, God of Isaac, God of Jacob, not of the philosophers and the wise," brought "forgetfulness of the world and of all save God" and was accompanied by feelings of joy and certitude.[28] William James describes experiences of conversion such as these as due to an irruption into consciousness, often sudden and forcible, of what has been developing below the level of consciousness, with the result that the whole personality becomes reoriented and unified around a new center, i.e., a new belief and sentiment.[29] Whatever the psychological explanation may be, conversion involves "a surrender of man's own power in favour of one that utterly overwhelms him and is experienced as sacred and as 'wholly other'," so that "it is not man who converts himself, but God who converts him: God bestows life." [30]

However, sin persists even after the self has been reconciled to God through conversion. Reinhold Niebuhr has repeatedly insisted upon this fact and hence upon the necessity of repentance and forgiveness to the end of life. He speaks of "the intolerable pretension of saints

[24] Malinowski, B.: "Magic, Science and Religion" in Needham, (ed.), *op. cit.*
[25] Psalm 51:10.
[26] John 3:3.
[27] Augustine: *Confessions*, Bk. 8.
[28] Pascal, B.: "Memorial," quoted by Van der Leeuw, *op. cit.*, Vol. II, p. 532.
[29] James, William: *Varieties of Religious Experience*, New York, Modern Library, 1936, Lecture IX.
[30] Van der Leeuw, *op. cit.*, p. 534.

who have forgotten that they are sinners." [31] Hence, the religious experience for Western theists is far from being a continuous and uninterrupted state of peace and joy. The man of faith must not only continue to struggle with sin and suffer from the consciousness of guilt; he must also face doubts and periods of spiritual dryness when God seems remote or completely absent. Thus, *peace* and *joy* are interspersed with *conflict* and *suffering* in the religious life, because it is only through self-denial and suffering that self-fulfillment and salvation can come. But despite the persistence of sin, the assaults of doubt, and the pain involved in self-renunciation, the religious life of the theist is dominated by a deep and abiding trust in God accompanied by peace and joy and hope for the future. For the man of faith lives in communion with God and is not alone when he faces suffering but is supported by a power greater than his own.

The religious experience of Hindu monism as represented by Sankara and his followers is very different. The primary evil which stands in the way of the realization by the self of its proper relationship to Brahman is not sin but suffering. The cause of this suffering is not the sinful opposition of the self to the divine will, but ignorance of its true nature. It can attain liberation from its suffering only by coming to knowledge of the identity of the true or essential Self with Brahman.

The kind of religious experience which lies behind these beliefs is very different from the religious experience of Jewish and Christian theism. Van der Leeuw characterizes theism as essentially a "religion of unrest" in which God is "never-resting Will, which governs all human life" and will never "leave His people in repose." [32] "The God who descends to destroy the Tower of Babel," he says, "descends a second time to deliver mankind; whether in anger or in compassion, He never leaves humanity in peace. Wherever man goes, God's creative love pursues him." [33] Van der Leeuw contrasts this theistic "religion of unrest" with "the main stream of Hindu religious sentiment" which "directs itself towards the infinite and attempts to attain it by asceticism." [34] Through an ascetic discipline the self seeks to liberate itself from the ignorance which binds it to the world of appearance in order to experience union with the infinite, eternal Brahman. For it is only by merging with the repose and bliss of the Brahman that it can hope to free itself from the suffering of mortal existence and attain repose and

---

[31] Niebuhr, R.: *The Nature and Destiny of Man*, New York, Charles Scribner's Sons, 1943, Vol. II, p. 126.

[32] Van der Leeuw, *op. cit.*, Vol. II, p. 607.

[33] *Ibid.*, p. 608.

[34] *Ibid.*, p. 626.

bliss itself. Clearly this "religion of repose" is the antithesis of the theistic "religion of unrest," since the Brahman is at rest in Itself and the self finds rest by losing itself in Its infinite being.

The form of religious experience through which this goal is attained is mysticism. That which distinguishes mysticism from ordinary religious experience is that the mystic seeks to break down the barriers that separate him from God and to become one with Him. In order to attain complete union, he eliminates all the contents of his consciousness, including his ideas and images of God as well as his earthly desires. When he has left the world behind and reduced his own self to nothingness, he realizes his goal of union and is filled with peace and joy. For him, the scriptures, ritual acts, and dogmas of organized religion are subordinate to his experience of union. Even moral conduct is secondary, although moral discipline purifies the soul and thus prepares it for the union it seeks with God. Thus, the mystic witnesses to the possibility of gaining an immediate experience of union with God by removing the obstacles which separate most religious people from Him. Although he may enjoy the union he seeks very rarely, it gives him an experience of that fullness of life and joy which constitutes salvation.

Van der Leeuw points out that mysticism in some form has arisen in virtually every religion and that it is an essential element in all religions. But he adds that it is seldom "pure" and that a religion can incorporate mystical elements within itself "only insofar as they do not contradict its own essential character." [35] For example, mysticism is limited in Islam and Judaism by the commandments of God and in Christianity by the one absolute commandment of love, i.e., by the ethical element in each of these religions.[36] Moreover, the "numinous" experience of God as transcendent and "other" than His creatures has been dominant in Western theism, and it has emphasized the radical distinction between God and man. Hence, although mysticism has had a considerable influence on Western religions,[37] it has not been the primary determining factor in them. In contrast, it has been dominant in Hindu monism and has largely determined the conception of the Brahman and Its relation to the self.

[35] *Ibid.*, p. 508.

[36] *Ibid.*, p. 508.

[37] For an analysis and evaluation of the Christian mystic Meister Eckhart and the differences between theistic and monistic mysticism, see the author's *Religious Philosophies of the West*, Ch. 4, and Zaehner, R. C.: *Mysticism, Sacred and Profane,* Oxford, The Clarendon Press, 1957.

Cognitive Value: Critical

The diversity of interpretations of religious experience which we have illustrated by these differences between Western theism and Hindu monism, as well as the difficulty of verifying any of these interpretations with certainty, has led a number of recent philosophers to criticize the claim of religious experience to give us knowledge.

(1) One of the strongest of these critics was F. R. Tennant. As an empiricist, Tennant maintained that all our knowledge of reality, with the exception of knowledge of the soul, is derived from sense perception. Therefore, although he was a theist, he rejected the claim that religious experience gives us knowledge of a divine reality. He acknowledges that it *seems* to religious people that they are experiencing an objective divine reality, but he maintains that the object that is before them may be an image or idea in their own minds rather than a real being. Hence, he thinks that religious experience cannot be the source of belief in God but presupposes that that belief has already been attained in another way. "We may believe in the Beyond, or in God, on less direct grounds reached by more circuitous paths, and then reasonably interpret numinous or religious experience in terms of the theistic concept and world-view: on the way back [from belief], so to say, as distinguished from the way out [to belief]." [38]

The main arguments of Tennant for this conclusion can be briefly stated. First, a divine object is not known in the religious experience with an immediacy like that of an object of sense perception. Whereas in the latter a particular quality is given, "there seems to be no corresponding or quasi-impressional *quale* presented in alleged apprehension of the numinous Reality." [39] In other words, the object presented is too vague and indefinite to give us any assurance that it is God that is being experienced. Second, while religious experience may *seem* to the religious person to provide an immediate knowledge of God, he may be unaware that this conviction is actually being mediated to him by an image or idea of God in his mind. [40] For imaginal or ideational objects are as capable of evoking profound and intense feelings as real perceptual objects are, and this may lead the religious person to think he is "reading off" reality what he is actually "reading in." [41] Finally, the fact that "the numinous Real is indeterminate enough to enter equally well into a number of diverse mythologies and religions" sug-

[38] Tennant, F. R.: *Philosophical Theology*, Cambridge, Mass., Cambridge University Press, 1928, Vol. I, p. 311. Brackets added.
[39] *Ibid.*, p. 309.
[40] *Ibid.*, pp. 309, 310.
[41] *Ibid.*, p. 309.

gests that in each case it is actually derived from beliefs already held in a particular religion and shared by the individual.

Tennant's criticism of the cognitive claims of mystical experience is even sharper. If the experience is "ineffable," as often said, it is indescribable and therefore cannot provide us with truth.[42] On the other hand, if it takes the form of visions which claim to offer specific truths, the diversity of such truths offered by mystics of different religions should warn us that these truths have probably been derived by them from their various religious traditions. Thus, when Christian mystics have seen visions which have disclosed to them the mysteries of the Trinity, the Creation, and the Assumption of the Virgin Mary, it is obvious that "they have seen what they were by education predisposed to see." [43] Moreover, the discipline imposed by the mystic upon himself in order to attain his goal of union, i.e., his elimination of all the contents of his consciousness and his intense concentration upon a single object, may provide a psychological explanation for the ineffability of his mystical experience and for the negations he uses to describe it.[44]

These criticisms are largely determined by Tennant's narrow empirical theory of knowledge. Since he holds that all knowledge begins with perception, he is bound to reject all claims of religious experience to offer an intuitive apprehension of a supersensible reality. He is also motivated as a philosophical theologian by the desire to develop a theistic world view which is based upon evidence available to all, religious and nonreligious alike, and which can therefore commend itself to scientists and philosophers lacking in religious experience. It is this empiricism which leads him to deny that religious experience presents us with a "quale" comparable to that experienced in sensation and to conclude from this that it is too "vague" to give us knowledge.

Now, it is certainly true that religious experience differs from sense perception in the quality of its object, for its object is the "Holy" which transcends all objects of sense and therefore has qualities very different from any quality they possess. But it does not follow from this that its object is "qualityless," "vague," and "indeterminate," although its qualities may be very difficult to describe. Of course, the descriptions of it by phenomenologists and philosophers such as Otto, Oman, and Van der Leeuw present qualities which cannot be pointed out to all and observed through the senses. But their widespread acceptance as correct descriptions of the divine object, insofar as its transcendence permits description, is strong evidence that men *do* ex-

[42] *Ibid.*, p. 314.
[43] *Ibid.*, p. 319.
[44] *Ibid.*, pp. 322, 323.

perience these qualities. Similarly, Tennant misinterprets the statement of mystics that their experiences are "ineffable." They make this statement not because they have experienced no real object but because the Divine transcends every finite thing or quality with which we are familiar and cannot be fully expressed in words derived from finite things. And it is significant that despite this difficulty mystics pour out one image or analogy after another to express the fullness of being and value of the Divine which they have experienced.

It is because Tennant's empiricism will not allow him to accept an intuitive apprehension of a supersensible reality that he is forced to offer a psychological explanation of the object of religious experience, suggesting that a religious person is really experiencing only an image or idea in his own mind. Of course, if one holds that knowledge can be attained only through the data of the senses and inferences based upon them, one is bound to regard the conviction of religious people that they have experienced God as an illusion. But the empiricism which leads to such a conclusion would result in complete skepticism if it were applied consistently in all fields of experience. If one is not prepared to accept such an all-embracing skepticism as this, one must reject Tennant's empiricism which leads to it.

However, Tennant's criticism is valuable because he points out that the content of the religious experience is affected by the beliefs brought to it by the religious person. Since religious experience cannot be isolated from the rest of experience, ideas and images based upon the religious beliefs of the individual and ultimately derived from his religious tradition inevitably influence his interpretation of the object of the experience. Indeed, it is difficult, if not impossible, to separate completely the object as experienced from the object as interpreted because every experience is conditioned by the attitudes and beliefs of the individual. Therefore, Tennant is justified in saying that much which a religious person may think he is "reading off" the object he is actually "reading in." How could it be otherwise? He enters the religious experience not with an empty mind but with dispositions, feelings, and beliefs developed in a particular religious community at a particular time in history. Moreover, modern psychology has made us aware that there is much in his mind of which he is unconscious. It is not strange, therefore, that the content of the visions which some (by no means all) mystics have reported, e.g., the nature of the Trinity or the Creation, is found to be conditioned by beliefs derived from their religious traditions. The implication of this is clear: although the claim that religious experience involves an apprehension of God can be maintained, many of the claims made by religious persons concerning specific truths gained directly from it are exaggerated. Hence, these claims should be critically examined in the light of experience as a whole and of reflection upon it.

(2) The objections raised by Ronald Hepburn in his *Christianity and Paradox* are directed mainly against the view of Martin Buber, Emil Brunner, and others that in a direct personal "encounter" between a human "I" and a divine "Thou" we attain knowledge of the existence and nature of God that is "self-authenticating" and needs no support from rational theology. Hepburn points out that the relation of an "I" with a human "Thou" depends upon relations with the latter as an object or an "It," relations which are mediated by sense perception of his behavior, gestures, and talk.[45] Moreover, mistakes in interpreting another person are possible and can be corrected only by observing his behavior further and more carefully.[46] He implies that this is not possible in the case of God when He seems to be encountered as a "Thou" who should never be an "It" and that this casts doubt upon the belief that He can be known directly as a divine "Thou" analogous to a human "Thou." Since we cannot make use of "bodily features, sounds, and appearances" to mediate knowledge of Him and to correct mistakes about Him, we have no "checking procedures" to test assertions about Him. This suggests that Freud may be right in thinking that a religious "encounter" is not really a meeting with a divine "Thou" but involves the projection of human personality upon an impersonal cosmos.[47] At the very least, "the transition from 'numinous awe' to 'therefore experience of the transcendent'—of the 'wholly other' —is far from a reliable one, cannot be honestly called immediate or self-authenticating." It is necessary, therefore, to "step outside the felt experiences themselves" to determine whether this transition to an objective divine reality is valid.[48]

Of course, it might be maintained, Hepburn continues, that there is a reciprocal personal relationship with God which is mediated through events of nature and history, so that a person is assured of His "presence" but is given no "conceptual" knowledge about Him.[49] The difficulty with this view is that a person might be mistaken in thinking that he was in communication with a personal God distinct from ("behind") the world, when in fact he was only in communication with those aspects of the world itself through which the experience came to

[45] Hepburn, R. W.: *Christianity and Paradox*, London, Watts, 1958, pp. 32–34.
[46] *Ibid.*, pp. 34–37.
[47] *Ibid.*, p. 45.
[48] *Ibid.*, pp. 47, 48.
[49] *Ibid.*, p. 52.

him.[50] Moreover, even if the claim of the person that he was communicating with a personal God could be verified, there would still be
a question "what sort of God" was encountered, for men have thought
they encountered many different sorts of gods.[51] If the term "God" is
taken simply as a proper name for the Thou who seems to be met in
prayer, the assertion by the theist that He is also Father and Creator
adds new information about Him which is not immediately given in
the encounter.[52] Hence, this assertion must be established in some
other way. Therefore, we must abandon the claim that the personal
encounter with God is immediate and self-authenticating and recognize
the necessity to supplement the encounter-experience with philosophical reflection.[53]

These criticisms are more subtle and less dogmatic than those of
Tennant. For Hepburn does not seem to deny the *possibility* of a
direct intuition of God in the religious experience; rather, he raises
difficulties that must be faced by those who assert that they have
actually had such an intuition. How can we know that that which is
encountered is a personal Being analogous to human persons, since we
come to know the latter only with the aid of observation of their bodily
behavior and talk? Even if the claim is made that we can encounter
Him through events of nature and history, how can we know that we
are encountering a personal Thou "behind" the events, and if so
whether He is also the Creator and Father of theism rather than some
other kind of God?

These difficulties must be taken seriously by theists, and they seem
fatal to the claim that the religious experience gives us detailed
knowledge of God's reality and His nature. We know a human person,
a Thou, only when we know about him as an object, an It, through
observation of his bodily behavior, which is impossible in the case of
God; and we cannot *know* with certainty that we are encountering Him
indirectly through His manifestations in nature and history. This
should warn us against the exclusive reliance of Buber and Brunner
upon the experience of personal encounter to give us direct knowledge
of both the existence and the nature of God. As Hepburn says, there
are no "checking-procedures" in the case of God comparable to those
by which the claim to know a human person can be verified or falsified.
How could there be, if God is a transcendent Being distinct from the
world, as theists believe Him to be? Moreover, while the diversity of

[50] *Ibid.*, pp. 52–54.
[51] *Ibid.*, p. 55.
[52] *Ibid.*, p. 57.
[53] *Ibid.*, p. 59.

interpretations of the object of the religious encounter does not prove that *all* of them are false, it raises the question whether the claim of any *one* of them to be true while the *others* are false may not be arbitrary. From this we must conclude that Buber and Brunner make exaggerated claims for the cognitive value of I-Thou encounters. If the claim that such encounters give us knowledge of the existence and nature of the God of theism is to be more than a blind faith, it must be supported by other types of experience and be compatible with experience as a whole. We shall return later to the question raised by the fact that some religions have interpreted the object of the religious experience as another "sort" of God than the Creator and Father of theism, for this question troubles many in our time when historical relativism concerning religious beliefs is so widespread.

The basic weakness of Hepburn's argument is his apparent assumption that the *only* way to evaluate critically the cognitive claim of a religious experience is to "step outside" religious experience altogether and consider other kinds of evidence. This assumption is probably due to the fact that the only sort of "checking-procedure" he seems to acknowledge is observation of behavior and other natural and historical phenomena through the senses, a view which shows the influence of empiricism upon his thinking. On the contrary, we would maintain that the cognitive claim of a religious experience can be supported, even if not conclusively verified, by other religious experiences of a similar kind, especially when they have been enjoyed by persons in several different religions which have developed in independence of each other, e.g., the experience of devotion to a personal God in Bhakti Hinduism and a certain sect of Mahayana Buddhism as well as Judaism and Christianity, or the widespread experience of mystical union. This may not *prove* the objective reality of God but it strongly *supports* the belief in Him. Thus, while we would agree with Hepburn that it is necessary to examine critically the cognitive claim of a religious experience, we would insist that among the most important kinds of evidence to be examined in testing that claim are other religious experiences. To deny this would require us to dismiss as illusory a kind of experience which, if not universal, has been so widespread that it would be arbitrary to rule it out of court as providing no evidence concerning the nature of reality.

(3) The major criticism of religious experience by C. B. Martin is that there are no tests which could establish the genuineness of an experience of God. If a believer says, "I am a changed man since 6:37 P.M., May 6, 1939," we can test the assertion because we may find evidence of a bad conscience and remorse that had not been present before that date. But if he says that he has had "a direct experience of

God" at that time, we cannot check the truth of his statement.[54] If a person wants to know whether he really saw a star, he can take photographs and look through a telescope. He can also ask others whether they saw a star, and if many of them deny having seen it he "will be considered irrational or mad if he goes on asserting its existence." [55] But there are no comparable "checking-procedures" to test the claim that a person has seen God, and he has only "the testimony of his own experience and the similar testimony of the experience of others." [56] Martin concludes from this that the claim shows a "distressing similarity" to a psychological statement about the subjective feelings and experiences of the believer.[57]

Now, it must be admitted that there are no checking-procedures to test whether a person has really had an experience of God comparable to those which can be used to test whether one has really seen a star or some other physical object. The nature of God as a transcendent Being who is quite different from physical objects obviously makes such checking-procedures impossible. But does it follow that "statements concerning a certain alleged religious way of knowing betray a logic extraordinarily like that of statements concerning introspective and subjective ways of knowing" [58] and that they are therefore more like "psychological" statements about one's own feelings than "existential" statements about God? Religious people themselves regard them not as psychological facts of a subjective kind but as experiences of an objective reality present to them. Of course, it is possible that they have been deluded and that what they thought was God was only a projection of their own minds. But if one is not convinced on other grounds of the truth of a naturalistic philosophy which rules out the possibility of any supersensible reality, the most reasonable explanation of a man's conviction that he has experienced God may be that he has really done so. Moreover, Martin admits that the claim of the believer is supported by the testimony of many others that they have had similar experiences of God. It is true that there are some who say they have not had such experiences, so that the claim cannot be confirmed by everyone, as one's claim that one has seen a star can be verified by everyone with normal vision who looks through a telescope. But religious experiences are not alone in not being verifiable by everyone, e.g., there is also no universal agreement about moral judgments. As we have said, it is only in

---

[54] Martin, C. B.: *Religious Belief*, Ithaca, N.Y., Cornell University Press, 1959, pp. 67, 68.

[55] *Ibid.*, pp. 73, 74.

[56] *Ibid.*, p. 74.

[57] *Ibid.*, p. 75.

[58] *Ibid.*, p. 81.

natural science that statements about reality can be verified by every-one, and it is arbitrary to demand a type of verification for judgments of *all* kinds which is suitable for *scientific* judgments alone.

Cognitive Value: Constructive

We have now examined some typical criticisms by empiricists of the cognitive claims of religious experience. We have argued that these criticisms are convincing only to those who have accepted a narrowly empirical theory of knowledge, who therefore acknowledge only sense perception as evidence, and who insist upon verification by tests of a kind suitable only for physical objects. If God is a transcendent, super-sensible reality, as religious people assert, it is obvious that He does not possess qualities similar to those of sensible objects and cannot be veri-fied by tests based on sense perception. The conclusion to which we have been led is that religious experience, at least in its higher forms, may provide men with intuitions of a transcendent, divine Reality.

This conclusion may be stated in the words of a tough-minded Eng-lish philosopher, C. D. Broad. "When there is a nucleus of agreement between the experiences of men in different places, times, and tradi-tions, and when they all tend to put much the same kind of interpreta-tion on the cognitive content of these experiences, it is reasonable to ascribe this agreement to their all being in contact with a certain objec-tive aspect of reality *unless* there be some positive reason to think other-wise. The practical postulate which we go upon everywhere else is to treat cognitive claims as veridical unless there be some positive reason to think them delusive. . . . I think it would be inconsistent to treat the experiences of religious mystics on different principles. So far as they agree they should be provisionally accepted as veridical unless there be some positive ground for thinking that they are not." [59] When Broad goes on to consider whether there *is* "some positive reason to think them delusive," his answer is that there is not.

"It is alleged," he says, "that founders of religion and saints have nearly always had neuropathic symptoms or certain bodily weaknesses, and that these would be likely to produce delusions." [60] Broad replies that it is equally true that many of them have had great endurance and power of organization and that few people of extreme genius in *any* field have been perfectly normal in all respects. Moreover, it is probable that "some degree of mental and physical abnormality would be a necessary condition for getting sufficiently loosened from the objects of

[59] Broad, C. D.: *Religion, Philosophy and Psychical Research*, London, Routledge & Kegan Paul, 1953, p. 197.
[60] *Ibid.*, p. 197.

ordinary sense perception to come into cognitive contact" with the religious aspect of reality.[61] It has also been charged that religious experience originates from sexual emotions, irrational fears, and false ideas about nature and man, and that the experiences and beliefs which arise from such sources are likely to be delusive.[62] Broad replies that, even if it could be shown that there is some correlation between such emotions and religious experience, they often exist in persons with little or no religious experience and there is no evidence that religious experience can be reduced to them. Moreover, false beliefs and irrational fears among primitive peoples have led on at a later stage to true beliefs and appropriate feelings of reverence.[63] "There has obviously been a gradual refinement and purification of religious beliefs and concepts in the course of history, just as there has been in the beliefs and concepts of science." [64] Broad concludes that our knowledge of the conditions under which religious beliefs have arisen does *not* require us to think that "they are *specially* likely to be delusive or misdirected." [65] Hence, he regards as "far-fetched" the view that "the whole religious experience of mankind is a gigantic system of pure delusion." [66]

However, this cautious but positive conclusion with respect to the cognitive claims of religious experience is qualified by a warning of its limitations. "It is reasonable to think," says Broad, "that the concepts and beliefs of even the most perfect religions known to us are extremely inadequate to the facts which they express; that they are highly confused and are mixed up with a great deal of positive error and sheer nonsense; and that, if the human race goes on and continues to have religious experiences and to reflect on them, they will be altered and improved almost out of recognition. But all this could be said, *mutatis mutandis*, of scientific concepts and theories." [67] Broad may here exaggerate the extent to which the beliefs of the highest religions we know will have to be altered in the future, but his warning is salutary. It brings us back to the point we made in our discussion of Tennant and Hepburn: *excessive claims* for the knowledge derived from religious experience are as unwarranted as complete skepticism about them. Since they are not self-authenticating, we must subject them to *critical examination* to determine whether they are supported by other

[61] *Ibid.*, pp. 197, 198.
[62] *Ibid.*, pp. 198, 199.
[63] *Ibid.*, p. 199.
[64] *Ibid.*, p. 200.
[65] *Ibid.*, p. 200.
[66] *Ibid.*, p. 201.
[67] *Ibid.*, p. 200.

religious experiences and by experience as a whole. If they are not supported by the religious experiences of others and are not consistent with other kinds of experience, they are bound to be regarded as doubtful, if not false.

This critical examination is the more necessary because of the *diversity of interpretations* given to religious experience in different religions, a diversity which we have illustrated by contrasting the beliefs of Western theism and Hindu monism. It will be remembered that one of the strongest criticisms of both Tennant and Hepburn was based upon the fact that the knowledge religious persons claim to have derived from religious experience has varied greatly. How can we account for such a diversity of interpretation? We shall conclude by attempting a partial answer to this question.

In the first place, religion is one strand in the complex pattern of experience and is interwoven with and affected by all the other strands. Many of the crude beliefs of primitive religions and the irrational elements of ancient polytheism can be accounted for by the undeveloped state of scientific knowledge and other *cultural factors* which influenced their interpretation of religious experience. The development from lower to higher forms of belief and practice has been due not only to the creative insights of religious prophets and founders but also to the growth of science, philosophy, and social organization. Even the differences between the advanced religions of Hebraic-Christian theism and Hindu monism were partly due to the influence of extrinsic factors such as these. Hence, it is not necessary to assume that religious experience is merely subjective in order to account for the diversity of beliefs which have resulted from it.

In the second place, the interpretation of religious experience has always been affected by the nature of the finite things, events, or persons through which the presence of the Holy has been *mediated* to men at different times and places. For example, the dependence of the ancient Egyptians upon the Nile for the fertility of the soil from which their food supply was derived and the nature of their political organization under the Pharaoh had a profound effect upon their conception of the gods. In contrast, the ancient Hebrews from the time of Moses seem to have experienced the presence and power of Yahweh primarily in historical events, although they were also aware of their dependence upon Him for the fertility of their flocks and fields. Finally, Christians from the beginning interpreted God as He was experienced through a human person, Jesus of Nazareth. Thus, the finite things, events, or persons in which God was originally experienced in each religion profoundly affected the interpretation of Him, e.g., as a powerful force manifested in a natural phenomenon such as the stormy sea (the

Greek Poseidon) or as a personal and gracious Will active in history (the ancient Hebrew Yahweh) or as a loving Father known through His Son (the Christian God).

Finally, when we consider conceptions of God not from the human side but from the divine side, it is obvious that their diversity was inevitable in view of His transcendence and otherness. Since He is the *mysterium tremendum* who cannot be fully comprehended by human concepts and images, men have approached Him from many different angles and have used analogies drawn from the many different kinds of things which have impressed them as manifestations of the superior Power confronting them. In this way they have seen different facets of His nature. The overarching sky, the light- and life-giving sun, and the vast sea; the powerful elephant, the bull, and the soaring falcon; the great men of the past and present; the Word of the prophet which seems to come from beyond himself; and the love of a person who serves and dies for others—all of these and many more things and persons have seemed to men at different times to disclose aspects of the nature of the Holy. Men have had to speak of God in terms of what they have seen; and they have never seen Him "face to face" but always "in a glass darkly."

These are some of the reasons for the diversity of interpretations of the divine object of the religious experience. As we have seen, this diversity makes it imperative that we critically examine the cognitive claim of any particular interpretation of it. In making such a critical examination of the claims of Western theism, it is necessary to compare it with Western pantheism, on the one hand, and Hindu monism, on the other. For the former has had considerable influence in the West and the latter has been the dominant religious philosophy of India. In the next chapter, we shall consider in turn Spinoza's pantheism and Sankara's monism, reserving our examination of theism for the following chapters.

4

Pantheism and Monism

The Nature and Sources of Pantheism

Although pantheism has taken different forms, it is possible to indicate its general character. "Pantheism is the theory which regards all finite things as merely aspects, modifications, or parts of one eternal and self-existent being; which views all material objects and all particular minds as necessarily derived from a single infinite substance. The one absolute substance—the one all-comprehending being—it calls God. Thus God, according to it, is all that is; and nothing is which is not essentially included in, or which has not been necessarily evolved out of, God. . . . In order that there may be pantheism, monism and determinism must be combined." [1] The merit of this definition by Robert Flint is that it distinguishes pantheism from pluralistic and dualistic philosophical theories by emphasizing the fact that pantheists regard the many finite things and persons of experience as modes or appearances of one reality (monism), and that it contrasts pantheism with theism by stressing the production of the many from the one reality by necessity (determinism) rather than free creation. However, it is essential to bear in mind that pantheism has been not only a metaphysical theory but also a religious belief or attitude, since it has always affirmed that the way to blessedness is through a relationship with the one ultimate reality or God.

With this definition before us, we must now inquire into the *sources* of pantheism. It is possible to distinguish at least three major sources, religious, philosophical, and scientific, although they have not been equally present in every form of pantheism.

(1) The *religious* source of pantheism is evident in the fact that ancient pantheism developed out of polytheism in both India and

[1] Flint, Robert: *Anti-theistic Theories,* Edinburgh, Wm. Blackwood and Sons, 1889, p. 336.

86

Greece. In the speculative writings of ancient India known as the *Upanishads,* the many gods of the earlier Vedic hymns became names of different manifestations of one divine reality, the *Brahman.* In Greek Stoicism a somewhat similar development can be noted in which the gods became different names for Zeus and he was identified with the divine *Logos* immanent in all things.[2] Among the modern pantheists Spinoza was deeply influenced by Jewish and Christian thinkers and was also inspired by a certain kind of mystical experience.

The positive religious impulse which expresses itself in pantheism seems to be the longing of man in his finitude to participate in an infinite reality and to enhance his sense of significance by feeling himself to be part of an all-embracing and perfect Whole. At the same time, pantheism fosters in man a sense of his absolute dependence upon the Whole for his fulfillment and an attitude of humble acquiescence in his role as a part of the Whole. Negatively, it reflects the dissatisfaction of many thinkers with the uncritical anthropomorphism of popular theistic religion and their desire to eliminate mythical elements from religion which seem to them to be inconsistent with a rational world view.

(2) The *philosophical* impulse behind pantheism has been the drive of reason for unity in its view of the world. The multiplicity and diversity of phenomena challenge reason to relate them to each other in a comprehensive system based upon a single principle of unity. For the philosophical reason cannot be content with the description of different fields of phenomena by the special sciences; it seeks for a principle from which all phenomena have been derived. This drive of the theoretical reason for unity in a metaphysical system is accompanied by a demand of the practical reason for an ethical ideal based upon the nature of man and his place in the world to guide him in his quest for self-fulfillment. For it is clear that in the pantheism of both the East and the West the quest of man for a happiness which is rooted in something deeper than personal desires and pleasures is an important factor. It is not surprising, therefore, that Western pantheistic philosophies such as Stoicism and Spinozism combine a metaphysical world view with an ethical ideal.

(3) In the modern period these religious and philosophical sources of pantheism have been supplemented and strengthened by a *scientific* one. From the time of Giordano Bruno the scientific vision of the world as an infinite system of which the earth and man are only a small part has stimulated the imagination of men, has humbled them by making them aware of their own weakness, but has also exalted

[2] Copleston, Frederick: *A History of Philosophy,* Westminster, Md., The Newman Press, 1959, Vol. I, p. 394.

them as they have contemplated the immensity of the world. Copleston
has pointed out that Bruno was deeply influenced by the Copernican
astronomy, regarded our sun as merely one star among others, and
denied that our earth had a privileged position among the multitude
of heavenly bodies in limitless space. "He thus entirely rejected the
geocentric and anthropocentric conception of the universe both from
the astronomical point of view and in the wider perspective of speculative philosophy. In his system it is Nature considered as an organic
whole which stands in the centre of the picture, and not terrestrial
human beings who are *circonstanzie* or accidents of the one living
world-substance," [3] etc. Thus, in the early modern period the scientific
effort to discover and describe the laws of nature stimulated the
philosophical quest for unity which we have mentioned. This is important for an understanding of Spinoza, who was a philosopher rather
than a scientist but who was profoundly affected by the scientific vision
of the world.

This general account of the nature and sources of pantheism should
be qualified by a recognition that there has been an important difference of emphasis among pantheists. This has to do with the relation
between the one ultimate reality or God and the many finite manifestations of it in space and time. One form of pantheism has stressed the
sole reality of God and has denied the reality of finite things. Hence, it
is usually called "monism." Another has affirmed the reality of the
many finite things, although it has regarded them as only modifications
of the one ultimate reality. Thus, in the first form "God is all" and the
many are only appearances of Him, while in the second "The world or
nature is all" and God is identified with nature as a whole. The first
form has had its greatest influence in the East, especially in India, the
second in the West. The first is idealistic and mystical, since it views
the One as Universal Self or Spirit and is partly inspired by "introvertive" mysticism which seeks union with the One in the depths of
the soul. The second, which is more naturalistic and this-worldly,
identifies God with Nature viewed as an eternal and immutable system.

Western Pantheism: The Stoics and Spinoza

According to the ancient Stoics, the divine substance of the world
is both material and rational. It is all-pervasive fire, but also active,
rational soul. It is one, intelligent, and purposeful. The universe which
is ordered by it is a beautiful, good, and perfect whole, all of whose
parts are in harmony. The divine *Logos* is related to matter as the soul
is related to the body, so that it is the soul or reason of the world, and

[3] Copleston, F.: *History of Philosophy*, Vol. III, pp. 260, 261.

all the germs or seeds of life, *spermata,* are contained in it. This divine *Logos* is conceived as like the God of theism in certain respects: it has prevision and will, is benevolent, and cares for everything. However, it is not a free personal being, the creator of the world, but a substance from which everything proceeds with the necessity of a natural process. Everything is determined, and man's freedom is simply his ability to do consciously and with assent what he must do. But since this necessity is derived from the divine *Logos,* it orders all things for the best; and man has inner freedom in that he can control his attitude towards events and welcome them as an expression of Providence.[4] Moreover, the world is good and perfect. The evils in it are only relative and are necessary to the perfection of the whole or means of realizing good. And moral evil is necessary that virtue may be strengthened in combatting it. Thus, the universe is a beautiful, good, and perfect whole, in which everything has its purpose. Finally, the reason of man is part of the *Logos* or universal Reason, a spark of the divine fire.

The greatness of Stoicism does not lie in its metaphysics, for the conception of a universal fire which is at the same time rational is an incoherent attempt to identify material with spiritual reality. Rather, it has always been respected for its noble conception of the rational soul as capable of self-mastery through the control of its passions. Although this ethical ideal was carried to an extreme through an assertion of the desirability of passionlessness, *apatheia,* and sometimes fostered spiritual pride, it emphasized an essential element in the moral life. The Stoics also advocated acquiescence in the external circumstances of life, whatever the vicissitudes of a person's fortune might be. For these are beyond his control and are to be cheerfully accepted as bestowed by Providence.

It is necessary to consider Spinoza more fully, since he was the greatest pantheist the West has produced. Using the deductive method of geometry and starting from definitions and axioms he regarded as self-evident, Spinoza developed a rationalistic *metaphysics* and a conception of religion and morality based upon it. There is only one "Substance," Nature, which is infinite, eternal, and perfect. Thought and extension, which dualists such as Descartes regarded as distinct substances, are "attributes" of this Substance which is identical with God. The many things and persons of time and space, which were traditionally regarded as substances, are only "modes" of the one Substance, Nature or God. In contrast to the theistic view that Nature is a creation of God and hence distinct from Him, Spinoza holds that God and Nature are the same.

God's causal activity is never "transitive," i.e., He does not act upon

4 Copleston, *op. cit.,* Vol. I, p. 389.

nature from without, but "immanent," i.e., He acts within it. However, Spinoza distinguishes between nature as causal activity, *natura naturans,* and nature as the effect of this activity, *natura naturata.* He also rejects the theistic view that God is free to create or not to create or free to create things in addition to or different from those that actually exist. God is free only in the sense that He acts from the laws of His own nature alone, so that His freedom is the same as the necessity of His nature. Hence, "all things have necessarily followed, or continually follow by the same necessity, in the same way as it follows from the nature of a triangle from eternity and to eternity, that its three angles are equal to two right angles." [5] In consequence, nature is a system in which every event is determined by causes. There is no freedom of the human will. A man is a part of nature, a "mode" of the one Substance, and his mind and body are simply parallel aspects which are ultimately identical with one another.[6]

The *theological* implications of this metaphysical theory are strikingly different from those of traditional theism, and Spinoza emphasizes the differences again and again. Although his God or Nature is asserted to be infinite, eternal, immutable, and perfect, like the God of medieval scholasticism, Spinoza maintains that "extension" is one of His "attributes" as well as "thought," i.e., there is a bodily as well as an intellectual aspect of His nature. Again, Spinoza rejects the view that God possesses a will and intellect analogous to ours. For "will and intellect are modes of God on the same level as other modes." If they belong to His eternal essence, they "would have to differ entirely from our intellect and will, and could resemble ours in nothing except in name. There could be no further likeness than that between the celestial constellation of the Dog and the animal which barks." [7] Moreover, we must not speak of Him as acting for the sake of the good, for this would imply that He is not perfect but is in need of something. Hence, we should not seek for the explanation of anything in God's will, for He does not act for the sake of ends. Every event that occurs in nature is the result of efficient causes and "final causes are nothing but human fictions." [8] Finally, men's judgments of value are not objective but express their anthropocentric attitude to things. "Good" is not a quality of things but is simply that which is conducive to an increase in man's health or vitality, while that is "evil" which tends to diminish it. Since these distinctions of nature are relative to man alone, we should

[5] Spinoza, B.: *Ethics,* in *Selections,* New York, Scribner's, 1930, Pt. I, Pr. 17, Sch.
[6] We have given a more adequate account of Spinoza's philosophy in *Religious Philosophies of the West,* ch. 7.
[7] *Ethics,* Pt. I, Pr. 17, Sch.
[8] *Ibid.,* Pt. I, Appendix.

not complain about the "evil" in the world and criticize God for bringing it into being. God or Nature is perfect, and everything that exists possesses some degree of perfection.

According to Spinoza's *Ethics,* men are in bondage to their passions or "passive affections" as long as they are moved by desires to possess and fears to lose finite things, which are of limited value and which can be taken from them. But they can free themselves from this bondage by replacing "inadequate" and "confused" ideas derived from sensation by "adequate" and "clear" ideas conceived by reason. For reason is the distinctive property of man and the source of truth, and he expresses his nature most fully when he acts in accordance with reason. By an "intuitive knowledge" of Nature and of himself as a part of the whole, he can attain an "intellectual love of God" which will liberate him from his passions and bestow blessedness upon him. He will then be able to see everything in time, including himself, "under the aspect of eternity," i.e., in relation to the eternal system of Nature of which everything is a part, and to accept the role he is determined by his place in the whole to play. He can also know that the intellectual element in him which even now lives in the light of eternity will survive the death of the body. He cannot and should not hope for personal immortality, but the intellectual element which is the highest part of him will participate eternally in the infinite intellect of God. To those who object that, if men will not enjoy personal immortality, they will not be rewarded for their virtue, Spinoza replies scornfully that "virtue is its own reward," and should be sought for its own sake. "Blessedness is not the reward of virtue, but is virtue itself." [9]

It is extremely difficult to interpret certain aspects of Spinoza's philosophy of religion, and he has been attacked as an atheist by some and venerated as a "God-intoxicated man," a sort of lay saint, by others. Since he was outspoken in his criticism of theism, it is easy to understand why he has been regarded by some as an atheist. However, there is no question about the genuineness of his religious attitude towards the world. The existence of a mystical element in his thought, which is expressed in the phrase "intellectual love of God," has been denied by some modern philosophers who have interpreted the phrase to mean nothing more than the scientist's intellectual contemplation of the order of nature. But mysticism has taken many forms and Spinoza is clearly a mystic of the "extrovertive" sort.[10] It is true that, unlike

[9] *Ibid.,* Pt. V, Pr. 42. For a critical analysis of Spinoza's conception of the "intellectual love of God" and of eternal life, see the author's *Religious Philosophies of the West,* pp. 185–190.

[10] For the distinction between "introvertive" and "extrovertive" mysticism see Stace, W. T.: *Mysticism and Philosophy,* Philadelphia, J. B. Lippincott Co., 1960.

most mystics, he does not think that one must leave all knowledge behind before one can come to the contemplation of God; rather, he advocates an "intellectual love of God" which arises from an "intuitive knowledge." However, if the term "mysticism" is used in a broad sense, it is impossible to deny a mystical element in his attitude towards Nature.

Others have denied that Spinoza's philosophy is religious in its nature because of the naturalistic element in it. Undoubtedly, the scientific vision of nature of Galileo, Descartes, and others had a powerful influence upon his thought. This is evident in his view of nature as an eternal and immutable system in which every event is determined by efficient causes and final causes are completely eliminated. Nevertheless, it is a mistake to regard him simply as a modern naturalist in his philosophy. He asserts that the attribute of "thought" as well as that of "extension" belongs to God, and that the "modes" of the divine Substance follow by necessity from the essences contemplated by His intellect. Thus, thought has a higher place in his view of Nature than it has in naturalism. Moreover, the religious culmination of his philosophy in the "intellectual love of God" is interpreted by him as a love of God for Himself and for men as modes of Himself, which implies that the attribute of "thought" in Him is associated with love of some kind.

A Critical Evaluation

Since pantheism is not only a form of religious belief but also a philosophical theory, any evaluation of it must answer two different questions: Is its metaphysical world view acceptable? Is its conception of religion adequate? In attempting to answer these questions, we must bear in mind the difference between the two forms of pantheism we have distinguished, idealistic monism and naturalistic pantheism. Here we shall consider only the naturalistic pantheism we have been describing, especially that of Spinoza. However, some of the comments we shall make apply equally to idealistic monism.

(1) As we indicated, the basic principle of pantheism as a metaphysical theory is *monism*. The drive of reason for unity of explanation has taken different forms in the history of philosophy. Parmenides solved the problem of the relation of the one and the many in a radical way by affirming that Being is one and denying that the many things that appear to the senses have being. Western pantheists have not been as radical in their monism as Parmenides. Neither the Stoics nor Spinoza regarded the many as illusory or mere appearances. However,

both subordinated them to one ultimate reality, the universal *Logos* or Nature.

This reduction of the many things of experience to modes of one reality cannot be justified. It rests upon a disparagement of the evidence of the senses for the existence of a plurality of individual things and persons in space and time, on the one hand, and upon a misunderstanding of the nature of the unity demanded by reason, on the other. It is true, of course, that the evidence of the senses cannot be accepted uncritically. A table which appears at first sight to be one thing can be seen on closer observation to be made up of many parts, and modern physical science tells us that it consists of an immense number of invisible entities, just as the human body is one organism but is composed of countless cells each of which has a complex structure of many parts. Moreover, the many entities contained in each thing or organism are closely related to each other and the pattern constituted by them is often extremely complex. Spinoza was fully justified in insisting that "sensation" and the "imagination" which is based upon it constitute only the first and lowest level of knowledge and that it is necessary to resort to "reason" which employs "common notions" such as extension and motion in explaining the things and events of nature.

But it does not follow from this that the plurality of things experienced by the senses are only modes of one Substance. Modern science seeks to interpret the facts of experience by means of laws which describe regular patterns of experience, e.g., Kepler's laws of planetary motion and Boyle's law correlating the volume of a gas with its pressure. It also develops theories which are more comprehensive and general. From a theory previously known, laws can be deduced, as Kepler's laws could be deduced from Newton's theory of gravitation and Boyle's law from the kinetic theory of gases.[11] But the attempt of science to attain unity of explanation in this way has not led scientists to deny the plurality of things. Indeed, the development of more inclusive theories by science has been accompanied by a discovery of the immense number of the elementary entities of nature. It is clear, therefore, that the assertion by Spinoza and others that there is only one substance and that the many things of experience are only modes of it is an error. It was due partly to the disparagement of knowledge gained through the senses and partly to the influence of the deductive reasoning of mathematics upon rationalists who have sought to deduce the plurality of things from a single principle. We must simply accept the

[11] Barbour, Ian: *Issues in Science and Religion*, Englewood Cliffs, N.J., Prentice-Hall, 1966, pp. 140, 141.

plurality and individuality of things as given, contingent facts of experience.

There is also an ethical reason for rejecting monism. Every person experiences himself as one among many persons. He is conscious of himself as an individual self with a capacity for self-determination rather than as a mere mode of a more ultimate reality, i.e., as something more than a merely "adjectival" reality. He is also conscious that other persons have the same kind of distinct, individual existence and freedom as himself. This is the source of his (and their) dignity and of his (and their) right to be treated with respect as persons, and without it there would be no sense of moral responsibility. Thus, morality presupposes the distinction of individual selves from each other as well as their participation in a common human nature. To deny this by reducing men to modes of one Substance is to destroy their dignity as persons and their claim to be treated with respect and love by others.

(2) The monism of naturalistic pantheism is necessarily accompanied by *determinism,* for the many are regarded by the monist not as distinct centers of activity capable of initiating conduct from within but only as manifestations of the one Substance or God which are determined by their relation to Him and to each other. As we noted, the Stoics were determinists, although they inconsistently affirmed the freedom of man to master his passions by reason and attain virtue. Similarly, Spinoza asserted that it is only men's ignorance of the hidden causes of their acts which leads them to think that they are free. As we shall see,[12] this denial of freedom of will implies that man is simply a part of nature and runs counter to his consciousness of his capacity within limits to act in accordance with his own purposes rather than be determined by natural laws. Moreover, Spinoza's determinism is inconsistent with his ethics. Although men are in bondage to their passions, he affirms, they can liberate themselves by turning away from inadequate to adequate ideas, from passive to active affections. The whole argument of the concluding part of Spinoza's *Ethics* assumes that the individual can make this choice and loses its point if he cannot do so. The statement that "all noble things are as difficult as they are rare" [13] becomes meaningless if men cannot by striving follow the difficult path to virtue and happiness Spinoza has described.

(3) The monism and determinism of Spinoza's pantheism inevitably lead to a conception of *man* which reduces the individual self to a mere mode of the one Substance or Nature. We have already shown how this weakens, if it does not destroy, the sense of moral responsi-

---

[12] Ch. 10.
[13] Spinoza, *Ethics,* Pt. V, Pr. 42.

bility. It also results in a subordination of creative activity to a theo-retical, contemplative attitude. For man is reduced to the status of a part of the system of nature, whose acts are determined by eternal and immutable natural laws. Spinoza also affirms that the mind and body are only different aspects of man (under the attributes of thought and extension) and are ultimately identical. Although he asserts that there is a parallelism between the series of mental states and the series of bodily events and that a mental state is caused by other mental states rather than by bodily events, his emphasis upon the capacity of the body to perform acts usually attributed to the will tends to subordinate the mind to the body.[14] In this way, as well as by his determinism, Spinoza prepared the way for modern naturalism and the reduction of the mind to a series of epiphenomena of the body or to behavior. This conception of man would make impossible the control of reason over the passions upon which Spinoza's own ethics depends. Thus, not only his determinism but also his subordination of the individual to the whole and stress upon the identity of mental with bodily states are inconsistent with his own independent spirit and moral seriousness. A similar paradox has often been noted in Stoicism. For the Stoics regarded the individual as only a spark of the divine Fire whose acts are strictly determined, and yet affirmed that he is able as a rational being to master his passions and live in accordance with reason.

(4) We have been considering fundamental errors in the metaphysics of pantheism in its Western form: its monism which reduces the many things and persons to mere modes of one Substance or Nature; its determinism which identifies God's freedom with the necessity of His nature and denies man's freedom altogether; and its reduction of man to the status of a part of the system of nature at the cost of disparaging his creativity as an individual and the independence of his mind in relation to his body. We must now inquire into the *religious adequacy* of the beliefs associated with this metaphysical theory, beginning with the conception of God.

A complete answer cannot be given to this question until we have considered the theistic view of God which has been the major alterna-tive to pantheism in the more advanced religions. But a critical com-ment can be made at this point. Much of the appeal of pantheism, we said, lies in the fact that it gives man a sense of participating in the infinite and eternal Whole upon which he depends for his existence. By doing so it enables him to escape from narrow preoccupation with himself and his own interests. It also provides the basis for a feeling of "natural piety," of reverence and gratitude towards nature, which

[14] *Ibid.*, Pt. III, Pr. 2.

was one of the more attractive aspects of ancient paganism but is rare in the modern world except in nature mystics such as Wordsworth. An experience of the presence and power of the eternal in the temporal, the infinite in the finite, has been an important aspect of the piety of theists such as Schleiermacher, and it has been due in large part to the influence of Spinoza upon them.

However, naturalistic pantheism lacks that feeling of awe in the presence of the Holy as transcendent and "other" which Otto has described as essential to the religious experience and that attitude of absolute devotion to it as Sacred which Oman has also emphasized. Man cannot worship that which is not transcendent to and other than himself and every other finite being, and he cannot give absolute devotion to and serve that which is not the highest good. Now, although nature is infinitely greater and more powerful than man, it is not qualitatively superior to him. Much less, despite Spinoza, is it perfect. Therefore, while man is dependent upon nature and should feel gratitude and even love for her, he cannot really worship and surrender himself to her.

(5) In determining whether pantheism is religiously adequate it is also necessary to consider its attitude toward the problem of evil. Since the distinction between good and evil is relative to man, says Spinoza, he should not complain against the "imperfections" of nature as if evil existed in nature itself. God is perfect, and, as God and Nature are identical, Nature is perfect. This is Spinoza's solution of the problem of evil. Since God is perfect and everything follows by necessity from His nature, there is no imperfection; there are only different degrees or levels of perfection. There is no imperfection even in sin. "And therefore," says Spinoza of Adam's disobedience to God, "we shall be able to find no imperfection in the decision of Adam when we consider it in itself, and do not compare it with other things which are more nearly perfect, or show a more nearly perfect state," since "the evil in it was no more than a privation of a more perfect state." [15] Thus, Adam's desire for pleasure "was evil only in relation to our understanding and not in relation to that of God." [16] As we have seen, the Stoic view of evil is somewhat similar. Since the *Logos* is the immanent rational principle in everything, the world is an orderly and perfect whole, and what appear to man to be evils are necessary to the good of the whole.

This conception of evil has had a long history in Western thought. However, like Spinoza's denial of the plurality of things, it is contrary

[15] Spinoza, B.: *Ibid.*, Letter XIX, p. 420.
[16] *Ibid.*, Letter XXI, p. 420.

to man's experience. Man experiences evil as real and as opposed to good, and to deny that the distinction between evil and good exists in reality is to fall into skepticism concerning all his judgments of value. To deny the reality of evil also leads logically to a passive acquiescence in or at least a weak submission to it and hence to a paralysis of the moral will.

(6) What are the *ethical* implications of pantheism? It cannot be said that pantheists have been indifferent to morality. Indeed, both the Stoics and Spinoza made significant contributions to ethical theory, although we have noted that their ethics is inconsistent with their determinism. The most important ethical insight of the Stoics was that man should master his passions and control his acts by reason. They also affirmed that he should accept the external circumstances of his life as beyond his control and affirm them as the work of Providence rather than rebel against them, whether one was a slave like Epictetus or an emperor like Marcus Aurelius. Since every person must exercise his freedom within the limits set by many contingent circumstances, this is an important aspect of the truth, although it must be qualified and balanced by a recognition that some circumstances of a person's life are evil and he should struggle against them.

The ethic of Spinoza has much in common with these Stoic ideas. For Spinoza also asserts that the passions are the source of man's misery, that he can free himself from his bondage to them by reason, and that he should accept without complaint the determination by nature of the circumstances of his life. This is in some ways a noble and inspiring ethical ideal, and Spinoza's picture of the wise and virtuous man has been respected and admired by many. But it also has serious limitations. Since Spinoza's God has no will analogous to that of man and no purpose for man in history, his ethical ideal cannot inspire a dynamic and creative religious morality. For such a creative morality requires more than rational self-control and a cheerful acceptance by the individual of his place in nature. Motivated by love of God and obedience to His will, it manifests itself in active service of others and in struggle against the evils from which they suffer. Spinoza's impersonal conception of God, his view of man's will as determined in all its acts, and his attitude towards evil make such a dynamic, creative morality logically impossible for him.

Hindu Monism: Sankara

The Hindu monism of Sankara is idealistic rather than naturalistic, since it conceives of ultimate reality as spiritual. Although it is only one of the schools of Vedanta philosophy, it has had a profound influence upon Indian religious philosophy. Since the nineteenth century it has also fascinated many Western historians of religion, and in the twentieth century it has been interpreted for Western readers by a number of Indian philosophers such as Dasgupta.[17]

Sankara, who lived about the end of the eighth century, was a deeply religious man as well as a philosopher, wrote hymns to popular deities, and established several monasteries for the study of the Hindu Scriptures. He based his idealistic monism, with which we are here concerned, upon the *Upanishads*, the revealed writings that are the fountainhead of Indian philosophy. Although the *Upanishads* can be and have been interpreted in various ways, Sankara based his philosophy upon the monistic elements in them and became the founder of the *advaita* or "non-dualist" school of Vedanta philosophy. We shall offer only a brief summary of his most important ideas.

Brahman is the Reality behind phenomena, "One without a second." It is beyond man's power to comprehend or describe, and we miss its essential nature when we try to grasp it as an object in the categories of our reason. Hence, we can speak of it only in negative terms: it is *"neti, neti,"* "not this, not this." We can characterize it in abstract terms as *Sat, Chit,* and *Ananda,* "Being, Consciousness, and Bliss," to indicate that it is the ultimate Reality, that it is not an object but a subject or pure Consciousness, and that it enjoys absolute serenity and repose. But we can ascribe to it no qualities, relations, or acts, so that it is absolutely indeterminate and undifferentiated. Among other things, this implies that personal attributes such as will and love and acts such as creation cannot be ascribed to it. Thus, it is impersonal. Also, it is beyond good and evil and cannot be said to have a purpose for man.

The world of finite things and persons which are apprehended by the senses and ordered by reason constitutes a realm of *maya,* "appearance." This is deduced from the principle that Brahman is the sole reality. *Maya,* which seems to be conceived as an inherent power of Brahman, "superimposes" or projects the world of plurality upon the ultimate reality of Brahman and in doing so conceals the latter behind the many things of the world as behind a screen. Thus, it is the source of *avidya,* "ignorance," concerning the true nature of the world. The *jiva,* or empirical self of the individual person, belongs to the realm of *maya* and consequently partakes of the unreal character of the latter in both its bodily and its mental aspects. In its ignorance of its true nature, it thinks of itself, as it thinks of other selves, as one separate and distinct being among many. Thus, the phenomenal world is unreal, like

[17] Dasgupta, S.: *Indian Idealism,* Cambridge, Cambridge University Press, 1933, ch. VI.

a mirage, or a dream, or a rope that is mistaken for a snake. These metaphors are meant, it seems, to express the fact that the world, although not ultimately real, is yet not utterly unreal. "The world is only an appearance. It is not ultimately real. . . . But so long as we are in this world, we cannot take it to be unreal. . . . It is the Real which appears and hence every appearance must have some degree of truth in it, though none can be absolutely true. Objects seen in a dream are quite real as long as the dream lasts. . . . Similarly, so long as we are engrossed in Ignorance, the world is quite real for us. . . . It is relative, phenomenal, finite. But it is not illusory." [18]

Sankara speaks of a "lower" or "qualified" Brahman whom he calls *Isvara*, "Lord," and whom he pictures as Creator, Preserver, and Destroyer of the world. *Isvara* is the personal appearance of the impersonal Brahman. Thus, He is an object of devotion, a personal God. But He belongs, like those who worship Him, to the realm of *maya*. He is only an appearance of Brahman to the self, and when the essence of Brahman is known or realized He vanishes along with the world and the self which are His creation.[19] "In higher truth," says the Hindu in Ninian Smart's *A Dialogue of Religions*, "Brahman is without attributes, save those of Being, Consciousness and Bliss; in lower truth, It appears as the *Isvara* or Lord, who is all-knowing, almighty, providential, who creates, maintains, and dissolves the universe, who pervades it in His capacity as Inner Ruler. What better description could you have of the theistic ideas of divine transcendence and immanence? Yet all this is part of the lower knowledge. And so our belief in such a Being is itself a kind of ignorance: just a preliminary picture." [20] Thus, Sankara makes a place in his monistic and impersonal view for theism with its worship of a personal God, but at the same time he regards Him as only an appearance produced by ignorance and belonging to *maya*.

As long as the self remains without knowledge that it is only an appearance without ultimate reality, it is bound to *samsara*, the wheel of rebirth, condemned to undergo transmigration again and again. For, according to the law of *karma*, it must suffer the consequences of its deeds in its present and previous existences. But if it strips away all its desires and other contents of consciousness by a rigorous discipline of moral purification, bodily control, and intense meditation, it can attain an intuitive knowledge, *vidya*, of the truth. In a mystical experience, it can come to a realization that its true Self, *Atman*, is identical with

[18] Sharma, Chandradhar: *A Critical Survey of Indian Philosophy*, London, Rider and Co., 1960, pp. 277–279.

[19] *Ibid.*, pp. 280–282.

[20] Smart, Ninian: *A Dialogue of Religions*, London, SCM Press, 1960, p. 62.

Brahman, the ultimate Reality. "That art thou" is the formula in which this identification is expressed. When knowledge comes, it involves no real change in the status of the Self. It does not *become* identical with the Brahman, for it has *always been* the Brahman but has hitherto been ignorant of it. The final state of *samadhi*, the merging of the self with the Brahman, occurs only when the distinction between the subject (the self) and the object (Brahman) completely disappears.[21]

Through this intuitive knowledge the self experiences *moksha*, "liberation" or "release." As long as he lives, he continues to be associated with his body and its functions. The consequences of his past actions from his present and from his previous lives maintain his appearance as an individual. But he is no longer disturbed by ignorance, the effects of his actions fade gradually, and he lives in serenity. "He continues to move among the shapes and events of time but abides forever in peace. When the moment arrives for his ultimate liberation . . . and this vestigial shell of his earlier false impression of himself drops away, nothing takes place in the sphere of eternity in which he really dwells—and in which, if we but knew, we all really dwell." [22]

We noted that the discipline which is required to attain the mystical experience of identity with Brahman includes moral purification, for only the pure self can know Brahman. After the dawn of this knowledge, the habits which conduce to virtuous acts continue as before, for they are "kept as so many ornaments." But the true Self, *Atman*, is beyond virtues as well as other qualities. "They are not actually part of him, any more than jewels are part of the body; and so we read: 'Such virtues as non-hatred arise and abide of themselves with one in whom the Awakening of the Self has come to pass. In this case they are not of the nature of requirements or implements necessary to any task." [23] For moral actions are necessary only to purify the self and prepare it for knowledge of Brahman, i.e., for those who are still in ignorance. They are not prescribed for those who have attained enlightenment and liberation, although the liberated one performs actions without any attachment to their fruits or consequences.[24] Thus, it is not true, as some Western writers have charged, that the Hindu monist is completely indifferent to morality. However, while virtuous actions may continue after knowledge has come, they are not

[21] Zimmer, Heinrich: *Philosophies of India*, New York, Meridian Books, 1960, p. 439.
[22] *Ibid.*, p. 441.
[23] *Ibid.*, p. 445.
[24] Sharma, *op. cit.*, p. 286.

prescribed or demanded of him. For his actions, like his individual self, belong to the realm of *maya* and are not essential elements of his spiritual state after his liberation.

A Critical Evaluation

How are we to evaluate this idealistic monism?

(1) In our criticism of naturalistic pantheism we stressed the fact that its monism is incompatible with our experience of the plurality of things through the senses and with the distinctions between them made by our reason. However, this criticism would not trouble the Hindu monist, because he regards the kind of knowledge that is attained by sense and reason as limited to appearances in the realm of *maya* and is convinced that only an intuitive awareness through the mystical experience can give us knowledge of ultimate Reality, the Brahman. Although Sankara accepted monism in the first place as a truth revealed in the *Vedas* and *Upanishads,* he would not have defended it with such persistence and passion if it had not seemed to him to be confirmed by the mystical experience of the authors of those religious scriptures and others.

Now, there is no doubt that mystics in both the East and the West have experienced the divine as one and have felt themselves to be united with it in an intimate way. But the crucial question is whether Sankara and other monistic mystics have been right in interpreting this as an experience of *undifferentiated unity* in which the self is *identical* with the divine. We would deny this. Many mystics, including most Western mystics, have not accepted this interpretation of their experience of union with God, and therefore they have refused to accept the inference that the Brahman or God is without qualities and relations and that only negative assertions can be made about Him. They have also denied that in the mystical experience of union the self is identical with Brahman or God so that there is no distinction between them.

For example, Ghazali, the great mystic of Islam, describes the state of union of mystics with God as a kind of drunkenness in which their reason has collapsed. In this state, he says, "nothing was left to them but God," but "when their drunkenness abates and the sovereignty of their reason is restored,—and reason is God's scale on earth,—they know that this was not actual identity, but that it resembled identity," as if one "should see wine in a glass and think that the wine was just coloured glass." "This condition is metaphorically called *identity* with reference to the man who is immersed in it, but in the language of truth (it is called) *union*." [25] Thus, the monistic mystic tends to confuse the ecstatic union he experiences with identity. Moreover, this tendency is strengthened by the fact that he has emptied his mind of all specific contents by the mystical discipline of meditation in the attempt to overcome completely the duality between himself and Brahman, so that there is no longer anything in his consciousness by which he could differentiate between aspects of Brahman or between Brahman and himself.

In an able defense of monistic mysticism, Walter Stace has maintained that common to the mystical experiences of all the great religions has been the experience of undifferentiated unity and that in this experience there has been no distinction between the human subject and the divine object. The mystical experience, he argues, is neither "subjective" nor "objective" but "transsubjective," i.e., the human subject experiences the divine as a Universal Self or Subject and himself as identical with it. Stace acknowledges that mystics of the three monotheistic religions, Judaism, Christianity, and Islam, have usually interpreted their experience in another way, i.e., they have asserted that they experience God as possessing personal and moral qualities and themselves as in communion rather than as identical with Him. However, he argues that this theistic interpretation of their experience was a distortion of it which was imposed upon the Christian mystics by the orthodox theologians of the Church. Hence, he concludes that monistic mystics such as Sankara have interpreted mysticism rightly and that it justifies a pantheistic view of God.[26]

This attempt to defend the monistic interpretation of the mystical experience is unconvincing. The fact that many Eastern and most Western mystics have interpreted their experience as involving communion rather than identity with God is strong evidence, to say the least, that there is a distinction between the self and God. This obviously supports a theistic rather than a pantheistic view of God's relation to the world, although it is not sufficient by itself to prove the truth of theism. Stace's assertion that this theistic interpretation was imposed upon Western mystics such as Eckhart by orthodox authorities of the Church but that Eastern mystics were free from external pressure in their monistic interpretation is unjustified. It is true that Western mystics have tended to interpret their experience in the light of beliefs derived from their own religious tradition. But Hindu monists have been influenced by their own religious tradition no less than Christian theists. It is significant, for instance, that Sankara based his monistic

---

[25] Quoted in Zaehner, R. C.: *Mysticism Sacred and Profane*, Oxford, The Clarendon Press, 1957, pp. 157, 158 (italics mine).

[26] Stace, W. T. *op. cit.*, chs. 3, 4.

interpretation of reality upon the Vedic revelation of Brahman as interpreted in the *Upanishads*. Therefore, it is arbitrary to charge Christian mystics with distortion of their experience because of pressures from outside, but to assume that Hindu mystics described their experience as it really was, unaffected by beliefs taken over from their Hindu tradition.

Moreover, it should be noted that Sankara's monism was not the only interpretation of the mystical experience in Indian thought. Ramanuja's "qualified non-dualism" has much in common with Western theism, since he affirms that the Brahman has personal attributes and that the experience of union with Him through faith and devotion is one in which the self remains distinct from Him. In short, the monistic interpretation of mystical experience is only one of several interpretations and there is no compelling reason to consider it the normative one.

(2) Sankara attempts to meet one of the major religious criticisms of monism, namely, that man in his weakness and sin needs the help of a personal God who cares for him, by making a place for the theistic religion of devotion to a personal God such as Vishnu or Siva. As we noted, he speaks of *Isvara,* the "Lord" who is worshipped with faith and love in popular Hindu theism, as a personal appearance of the impersonal Brahman. However, *Isvara* belongs to the realm of *maya,* like those who worship Him, and with the coming of knowledge of the Brahman He vanishes. This is the source of one of the major differences between the "unqualified non-dualism" of Sankara and the "qualified non-dualism" of Ramanuja, since the latter maintains that Brahman is personal and that his worshippers are real rather than mere appearances.

Sympathetic interpreters of Hinduism sometimes argue that Sankara's concept of *Isvara* provides an adequate place for theistic worship of a personal God and therefore meets the needs of simple religious people as well as sophisticated philosophers. For example, Huston Smith says that "the conclusion that does most justice to Indian history as a whole" is that both Sankara's impersonal and Ramanuja's personal conceptions of Brahman "are equally correct." [27] Whether this is Smith's own view or he is merely stating the view of Hindus is not clear. But the grounds for the view, as stated by him, are unconvincing. The first is that, since all of our ideas of God are very limited, contradictory ones may be complementary. "As he is in himself, God may not be capable of being two contradictory things. . . . But concepts of God contain so much alloy to begin with that two contradictory ones

[27] Smith, Huston: *The Religions of Man,* New York, Mentor Books, 1959, p. 75.

may be true from different points of view, as both waves and particles may be equally accurate heuristic devices for describing the nature of light." [28] The second ground is that Hindus may accept either the personal or the impersonal concept of the Brahman "depending on which carries the most exalted meaning for the particular mind-set." [29]

Now, it is true that there is much "alloy" in all of our concepts of God. But it is difficult to see how this can justify our acceptance of two contradictory concepts of Him. It is also true that people have different "mind-sets" and that some find the concept of a personal and others the concept of an impersonal God more congenial to them. But this psychological fact also does not warrant the acceptance of such contradictory concepts. The extension of the "principle of complementarity" from physics to theology, as suggested by Smith in his reference to the wave and particle theories of light, is most misleading. The wave and particle theories are regarded by physicists as "complementary" because both seem to be needed to explain different aspects of the phenomenon of light. But they are not "contradictory" to each other. In contrast, Sankara speaks of the "unqualified" Brahman as impersonal and the "qualified" Brahman or *Isvara* as personal not to indicate that they are complementary aspects of It but to contrast Brahman as It is *known* in its essence to be and as It *appears* to one who is still in "ignorance," *avidya.* That he does not mean that Brahman is both personal and impersonal but only that It *is* impersonal but *appears* personal to one in "ignorance" is shown by the fact that when "knowledge," *vidya,* comes *Isvara* disappears. Even if he regarded *Isvara* as having a sort of relative reality, his view would be religiously unsatisfactory because he asserts that "liberation" or salvation comes only through identification with the impersonal Brahman.

However, there is an important element of truth which is suggested by Smith's statement. It points to the fact that man's experience of God, in Western as well as Eastern religions, seems to disclose both personal and nonpersonal attributes in God. The experience of awe and wonder in the presence of the Holy implies that God's nature transcends the limitations of all finite objects and persons, that there is what is sometimes called an "ontological gulf" between Him and them. This is the reason why theists as well as monists have conceived of Him as infinite, eternal, unchanging, and perfect, and why great theologians such as Aquinas have developed a negative theology to safeguard His transcendence of all His creatures. The difference between theists and monists in speaking about Him is that theists have *also* ascribed personal attributes and acts by analogy to Him and that they have taken

[28] *Ibid.*
[29] *Ibid.*

these affirmations seriously. In other words, Western theism attempts to do justice to the nonpersonal or "metaphysical" aspects of God's nature but does so without denying or disparaging the personal aspects by relegating them to a realm of mere appearance.

(3) The doctrine that the world of things and persons constitutes a realm of appearance, *maya*, is a consequence of Sankara's unwarranted view that mystical intuition is the sole source of knowledge of ultimate reality, *vidya*, and his disparagement of the cognitive value of both sense experience and reason. One advantage of the theistic interpretation of mystical experience is that it does not require the acceptance of this exaggerated claim for mysticism, since it affirms the reality of the many things and persons of the world of space and time as known by sense and reason.

The doctrine of *maya*, according to some writers, has been as morally stultifying as it is philosophically unjustified. In the conclusion to his careful study of the concept of *maya* in Hindu philosophy, Paul Devanandan remarks that, although the concept does not necessarily mean that the world is an "illusion," "it is obvious that the nearer it approaches such an assertion, the more devitalizing is its effect upon activity, and therefore upon progress." [30] He also maintains that the denial of the reality of the material world results in a neglect of natural science, since the aim of science is the investigation and description of natural phenomena.[31] However, a revolution has been going on in Indian life and thought for more than a century which has involved a reinterpretation of the doctrine of *maya*. This has led to a greater appreciation of the material world and a higher estimate of the value of human life in time. As a result, recent Hindu philosophers such as Radhakrishnan deny that the concept of *maya* leads to world negation. "It is not true to contend," he says, "that the experience of the pure realm of being, timeless and perfect, breeds in us contempt for the more familiar world of existence, which is unhappily full of imperfection. . . . Those who have the vision of perfection strive continually to increase the perfection and diminish the imperfection. Life is forever striving for its fuller creative manifestation." [32]

(4) Sankara's view that the true, inner *Self* is identical with Brahman is untenable on both philosophical and religious grounds. It rests upon the idea that the empirical self belongs to the realm of *maya* and hence has no ultimate reality and the assumption that the inner Self has

---

[30] Devanandan, Paul: *The Concept of Maya*, London, The Lutterworth Press, 1950, pp. 218, 219.

[31] *Ibid.*, p. 220.

[32] Radhakrishnan, S.: *Eastern Religions and Western Thought*, Oxford, The Clarendon Press, 1939, p. 31.

characteristics wholly different from those of the empirical self. Neither of these views is in accord with our experience of ourselves, and both are simply corollaries derived from the monistic principle that Brahman is the sole reality. Moreover, Sankara's identification of the true Self with the Brahman is unacceptable from the religious point of view. The "numinous" experience of God, as described by phenomenologists of religion such as Otto and van der Leeuw, clearly implies His transcendence of every finite being, including the self. While He is experienced as holy, majestic, and pure, man feels himself to be finite, weak, and "unclean." [33] Therefore, the monistic idea that there is an identification or merging of the self with God is inconsistent with the most fundamental characteristic of numinous religious experience and makes worship impossible. In the words of Devendranath Tagore, "What we want is to worship God; if the worshipper and the object of worship are one, how can there be any worship?" [34] Furthermore, man's awareness of his finitude and of the gulf made by his sin between himself and God implies that even the most saintly man cannot claim to be identical with God without presumption and spiritual pride. Yet it is one of the paradoxes of Sankara's monism that, while it deifies the hidden Self within, it does so at the cost of denying the reality and worth of the empirical self which is the only self we know in our ordinary experience.

(5) Although there is much that is admirable in Hindu ethics, e.g., the ideal of *ahimsa* or "non-killing," morality has only a very subordinate place in Sankara's monism. We noted that moral purification is necessary as a preparation for the knowledge that brings liberation, but that moral acts are not prescribed for those who have attained that knowledge and are awaiting final absorption in Brahman. Since moral acts are concerned solely with a man's duties in the world, they belong to the lower sphere of *maya* and are not an essential part of the life of the liberated man. There is nothing in Sankara's monism comparable to Eckhart's praise of the practical activity of Martha as superior to the purely contemplative life of Mary because the mystic should give out in deeds of love that which he has received in his union with God. Moreover, Sankara's conception of the Brahman does nothing to enhance the importance of moral action or raise it to a higher level. Since Brahman has no attributes or relations, moral goodness is not ascribed to It and It makes no moral demands upon men. Hence Sankara's monism offers no ethical ideal corresponding to the Jewish Messianic hope of justice and peace or the Christian ideal of a Kingdom of God based upon love of God and love of man. Moral conduct is simply

[33] Isaiah 6.
[34] Quoted by Smart, N.: *op. cit.,* p. 67.

equated with conformity to the fixed pattern of duties prescribed in the *dharma* and falls short of the creative activity which goes beyond moral rules and seeks to realize what Bergson called an "open society." [35]

An Appreciation

In view of such criticisms of Hindu monism, many Western thinkers have dismissed it as a tissue of errors which has neither philosophical nor religious value. Others have sought to explain it as merely an effect of an enervating climate, political chaos, and other environmental forces which imposed such a burden of suffering upon sensitive men that they sought to escape by renunciation of the world and the self and cultivation of mystical union with the eternal. Such views are too simple, and they cannot possibly account for the respect of Western philosophers such as Hegel for Hindu monism and the admiration of many Western religious thinkers for Hindu spirituality. What has been the source of the appeal of this monism and mysticism to the West?

The answer is to be found, not in the conceptions of Brahman, the world, the self, and morality which we have criticized, but in the monist's profound conviction of the *primacy of the spiritual life* and the intensity with which he has sacrificed every worldly interest and value to the attainment of his spiritual goal. One may not accept the conception of the spiritual goal as liberation through knowledge of the self's identity with the Brahman, but one cannot but respect the passion with which Hindu holy men have disciplined their bodies and minds in order to arrive at that goal. Even a superficial study of the rigorous ascetic discipline which is necessary to bring all the functions of the body and the mind into complete subjection and to focus all the energies of the self upon the attainment of mystical union is bound to impress any thoughtful and open-minded reader.[36] Whatever defects there may be in his spiritual ideal, the Hindu holy man has been willing to devote himself with single-minded passion to the realization of it. This is why it is often said that Hindu spirituality has much to teach the modern materialistic West which has almost forgotten the ideal of saintliness and is scornful of ascetic discipline.

Again, although we have criticized Sankara's denial of the reality of the empirical self, it has had beneficial as well as harmful effects. While it has led to a depreciation of the worth of the individual person, it has also helped Indians to avoid the *excessive individualism*

[35] Bergson, Henri: *The Two Sources of Morality and Religion*, New York, Henry Holt, 1935, p. 256.
[36] Zimmer, *op. cit.*, pp. 433–440.

which has been the source of much evil in modern Western societies. For it does not allow a person to forget that he is only a small part of a complex society during his existence in time and that his spiritual fulfillment depends upon his relationship to the eternal. In contrast, it must be admitted that Jewish and Christian theism has emphasized the intrinsic worth and dignity of the individual self so strongly that the value of independence and self-assertion has often been highly exaggerated in the West. As a result, the dependence of the individual upon society for his temporal welfare and upon God for his eternal destiny has all too often been forgotten.

There is another danger in Western theism that Hindu monism could help to counteract, i.e., the moral *activism* which has resulted, in part at least, from the strong demand of Judaism and Christianity for obedience to God's will in moral action. The urgent demand of the Hebrew prophets for justice and mercy and of Jesus and Paul for love of the neighbor was based upon the belief that God requires above all obedience to His righteous and loving will in moral conduct. But this religious motive for moral action has been seriously weakened in the modern world, and as a result man's struggle for social justice and his concern for the needs of individuals have been cut off from their religious root. Moral action has been increasingly grounded in humanitarian concern for human happiness, so that men have thought more of the social consequences of their acts than of their relation to God's will. Eckhart warned against moral acts that do not arise from a will that is essentially good. He insisted that only when the deeper springs of action in the soul have been purified by union with God can the will spontaneously pour forth deeds of love. But this warning has seldom been heeded in the modern age when men have been restlessly active in discovering the secrets of nature, harnessing her energies to serve their needs, and constructing or reforming social institutions to further their earthly happiness. In consequence, the lives of many modern Jews and Christians have been characterized by an excessive activism which has been increasingly secular in its motivation. Since the relation of moral conduct to God's will has been largely forgotten, moral action has often come to be regarded as merely a means to worldly ends such as success and power. If the Hindu monist's spirituality often seems to be barren of moral fruits, the Western theist's morality as often appears to be cut off from its spiritual roots.

Finally, the metaphysical *idealism* of Sankara, although it is expressed in an extreme way in the doctrine of *maya*, contains a most important truth. Although the material world is not a mere illusion or appearance, one of the fundamental insights of high religion is that the meaning of matter is to be found in the fact that it is instrumental to spiritual purposes, divine and human. Christian theists as well as Hindu idealists have stressed this truth. William Temple, for example, describes the material world as a "sacramental universe" in which matter is a vehicle or medium for the realization of spiritual ends.[37] Unfortunately, this has been almost forgotten in the West, where the development of science and technology and the exploitation of natural resources by our industrial society has led to naturalism in philosophy and practical materialism in life. As a result, the belief of theism in the reality and value of the material world has for many been replaced by the erroneous view that the material world is everything. Hence, the idealistic world view of Sankara has great value as a corrective of the modern materialism against which both Hindu monism and Western theism are struggling in our time.

[37] Temple, William: *Nature Man and God,* London, Macmillan, 1940, ch. XIX.

5

Theism and Religious Experience

The Nature of Theism

A critical examination of the claim of theism to truth must begin with a careful analysis of its nature. This is not an easy task. Since theism has had a long historical development and many thinkers have contributed to the formulation of its beliefs, there have been considerable differences between the interpretations of it at different times and places. One has only to recall that religious thinkers as diverse as Isaiah, Job, Augustine, Aquinas, Kant, Kierkegaard, and Buber were all theists to realize that theism has been a very complex historical phenomenon. Consequently, an evaluation of its beliefs which may be largely justified when applied to one thinker or one period may be quite misleading or unfair when applied to another. Furthermore, theism is still developing as contemporary theists take account of new knowledge and respond to new challenges by rethinking their beliefs. The easiest way to score a cheap and easy victory over a theist of the present day is to attribute to him precisely the same views with respect to faith and reason or God and His relation to man as those which were held by most theists of the medieval or early modern period, despite the fact that he may never have held them or may have rejected them long ago. Theism is not a static, monolithic system; it is a dynamic, evolving point of view.

Although there are important theistic elements in Hinduism and Mahayana Buddhism, and Islam has always been a theistic religion, we shall confine our attention to Western theism. The first thing we should note about it is that Western theism is the product of a synthesis of Hebraic and Christian faith with philosophy. It is a religious philosophy which originally sprang from a religious faith but was formulated by theological and philosophical reflection.

110

It is necessary to emphasize both of these points. The ancient Hebrews and early Christians were men of faith rather than philosophers, and religion was primarily a practical rather than a theoretical matter for them. It did not arise from abstract speculation but from religious experience and insight. Also, the theistic elements in the philosophies of Greek thinkers such as Plato and the Stoics were obviously expressions of a deeply religious attitude towards the world as well as products of philosophical reflection. It is misleading, therefore, to define theism, in the terms of A. E. Taylor, as "the philosophic conception of God as the ultimate ground of things" or as "a philosophic theory as distinct from a practical religious faith." [1] Theism in the sense of "the philosophic conception of God as the ultimate ground of things" is an abstraction from the actual theism of the West, for this has always been rooted in religious experience. On the other hand, Western theism is more than a religious faith and way of life; it is also a philosophical theory. This is obvious in the case of Plato and his successors in the history of philosophy. It is also true of Jewish and Christian theists from the time they came into contact with Greek philosophy, as the examples of Philo and Clement of Alexandria show. From the second century onward theism has used the categories, arguments, and conclusions of one philosophy after another in order to express the implications of its faith in a comprehensive view of the world.

What have been the major beliefs of theism? (1) It is a serious mistake to equate it simply with belief in *one* God, for it shares that belief with deism. That which is distinctive of it is belief in a *living* God, a God who is active in nature and history, rather than the absentee God of deism, e.g., the Prime Mover of Aristotle or the Divine Clockmaker of the Age of Reason. The God of theism is also a *personal* God in some sense, rather than an impersonal being like the God of pantheism. However, there has never been complete agreement among theists as to the way the "personal" character of God should be conceived, and the issue is still an open one with which contemporary theists are deeply concerned. Broadly speaking, the question is whether God should be regarded as "a person" who is one among but superior to other persons and whose personal attributes should be interpreted in the same sense as those of human persons, or whether He is to be understood as the ultimate Spiritual Reality who possesses personal attributes *analogous* to those of human persons and who is therefore capable of personal relationships with men.

(2) This living, personal God is also conceived as the Ultimate Real-

---

[1] Taylor, A. E.: "Theism" in Hastings' *Encyclopedia of Religion and Ethics*, New York, Charles Scribner's Sons, 1922, Vol. XII, p. 271.

ity who is the *Ground* or *Creator* of all finite things and events. Here again it is necessary to point out that the sense in which God should be regarded as the Ground or Creator has varied with different theists and in different times. Most theists of medieval and early modern times have conceived Him as the Creator of the world out of nothing, but many recent theists have maintained that He is the creative Ground of everything but that the creation may not have had a beginning. In the latter view, God has been creating from all eternity and the creatures have cooperated with Him in some measure in their creation.

(3) God is also *perfect* and His perfection includes not only *supreme reality* but also *pure goodness*. As such, He is the only being worthy of worship and absolute devotion. While many medieval and early modern theists interpreted Him as perfect in the sense of complete and wholly actual, some recent theists have affirmed that there is potentiality in God and that this involves change in Him. Again, while all Western theists have included goodness in God's perfection, some modern theists such as Rudolf Otto in their attempt to counteract the excessive moralism of the eighteenth and nineteenth centuries have emphasized the non-ethical aspects of the Holy. Doubtless this interpretation has been in a measure justified, since God's perfection includes not only goodness but also other attributes. But Western theism, from the time of the eighth century prophets of Israel and the time of Plato in Greece, has always stressed the goodness or righteousness of God and any conception of Him which minimizes or subordinates it is a distortion of theism.

(4) Although belief in God conceived in the manner we have described is the primary belief of theism, it is by no means the only one. For our present purpose, it is necessary to mention only a few of the beliefs which have been associated with it. One of the most important is the belief that, while the *world* of finite things and persons is dependent on Him as its creative ground, it is *distinct* from Him. As we have indicated,[2] this distinguishes theism from Hindu monism which reduces finite things and persons to the status of appearances of Brahman. Theism views finite things and persons as real and endowed with at least a relative independence of their own. Recent theistic philosophers and theologians have emphasized this point more strongly than medieval and early modern ones, insisting especially upon the independence and freedom of man and his responsibility to cooperate with God in His creative and providential work.

(5) According to the theistic worldview, *man* has a pre-eminent place among finite things. This has been the basis of the theocentric humanism which resulted from the convergence of the Biblical view of man

[2] Ch. 4.

with classical humanism. According to the Biblical view, man alone is made in the image of God and hence is pre-eminent among the creatures. As such, he is a rational being, capable of being addressed by God in His "Word" and responding to Him by a free decision to obey or disobey. If he obeys, he will attain happiness, fulfill God's purpose for Him, and further the good of his fellows. If he disobeys, he will be estranged from the divine source of his being and bring misery upon himself and others. The contribution of Greek philosophers such as Plato to the theistic view of man was somewhat different. Man, they affirmed, is superior to the animals through his possession of reason. He is capable of using his reason to control his appetites and devote himself to spiritual values such as truth and goodness. This humanistic view supplemented the Biblical view, stressing the dignity of man and his capacity to realize values worthy of a rational being as the Biblical view insisted upon his obedience to God's will and service of his fellows.

(6) Western theism has affirmed that God is seeking to fulfill a purpose for man in *history* and that through His *Providence* man is being directed towards the end for which God has destined him. Although Jewish and Christian theists have conceived the fulfillment of the divine purpose in somewhat different terms, there has been a basic similarity between their views on the major point, i.e., that God's purpose is to establish a new order of justice, peace, and love among men. They believe that divine Providence is at work in every historical situation to guide men towards this end and that it will be realized either within history or beyond history.

(7) It is obvious that these beliefs concerning God, the world, man, history, and Providence have required *faith*. Since God transcends the world, He cannot be discerned by the eye or the other senses. Hence, it is natural that sense-bound man should find it difficult to conceive Him. This is one of the reasons that belief in the gods of polytheism is easier and in a sense more natural for man than theism, since natural phenomena such as the heavenly bodies and human concerns such as victory over enemies are concrete and visible. In contrast, the transcendent God of theism is invisible, and even His immanence in finite things cannot be discerned by the senses. Moreover, the activity of God in concrete historical situations and the meaning and purpose of history as a whole are notoriously difficult to discover. Indeed, scientific historians tend to dismiss philosophical and theological interpretations of history as mere products of imagination or *a priori* speculation without a basis in the facts. Hence, the theistic view of God and His activity in history has always required faith for its acceptance, since it goes beyond what the senses can apprehend or reason can prove. However, this does not imply that these and other basic beliefs of theism are merely

irrational products of the myth-making imagination. The fact that some, although not all, of them were developed in Greece by a process of philosophical reflection which was not dependent on revelation is an evidence of this. Hence, the dominant strand in Western thought has affirmed that faith goes beyond reason but is not contrary to it.

Origin in Religious Experience

Since Western theism originated primarily in the religious experiences of ancient Hebrews and early Christians, the critical evaluation of its truth claims will be aided by an analysis of the nature of those experiences. The objection could be raised that the religious experiences of men two thousand or more years ago are not normative for men of today. But we would point out that men have continued to affirm the beliefs of theism since that time largely because they have had similar religious experiences which have seemed to them to confirm the basic beliefs of the Biblical writers. We shall face later the question whether, as is sometimes said, it is no longer possible for men of our time to enjoy such experiences.

We shall begin by recalling that the interpretations of their religious experiences by Hindu monists and Western theists have been very different, and the contrast throws light on the distinctive characteristics of theistic religious experience. Hindu monists have asserted that man must attain liberation or salvation from the ignorance that binds him to the realm of appearance by coming to a knowledge of the identity of his true Self with Brahman through mystical experience of the "introvertive kind." [3] In contrast, the ancient Hebrews and early Christians experienced the reality of God, not by detaching themselves from the world of space and time but by discerning His activity primarily in their *history,* past and present. They knew Him in His "mighty acts," from the call of Abraham through their liberation from bondage in Egypt under Moses to the establishment of their national kingdom under the leadership of David. Similarly, the early Christians experienced Him in the earthly career of Jesus of Nazareth and in the spread of the Gospel in the early Church. Thus, the ancient Hebrews and early Christians found God not through a mystical experience in the depths of the soul but in the midst of life within the world, especially in times of national or personal crisis. Moreover, they experienced Him not as a self-sufficient spiritual being, serene in eternal peace and joy apart from the concerns of the world and of time, but as a dynamic and creative force that was active in every situation. More specifically, they were

[3] For the meaning of "introvertive mysticism" see Stace, W. T.: *Mysticism and Philosophy,* Philadelphia, J. B. Lippincott Co., 1960, ch. 2.

confronted by Him as a Personal Will acting in and upon them to realize His purposes in their history. They felt the pressure of the divine will upon their own wills, commanding them to act in certain ways, rewarding them when they obeyed and punishing them when they disobeyed.

The nature and purpose of God, as manifested in His activity, were interpreted by prophets who believed themselves to be "called" and commissioned by God to speak for Him, so that the message they spoke was not their own but was given to them by God. This is often expressed by saying that the prophet was "inspired," and there is no doubt that the prophets felt themselves to be possessed by God's Spirit and to be His spokesmen. But the traditional view that inspiration involved the supersession of the prophet's own faculties by God so that his message was simply dictated to him is false. It implies that he was in a purely passive state and contributed nothing from his own experience and insight to the message he spoke. In reality, the great prophets did not merely speak words put into their mouths by God while in a state of frenzy. As R. B. Y. Scott says, their "grasp of the moral and spiritual realities of a given situation" and the fact that the "Word" they spoke conveyed a definite message marked them off from the spirit-possessed ecstatics.[4] Also, their predictions of future events were based upon their own insight into the moral realities of the present situation when understood in the light of God's covenant with their people and His moral will. The prophet made clear to his people the moral crisis in which they were standing, the demand of God's will upon them in that crisis, and the consequences that would follow their obedience or disobedience to Him. "The prophet reveals the moral and spiritual reality behind appearances, *what is,* as against what seems, what is felt on the level of the senses, or what is desired or feared. He interprets the present experience of his auditors in the light of wider experience, that of his own call and communion with Yahweh and that of his people's religious history." [5] Thus, he proclaims God's will and interprets His nature and purpose for men.

However, the ancient Hebrews did not feel that the divine will was imposing demands upon them in an arbitrary way and without concern for their welfare. They experienced God's demands as coming from One who cared for His people, as He had shown when he delivered them from bondage in Egypt and entered into a covenant with them on Mt. Sinai. Hence, they viewed the commandments revealed through Moses and the oracles spoken through the prophets as expressions of

[4] Scott, R. B. Y.: *The Relevance of the Prophets,* New York, Macmillan, 1968, pp. 92, 93.

[5] *Ibid.,* p. 113.

God's *love* for His people and His concern for their happiness. Indeed, they believed that He was faithful to His promises to them even when they were faithless toward Him and wandered from His ways. Although He punished them for their idolatry and their injustice to others, they were sure that He was ready to forgive them when they repented and turned back to Him. Their conviction that God cared for them even survived the destruction of Jerusalem, their national capital and religious center, for their great prophets continued to have faith in Him in the dark days of the Babylonian Exile and kept alive their hope for the future by visions of a Messianic age of justice and peace.[6] Thus, their religious experience centered not only on the *power* of God as shown by their liberation from Egypt and His *righteousness* as manifested in the giving of the Law to them, but also on His *love* for them and *concern* for their welfare.

In the early stages of their religious development, they seem to have believed that He was concerned only for their happiness, as was customary in tribal and national religions. But this narrow view, which had been challenged by the prophet Amos, gave way after the disillusioning experiences of the Babylonian Exile, and nobler writers such as the Second Isaiah[7] and the author of the Book of Jonah saw that the purpose of God for history extended to Gentiles as well as Jews. This development of universalism was continued in the New Testament with the recognition by the early Christians of the universality of God's love and the inclusion of Jews and Gentiles alike in the Church.

The ancient Hebrews experienced God as both *transcendent* and *immanent*. Some passages in the earlier books of the Old Testament picture Him in a crudely anthropomorphic way which virtually reduces Him to the level of a finite being, as when Adam and Eve hear Him walking in the Garden of Eden after their disobedience or when He goes into battle before His people as their Lord and overthrows their enemies.[8] But in the great prophets His transcendence and otherness are emphasized. Thus Isaiah has a vision of Him as "high and lifted up" in His holiness and shrinks back from Him as a sinful creature.[9] The Second Isaiah exalts Him as the Creator who "sits above the circle of the earth, and its inhabitants are like grasshoppers," and before whom "the nations are like a drop from a bucket, and are accounted as the dust on the scales." [10] Moreover, His thoughts and acts are unlike those of man: "For as the heavens are higher than the

---

[6] See especially the prophecies of the Second Isaiah in Isaiah, chs. 40–55.
[7] Amos 9:7, 8; Isaiah, chs. 40–55.
[8] Genesis 3:8; Judges 5.
[9] Isaiah 6:1.
[10] Isaiah 40:22, 23, 15.

earth, so are my ways higher than your ways and my thoughts than your thoughts." [11]

However, the emphasis upon God's transcendent holiness did not lead the Hebrews to think of Him as remote and detached from the world like Aristotle's Prime Mover, for He is also *immanent* in both nature and history. He is everywhere, in heaven above, in "the uttermost parts of the sea," and in darkness and light alike, so that it is impossible to flee from His presence.[12] He knows every man's thoughts and ways; He even knows a man's words before he speaks them.[13] Moreover, His knowledge of men is accompanied by a deep love and concern for them. He manifests "steadfast love and mercy" toward them and pities those who fear Him "as a father pities his children." [14] This experience of the immanence and nearness of God not only in the sense of His omnipresence but even more in the sense of His love and care for all His creatures is continued in the New Testament, and St. Paul is represented as quoting to the Athenians the words of a Stoic poet, "In Him we live and move and have our being." [15]

While the ancient Hebrews experienced God primarily through His activity in history, they were also conscious of His wisdom, power, and goodness as manifested in *nature*. The great myth of Creation in the Book of Genesis pictures Him as creating the order of nature out of a primordial watery chaos by a series of mighty acts. After several of these acts, He expresses His approval of the result, "And God saw that it was good";[16] and when He has finished His work the author says, "And God saw everything that he had made, and behold, it was very good." [17] Clearly, the author of this myth had come to believe that the power which had put limits to the stormy waters, peopled the earth with plants and animals, and finally created man must be a divine will guided by wisdom.[18] The order of nature must be the product not of random motions and transformations of matter but of a creative will whose purpose was to realize good through His creatures. Great nature poems such as Psalm 104 also picture Him manifesting His goodness to all the species of living creatures He has made by providing them with food and drink to sustain them.[19] Thus, the ancient Hebrews saw in

---

[11] Isaiah 55:9.
[12] Psalm 139:1–12.
[13] *Ibid.*
[14] Psalm 103:4, 13.
[15] Acts 17:28.
[16] Genesis 1:10, 12, 18, 21, 25.
[17] Genesis 1:31.
[18] Proverbs 8:22–31.
[19] Psalm 104.

both the order and the bounty of nature evidence of God's wisdom, power, and goodness.

There was an increasing awareness among the Hebrews, especially after the destruction of Jerusalem and the Temple by the Babylonians, of the need for a *personal relationship* with God. This is expressed first in passages of the Book of Jeremiah. The Book of Psalms also expresses in a deeply moving way many aspects of this personal relationship, from joyful praise and thanksgiving for God's blessings to anguished petitions for help in sickness and protection against personal enemies. It would be a mistake, therefore, to emphasize the Hebrews' experience of God's activity in their national history so strongly as to overlook or minimize the importance for them of personal communion with God. The Gospels and Letters of the New Testament also contain many passages describing the personal relationship of Jesus and the early Christians with God.

This personal religious experience of the ancient Hebrews and the early Christians was characterized not only by inner peace and joy but also by *struggle* and *suffering*. They rejoice in God's presence and praise Him for His blessings; they also long for Him when they feel Him to be absent and plead with Him to restore them to favor when they feel His displeasure. Above all, their religion is marked by a sense of *sin* and *guilt*. Although "sin" often refers merely to a ritual fault, the sense of sin was sometimes profound and was accompanied by an intense longing for forgiveness. The Psalmist prays, "Have mercy on me, O God, according to thy steadfast love; according to thy abundant mercy blot out my transgressions." [20] Since he is aware that his transgressions are the result of a sinful condition of the self within, he cries, "Create in me a clean heart, O God, and put a new and right spirit within me." [21] For deliverance from sin which alienates one from God, he believes, requires a radical transformation of the self which springs from repentance and faith and results in a new heart and a new spirit. The New Testament continues this theme in both the Gospels and the Letters. Jesus begins his ministry by proclaiming that the kingdom of God is imminent and urging men to repent and believe the good news,[22] and in the Gospel of John he says, "Unless one is born anew, he cannot see the kingdom of God." [23]

This is significant because to the greatest Biblical writers estrangement from God by sin meant separation from the ultimate source of meaning in life and hence was a cause of acute suffering. This suffering

[20] Psalm 51:1.
[21] Psalm 51:10.
[22] Mark 1:15.
[23] John 3:3.

made a person more aware of his absolute dependence on God and drove him to turn back to God and seek a reconciliation with Him. When God in His mercy forgave him, he experienced another aspect of God's goodness, His *grace*. For God's goodness was experienced by the Biblical writers not only in his activity on behalf of His people in history, but also in His compassion for individual persons in their weakness and His willingness to save them from their sins. As one of the Psalmists expresses it, "For as the heavens are high above the earth, so great is his steadfast love toward those who fear him; as far as the east is from the west, so far does he remove our transgressions from us. As a father pities his children, so the Lord pities those who fear him. For he knows our frame; he remembers that we are dust." [24]

Thus, the experience of alienation from God by sin, as well as the traumatic experience of exile, deepened the faith of many ancient Hebrews by leading them to an experience of His mercy and grace. The emphasis of Jesus upon the love of God for just and unjust alike and his own special concern for outcasts and sinners, followed by Paul's insistence that salvation must come through God's unmerited grace rather than man's good works, continued this aspect of Israel's religious experience. As a result, Christianity became above all a religion of redemptive love. It is a paradoxical fact that the experience of God's reality and goodness has come to man as often in times of frustration and anxiety as in times of fulfillment and joy.

Contemporary Religious Experience

We have attempted to show how the religious beliefs of Western theism arose from the religious experiences of the ancient Hebrews and early Christians. If we were right in arguing[25] that religious experience may provide valuable evidence for the truth of religious beliefs, the religious experiences described by the Biblical writers must be weighed along with experiences of other kinds in evaluating the truth claims of theism. Before we undertake such an evaluation, however, we must face the objection that the thinking of contemporary man has been so profoundly affected by science and technology that religious experiences like those of the ancient Hebrews and early Christians are no longer possible in our time. For this seems to be the assumption behind much of the thinking of those who speak of the "death of God."

The only way to deal responsibly with this objection is to examine the experience of contemporary men and to inquire whether or not

[24] Psalm 103:8, 11–14.
[25] Ch. 3.

it includes religious experiences corresponding to those described by the Biblical writers. For this purpose it is not sufficient to examine the experience of theists alone, since the objector might concede that they have had such religious experiences but maintain that they constitute a minority in an increasingly secular world. Therefore, we must also examine the experience of those who are not theists in order to determine whether it includes kinds or dimensions of experience which may be reasonably interpreted in theistic terms.

(1) One of the fundamental aspects of the religious experience described by the Biblical writers is that it is an experience of a *transcendent Being*, one who is holy in the sense of other than and superior to all finite beings, although also immanent in them. Now, it is frequently said that contemporary man has completely lost his sense of the transcendent. Scientism has fostered the belief that the only source of knowledge is the scientific method which acknowledges no reality that transcends the world of the senses. Moreover, technology has encouraged men to exploit nature for their own ends rather than to feel wonder before her mystery or awe in the presence of her beauty and sublimity. There is truth in this, and we have ourselves emphasized it in our analysis of the contemporary crisis of belief.[26] However, many contemporary men have simply turned away from traditional dualistic interpretations of the divine transcendence and are experiencing it in ways which require a different interpretation of it. We shall mention several examples of this tendency among recent theistic thinkers.

Rudolf Bultmann has pointed out that the cosmology of the New Testament pictured the world as consisting of three levels: heaven above, hell below, and the earth between them. Since God, accompanied by the angels and the redeemed, occupied heaven, He was pictured by men on the earth as living in another world which was conceived as supernatural and hence quite different from the natural world. This ancient cosmology is not acceptable to modern man not only because science knows only one world but also because the picture of a world consisting of three levels is mythological in character and therefore not to be taken literally.[27]

Other recent theists have pointed out that the traditional supernaturalism seems to deny God's immanence in the world of nature and man and to limit His activity to occasional miraculous interventions. For this and other reasons, they interpret the divine transcendence in ways which will not separate God from nature and history and therefore will be more compatible with His immanence. This point of view

[26] Introduction.
[27] Bultmann, R.: *Jesus Christ and Mythology*, New York, Charles Scribner's Sons, 1958.

is well illustrated by Martin Buber. The "eternal Thou," he affirms, is present in our relations with "temporal Thous." [28] This implies that, while the eternal Thou is transcendent to, He is also immanent in, the finite Thous and is experienced along with them. The criticism of the traditional conception of transcendence by Dietrich Bonhoeffer is somewhat different. "The transcendent," he asserts, "is not infinitely remote, but close at hand." [29] Referring to Jesus as "one whose only concern is for others," he writes, "This concern of Jesus for others [is] the experience of transcendence. . . . Our relation to God [is] not a religious relationship to a supreme Being, absolute in power and goodness, which is a spurious conception of transcendence, but a new life for others, through participation in the Being of God." [30] Finally, a recent Catholic philosopher, Leslie Dewart, asserts that the revelation of Jesus profoundly affected men's understanding of the transcendence of God. "Henceforth God should not be understood as having the paradoxical qualities of transcending creation yet entering into communication with man. . . . God was a transcendent *presence,* that is, he 'lived in,' was immanent within, all being, all existence and most particularly in all men. . . . He is a reality *other* than being who is *present* to being (by which presence he makes being to be). . . . In brief, God no longer 'sent word' or 'spoke' to us from on high. He now lived with us 'here below,' and shared our history, our humanity, our nature and our life." [31] Thus, Jewish, Protestant, and Catholic thinkers alike reflect the recent tendency to conceive God's transcendence in a way different from that of traditional theism. A somewhat similar tendency may be seen in philosophers of process. Whitehead's "principle of relativity" means that God, like every other actual entity, influences and is influenced by others, so that He is not absolutely transcendent in the sense of independent of all finite beings. However, He is transcendent in the perfection of His experience.[32]

We have mentioned these different conceptions of the divine transcendence to indicate that many contemporary religious thinkers are interpreting it in ways which reflect the experience of men in our time. What is common to these thinkers is that they discern God's transcendence precisely in and through His immanence, i.e., His presence as a

[28] Buber, Martin: *I and Thou,* Edinburgh, T & T. Clark, 1947, p. 101.

[29] Bonhoeffer, D.: *Letters & Papers from Prison,* New York, Macmillan Paperbacks, 1953, p. 233.

[30] *Ibid.,* pp. 237, 238.

[31] Dewart, L.: *The Future of Belief,* New York, Herder & Herder, 1966, pp. 138, 139.

[32] Christian William: *An Interpretation of Whitehead's Metaphysics,* New Haven, Conn., Yale University Press, 1959, pp. 364–380.

creative and redemptive power in nature and human life. Thus, White-head's conception expresses his experience of the creative Eros in nature and man which is always realizing values by bringing new actual entities into existence and which preserves them in its own everlasting life. Buber experiences the reality of the "Eternal Thou" as present in but not reducible to the temporal "Thous" with whom the "I" enters into personal relationships. Bonhoeffer and Dewart are conscious of God above all as present and active in history, showing His transcendence not by a display of His power from on high but by loving and suffering with man.

These philosophers and theologians are also significant because they are expressing religious experiences that are shared by many persons who do not regard themselves as theists in the traditional sense, men who are conscious of a transcendent and sacred Power present in the complex order of nature, the beauty of art and music, the love of other persons, and the struggle for social justice. If so, contemporary men still experience the transcendence of God, like the ancient Hebrews and early Christians, through His presence and activity in nature and history, although they may be reluctant to express their experience in the traditional language of theism.

(2) Western theism has always affirmed not only the transcendence of God but also the *absolute dependence* of men upon Him for their existence and for the meaning of their lives. Do contemporary men experience the feeling of absolute dependence? At first sight, it seems that our secular age is almost wholly lacking in this experience. As we have indicated, modern man has been tempted by the scientific and technological revolution and the power it has put into his hands to think that he is dependent upon nothing but his own intelligence and will for his self-fulfillment. This is why the religious humanists had such a strong influence in the nineteenth century when men had unbounded confidence in themselves and their future possibilities. Of course, modern men have recognized that they are dependent on nature for the physical conditions of life and that they violate her laws only at their peril. But they have not believed that they are absolutely dependent on her; they have regarded her as a source of raw materials and forces to be exploited for human purposes. It is only as they approach death that they become fully aware of her ultimate power over them, and they have found many ways to keep that grim reality out of sight as long as possible.

But although modern men have not usually been willing to acknowledge their absolute dependence on anything, they are in fact limited by and dependent upon powers beyond their control. Pride, individual or collective, may blind man for a time to this basic reality of his finite and conditioned existence; but sooner or later he is forced to recognize the limitations of his own power and his dependence on nature and man. Of course, it is possible for a man to be aware of his dependence upon nature (like the pantheist) or his dependence upon other men (like the humanist), but to be wholly unaware of his ultimate dependence upon God. He can adopt a naturalistic view which affirms that nature is self-explanatory and that man is only a part of nature. If so, he will not be conscious of the absolute dependence of both nature and himself upon God as their creative and sustaining ground and will explain away as illusory the religious experience of creatureliness men have felt in the presence of the Holy.

Nevertheless, contemporary men do experience the finite and conditioned nature of their existence and may be led by it to a belief in theism. Recent existentialist philosophers have made us deeply aware of the insecurity of man because of the limitation of his powers and achievements and the contingency of his existence. Karl Jaspers has described some of the "limit-" or "boundary-situations" which confront man, e.g., suffering, struggle, guilt, and death. For example, guilt is inevitable because of man's finitude, for every moral choice involves the fulfillment of some claims at the cost of rejecting others. And death, when it is faced squarely as the inevitable end of life, puts in question a man's whole existence. In such a situation a man experiences deep anxiety and may fall into despair. He may come to feel that existence is meaningless and absurd, like some recent atheistic existentialists. However, he may be led in his freedom to affirm his faith in and dependence upon the Transcendent beyond the world of phenomena.[33] Paul Tillich also has described the condition of human existence as one of anxiety due to the "threat of non-being" or the threat of meaninglessness. Man can be saved from despair, he affirms, by faith in God as the power of being which can overcome the threat of non-being and give man the "courage to be." [34]

Thus, the existentialists have made us aware that under the surface contemporary men are painfully aware of the contingency of their existence and of the reality of guilt in their lives, as the Biblical writers were. The fact that our time has been called the Age of Anxiety and that so many people are forced to seek the aid of psychiatrists is evidence enough of this. The difference between our contemporaries and the ancient Hebrews or early Christians is that many men of our time are prevented by their distrust of feelings and insights which

[33] Jaspers, Karl: *Way to Wisdom*, New Haven, Conn., Yale University Press, 1964, pp. 19, 20.

[34] Tillich, Paul: *Systematic Theology*, Vol. I, Chicago, University of Chicago Press, 1951, pp. 208–210.

cannot be verified by the scientific method from affirming their absolute dependence upon God as the ground of their being.

(3) However, many persons would admit that there are grounds in contemporary experience for affirming a transcendent Power of some kind and man's absolute dependence upon it, but would deny that there is any such ground for affirming that it is *personal*. Primitive man, they would say, believed quite naturally that the invisible powers upon which he depended were personal like himself. Since he had not yet learned to distinguish clearly between matter, life, and spirit, he interpreted everything that seemed to him to be endowed with power as a living spirit like himself. Acceptance of this primitive animism led ancient man to personify the invisible powers he worshipped as gods. The theistic belief in a personal God was simply a survival from this primitive way of explaining the power experienced in natural phenomena or human activities. But modern science has made it impossible for contemporary man to explain natural or human forces by reference to personal beings—or one Personal Will—acting in and through them. Moreover, to introduce a Personal Will into natural or historical science as an explanatory principle would destroy it as a science.

This modern exclusion of Personal Will from the explanation of events has been accompanied by the widespread reduction of personal relations to impersonal ones in our civilization. The depersonalization of men in modern mass society has been described so fully by existentialists such as Karl Jaspers and Gabriel Marcel that it is necessary only to mention it at this point.[35] For example, when men regard others as producers of goods for the sake of profit to themselves or as consumers of goods to be manipulated by advertisers for the same purpose, they treat them as objects rather than persons, "Its" rather than "Thous." It is not surprising, therefore, that in our scientific and industrial civilization many persons find it difficult to believe that a Personal Will guided by wisdom and motivated by love is the ultimate source of all existence and value.

Nevertheless, contemporary man experiences the presence and power of personal qualities and relations in many situations. He knows that impersonal natural laws are discovered and described by the personal intelligence of the scientist and that the machine which enables him to exploit the resources of nature was made possible by the imagination of the inventor. He is aware of the crucial role of dynamic persons in the drama of political activity, whether they are charismatic but demagogic "leaders" or constructive statesmen. Above all, in his every-

[35] Jaspers, Karl: *Man in the Modern Age*, London, R. & K. Paul, 1951, and Marcel, Gabriel: *Man Against Mass Society*, Chicago, Regnery, 1962.

day life he is very conscious that happiness depends largely upon mutual love and respect. He usually confines such relationships to members of his own family or his circle of friends, but he protests at times against the treatment of members of a minority race as things rather than persons, as in the recent civil rights movement. Thus, contemporary man has not lost sight of personal qualities and relations as a powerful force in human life.

But is it possible for him to feel, as the ancient Hebrews and early Christians felt, the presence and power of a divine Personal Will? The wide influence of Martin Buber's *I and Thou* and his other works during the last generation suggests that it is. It also suggests that contemporary man usually encounters the divine Thou in and along with human Thous, i.e., as immanent in the human Thous with whom he enjoys genuinely personal relationships. For he finds it difficult, as we have indicated, to conceive of God as transcendent in the sense of separate from and above the world of nature and man. Hence, it is easier for him to experience the divine Personal Will as it acts in and through persons than to discern its activity in the vast movements of history. Also, every person has felt at times a pressure upon his will which seems to urge upon him a course of action that goes against his desires. H. H. Farmer refers to the experience of "value-resistance" to the ordinary interests of the self and argues that it is evidence for the action of the moral will of God upon our wills.[36] This experience is familiar to everyone, although it is inadequately described by the term "value-resistance" because the pressure upon our wills sometimes seems to act upon them not by resisting natural desires but by awakening higher desires. Perhaps it was this kind of pressure that St. Paul had in mind when he wrote that, although the Gentiles were without the revealed Law, the law was written in their hearts. His vivid description of conscience as "accusing" or "excusing" them may have been his way of explaining the way the divine will sought to make that law effective in their lives.[37]

Thus, it can be argued that contemporary man experiences God as personal both when He is encountered as the Eternal Thou in intimate personal relationships and when He acts upon the wills of men from within to restrain their selfish desires and to awaken in them the desire to serve wider purposes. Was it not by experiences similar to these that the ancient Hebrews were led to believe that the transcendent Power upon which they felt themselves to be absolutely dependent was not a blind impersonal force but a Personal Will? There is much evidence in the Old Testament that this was the case, e.g., the demand laid upon

[36] Farmer, H. H.: *Towards Belief in God,* New York, Macmillan, 1943, pp. 46, 49.
[37] Romans 2:14–16.

Moses by God to deliver Israel from bondage[38] and the sending of
Nathan the prophet to David to rebuke him for his adultery with
Bathsheba and the killing of her husband.[39] Perhaps the difference
between the ancient Hebrews and many of us is not that they had
religious experiences of God as Personal Will which are denied to us
but that they were not as inhibited as we are by impersonal modes of
thinking and impersonal relations with others from recognizing His
presence in these experiences.

(4) Although the ancient Hebrews and early Christians were conscious of the presence of God primarily through His activity in their
history, we pointed out that they regarded the *order of nature* also as
the handiwork of a transcendent Creator and as evidence of His wisdom, power, and goodness. Although they were well aware of the wild
and destructive forces of nature, as the story of the flood shows, and
were haunted by the problem of suffering and death, they were impressed above all by the goodness of the Creation and the blessings of
life. Therefore, although they were not tempted to make nature their
God, their attitude toward her was one of wonder and gratitude.

The attitude of most contemporary men toward nature is very different. As we have said, they tend to think of nature as a system of things
and events which can be described by the scientific method and which
itself requires no further explanation. They seek to master her in order
to exploit her resources for their own purposes. Although they may at
times admire the beauty and complexity of natural things, it seldom
occurs to them to be grateful to her—much less to her Maker—for her
many blessings to them and to other living beings. She is neither
Mother Earth, as she was to the pagans, nor God's Handiwork, as she
was to the Hebrews.

Nevertheless, the same experiences which led the author of the first
chapter of Genesis to write his great myth of the Creation and the
nature Psalmists to write of the care of the Creator for all living
creatures are possible for contemporary men. Indeed, they can appreciate the wonders of nature far better than the ancient Hebrews or the
early Christians. They have learned from modern science how much
more complex is the order of nature, even in the single cell, than the
Biblical writers knew. They know something of the immensity of space,
the length of time it required for the earth to develop and living
organisms to evolve, the fearful power enclosed in the atom, and the
intricate mechanisms involved in heredity and growth. Thus, they are
in a far better position to discern the wisdom and power manifested in
nature than the ancient Hebrews. Hence, it is not because men of today

[38] Exodus 3.
[39] II Samuel 12:1–15.

lack experiences of nature similar to those of the Hebrews that many of them view the world as a product of blind, purposeless forces rather than of divine wisdom and goodness. It is because they have uncritically accepted the scientific description of natural phenomena as the whole truth that they raise no questions about the ultimate ground of nature as a whole.

(5) In our analysis of the religious experience of the Biblical writers, we noted that they experienced God's presence in times of adversity and suffering as well as in times of fulfillment and joy. God often seemed to be hidden from them and to have withdrawn his care from them, and they were very conscious that they had put a gulf between Him and themselves by their sin. Is it not possible to regard the contemporary "absence" of God in a somewhat similar way, especially if we think of it, with Buber, as really an "eclipse" for which men are themselves primarily responsible?

Indeed, the sense of God's *absence* may itself be indirectly a witness to His reality and to His hidden presence. Since the time of St. Augustine many Christian thinkers have affirmed that man has a natural desire for communion with God and can fulfill himself only through love of Him. St. Augustine's famous words are a classic expression of this affirmation: "Thou hast formed us for Thyself, and restless are our hearts until they find their rest in Thee." Fred Berthold maintains, in line with this tradition, that anxiety has a positive as well as a negative aspect. As a being made in the image of God, man has a natural tendency and inclination to communion with God. This tendency is threatened from many sides and is blocked to some extent in all men, not least by their evasion of the demand of God for unselfish love and their attempt to find security in finite things. Anxiety arises from this natural desire for God in the presence of a threat to it. "Without love, or desire for what is felt to be good, anxiety could not arise," so that anxiety is a sign of "a love which is embattled" and "whose end is far from secured." [40]

Tillich's view of anxiety is somewhat similar. Anxiety arises from the threat of non-being to the self, a threat which in our time tends to take the form of a sense of meaninglessness. This seems at first sight to be a completely negative view of anxiety. But Tillich also affirms that even in the state of despair to which this anxiety may lead man can experience the "power of being" which is able to overcome the threat of non-being and through faith in it can find the "courage to be" despite his anxiety.[41] The reason he can do so is that he is a finite being

[40] Berthold, Fred: *The Fear of God*, New York, Harper and Bros., 1959, pp. 143, 144.

[41] Tillich, Paul: *The Courage to Be*, ch. 6.

who is estranged from but, at the same time, participates in God the "ground of being," so that God is present in His very absence.

Thus, it is possible to see in the sense of meaninglessness which has led to the widespread anxiety in our time an experience of the emptiness of life apart from God and hence an indirect evidence that man has an inherent desire and need for communion with Him. He cannot find fulfillment in "restless" pursuit of finite things and values, as St. Augustine tried to do before his conversion, but can find his "rest" only in the love of God which is a response to God's love for him. Of course, he is free to accept or reject the faith which can make this possible, for faith is an act of free decision; but he experiences the consequences of its absence and this points to the need for God's presence to give meaning to his life.

Modern Empiricism and Religious Experience

We have shown that religious experiences like those which led ancient Hebrews and early Christians to believe that a *transcendent* God exists, that all finite beings are *absolutely dependent* on Him, that He manifests Himself to men in their history as a *personal and moral Being*, that He shows His *wisdom and power* in nature and that His presence is experienced even through His *absence* can be—and sometimes are—enjoyed by men of our time. Thus, the experiences which led the Biblical writers to belief in theism are available to men today and can be for them also a primary ground for religious belief.

We have also suggested that the main reason many of our contemporaries are not convinced by these experiences is that they put an interpretation upon them that is very different from that of the Biblical writers. The interpretation of experience depends upon the presuppositions with which men approach it, and the presuppositions which are dominant in our time are opposed to the theistic interpretation of experience. These presuppositions are epistemological, on the one hand, and metaphysical, on the other. The epistemological one is a narrow conception of experience; the metaphysical one is the naturalistic view that there is no reality which transcends the natural order. These presuppositions are interdependent, each supporting the other, and they are so widespread and powerful in their influence that many persons simply take it for granted that religious experience is only subjective and without cognitive value.

Although we have already mentioned the conception of experience which has dominated empiricism since Hume,[42] it is necessary to deal

[42] Ch. 3.

with it more fully at this point. It is based upon Hume's assumption that the origin of all our knowledge is from "impressions," i.e., the immediate data of experience, and that "ideas" are only faint copies or images of impressions. Hume uses this principle to test the cognitive value of a number of fundamental ideas by inquiring whether they can be traced back to external or internal impressions. "When we entertain, therefore, any suspicion that a philosophical term is employed without any meaning or idea (as is but too frequent), we need but to inquire, *from what impression is that supposed idea derived?* And if it be impossible to assign any, this will serve to confirm our suspicion." [43] When he tests several fundamental ideas in this way, he finds that each of them cannot be traced back to an impression and concludes that its claim to give us knowledge is not rationally justified. For example, the idea that there is a "necessary connection" between a cause and its effect does not originate from an impression of such a connection but only from the "constant conjunction" of the two in the past.

The general conclusion Hume drew from this skeptical analysis of fundamental ideas was that our knowledge is confined to physical and psychical phenomena, although for the practical purposes of life we must act upon "natural beliefs" such as the existence of external substances and causal relations between events. The implication for metaphysics and rational theology was devastating. "If we take in hand any volume, of divinity or school metaphysics, for instance, let us ask, *Does it contain any abstract reasoning containing quantity or number?* No. *Does it contain any experimental reasoning concerning matter of fact and existence?* No. Commit it then to the flames: for it can contain nothing but sophistry and illusion." [44] This means that our knowledge is limited to mathematics and the empirical sciences and that all metaphysical and theological efforts to interpret the nature of reality are arbitrary and illusory constructions of the imagination. Thus, Hume's empiricism resulted in phenomenalism with respect to our knowledge of nature and man and skepticism with respect to the possibility of any metaphysical or theological explanation of reality.

The powerful influence of this view of experience upon empiricists since the time of Hume has been largely due to the prestige of the scientific method. The model of knowledge for Hume was Newtonian natural science which was based upon the observation of natural phenomena as apprehended by the senses and the verification of hypotheses by sense experience. Now, the method employed by natural science does not deny the reality or importance of aspects of the world which

[43] Hume, David: *Enquiry Concerning Human Understanding*, Oxford, Oxford University Press, 1951, p. 22.
[44] *Ibid.*, p. 165.

are *not* apprehended by the senses; it simply investigates and describes those which *are,* especially those which can be measured and described in mathematical terms. However, the picture of nature that was developed by modern scientists from Galileo to Newton seemed to many persons to imply a denial of the objective reality of other aspects of nature than those described by the scientists. Final causes were banished from natural science by Galileo and Descartes, and all natural events were explained mechanically by efficient causes. Secondary qualities such as color, sound, and heat were regarded not as qualities of objects but as effects of primary qualities upon our senses.[45] The effect of these and other scientific developments upon many modern minds was to make them question the reality or at least the importance of aspects of the world which are not experienced through the senses. Whitehead and others in our time have completely rejected this interpretation of experience and the materialistic conception of nature which resulted from it,[46] but it had a powerful influence upon philosophy in the eighteenth and nineteenth centuries and still dominates the thinking of many empiricists today.

The Necessity of a Broader Empiricism

It has been increasingly recognized that, while metaphysics and the philosophy of religion must be empirical in their basis, the conception of experience we have been analyzing must give way to a broader one. The necessity of a broader view may be illustrated by a brief discussion of several types of experience which have been regarded by many empiricists as "merely subjective" and therefore as having no cognitive value.

The first of these is the experience of *value.* Beauty, for example, has been treated by many modern empiricists as a purely subjective state, e.g., a feeling of pleasure, rather than a quality which is independent of the appreciation of human subjects or which is potentially in the object but is actualized by the appreciation of human subjects.[47] Obviously, one reason for this subjective theory of beauty is that the quality of beauty is not apprehended by sense impressions, although the intuition of it is mediated through them. Consequently, if one has accepted the empiricism we have been criticizing, one will naturally deny that beauty points beyond the "sensuous surface" of the object to

[45] Burtt, E. A.: *The Metaphysical Foundations of Modern Physical Science,* New York, Harcourt, Brace and Co., 1925.
[46] Whitehead, A. N.: *Science and the Modern World,* New York, Macmillan, 1926.
[47] The latter is the view of William Temple in *Nature Man and God,* London, Macmillan, 1951, p. 154.

a transcendent, ultimate ground. Hence, both the idealistic view of Plato that beautiful objects are manifestations of Absolute Beauty and the theistic view that natural beauty is a revelation of the wisdom and goodness of the Creator will be discredited. This is why beauty has ceased to have either philosophical or religious significance for so many modern men and has become merely an ornament and source of pleasure. Both Shelley's praise of "Intellectual Beauty" and the Bible's praise of the "beauty of holiness" have lost all meaning for them. Yet a reduction of beauty to its sensuous element and to the human pleasure stimulated by it ignores precisely that dimension of beauty which has always made it seem so important to man and has made it a natural ally of religion.

The interpretation of *moral value* as subjective is still more serious from the religious point of view. It would be unjust to accuse modern empiricists of indifference to morality, as many of them have contributed to ethical theory and have sought to promote human happiness by social reforms. But the type of morality advocated by many of them has been almost completely human and has lacked any foundation in a moral order that is grounded in ultimate reality. For empiricism has usually been associated with the utilitarian ethical theory according to which an act is right when it is conducive to the attainment of the greatest happiness—or, in its non-hedonistic form, the greatest good—of the greatest number or on the whole. The presupposition behind this theory has been that the rightness or wrongness of an act is determined solely by its consequences for men. This implies that there is no moral order to which men should conform in their acts and which is the source of unconditional moral demands upon them. Moral acts are merely useful means of attaining the pleasure or other values desired by men. This is why Kant attacked the view that the morality of acts is determined by their consequences and insisted that morality is governed by "categorical" or unconditional imperatives rather than by "hypothetical" imperatives which merely prescribe the right means one should take to attain one's ends. Doubtless Kant's ethic of conformity to law is as one-sided as the utilitarians' ethic of consequences, as both the inner character of the good will and the intention to bring about good consequences are indispensable in moral conduct. But his emphasis upon the absolute worth of the good will and his affirmation that the self belongs to the supersensible as well as the sensible world point to a dimension of moral goodness which cannot be apprehended by the senses but is nonetheless real and religiously significant.

A second consequence of the narrow conception of experience is that it has led most modern empiricists to deny the unity and continuity of the *self* as a spiritual reality through its changing experiences. Hume's criticism of the idea of "personal identity" because he could find no impression of such an idea when he looked within led to the modern empirical concept of the self as only a series of changing states.[48] Behaviorism has simply gone a step further and reduced mind to behavior of the organism. As we shall see, the basic reason for these reductionistic views is that we cannot know the existence of the self or mind by an immediate impression, since minds are not objects which can be apprehended (as their changing states can) by immediate impressions.

The same misconception lies behind the denial by many empiricists since Hume of *freedom* of the will or the identification of it with a "soft determinism." For when acts of the will are conceived as events like those which occur in objects, they are bound to be viewed as determined by antecedent events rather than as expressions of decisions made by the self which is a creative subject of activity. Ian Ramsey has pointed out that we know the self through the "disclosure" that it cannot be reduced to its publicly observable behavior, as in behaviorism, but is that "and more." [49] This seems to be a way of saying that we intuitively know the self as a subject of activity over and above the outward expression of itself. No theory of knowledge can claim to be genuinely empirical if it fails to acknowledge and take seriously such intuitions of the subjectivity and freedom of the self, as well as the objectivity of values such as beauty and goodness which it acknowledges.

Again, there has been a tendency in modern empiricism to deny the cognitive value of *feeling* in contrast with sense and reason. The assertion of A. J. Ayer that moral judgments are merely "emotive" and cannot be verified by sense experience leads him to the conclusion that they are "meaningless." [50] While we would reject the view that moral judgments are *only* expressions of feeling, we would maintain that feeling has an important function in morality. The intuition of values is accompanied by feeling; and sympathy makes men aware of their solidarity with each other and awakens concern for the needs of others. Above all, love is fundamental to the highest morality not only as a motive for right conduct but also as a source of insight. Although skeptics and cynics have delighted in pointing out that love is blind to faults and sees virtues in the loved one that others cannot see, it is able to appreciate worth and possibilities in the loved one which are not

[48] Hume, David: *A Treatise of Human Nature,* Oxford, Clarendon Press, 1949, Part IV, sec. VI.

[49] Ramsey, Ian: *Freedom and Immortality,* London, SCM Press, 1960, p. 26.

[50] Ayer, A. J.: *Language Truth and Logic,* New York, Dover Publications, 1946, Ch. VI.

visible to others who do not care enough to look beneath the surface.

As John Macquarrie has pointed out, ". . . every feeling includes a reference to a situation in the world (it is, in Brentano's expression, 'intentional'), and it arises in the interaction of the self and the world." [51] Moreover, in its intentionality it involves at least a vague understanding of the nature of the situation to which it refers, e.g., fear contains an awareness of the menacing character of something.[52] Heidegger uses the term "state" or "condition" to express the "way one finds oneself" in a situation.[53] Such a state of feeling or "mood" discloses something about the situation which is different from anything perceived through the senses, i.e., the pattern or structure of the situation and the relation of the individual to it.[54] Thus, it reveals aspects of man's existence and relation to the world which are not accessible to reason or sense perception.

Heidegger's phenomenological analysis of anxiety, *Angst*, illustrates the cognitive value of affective states or moods, for anxiety reveals the situation of man as "being-in-the-world." It discloses the "facticity" of man's existence as possibility "thrown" into a world which is alien to him. Unlike fear, anxiety has no definite object. That which is disclosed by it is man's possibility limited and threatened by the facticity of his contingent existence, his imprisonment within the alien being of the world. Above all, man's existence is faced by the possibility of death; his existence is "being-unto-death." This possibility is certain to become an actuality for each of us, although we cannot know when. Thus, anxiety discloses the crucial fact that man's possibilities are limited by his facticity and ended by his death.

Obviously, the understanding of man's existence in the world which is provided by feeling is fallible. Some moods are misleading or at best partial in what they disclose, e.g., the understanding of man's existence derived by Sartre from the feeling of disgust. For this reason, it is necessary to have a criterion for use in judging the truth of assertions based on feelings or moods. But the criterion which is used to test the truth of scientific propositions, an appeal to sense perception, is obviously unsuitable for this purpose. Ultimately, the appeal must be to the results of thorough phenomenological analysis and description. The phenomenologist seeks to understand a phenomenon such as anxiety or hope by freeing it from all interpretations and preconceived views. This "phenomenological reduction" makes it possible for him to attend

---

[51] Macquarrie, John: *Studies in Christian Existentialism*, London, SCM Press, 1966, p. 33.

[52] *Ibid.*, p. 34.

[53] *Ibid.*, p. 35.

[54] *Ibid.*, pp. 35, 36.

to it as it appears to his consciousness and to gain an intuition of its essence simply as it shows itself to him apart from metaphysical speculation. Of course, a phenomenological description of a feeling-state may itself be fallible. The test of its adequacy, however, is not whether it agrees with a scientific description, but whether the picture it gives of a phenomenon is convincing, whether it can be seen by anyone who will look attentively at the phenomenon, and whether it makes an aspect of reality understandable.[55]

We have argued that, if the empirical method is to be adequate for an evaluation of the truth claims of theism, it must take seriously not only sense impressions but also experiences of values such as beauty and goodness, intuitions of the self as a subject and free agent, and feelings or moods such as love and anxiety.

With respect to the claims of *religious* experience, it is necessary only to recall what was said in an earlier chapter.[56] Religious experience, no less than sense experience, is an encounter with reality and therefore has an objective side, so that it cannot be dismissed as merely subjective. Although knowledge of its object cannot be "read off" it immediately but must be interpreted and any interpretation of it is subject to the possibility of error, there is no reason for general skepticism about its cognitive value. However, since there is a diversity of interpretations of religious experience, the truth claims of theism which have arisen from the kinds of religious experience described in this chapter must be critically examined. We would only insist that the examination be approached with a mind which has not already prejudged the issue by previously accepting a view of experience which minimizes the significance of every kind of experience except that of the senses. It will then be seen, we think, that the basic insights arising from the religious experience of the prophets and other Biblical writers are confirmed in their essentials by the similar religious experience of many generations of Western theists, including our own, and are also confirmed in some respects by the religious experience of theists in the East. At the very least, this is important evidence for the reality of the God of theism and His relation to man, although it will still be necessary to inquire whether the major beliefs of theism are also supported by evidence derived from other aspects of experience and provide an adequate interpretation of experience as a whole. To such an inquiry we shall now turn.

[55] Tillich, Paul: *Systematic Theology*, Vol. I, p. 118.
[56] Ch. 3.

6

The Existence of God

Can God's Existence Be Proved?

There are several different views among contemporary philosophers with respect to the question, can God's existence be proved? The first, which is held chiefly by Thomists, is that the existence of God *can* be proved and can be proved with *certainty*. The second, which is maintained mainly by naturalists and positivists but also by religious existentialists, is that His existence *cannot* be demonstrated by human reason. The third, which is held by a number of British and American theists, denies that rational arguments can *demonstrate* His existence but affirms that one or more of them can be formulated in such a way as to *support* belief in His existence which has arisen from religious experience.

(1) The first view has been held by many outstanding philosophers from the classical period of Greek philosophy to contemporary Thomists. Nevertheless, there are several weighty reasons for rejecting it. First, if the test of the effectiveness (if not the validity) of an argument is its power to convince all or most men capable of understanding it, the traditional arguments have failed to meet the test. While one or more of them have been accepted by great philosophers such as Plato, Descartes, and Leibniz, none of them has ever succeeded in convincing all philosophers. Of course, this does not prove that they are not logically valid, because a valid argument may fail to convince those who approach the evidence with inattentive minds or strong prejudices. This should warn us against dismissing the traditional arguments without a fair hearing merely because many modern philosophers since Hume and Kant have not accepted them. The fact remains that they have not convinced many thinkers whose ability to understand them is beyond question. One of the main reasons for this is that the traditional arguments were developed by Greek and medieval philosophers

135

who had great confidence in the capacity of reason to demonstrate metaphysical propositions, whereas it has become very difficult for modern philosophers to share that confidence. As a result, even those who continue to believe in the value of the traditional arguments do not usually claim certainty for the conclusions reached by them.

Again, the nature of God as He is conceived by theists makes it philosophically rash and religiously presumptuous to claim that His existence can be demonstrated with certainty. If God is transcendent and other than everything finite, it is incredible that man's reason should be able to comprehend His nature or prove His existence beyond all doubt. For every proof must start with evidence derived from the experience of finite minds and be expressed in concepts derived from the same source. "He cannot be demonstrated," says Austin Farrer, "in the ordinary sense; for no principle can be found for a proof . . . He cannot be demonstrated *a posteriori* either, i.e., from effects, because we must first know that they are effects, and effects of a perfectly unique activity." [1] It is also religiously presumptuous to suppose that a demonstration of God's existence is possible, because there is a "numinous" aspect of God which is incomprehensible to reason. As Farrer says, "The matters we are dealing with are mysteries, and it is impious of the philosopher to suppose he can handle them with demonstration, as plainly as he might chalk and cheese." [2] A God who could be perfectly demonstrated or fully comprehended by reason would not be the God worshipped by men of faith.

(2) According to the second view, rational arguments are completely unconvincing and therefore useless. Some Neo-orthodox theologians have even agreed with Kierkegaard's denunciation of them as not merely useless but an indication of unbelief. They are useless because the reason of men cannot know anything about God save as He has revealed Himself to them; they are a manifestation of unbelief, because only those without faith would need a proof of God's existence. Neither of these charges can be substantiated. The first of them implies a profound distrust of man's capacities and would lead logically to the conclusion that men are unable even to understand the revelation of God to them. Moreover, it is a plain historical fact that men such as Plato who were without knowledge of the revelation in the Bible have claimed to know God's existence in other ways, e.g., from the order and beauty of nature. The "theological veto" on the philosophy of religion should, therefore, be set aside; it is presumptuous to limit the ways in which God can be known by man.

With respect to the charge that attempts to prove the existence of

[1] Farrer, A.: *Finite and Infinite*, Westminster, Dacre Press, 1943, p. 7.
[2] *Ibid.*, p. 4.

God are an evidence of unbelief, one need only recall that many philosophers who have developed arguments for His existence have been strong believers who were seeking to understand their faith or to convince others who did not share it. Of course, other believers have been interested in the arguments because they have had doubts. But doubt is not necessarily caused by sin, as some theologians think. When it is caused by intellectual difficulties such as those raised by naturalistic philosophy, the only honest way to deal with it is to examine all the evidence available to determine whether one's beliefs are reasonable. There are also some persons who are not believers but who are seeking for a faith which can command their assent as reasonable. To these, as well as to believers who are troubled by doubts, arguments for God's existence may be of assistance.

Philosophers who reject the arguments do so for different reasons. Some of them have been convinced by the criticisms of Hume, Kant, and other philosophers; others have embraced world views or theories of knowledge which rule out the possibility of knowing His existence. It is unlikely that even the most persuasive rational arguments will convince philosophers of the latter kind. They are not likely to listen to any attempt to argue for that which from their perspective it is impossible to believe. Only if they abandon their world view or theory of knowledge will rational arguments developed from another perspective have any effect upon them. However, rational arguments for God's existence may have some weight with philosophers who have hitherto accepted the criticisms of the traditional arguments as conclusive but who have not definitely committed themselves to a philosophical perspective which rules out the existence of God. For belief in God's existence does not stand or fall with arguments as they have been formulated in the past. Like other ultimate issues of philosophy, the question of God's existence is a perennial one. Since the evidence admits of different interpretations, the question may never be finally answered, but it is important—and inevitable—that it be raised anew in every generation and that new approaches to an answer be explored.

Of course, it is improbable that wholly new proofs will be discovered. Belief in the God of theism is about three thousand years old, and it has been critically examined by capable philosophers since the time of Plato. But although the major approaches have doubtless already been discovered, the way they have been explored in the past may have been inadequate. For even great philosophers such as Aquinas and Kant have expressed their insights in terms which may be no longer acceptable, and it may be possible to express these insights in a more convincing manner and to strengthen the arguments based upon them by new evidence derived from modern experience.

(3) The third view of the arguments seeks to do justice to the elements of truth in both of the other views but refuses either to accept the traditional arguments uncritically or to reject them completely. It is the view that, while these arguments are not demonstrations, they can be formulated and related to each other in such a way as to *support* belief in God's existence and form the basis of a theistic interpretation of the world which is more adequate than other world views.

This view is based upon the idea that the function of the arguments is to analyze and draw out the implications of certain aspects of experience which seem to point towards the existence of God and then to show that they offer the most reasonable explanation of the world and man. It presupposes an empirical conception of the method of philosophy but has been developed by thinkers who do not accept the narrow view of experience that has characterized many empiricists from Hume to the present. When questions such as the existence of God are approached from this point of view, it is necessary to set aside *a priori* reasoning such as that employed by the rationalists and to depend upon experience. However, the whole range of experience must be taken into account and evidence derived from different areas of experience must be taken seriously.

A recent representative of this view is Austin Farrer, who maintains that, while the existence of God cannot be "inferred," it can be "apprehended" and argument can help men to apprehend it. This is possible because our minds grasp His presence "in and through and with His effects." [3] Therefore, the philosophical theologian should seek to give an account of God as present and active in the world, with the hope that others will recognize it to be a description of what they also apprehend.[4] Farrer assumes that God's presence in the world does not go unnoticed, even by the unbeliever, so that "it is likely that those who habitually look at it have some crypto-theism in some parts of their interpretation of it, some sub-awareness of certain aspects of the divine activity." [5] The philosophical theologian starts by analyzing these elements of "crypto-theism" and attempts to "show how these can only be upheld in a full theistic position and how the denial of such a position removes them wholly." [6] This implies that God's presence in the world is already implicit in the experience of those whom the philosophical theologian seeks to persuade although they may have been only vaguely aware of it. His task is to make this implicit or latent theism in them explicit, to make men fully aware of it. He

---

[3] *Ibid.*, p. 8.
[4] *Ibid.*, pp. 9, 10.
[5] *Ibid.*, p. 10.
[6] *Ibid.*, p. 10.

should not attempt to produce "knock-down" proofs like a mathematician; he should simply try to persuade men that theism offers a more nearly adequate account of what they apprehend in their experience than other interpretations.

A somewhat similar view has been expressed by Ian Crombie. There are elements in experience, he points out, that do in fact lead people to belief in God. Among these are "a sense of contingency," "moral experience," "the beauty and order of nature," and "religious or mystical" experiences.[7] The theist does not suppose that there is any inductive or deductive argument that can lead from any of these experiences to the conclusion that God exists. "All that is necessary is that he should be honestly convinced that, in interpreting them, as he does, theistically, he is in some sense facing them more honestly, bringing out more of what they contain or involve than could be done by interpreting them in any other way." [8] These elements of experience are obviously among the sources of the "crypto-theism" or "sub-awareness" of God mentioned by Farrer, and the reader will doubtless have noticed that there is a traditional argument for the existence of God corresponding to each of them.

There are two reasons for thinking that this conception of the method of the philosophical theologian offers more hope for advance than the method usually followed in arguments for God's existence in the past. One is that, while it is empirical in its starting-point, it has a broader conception of experience than has been characteristic of British empiricists, e.g., Crombie includes a sense of contingency and religious experience among the elements of experience he lists. The other is that rational arguments have often—indeed, usually—failed to convince persons who have not enjoyed such experiences or have been prevented by prior acceptance of a secular attitude from recognizing that these experiences have religious significance. For rational argument cannot convince a person by merely leading him through a series of propositions to a conclusion in logical order; he must also understand and assent to each proposition, especially the premises, in the light of his own experience.

This is true not only of arguments concerning God but also of arguments in other fields. For example, a person cannot understand or be convinced by an ethical argument unless he has learned from experience to distinguish good from evil or a political argument for democracy unless he has had some experience of the benefits of freedom. Philosophical thinking is not carried out by pure reason ab-

[7] Flew, A. & MacIntyre, A.: *New Essays in Philosophical Theology*, New York, Macmillan, 1955, pp. 111, 112.

[8] *Ibid.*, p. 112.

stracted from the rest of the self and unaffected by its total experience. Hence, rational arguments for God's existence will be convincing only to those who have enjoyed experiences that seem to point beyond themselves to something transcendent, something whose presence is felt but not seen and which awakens a sense of awe. For example, a person who has had no vivid experience of the contingency of human existence is not very likely to be impressed by the cosmological argument; and one who has not shared Kant's feeling of awe at the sight of the starry heavens above and the moral law within is hardly going to be convinced by the teleological and the moral arguments. One of the aims of the philosophical theologian, therefore, must be to raise to the level of clear awareness experiences such as these which lie behind the arguments.

John Smith has spoken of an "antinomy" between rational demonstration and religious faith. Demonstration is not regarded as rigorous unless the movement of thought proceeds independently of the thinker's own experience and concern to a conclusion that is universal and necessary, whereas religious faith requires the involvement of the thinker through his experience, an openness towards God and a turning toward Him.[9] Thus, rationality demands that the reality of God be shown to be objectively necessary, while faith demands personal participation through experience of Him.[10] The solution of this antinomy is to be found in a distinction between "formal" reason, which is governed by the logical necessity of pure thought, and "living" or concrete reason, which "starts from certain direct experiences and moves toward the discovery of rational pattern and meaning within these experiences." [11] Philosophical rationalists have always supposed that it is "formal" reason which provides the model of reason. But Smith points out that it is "living" reason which is required in the concrete thinking of art, morality, politics, and religion, since the whole self and its experience are involved.[12] "It is only when the self begins with its own experience, lives in and through it while seeking to trace out the rational pattern implicit in that experience, that the conclusions of thought at once persuade and engage the entire self." [13]

The implications of this view of "living" or concrete reason for the arguments for God's existence are radical. Men must consider whether the belief in God which has arisen from religious experiences is supported by other forms of experience and renders reality as a whole

[9] Smith, J. op. cit., pp. 109, 110.
[10] Ibid., p. 110.
[11] Ibid., p. 111.
[12] Ibid., pp. 112, 113.
[13] Ibid., p. 114.

more intelligible. But, the pretension that reason can "demonstrate" or "prove" the existence of God must be abandoned; the function of reason is to show that belief in Him is reasonable because it provides the most adequate interpretation of experience.

The Ontological Argument

(1) The ontological argument is often called the *a priori* argument because it is the only one of the traditional arguments which does not appeal to experience. As formulated by Anselm, it deduces the existence of God in reality from the idea of a supremely great being in the understanding. Anselm had developed several arguments in the *Monologium* to prove the existence of God, the "supremely good, and supremely great, and the highest of all existing beings," as the source of all good things, all great things, and all existent things which men experience.[14] He then inquired in the *Proslogium* whether there was one argument which by itself alone would be sufficient. In Chapter II he presented the argument which resulted from his inquiry, and it is this which has usually been regarded as *the* ontological argument of Anselm.

It begins with the statement, addressed to God, "We believe that thou art a being than which nothing greater can be conceived," *aliquid quo nihil maius cogitari possit*. The question is then raised whether there is no such nature, since we are told in Psalm XIV.1 that "the fool hath said in his heart, there is no God." But even the fool, says Anselm, when he hears of "a being than which nothing greater can be conceived," understands what he hears and it is in his understanding, *in intellectu*, although he does not understand that it exists. Now, that than which nothing greater can be conceived cannot exist in the understanding alone, for "it can be conceived to exist in reality, which is greater." "Therefore, if that than which nothing greater can be conceived exists in the understanding alone, the very being than which nothing greater can be conceived is one than which a greater can be conceived. But obviously this is impossible. Hence, there is no doubt that there exists a being than which nothing greater can be conceived, and it exists both in the understanding and in reality, *in re*." [15]

A monk, Gaunilo, wrote *A Book in Behalf of the Fool* which raised a number of criticisms of this *a priori* argument. The most famous of these is that, if Anselm's reasoning from the *idea* of a supremely great being to His *existence* were to be accepted, one could claim by similar

[14] Anselm: *Monologium*, chs. I–III, in *St. Anselm*, La Salle, Ill., Open Court Publishing Co., 1962, pp. 37–43.
[15] *Proslogium, ibid.*, ch. II, pp. 7, 8.

reasoning that there exists a "lost island" more perfect than the Islands
of the Blessed, since there exists an idea of such an island in the mind
and it is more excellent to exist in reality also than to exist in the
mind alone.[16] To this objection Anselm replies concisely but effectively:
"Now I promise confidently that if any man shall devise anything
existing either in reality or in concept alone (except that than which a
greater cannot be conceived) to which he can adapt the sequence of my
reasoning, I will discover that thing, and will give him his lost island,
not to be lost again." [17] The point of this reply, of course, is that even
the most ideal island is only a contingent thing which derives its existence from beyond itself. It is only God, the supremely great being,
who does not derive His existence from something beyond Himself, so
that the logic of the argument applies to Him but to no other being.

In the seventeenth century Descartes restated the ontological argument in such a way as to make clear an assumption which lies behind
it. Defining God as "a supremely perfect being," Descartes asserts that
"existence can no more be separated from the essence [or definition]
of God than can its having three angles equal to two right angles be
separated from the essence of a [rectilinear] triangle, or the idea of a
mountain from the idea of a valley." From this he infers that it is as
"repugnant" to conceive a supremely perfect being who is lacking in
existence as to conceive a mountain which has no valley.[18] In this
restatement Descartes clearly treats existence as an attribute or perfection without which a "supremely perfect being" would be less than
perfect. Since it is necessary to attribute to God every perfection, he
says, "this necessity suffices to make me conclude (after having recognized that existence is a perfection) that this first and sovereign Being
really exists." [19] However, Pierre Gassendi, a contemporary of Descartes, questioned the assumption that existence is an attribute or perfection. "Existence," he asserted, "is a perfection neither in God nor in
anything else; it is rather that in the absence of which there is no
perfection." [20]

Kant did not direct his criticisms against the argument of Anselm
but against that of Descartes. According to that argument, God, the
ens realissimum, possesses all reality, and since all reality includes
existence the denial of His existence is self-contradictory. Of course, if
I presuppose existence in the idea of a being, says Kant, I can infer

[16] Ibid., In Behalf of the Fool, 6, pp. 151, 152.
[17] Ibid., "Anselm's Apologetic," ch. III, p. 158.
[18] Descartes, R.: Meditations, V, in Haldane and Ross, The Philosophical Works
of Descartes, Cambridge, The University Press, 1911, Vol. I, p. 181.
[19] Ibid., p. 182.
[20] Quoted in Hick, John, and McGill, A.: The Many-Faced Argument, New York,
Macmillan, 1967, p. 211.

from the idea that the being exists, but this is only a tautology. For I can conclude that the being exists from the concept of it only because I have previously put existence into the concept and have thus begged the question.[21] "God exists" is not an analytic judgment in which the predicate is contained in the subject. All existential judgments are synthetic, i.e., the predicate adds something to or amplifies the subject. Hence, the proposition "God exists" is synthetic and can be denied without contradiction.[22] Existence is not a "real predicate" which belongs to the concept of a thing as one of its elements. "It is merely the positing of a thing, or of certain determinations, as existing in themselves." Thus, if we say "God is," "we attach no new predicate to the concept of God, but only posit the subject in itself with all its predicates." [23] Hence, the existence of God is not included in His essence and can be denied without contradiction. In reality, the existence of any object cannot be known *a priori* from its concept but only *a posteriori,* from experience of it.

(2) We must conclude, with Kant, that the ontological argument is not valid as a logical proof.[24] But is this the only way it can be regarded? The prayers at the beginning and the end of the passage in the *Proslogium* make it clear that Anselm was an Augustinian who started from belief in God. Now, if the ontological argument in the *Proslogium* is viewed "from the inside" of belief in this way, it may be interpreted as an attempt to explicate an *intuitive awareness* of the reality of God as "the supremely good and great being" whose existence Anselm had attempted to demonstrate in the *Monologium*. It affirms that the idea of that Being is not a mere construct of the mind but is imposed upon it from beyond itself, so that God's existence in reality, *in re,* as well as in the understanding, *in intellectu,* cannot be doubted. Arthur McGill describes this view, as represented by some recent interpreters of Anselm, in an interesting passage. "Anselm's argument is grounded on an 'idea' in the realistic sense, on an idea that for one reason or another is taken as an apprehension of the real. . . . At the beginning

[21] Kant, Immanuel: *The Critique of Pure Reason,* New York, Humanities Press, 1950, B. 626.

[22] *Ibid.,* B. 625.

[23] *Ibid.,* B. 627.

[24] Norman Malcolm and Charles Hartshorne have argued that in chapter III of the *Proslogium* Anselm states the ontological argument in a different form and have contended that, while the argument is not valid in the first, it is valid in the second, form. The difference between the two forms is that the first seeks to prove that God has the attribute of *existence,* the second that He has the attribute of *necessary existence.* In the opinion of the present author, the second form is no more convincing than the first. Essays by Malcolm and Hartshorne on the second form of the argument (together with a refutation of them by Hick) are reprinted in Hick, John, and McGill, Arthur, *op. cit.,* pp. 301–356.

of the argument, then, Anselm is not looking at or thinking about some mental notion and wondering whether this is a true notion which represents a true object. *Through* this idea he is looking at and thinking about reality, specifically about the unique perfection of God's nature. There is an *aliquid,* a real something which stands over against his mind and which he initially knows in one of its aspects, namely, as that which is too 'great' for his conceiving to surpass. . . . Throughout the syllogism the mind is probing a real something at first aware only of its unsurpassability, but then, through this syllogism, becoming cognizant of its real existence." [25] Thus, the logical reasoning only makes fully explicit an awareness of the reality of God which was present from the outset, and the power of the argument depends not so much on the validity of its logic as on the initial awareness which it makes explicit.[26] In contrast to most modern scientists and philosophers who have been suspicious of ideas until reason has found evidence beyond their presence in the mind that they are true, Anselm's theory of knowledge is realistic. He did not regard the idea of God as an idea which had been constructed *by* the mind but was convinced that it originated from the presence of God as an objective reality *to* the mind. Of course, the fact that Anselm developed the ontological argument in logical form indicates that he intended it to be *more* than an affirmation of an intuitive awareness of God's existence. In his time argument was expected to take the form of demonstration of a truth in a series of steps. However, it may be possible in our time, when the rationalistic method of demonstration is no longer necessary in metaphysical thinking, to separate the kernel of the argument from its logical shell. If so, the steps in the reasoning may be viewed as only a way of making explicit the certainty of a Christian theist who had an intuitive awareness of God as an objective reality.

(3) For this reason Tillich is right in asserting that the ontological *argument* is a "failure" as a proof of the existence of God but that the ontological *approach* embodied in it is indispensable for philosophical theology.[27] For it states the conception of God in Western theism as "the supremely good and great being" and makes it clear that this involves the necessity of His being as contrasted with the contingency of all finite beings. This specifies the *nature* of the God whose existence all the arguments attempt to prove and thus provides the proper *starting-point* for them. For all the arguments are concerned with one who is nothing less than a Perfect Being, a being "than which nothing greater can be conceived."

[25] *Ibid.,* pp. 71, 72.
[26] *Ibid.,* p. 74.
[27] Tillich, Paul: *Systematic Theology,* Vol. I, pp. 204–208.

The Cosmological Argument

(1) The cosmological argument was first developed by Plato and Aristotle. However, it was the formulation of it by St. Thomas Aquinas which has had the greatest influence. Of his five "ways" to prove God's existence by reason, the first three are clearly versions of the cosmological argument. They infer from the motions or changes we observe in the world to an Unmoved Mover, from efficient causes to a First Cause, and from contingent beings to a Necessary Being.

It is generally agreed that it is the third of these which is most fundamental, because it seeks to account not merely for certain characteristics of finite beings but for their very existence. We observe things in nature, says Aquinas, which come into being and pass away, so that it is possible for them to be and to not-be and impossible for them always to exist. Now, if we assume that everything is contingent or can not-be, at some time there was nothing in existence. If this were true nothing would exist now, because at that time there would have existed nothing which could have brought things into existence. But since things do exist now, this is absurd. Hence, the assumption that everything is contingent is false, and there must be a being the existence of which is necessary and which brought into existence the things that now exist. If the necessity of this being were caused by another being and the necessity of that being by yet another being, we would be involved in an infinite regress of necessary beings. Therefore, we must admit the existence of a Necessary Being which does not derive its necessity from another being but is necessary of itself, and this Necessary Being men call God.[28]

Critics have often pointed out that, while the contingent beings *we observe* now have not always existed, this does not imply that at some time in the past no contingent beings *at all* existed. Therefore, they argue that we do not have to posit a Necessary Being to account for such beings, since other contingent beings preceded them and brought them into existence. But Aquinas' argument does not necessarily depend upon there having been no contingent being at some time in the past. Even if contingent beings have been coming into being and passing away from eternity, he could argue that their existence has depended upon a Necessary Being. For all contingent beings, he could say, must receive their existence ultimately from a Being which has the power to bestow existence upon them because it has its existence from itself. In other words, the main point of the argument is not that a Necessary Being must be posited to account for the *beginning* in time

[28] Aquinas, Thomas: *Summa Theologica*, Pt. I, Q. 2, a. 3.

of the contingent beings we observe, but that, whether there was a beginning of them or not, contingent beings cannot owe their existence to other beings as contingent as themselves but must derive it from a Being that exists of itself.

If so, Kant's criticism that the argument assumes the impossibility of an infinite series of causes in the sensible world and that this assumption is not justified is wide of the mark. As modern Thomists have pointed out, Aquinas does not deny the logical possibility of an infinite regress of causes, since reason cannot demonstrate that the world had a beginning in time, i.e., was created. But even if there was never a time when no contingent beings existed, a Necessary Being is required to account for their existence. As Richard Taylor has said, we do not answer the question *why* a thing exists by stating *how long* it has existed, or even by stating that it has *always* existed.[29] Therefore, even if the world had no beginning, "it can be asked why there is a world, why indeed there is a beginningless world, why there should have perhaps always been something rather than nothing." [30] A similar answer may be given to the objection of Hume that, if God is asserted to be the First Cause of the world, we must ask, "What was the cause of God?" For this objection, like that of Kant, seems to assume that the cosmological argument infers God's existence as the "first" cause in a temporal series of causes and effects, in which case it is possible to ask for a cause of God Himself. But in fact the cosmological argument infers God's existence as the "first" in the *logical* sense, i.e., as the ultimate cause, the primary rather than a secondary cause. He is not "first" in the sense of first in time but in the sense that He is the being upon which all other things ultimately depend for their existence.

The basic *presupposition* of the argument is that there is an explanation for the existence of everything whatever, a reason why it should exist rather than not exist. This is the "principle of sufficient reason," and although it cannot be proved it is presupposed in all thinking about reality. Now, the world exists, but it is not necessary that it should have existed since its nonexistence would involve no contradiction. It follows from the principle of sufficient reason that there must be a reason for its existence. Furthermore, it is improbable that the reason can be found in itself, i.e., that it can exist by its very nature. For anything which exists by its very nature must be eternal, whereas everything in the world seems to come into being and pass away. It is logically possible that the world itself might be imperishable despite the fact that it contains only things which are contingent. But this is not plausible, since nothing about it suggests that it exists by its

[29]Taylor, Richard: *Metaphysics*, Englewood Cliffs, N.J., Prentice-Hall, 1965, p. 88.
[30] *Ibid.*, p. 89.

own nature and we can imagine without any difficulty that it might never have existed. We must conclude that the world is contingent and depends upon something other than itself for its existence. And if that upon which it depends, depends upon something else, which itself depends upon another thing, and so on *ad infinitum,* it does not provide a sufficient reason for the existence of the world of contingent things. Ultimately, therefore, the world or totality of contingent things must depend upon a necessary being which exists by its own nature.[31]

(2) The most fundamental criticism of the argument by Kant is that it employs the causal principle in an illegitimate way. It assumes that the category of causality can be applied to a transcendent cause which is beyond the world of phenomena, whereas Kant has argued in his *Critique of Pure Reason* that categories and principles of the understanding have meaning and application only to objects of experience in space and time. A somewhat similar criticism has been expressed recently by Ronald Hepburn, who asserts that the cosmological argument removes "cause words" from their "natural habitat," the "observed concomitance of events." "We are instead," he says, "*uprooting* the vocabulary of cause and effect from its habitat in the language, in order to relate the known to the unknown and unknowable." [32] What answer, if any, can be given to this criticism?

It is well known that Kant's twelve "categories of understanding," of which "cause and effect" is one, were those required to make possible the description of phenomena in Newtonian science by synthesizing impressions presented to the mind by "sensibility." Since Kant believed that we have no faculty of "intellectual intuition" which can present "things-in-themselves" to the mind, he denied that the categories can be applied to any supersensible object such as the soul or God. It was on this ground that he regarded any extension of the causal principle to objects beyond experience as unjustified. However, we have argued elsewhere[33] that this restriction of the categories to phenomena is arbitrary. It was made necessary by Kant's acceptance of Hume's view that we are dependent for all our knowledge upon sense impressions. Yet it is clear that we have experience not only of objects of the senses but also of the soul or mind, although we have no "sensuous intuition" or sense impression of it. We also have experiences of God, if religious experience must, as we have argued, be taken seriously.[34] If so, there is nothing to prevent us from using categories such as causality in seeking to understand supersensible realities such as the soul and God.

[31] In this summary of the cosmological argument, we are indebted to the clear statement of it by Richard Taylor, *op. cit.,* pp. 85–93.

[32] Hepburn, *op. cit.,* p. 160.

[33] Thomas, G. F.: *Religious Philosophies of the West,* ch. 9.

[34] Ch. 3.

Does this involve "uprooting" the category of causality from its "natural habitat," as Hepburn asserts? Only if it is assumed that its "natural habitat" is science, where it is used to describe constant sequences or correlations of events and thus to make prediction of future events possible. But throughout the classical period of Greek philosophy, in medieval philosophy, and in modern philosophy which has not been wholly dependent upon scientific methods of thinking, the category of causality has *not* been used merely to describe the "observed concomitance of events." Rather, causes have been regarded as having a necessary connection with their effects, as producing and not merely preceding the latter. Nor is the Humian view of causation which seems to be assumed by Hepburn the commonsense view of it. "It is a highly sophisticated doctrine," as A. C. Ewing says, "which eviscerates causation by eliminating most of the content we have in mind when we use the term in daily life. We do not think of the cause as only followed regularly by the effect, we think of it as in some way necessitating and so explaining the effect." [35] Of course, when the category of causality is used to explain the existence of the contingent world by reference to a transcendent Necessary Being, it is used in an analogical sense. We cannot pretend to have a clear and distinct idea of the mode of the causal activity of the Necessary Being upon which contingent beings depend for their existence. But, as we shall see in the next chapter, this is true of all language applied by the theist to interpret the attributes and activities of God.

(3) Another criticism of the cosmological argument which has been made by Hepburn is that the world is not the sort of thing that can have a cause. "Whereas cause-words have their use in our language in the relating of limited thing to limited thing, the Cosmological Argument puts them to the work of relating an *infinite being* to the *totality of things*. It is from just such redirections of linguistic labour that breakdowns in meaning constantly occur." [36] "Universe," he says, is not a "thing-word." [37] Wallace Matson makes a similar criticism. Referring to a passage in Hume's *Dialogues,* he asserts that the "fallacy of composition" is involved in asking for a cause of the whole universe. "This error consists in arguing that since every member of a collection has a certain property, therefore the collection itself (as a whole) must also have that property." [38] On Hume's view, parts are united in a whole by an arbitrary act of the mind which "has no influence on the

[35] Ewing, A. C.: "Two Proofs of God's Existence" in *Religious Studies,* Cambridge University Press, Oct. 1965, Vol. I, p. 30.

[36] Hepburn, *op. cit.,* p. 161.

[37] *Ibid.,* p. 169.

[38] Matson, Wallace: *The Existence of God,* Ithaca, N.Y., Cornell University Press, 1965, p. 78.

nature of things," and the cause of a whole "is sufficiently explained in explaining the cause of the parts." [39]

The answer one gives to this criticism depends upon whether one takes the principle of sufficient reason to be universally applicable. As Taylor says, "it would certainly be odd to maintain that everything in the world owes its existence to something . . . and then to deny this of the world itself." [40] Of course, it is true that the whole universe need not possess every property of its parts, e.g., the spatial property of being "above" or "below" something else, but there is no good reason to think that it does not possess the property of contingency which is possessed by all the parts that compose it. Moreover, Hume's assertion that the whole needs no explanation beyond the explanation of its parts because the unity of the whole is arbitrarily imposed on the parts by the mind is false. For the universe is more than a mere aggregate of separate and distinct parts; it is a system of interdependent parts possessing a unitary pattern, and this system is as contingent as the parts that compose it.

The presupposition behind both of the criticisms we have been considering is a naturalistic conception of explanation. As Matson states this conception, explanation consists of the discernment of causal laws or patterns in nature connecting events with other events in time. These causal laws are explained by more general laws, the ultimate goal being the discovery of a most general law which will have to remain unexplained.[41] "To put it in a slightly different way, the universe is the framework within which causal explanations operate. And although these explanations show the linkage of one part of the universe to another, it is quite beyond their scope to link the universe to anything else." [42] This is equivalent to an assertion that, while we can give a causal explanation for events in the world, we can give no explanation for the world as a whole but must simply accept the fact that it happens to be rather than not to be. It assumes that the scientific description of causal patterns within the world is the only kind of explanation possible and that no sufficient reason for the world can be given. Thus, it denies the intelligibility of the world as a whole. We shall raise the question later whether another conception of explanation is possible, one which differs from the scientific description of natural events by efficient causes.

(3) Another criticism of the cosmological argument must be men-

[39] Hume, *Dialogues concerning Natural Religion*, ed. by N. K. Smith, New York, Social Science Publishers, 1948, Part IX.

[40] Taylor, *op. cit.*, p. 87.

[41] Matson, *op. cit.*, pp. 79–82.

[42] *Ibid.*, p. 83.

tioned briefly. Paul Tillich has charged that it proves at most the existence of God as a part of the world and thereby reduces Him to the level of the world itself.[43] This criticism is also made by Hepburn. "The God," he says, "at whom we would have arrived by tracing back the causal regress would be a God far too closely tied to his creation to satisfy Christian demands for his 'otherness' or transcendence. Whatever inaugurated the causal sequence would be part and parcel of the natural world in which it is causally operative." [44] Now, this would be the case if God were regarded as "first" cause of the series of contingent beings in a temporal sense, but not if He is regarded as "first" in the logical sense of the "ultimate" cause upon whom the world depends and hence is viewed as transcendent to it. Hepburn considers this possibility but thinks that it does not escape the difficulty. "Why not imagine a being entirely outside the universe, infusing energy into the universe, without becoming in any way part of it? Why is this absurd? It is absurd because in imagining this, we inevitably picture the world as a limited system with a boundary beyond which dwells the God who is the world's cause. But this would really be no different from thinking of a *part* of the world and of a being who dwells in *another* part but is in contact with the first." [45] Hepburn concludes that the cosmological argument leads to God as "the one who completes the world's pattern," "the missing piece of the cosmic jig-saw." [46]

This is, to say the least, a caricature of the theistic view of the relation of God to the world. Hepburn seems to be the victim of a crudely literalistic interpretation of spatial metaphors which are sometimes used to describe God's transcendence. No responsible theistic philosopher or theologian conceives of God as "entirely outside the universe," or as dwelling beyond the "boundary" of the world, or as dwelling in one "part" of the world, for He is regarded as immanent as well as transcendent and He is "outside" nothing in the world. But precisely because He is conceived as distinct from the world, He cannot be in any sense a "part" of it acting upon "another" part; rather, He is the transcendent Being upon whom it depends in all its parts. For the same reason, He is not conceived by theists as only "the one who completes the world's pattern." Rather, He is the *cause* of the world's pattern as a whole, not a *part* of it which merely completes it.

(4) Finally, we must consider Kant's criticism that, even if the cosmological argument succeeds in proving the existence of a Necessary

[43] Tillich, Paul: *Systematic Theology*, Chicago, University of Chicago Press, 1951, Vol. I, p. 205.

[44] Hepburn, *op. cit.*, p. 166.

[45] *Ibid.*, pp. 166, 167.

[46] *Ibid.*, p. 167.

Being, it cannot prove that this is the Perfect Being worshipped by religious people unless it falls back upon the ontological argument. Since Kant rejects the ontological argument, this means that the cosmological argument fails to prove the existence of the God of theism.

This criticism is not valid, since the cosmological argument does not claim to prove *more than* a Necessary Being and does not at any point appeal to the ontological argument in reaching its conclusion that the world of contingent beings depends for its existence upon a Necessary Being. However, Kant is right in thinking that it cannot by itself prove that the Necessary Being is identical with the Perfect Being of theism. Does this imply that it has no value as an argument for the existence of God? Not at all. For if it establishes the belief that the contingent world owes its existence to a Necessary Being, this provides the basis for a further inquiry into the nature of this Being. In other words, while it does not by itself prove the existence of the God of theism, it may provide an important first step in a cumulative argument for His existence. For the God who is worshipped by theists is *first of all* a Necessary Being upon which all contingent beings depend for their existence, although He is also *much more*.

(5) We have presented the cosmological argument from the contingency of the world as it was formulated by Aquinas and as it has been reformulated by modern philosophers. We have also shown that the criticisms of Kant and contemporary philosophers such as Hepburn and Matson are not convincing unless one accepts Kant's arbitrary restriction of the causal principle to phenomena or the empirical and naturalistic view of explanation presupposed by Hepburn and Matson. The final objection of Kant to the argument, i.e., that it does not prove the Perfect Being of religion, we have admitted to be true, but we have argued that this limits rather than destroys its value.

However, the cosmological argument is not a "demonstration" of God's existence, as theologians such as Aquinas and philosophers such as Leibniz believed it to be. However improbable it is that the contingent world does not depend for its existence upon a Necessary Being but exists of itself, the possibility that this is the case cannot be denied. Moreover, we have seen that philosophers who are deeply influenced by the scientific method do not admit the basic presuppositions that the principle of sufficient reason applies to the world as a whole as well as to its parts and that the causal principle can legitimately be used to explain the world by reference to a transcendent Being.

But the failure of the argument to convince many modern thinkers is probably due not so much to philosophical considerations as to the psychological attitude of most men of our scientific, technological, and this-worldly age. Whereas scientific interest in the description of causal relations within the world is very strong, metaphysical concern for an explanation of the world by an ultimate cause is very weak. The preoccupation with technological knowledge for the sake of power leads men to be absorbed in problems they can solve and indifferent to mysteries that resist solution. The prevailing this-worldliness of our time focuses men's attention almost exclusively on mundane things and values and makes them impatient with philosophical reasoning about the Transcendent. As a result, their tendency is to avoid ultimate questions which cannot be answered by science and technology and to distrust metaphysical speculation which attempts to answer them. For reasons such as these, the cosmological argument for a Necessary Being is bound to seem abstract and unreal to them.

Yet we have pointed out that many contemporary men are deeply aware of the contingency of the world and of their own lives.[47] They have been made sensitive to it both by the general insecurity of life in our century and by the expression of that insecurity in art and literature. Recent existentialists have offered penetrating phenomenological analyses of the contingency of human existence, e.g., Heidegger's description of the "facticity" which limits man's possibilities and the movement of his life towards death and Tillich's description of existence as marked by anxiety before the threat of non-being. To many men in our Age of Anxiety, therefore, the cosmological argument may be more persuasive than it was in the more stable and secure period which ended with the first World War. For it generalizes their experience of their own contingent existence and provides them with an ultimate explanation of the contingent world as a whole. As we have said, it does not prove the existence of the God of theism, but it can be an important first step in an argument that can support belief in Him.

The Teleological Argument

In the preceding section we pointed out that the cosmological argument is unable to show that the Necessary Being which is the ultimate cause of the world is also the Perfect Being men worship as God. Indeed, it seems to show only that the world depends for its existence upon an indeterminate first cause. In order to determine the nature of the Necessary Being it is necessary to go beyond the cosmological to the teleological and moral arguments, since these arguments are based not upon the mere existence of the world but upon specific characteristics of it.

Ninian Smart has suggested that by an "imaginative leap" we can

47 Ch. 5.

conceive of a creative activity of will analogous to that of a free human
will but unlimited by the spatio-temporal setting and natural conditions under which our wills must act.[48] This may well have been the
first step in the development of the teleological argument, since men
must have had the idea of such a creative activity of will before it could
occur to them to explain the order of nature as the product of an
intelligent Will active in realizing purposes. The value of the teleological argument is that it seems to offer evidence from nature that
there *is* such a creative will corresponding to the idea.

(1) The argument has taken two different forms. The first infers the
existence of a divine Mind from particular instances or kinds of
natural beings which seem to attain ends without being conscious of
doing so. Aquinas has stated this form of the argument concisely and
we cannot do better than to quote him. "We see that things which
lack knowledge, such as natural bodies, act for an end, and this is
evident from their acting always, or nearly always, in the same way, so
as to obtain the best result. Hence it is plain that they achieve their
end, not fortuitously, but designedly." [49] Up to this point Aquinas is
simply following Aristotle's argument in his *Physics* for final causes
immanent in nature.[50] But he departs from Aristotle in the latter part
of the argument, explaining the operation of final causes as due to a
transcendent divine intelligence. "Now whatever lacks knowledge cannot move towards an end, unless it be directed by some being endowed
with knowledge and intelligence, as the arrow is directed by the archer.
Therefore some intelligent being exists by whom all natural things
are directed to their end; and this being we call God." [51]

Although Aquinas like Aristotle believed that final causes or ends
are operative at all levels of nature, even in inanimate bodies, philosophers of the eighteenth century were impressed especially by the
apparent purposiveness of *living organisms* in their adaptation of
means to ends. Consequently, some of them based the teleological
argument especially on the distinctive nature of organisms. They emphasized the fact that in even the simplest organism the parts are not
merely juxtaposed in an external and mechanical fashion but are
organized in such a way that they serve each other and the whole as
they perform their functions. They argued that the organization of a
complex organism such as the human body, or even of a single organ
such as the eye, is so intricate that nothing less than a divine Mind,
analogous but vastly superior to the human mind, could have com-

---

[48] Smart, N.: *Philosophers and Religious Truth*, London, SCM Press, 1964.
[49] Aquinas: *Summa Theologica*: Q2, a. 3, "the fifth way."
[50] Aristotle: *Physics*, Book II, chs. VIII, IX.
[51] Aquinas, *op. cit.*

bined its many parts into a whole and related them to each other in such a way that each is both a means and an end to the others. In Hume's *Dialogues concerning Natural Religion,* even Philo the skeptic, who has made sharp criticisms of the argument throughout, describes the elaborate organization of the many different parts of the human body and confesses that they cannot but strike anyone who considers it as indications of design.[52]

For most philosophers, however, this form of the argument has been weakened by the Darwinian theory of evolution which offers an explanation of the origin of organisms quite different from that of a divine Mind. According to Darwin, species of living organisms have evolved through a process of natural selection by the environment. Those organisms in which variations have occurred helping them to adapt themselves to their environment have survived in the struggle for existence and have passed on the variations that favored them to their offspring. In this way new species have come into existence without the intervention of mind and purpose, since the favorable variations have occurred by chance and the selection of organisms for survival has been done blindly by the environment. Because of the general acceptance of this theory of the origin of species, the argument from evidences of design in biological organisms is not as persuasive to many as it was before Darwin. Indeed, some theists make no use whatever of it.[53]

(2) The second form of the teleological argument is based upon the order of nature *as a whole* rather than the evidence of design in a *particular class* of things such as organisms. As Aquinas expressed it, we observe things with different and contrary natures coming together under one order of nature "always or for the most part." There must therefore be some being by whose Providence the world is governed.[54] This form of the argument also had a profound influence upon the "natural religion" of the eighteenth century and was eloquently expressed by Cleanthes the theist in Hume's *Dialogues.* "Look round the world: Contemplate the whole and every part of it: You will find it to be nothing but one great machine, subdivided into an infinite number of lesser machines, which again admit of subdivisions, to a degree beyond what human senses and faculties can trace and explain. All these various machines, and even their most minute parts, are adjusted to each other with an accuracy, which ravishes into admiration all men, who have ever contemplated them. The curious adapting of means to ends, throughout all nature, resembles exactly, though it

[52] Hume, *op. cit.,* Part XII.
[53] E.g., Smart, *op. cit.,* pp. 110, 111.
[54] Aquinas, Thomas: *Summa contra Gentiles,* Ch. 13, ¶35.

much exceeds, the productions of human contrivance; of human design, thought, wisdom, and intelligence. Since therefore the effects resemble each other, we are led to infer, by all the rules of analogy, that the causes also resemble; and that the author of nature is somewhat similar to the mind of man; though possessed of much larger faculties, proportioned to the grandeur of the work which he has executed." [55] The reference to the "lesser machines" into which the "one great machine" is subdivided and to the adjustment of their "most minute parts" to each other indicates that Hume meant to consider not only the general order of nature but also particular kinds of order such as that of organisms as evidences of design.

His criticisms of the argument are well known. The argument, says Philo the skeptic, rests upon an analogy between the order of nature and a machine or other human artifact. But the analogy is weak. The world, like a machine, is made up of a number of parts interacting with each other, but there are also many differences and it is at least as much like a vegetable or animal as a machine. Moreover, mind is only one of the sources of order we observe in nature, for there are also vegetable growth, animal generation, and instinct. Why may we not conceive the cause of natural order by analogy with one of these? Since mind is confined to one species on one planet, why should we single it out rather than some other part of nature as the key to an understanding of the order of the whole? The fact is that every hypothesis about the origin of natural order is arbitrary. It is only the constant conjunction of one species of events with another which leads us to speak of one as cause of the other, whereas the world is unique and we have observed no constant conjunction between divine minds and the coming into existence of worlds like our own. Moreover, even if it is conceded that the argument proves a "remote analogy" between the cause of natural order and a human mind, it cannot prove that the cause is infinite, perfect, or even morally good.[56] For there is no logical warrant for ascribing to the hypothetical cause of natural order any qualities beyond those which are necessary to account for the effects we observe in nature. Since nature is finite and contains much evil, we are justified in inferring only a finite cause of it and one which is neutral between good and evil. Kant's criticisms at this point follow similar lines: it can prove at the most an Architect or Designer but not a Creator of the world; and it cannot prove the infinite or perfect Being who is the God of theism.[57]

[55] Hume, David: *Dialogues concerning Natural Religion*, ed. by N. K. Smith, New York, Social Sciences Publishers, 1948, p. 143.

[56] Hume, *op. cit.*, Parts V, X.

[57] Kant, I.: *Critique of Pure Reason*, B. 649–658.

These criticisms by Hume and Kant indicate that there are weaknesses and limitations in the eighteenth-century form of the teleological argument. It is another question whether they are fatal to every form of it. It is certainly true that the analogy between natural order and a human machine or other artifact is weak. Although the natural order is a whole composed of parts related to each other, its order seems not to be externally imposed upon it but to be the product of formative principles immanent in its various parts. However, the teleological argument does not stand or fall with the analogy between natural order and a human machine. Indeed, it is strengthened when the analogy is abandoned, since the order of nature, both as a whole and in its parts, is immensely more complex than that of any machine designed by the human mind.

Again, the criticism of Hume and Kant that we are not justified in attributing to the *cause* of nature qualities for which we have no evidence in nature *itself* is valid. Although there may be evidence in nature for a Mind that far transcends that of man, it does not warrant us in speaking of it as infinite, perfect, or morally good. However, this criticism, important as it is, indicates a limitation rather than a failure of the argument. It reminds us that the grounds for belief in God's infinity, perfection, and moral goodness are not to be found in the order of nature but elsewhere, e.g., religious and moral experience. The limitation of the teleological argument is that it can prove only an intelligent Designer, as Kant asserted. But this does not mean that it has no value; it means that the rational theology criticized by Hume and Kant expected too much from it and that it cannot stand alone.

This brings us face to face with the crucial issue: Is it arbitrary to think that the cause of natural order is an intelligent Mind rather than some "inherent principle of order" in nature which is without intelligence, e.g., animal generation, vegetable growth, or the motions of atoms? It is not strange that Hume regarded the explanation of natural order by mind as arbitrary, because he viewed all metaphysical theories as speculative fancies and mind as only a "weak agitation of the brain," an insignificant part of the immense whole. But if one does not accept his skeptical rejection of metaphysical explanation and his naturalistic view of mind, one may still think that the explanation of natural order by a divine Mind is more reasonable than any explanation of it by blind natural forces such as those Hume mentions.

(3) A. C. Ewing has recently restated the argument for a teleological explanation of *organisms* in terms of probability. "It is an argument to the effect that to posit a purpose is the only way of accounting for certain phenomena which will remove the stupendously unlikely coincidence that they should show all the features of the results of purpose

without there being a purpose . . . It does seem fantastically improbable that living bodies should show such extraordinarily detailed adjustments to ends as they do unless some explanation of this can be given." [58] Of course, the objection to such a teleological explanation could be made that *any* particular arrangement of matter is bound to be very improbable, so that the arrangement that actually exists in nature is no more improbable than any other that might have occurred. But the improbability that suggests a teleological explanation is not that of the actual arrangement *in itself;* it is the improbability of an arrangement occurring by chance when it *fits in with certain purposes.*[59] If a distribution of cards in which a person held all the trumps occurred not once but several times in succession, it would not be as reasonable to suppose that it happened by chance as to suppose that he was cheating.[60] "Yet the odds against this [distribution of cards] happening by chance, fantastically high as they are, can be shown to be less than the odds against the existence of such a vast number of bodies apparently purposive in such intricate detail being due to mere chance." [61] Although this argument is primarily "from particular features of certain beings" rather than from "the world as a whole," Ewing points out that the world as a whole is also involved. "For living organisms depend upon their inorganic environment and it is not reasonable to think of part but not the whole as created by a divine Mind." [62]

Other recent theists have based the teleological argument not on the apparent purposiveness of organisms stressed by Ewing but on the order of *nature as a whole.* Ninian Smart, for example, emphasizes the fact that the cosmos is not only orderly but that its orderliness is such that conscious life has been able to emerge from it and to evolve. We cannot suppose that, whatever the laws of nature were, conscious life would be bound to evolve. "The universe of buzzing atoms which we imagined would not bring forth the complexity required for sentient existence as we know it in the cosmos. Hence, there is something about the degree of orderliness in the actual cosmos which poses a problem. . . . Why should there be a cosmos containing so much orderliness? Why indeed should it be sufficiently orderly to give rise to conscious and rational life?" [63] Smart's answer to these questions is that the degree of orderliness we observe in the cosmos was a necessary condi-

---

[58] Ewing, *op. cit.,* p. 39.
[59] *Ibid.,* p. 40.
[60] *Ibid.*
[61] *Ibid.* Brackets added.
[62] *Ibid.,* p. 41.
[63] Smart, *op. cit.,* pp. 116, 117.

tion for the evolution of conscious minds and that without the existence of conscious minds there could be no values. "It is hard to see what value could be attached to a dead universe, one which was bereft of consciousness . . . a blind swirling of atoms and galaxies. It would go about its unconscious business; but there would be no value or virtue in it. There would be no enjoyment, no creativity, no struggles and successes. No, for the cosmos to produce value, it must first produce conscious beings." [64]

When the teleological argument is formulated in this way, it bears little resemblance to the form of it which was criticized by Hume and Kant. For it infers the existence of a divine Mind not from the fact of natural order *as such* but from the existence of the particular *kind* of natural order which has made possible the evolution of conscious beings and the realization of values by them. It has often been pointed out that the form of the teleological argument criticized by Hume and Kant virtually ignored the most remarkable thing about the order of nature: the fact that it was of such a kind that it could provide the conditions for the evolution of man as a conscious being capable of creating values. Now, one of the most significant things in the attempts of recent theists like Smart to reformulate the argument in modern terms is that it is precisely this fact which they regard as crucial. The objection may be raised, of course, that this gives a special importance to the evolution of human persons and is an anthropocentric way of looking at the world. But it is not necessarily an anthropocentric view. If a similar race of conscious beings should exist elsewhere than on the earth, it would have the same value as man. The important thing is that consciousness "adds a new dimension to the cosmos," since there would be no values without it.[65]

(4) There is a striking similarity between Smart's reformulation of the teleological argument and that of F. R. Tennant in his *Philosophical Theology*. Like Smart, Tennant does not base his argument upon a particular class of natural beings such as living organisms, but upon the order of nature as a whole and the fact that it has made possible the evolution of conscious persons capable of creating values. However, his argument is more elaborate and comprehensive than that of Smart. For he holds that the suggestion of intelligent design arises from "the conspiration of innumerable causes to produce, by their united and reciprocal action, and to maintain, a general order of nature." [66] In other words, the teleological argument is a cumulative

[64] *Ibid.*, pp. 116, 117.
[65] *Ibid.*, p. 126.
[66] Tennant, *op. cit.*, Vol. II, p. 79.

one based upon a comprehensive examination of several different fields of fact and their connections with each other.[67]

First, there is the mutual adaptation of thought and things which renders science possible. The world is a more or less intelligible cosmos, although it might have been a chaos in which similar events never occurred.[68] A naturalistic philosophy can assign no reason for this adaptiveness of the many things in nature to the requirements of intelligibility, but a sufficient reason for it is given if it is regarded as "due to an intelligent Creator designing the world to be a theatre for rational life." [69] The intelligibility of nature, Tennant adds, has been made possible by the association of the mind with parts of the body (the sense organs) which "are not merely bits of Nature to the soul but also its windows and telephone exchange-office mediating to it all its knowledge whatsoever, even its self-knowledge." [70] A somewhat similar argument is presented by Richard Taylor. It is based upon the fact that our sense organs, as well as brains and nervous systems, are remarkably complex and delicate.[71] Their complexity and refinement as such are not necessarily due to the purposeful activity of a Mind.[72] But the striking fact is that we rely on them to discover things which we suppose to be true and to exist independently of them,[73] i.e., they mediate knowledge of things outside themselves. Taylor concludes that, if we suppose that they are reliable guides to truths about things beyond themselves, "it is difficult to see how we can, consistently with that supposition, believe them to have arisen by accident, or by the ordinary workings of purposeless forces, even over ages of time." [74] In short, the adaptation of our cognitive faculties, including our brains and sense organs, to the attainment of knowledge of the outside world can hardly be a mere coincidence.

Second, there is the fact of adaptiveness in the realm of organisms. The Darwinian theory of evolution suggested that *particular* adaptations of means to ends and parts to wholes could be produced by mechanical causes. But an examination of the organic realm *as a whole* raises the possibility that the general trend of the evolutionary process may have been divinely controlled.[75] This possibility is strengthened by

[67] *Ibid.*, p. 81.

[68] *Ibid.*, pp. 81, 82.

[69] *Ibid.*, p. 105.

[70] *Ibid.*, p. 105.

[71] Taylor, *op. cit.*, p. 98.

[72] *Ibid.*, p. 99.

[73] *Ibid.*, p. 100.

[74] *Ibid.*, 101.

[75] Tennant, *op. cit.*, p. 85. Cf. Teilhard de Chardin's *The Phenomenon of Man*, N.Y., Harper's, 1959.

evidence that the inorganic environment is adapted to the life of organisms, by what L. J. Henderson has called "the fitness of the environment" for life. "The fitness of our world to be the home of living beings depends upon certain primary conditions, astronomical, thermal, chemical, etc., and on the coincidence of qualities apparently not causally connected with one another, the number of which would doubtless surprise anyone wholly unlearned in the sciences; and these primary conditions, in their turn, involve many of secondary order." [76] The probability that these many conditions for life were due to chance is extremely small.[77] Of course, the logician may object that, since the world we know is the sole instance of its kind, there is no way of estimating the antecedent probability of its occurring by chance. But when the teleologist speaks of the improbability of coincidence or chance on such a large scale, he does not have in mind mathematical probability but what Tennant calls "the alogical probability which is the guide of life and which has been found to be the ultimate basis of all scientific induction." [78] Therefore, we are justified in concluding that both the *evolution of species* and the *environmental conditions* favorable to life are probably due to the directive purpose of an intelligent Mind rather than to blind forces.

The last phase of Tennant's argument is based upon man's moral experience. Tennant maintains that morality can supply the "coping-stone" of his cumulative teleological argument. Since man is "organic to nature" and is the culmination of a gradual ascent of nature in the evolutionary process, it is possible to regard him as the end or goal of its creative effort.[79] Moreover, the fact that nature provides favorable conditions of order and raw materials of appetite for the moral development of persons indicates that the intelligent Mind which we have seen to be the probable source of natural order acts in accordance with the purpose of developing moral personality.

In summarizing his argument, Tennant emphasizes once more its cumulative character. The "interconnexions" of things—between the intelligibility of nature and man's mind, between living organisms and their inorganic environment, and between natural conditions and man's moral development—point to intelligent design as the probable cause of the order of nature as a whole. The "progressiveness" of the evolutionary process culminating in man suggests that it is directed towards an end. And the fact that nature is instrumental to moral life

[76] *Ibid.,* p. 86.
[77] *Ibid.,* p. 87.
[78] *Ibid.,* p. 88.
[79] *Ibid.,* pp. 101, 102.

completes the argument by specifying the end as the development of moral personality.[80]

Like Smart, Tennant denies that this conclusion involves an anthropocentric view of the world. It asserts that man is the only rational and moral inhabitant of the world known to us and that the end of the world-process is best discerned in him. But it does not assert that he is necessarily the *highest being* in the whole cosmos, or that he is the *final stage* of evolution, or that he is the *only end* of the divine purpose.[81] There may be rational beings akin to us in other worlds and lower creatures in our world are not necessarily "mere by-products of the making of humanity." [82]

Tennant is also aware that his complex argument consisting of many different lines of evidence which converge towards a conclusion that is probable rather than certain will seem unconvincing to rationalistic philosophers who are satisfied with nothing less than a logical demonstration. But he stresses the fact that the argument must be judged as a whole and that we can attain only probable knowledge of matters of fact or existence. Therefore, anyone who accepts an empirical rather than a rationalistic method in philosophy should recognize that all that can be expected of any philosophical explanation of the world is the most reasonable interpretation of all the facts. Of course, other explanations are possible, such as "groundless coincidence" and "immanent teleology." But these naturalistic explanations are not adequate to account for the facts. To say for example that chance could have given rise to either the intelligible order of nature or the human minds that are able to know it strains credulity to the breaking-point. And while the "immanent teleology" by which organisms attain ends without being conscious of them exists, it cannot explain facts such as the fitness of the environment for life or the culmination of evolution in man as a conscious moral being. Thus, neither "reductionistic," "lower" naturalism nor the "higher" naturalism which speaks of "emergent evolution" is adequate.

There are defects in Tennant's ambitious reformulation of the teleological argument. For example, his argument from the "progressiveness" of the evolutionary process to a divine directive purpose is based upon a selective treatment of the biological evidence. There have been other lines of evolution besides the one which culminates in man, and some of them have been eliminated while others have come to dead ends and remained static. Since Tennant was well trained in natural

[80] *Ibid.*, pp. 104–105.
[81] *Ibid.*, p. 113.
[82] *Ibid.*, p. 114.

science, he was aware of these facts and of the general problem of
dysteleology which is illustrated by them, but he does not deal sufficiently with them. And although it is one of the merits of his argument that he shows the close relationship between the inorganic and
organic aspects of nature and the development of human persons, he
tends (despite his attempt to avoid it) to interpret the purpose of the
natural order as a whole in too anthropocentric a manner. But despite
such defects as these, his form of the argument is far superior to that
which was criticized by Hume and Kant.

(5) However, critics of the teleological argument have maintained
that even the broader form of it defended by theists such as Smart and
Tennant cannot be said to be more "probable" than alternative explanations of the world. Indeed, some of them have argued that the
concept of "probability" is not applicable to interpretations of the
world. "Nothing can be said to be probable per se," says John Hick,
"but only in relation to data beyond itself." [83] In the case of our experience as a whole, upon which any total interpretation of the world
is based, there is nothing beyond itself which could furnish data that
would show it to be probable. For there is only one world, and it is
impossible to estimate the probable character of any total interpretation of it by comparing it with the already known characteristics of
other worlds.[84] From this he concludes that it is impossible to weigh
the probability of one metaphysical system against that of another, e.g.,
theism with its teleological interpretation against naturalism with its
non-teleological interpretation. Indeed, he maintains that every "total
interpretation" of the world is based upon "an individual impression
or feeling or 'hunch'." [85] Hence, when a theist tries to show that theism
is more convincing than naturalism, he uses "personal persuasion"
rather than "impersonal demonstration" or "argument." [86]

Now, it is true that there are no data outside the world which could
provide evidence for the teleological or any other total interpretation
of the world. But it is arbitrary to demand that the evidence needed
to render a total interpretation probable should be derived from data
outside the world. Obviously, a total interpretation must be based
upon evidence derived from data *within* the world, for the only way
the probability of a proposition about the world can be established is
to marshal evidence from the world itself. Since Hick has ruled out the
only evidence about the world that is available, he naturally concludes

[83] Hick, John: *Faith and Knowledge*, Ithaca, N.Y., Cornell University Press, 1957,
p. 135.
[84] *Ibid.*, pp. 135, 136.
[85] *Ibid.*, p. 138.
[86] *Ibid.*, p. 139.

that any total interpretation of it only expresses a personal feeling
about it and cannot be supported by argument. This conclusion implies that any critical inquiry to determine whether a total interpretation is probable in the sense of reasonable is futile and meaningless.
Hence, it would make metaphysics and rational theology impossible.

To summarize, we have attempted to show that the teleological argument, when it is based upon a particular class of things such as organisms, has weight but is vulnerable to the objection that the theory of
evolution has made it possible to explain the complexity of organisms
by natural selection; that when it is based upon the order of nature as
a whole and stresses the fact that nature's orderliness involves intercon-
nections between the inorganic, organic, and human realms and has
made possible the evolution of man as a conscious being, it offers a
more reasonable explanation of these facts than naturalistic explanations can do; and that it is therefore more probable than these rival
explanations not in the statistical sense of "probable" but in the sense
that it is supported by cumulative evidence of many kinds derived from
experience of the world.

The Moral Argument

It seems strange that it did not occur to philosophers before Kant to
base a rational argument for God's existence on the moral experience of
men. This is the more surprising in view of the fact that Western
theism had been an ethical religion since the Hebrew prophets affirmed
that God is righteous and demands justice and mercy from His children. Moreover, the moral argument has an obvious advantage over the
cosmological and teleological arguments. Unlike them, it starts not
from the characteristics of nature but from a familiar and important
aspect of human life. Since man knows natural phenomena only from
without but himself from within, he might have been expected to discover the presence of God more clearly in the "moral law within" than
in "the starry heavens above" or the contingency of nature in general.
The fact that he did not may have been due in part to the belief during
the domination of Western culture by Christianity that moral knowledge was derived from revelation and that moral goodness depended
upon divine grace. Since it was assumed that morality was based on religious belief, it did not occur to men that religious belief could be supported by morality. Another reason for the development of the moral
argument after the cosmological and teleological arguments was the
dominance of the Greek philosophical tradition with its primary interest in theoretical knowledge of the cosmos and its tendency to view
man as simply a part of the cosmic order. As a result, when philosophi-

cal theologians such as Aquinas sought to develop proofs for God's existence, they naturally followed the example of Greek thinkers such as Plato and Aristotle who had originally formulated the cosmological and teleological arguments. They adopted what Tillich calls the "cosmological approach," which moves from the external world of nature to God as its transcendent cause, neglecting what he calls the "ontological approach" of Augustine, which moves from man's inner experience of values such as truth to God as the unconditional source of them.[87]

Therefore, when Kant rejected the traditional arguments of rational theology and postulated the existence of God as a presupposition of the moral life, he started a revolution in the philosophy of religion. For philosophers of religion beginning with Schleiermacher have tended to start not from the world of which man is only a part but from the experience, especially the religious and moral experience, of man.

(1) Kant's statement of the moral argument for the existence of God was simple. The practical reason sets before man as the *summum bonum* virtue and happiness in proportion to virtue. Now, his happiness depends not on his own will but on the natural circumstances of his life, and these do not bring him happiness in proportion to his virtue. Therefore, if the *summum bonum* is to be attained, the existence of a wise and benevolent God who will bestow upon each person the happiness his virtue deserves must be postulated by the practical reason.[88]

The criticisms which have been directed against this argument are well known and require little discussion.[89] First, the assumption that practical reason demands happiness for each man in proportion to his virtue may be challenged on ethical grounds. Second, Kant seems to postulate God's existence only as a means to the attainment of happiness by men, although he makes it clear that God is also concerned with their virtue and hence their "worthiness" to be happy. To these ethical and religious criticisms must be added a metaphysical one. The moral order consisting of rational wills acting freely in accordance with moral laws is sharply separated by Kant from the natural order consisting of phenomena determined by causal laws. This dualism makes it difficult to see how the two orders can have any relation to one another. Hence, God seems to be introduced as a *deus ex machina* to bring them together in a harmony that is foreign to the nature of both,

[87] Tillich, Paul: "Two Types of Philosophy of Religion," in *Theology of Culture,* New York, Oxford University Press, 1959.

[88] Kant, Immanuel: *The Critique of Practical Reason,* Bk. II, ch. II, sec. V.

[89] We have dealt with them at some length in *Religious Philosophies of the West,* ch. 9.

since the natural order seems to be indifferent to the demand of practical reason for the attainment of the *summum bonum*. Thus, the postulate of God's existence by the practical reason is not supported by the knowledge of natural phenomena attained by the theoretical reason. As a result, later philosophers inevitably regarded the postulate of God as a mere product of wishful thinking which has no basis in reality as we know it.

(2) Despite these basic weaknesses in Kant's ethical theology it opened up the possibility of a new and fruitful approach to the existence of God. By focusing upon the fact that in the moral consciousness man is aware of himself not as a natural object but as a person confronted by unconditional moral imperatives, it stimulated several moral philosophers of the twentieth century to develop a moral argument different from that of Kant.[90] These philosophers have sought to avoid Kant's dualism between the natural and the moral orders and between the theoretical and the practical reason by insisting that moral values are an integral part of reality and that the theoretical reason must take account of them in its interpretation of the world. One of the best examples of this newer type of moral argument is that developed by W. R. Sorley in his Gifford Lectures, *Moral Values and the Idea of God*.

Sorley argues that Kant's great mistake was to assume that the natural and the moral orders are completely disparate and are separated by a gulf from one another. They are, he contends, "different aspects of the same reality" and the relations between them are "relations within one system of reality." [91] Hence, values are *objective* in the sense that they belong to things that exist or may be brought into existence. For example, the mere ideal of truth or justice is not in itself a value; it is only true propositions and just persons or societies which are valuable. Moreover, values such as truth and justice have a *claim* to existence; they "ought" to exist. Thus, values are distinguishable from but related to existence.

The theistic belief that the ultimate cause of the world is good must be based on the view that "the moral order is an objectively valid order." [92] Sorley argues that there are several characteristics of *moral laws* which support this view of the moral order. The first is that they are *categorical* or *unconditional*. As Kant had said, they are binding

---

[90] To a certain extent these philosophers have followed a suggestion Kant made in his *Opus Posthumum* that our awareness of moral obligation is itself a consciousness of the reality of God.

[91] Sorley, W. R.: *Moral Values and the Idea of God*, Cambridge, Cambridge University Press, 1921, p. 336.

[92] *Ibid.*, p. 337.

upon us whether they are in harmony with our natural inclinations or not. Secondly, they are *universally valid* in the sense that they are binding upon all men. Specific rules vary according to time and place, circumstances and needs, but general ethical principles are invariable. For example, Sorley points out that the principle that each person should seek the common good indicates the presence of a basic unity between the conduct of the head-hunter of a primitive tribe and that of a person whose sense of obligation is so broad that he seeks the welfare of all mankind. Thirdly, ethical principles form a *coherent system.* As we have just said, the specific rules of different societies are often inconsistent with each other. But these inconsistencies can be explained by reference to a higher principle which does justice to the elements of truth in the moral judgments of different peoples. For example, the hedonistic principle that men should seek pleasure and the ascetic principle that they should sacrifice pleasure for the sake of spiritual values can be reconciled by the higher principle that spiritual values are superior but that pleasure is an important although subordinate value.

Now, these unconditional, universal, and coherent ethical principles differ from natural laws in that they prescribe what men *ought* to do rather than describe what they *actually* do. They provide ideals of conduct which are realized in existence only insofar as men choose to govern their conduct by them. But they have meaning and validity for all *persons* who are free to determine their acts for themselves. Thus, they constitute an ideal order but are valid for all men.

What, Sorley asks, is the source of these moral principles and of their validity for all persons? The most reasonable answer is: the thought and will of a Supreme Mind characterized by goodness. "Further, persons are conscious of values and of an ideal of goodness, which they recognize as having undoubted authority for the direction of their activity; the validity of these values or laws and of this ideal, however, does not depend upon their recognition: it is objective and eternal; and how could this eternal validity stand alone, not embodied in matter and neither seen nor realized by finite minds, unless there were an eternal mind whose thought and will were therein expressed? God must therefore exist and his nature be goodness." [93] In other words, men acknowledge objective values and an ethical ideal which are valid for them although not fully apprehended or realized by them. When we ask, what is the ground of the validity of these values and this ideal, we must answer that it is neither material things nor the mind of any individual person and must therefore be the mind of God.[94] Thus,

[93] *Ibid.*, p. 349.
[94] *Ibid.*, p. 351.

whereas Kant postulated the existence of God in order that He might bestow happiness upon men in proportion to their virtue, Sorley maintains that He must exist as the ultimate ground of the validity of objective moral values and of the unconditional imperatives with which they confront persons.

(3) When the moral argument is based in this way upon men's awareness of the unconditional character of moral imperatives, these imperatives need not be viewed as imposed by God's will upon them in an arbitrary way without concern for their good. One of the reasons for the widespread modern reaction in the West against Jewish and Christian morality has been the legalistic interpretation of it as consisting of commandments revealed by God which must be obeyed even when they have no relation to the fulfillment of human persons. It has been assumed that a theistic ethic must be an ethic of law or duty, a "deontological" ethic, rather than an ethic of values or ends, a "teleological" ethic. In reality, the theistic ethic is teleological as well as deontological, for it is concerned not only with the performance of duties as commanded in moral laws but also with the fulfillment of human persons as individuals and in community. It is true that in Biblical theism the moral imperatives are expressed as laws, but this is due not to a lack of concern in God for human good but to the fact that the existence of man is characterized by estrangement from his essence or essential nature, so that the fulfillment of the latter requires the guidance and restraint of the former by moral laws.[95] Hence, moral laws or rules should be regarded not as arbitrary demands but as directions with respect to the kinds of acts which should be performed or avoided if persons in community are to attain fulfillment. What is their ultimate source?

Tillich asserts that the root of morality in experience is "person-to-person encounter." In an encounter with another person, one is limited by the claim of the latter to be acknowledged and treated as a person rather than a thing. Of course, the claims of many groups of persons to be treated as persons have been denied throughout history, e.g., slaves, women, enemies, and those of other races. But the circle of those considered to be persons has been enlarged until it has come to include, in principle if not in practice, all human beings. This is the root of justice, which demands that every person should be treated as a person and accorded liberty and equality with others. It is also the basic principle of rational ethical theories such as those of Kant and the Utilitarians.

Tillich points out that if others are rationally acknowledged as persons with complete detachment, it is possible to "achieve justice with-

[95] Tillich, Paul: *Morality and Beyond,* New York, Harper and Row, 1963, pp. 37, 38.

out creating a relationship" with them.[96] But *community* is possible only if there is also a mutual involvement and participation of persons in each other. This requires that men who have been separated and estranged from each other should be reunited. This reunion can be brought about only by *love,* since love is the desire for union with those who are separated. Hence, love is the "unconditional element" in justice and thus the source of "creative justice," [97] i.e., justice which is based not merely upon a rational acknowledgment of others as persons but also upon a mutual involvement with them in community. "In this way," Tillich concludes, "love becomes the ultimate moral principle, including justice and transcending it at the same time." [98] It is the ultimate source of all moral demands.

The analysis of morality by William Temple is similar. The consciousness of obligation arises from the fact that by their nature men are bound up with each other as members of a society in which the weal and woe of each is the weal and woe of all the others.[99] Moral progress involves the widening of the area in which obligations to others are acknowledged until all human beings are recognized as having claims upon each other.[100] Since one's duties are concerned with many kinds of persons and require "infinitely delicate adjustments" based upon sympathy,[101] the principle of morality in its highest form is love.[102] Although the nature of love is absolute and unchanging, it is relative and changing in its concrete applications. It opens the mind to the needs and possibilities of each situation and determines what should be done in the light of these. Hence, it liberates us from conventional, legalistic morality and makes possible a creative morality which seeks the fulfillment of all persons.[103]

Thus, love is the ultimate source of the unconditional imperatives of morality at its highest level. If so, the moral argument can best be expressed as an argument from the fact that creative morality is based upon love to the existence of a divine source of that love and of the moral imperatives it lays upon us. Temple states the argument in the form of a question. Referring to the fact that man's nature often prompts him to subordinate his own interest to that of others and sometimes even to sacrifice himself for them, he asks: "Does this not

[96] *Ibid.,* p. 38.
[97] *Ibid.,* p. 39.
[98] *Ibid.*
[99] Temple, William: *Nature, Man and God,* p. 185.
[100] *Ibid.,* p. 187.
[101] *Ibid.,* p. 192.
[102] *Ibid.,* p. 195.
[103] Tillich, *op. cit.,* pp. 42, 43.

mean that man is by his nature shown to be created for love? And does not this again imply that in the ground of his being, and therefore in the ground of that natural order of which he is the most elaborately developed product within our knowledge, there must be the spring of that love which thus wells up in him?" [104]

When the moral argument is based upon the nature of a creative morality which is conceived primarily in terms of love and only secondarily in terms of moral law, the objection that God cannot be regarded as the source of moral imperatives without denying the moral autonomy of man is overcome. For moral imperatives may have their ultimate source in God's will and at the same time be based upon man's nature and needs. As Tillich says, God's will is not "an external will imposed upon us, an arbitrary law laid down by a heavenly tyrant who is strange to our essential nature and therefore whom we resist justifiably from the point of view of our nature," but "is manifest in our essential being and only because of this can we accept the moral imperative as valid." [105] This also has implications with respect to the way men come to know God's will. For the disclosure of His will may be viewed not as a direct communication of commandments having no connection with human nature but as mediated through the insight of morally creative men such as the Hebrew prophets into the essential nature of man and the conduct necessary for its fulfillment.

Thus, the unconditional nature of moral imperatives and the love which is the source of them suggest that they have their origin in a transcendent Will which demands justice and love toward all men. Of course, this does not imply that all men *recognize* that a divine Will is the origin of these demands, since unbelievers as well as believers acknowledge them and respond to them in their conduct. As H. P. Owen has pointed out, in the "order of being" God may be the source of moral principles, while in the "order of knowing" man may be immediately aware of them as having validity in themselves without referring them to the divine will.[106] According to theism, the creation, including the moral order, enjoys a relative independence in its modes of operation, so that moral principles may be recognized as valid by the unbeliever although he does not see their relation to the divine will.[107] At the same time, the recognition by the believer of the ultimate dependence of moral principles upon the divine will is not incompatible with his moral autonomy, since he can be conscious that an

[104] Temple, *op. cit.*, p. 195.

[105] Tillich, *op. cit.*, p. 24.

[106] Owen, H. P.: *The Moral Argument for Christian Theism*, London, George Allen and Unwin, 1965, pp. 34, 35.

[107] *Ibid.*, pp. 35, 36.

action is both in accord with God's will and right on purely moral grounds.[108]

The moral argument is strengthened when it is fully recognized that unconditional moral imperatives make themselves known in a way quite different from the way natural objects are known. The nature of the relationship between the knower and what is known is quite different in the two cases. "In moral experience, a passive observer or spectator does not stand over against a dead, inert, unresponsive object"; rather, "values 'take the initiative', 'press upon' man, and 'act towards' him." [109] As H. H. Farmer puts it, moral obligations "thrust themselves into the midst of our ordinary likes and dislikes, wants and preferences." [110] This is related to the paradoxical fact that, while unconditional moral values are objective and hence in some sense "real," they are in another sense disclosed to us as "not yet real" but "to be realized" by us in the world.[111] Thus, they are not experienced by us as detached spectators, but press in upon us, thrust themselves upon us, and demand that they be realized by us. This makes it more reasonable to consider them as unconditional demands of a transcendent Will which urges them upon us because it is only by fulfilling them that we can fulfill ourselves and others.

(4) The moral argument should not be separated from other arguments, as it was by Kant. However, Tennant is not justified in his view that it is only the final stage of a cumulative teleological argument and has no independent value of its own. As we have seen, the objectivity of moral principles and values and their unconditional demands on man have seemed to many philosophers besides Kant to provide the basis for a convincing and religiously significant argument in support of belief in God, convincing because moral imperatives impose their demands upon men with authority as if they come from a transcendent source and religiously significant because the nature of these imperatives indicates that the transcendent source is morally good and concerned with the attainment of good by men. Thus, the most reasonable explanation of the unconditional moral imperatives which are required by love is that a divine Will confronts men with values to be realized by their effort and duties to be performed even when they run counter to natural desire. For man is not only an animal seeking to satisfy his natural desires, but also a spiritual being who can fulfill himself only by devoting himself to higher values such as truth and a social being

[108] *Ibid.*, p. 57.
[109] Richmond, James: *Faith and Philosophy*, London, Hodder and Stoughton, 1966, pp. 113, 114.
[110] Farmer, H. H.: *Towards Belief in God*, London, SCM Press, 1942, p. 162.
[111] *Ibid.*, pp. 196, 197.

who can help others fulfill themselves only by performing the duties laid upon him by their needs.

When the moral argument is developed in this way, it is not only an important aspect of a cumulative argument for the *existence* of the God of theism, but also an indispensable argument for His *goodness*. For it goes beyond the cosmological and teleological arguments by showing that God is not merely a Necessary Being and an Intelligent Mind but also a Holy Being characterized by Goodness and concerned for the goodness of His children. Of course, it will not be convincing to those who regard morality in psychological and sociological terms as only a means by which man's biological drives and his interests are integrated in a pattern of conduct that will insure his personal happiness and at the same time serve the purposes of society. But for those who regard moral values as objective and feel awe in the presence of unconditional moral imperatives, the moral argument offers invaluable evidence for the existence and goodness of God.

The Fundamental Issue:
Theism vs. Naturalism

We have now completed our critical examination of the major arguments for the existence of God. In an earlier chapter,[112] we pointed out that men originally came to believe in God and have continued to believe in Him not because they could prove His existence by reasoning but because they have experienced His reality. But men are rational as well as religious beings, and when they have reached a certain level of intellectual development they have not been content to accept their religious beliefs on authority. Acutely aware of the difference between opinion and knowledge and perplexed by the fact that others hold religious beliefs different from their own, they have demanded grounds for their beliefs. When this point of development has been reached, philosophers committed to the quest for truth have sought for rational grounds for the existence of God or the gods in whom men have believed.

Thus, the function of arguments for the existence of God has not been to *discover* a God who was unknown before but to inquire whether the belief in Him which had previously arisen from religious experience could be *supported* by evidence drawn from other areas of experience. This does not imply that the arguments have added nothing to the previously held belief and have been nothing more than "rationalizations" of it. Since they have been based upon evidence derived from other sources than religious experience, they have sought

[112] Ch. 3.

to provide a basis for a reasoned belief. In addition, they have shown how such a belief offers an explanation of those characteristics of the world and man upon which the arguments have been based. Thus, they have not only supported or confirmed belief in Him; they have also *interpreted* the nature of the world and man in relation to Him.

We have approached the traditional arguments with this view of their primary function in mind. We have regarded them not as *proofs* which were intended to replace religious experience as the primary source of religious belief, but as attempts to show that religious belief can be *confirmed,* in some measure at least, by evidence from other sources than religious experience. The general conclusion at which we have arrived is that the ontological argument fails to prove God's existence but provides us with a religiously adequate concept of the God of theism and that the cosmological, teleological, and moral arguments, especially when they are combined to form a cumulative argument, provide grounds for a reasonable belief in His existence. We have acknowledged that *alternative* explanations of the facts are possible, e.g. the naturalist denies that the world as a whole requires a sufficient reason, asserts that natural order can be explained without reference to mind and purpose, and regards moral imperatives as products of social and psychological forces. We have only contended that belief in the God of theism offers the most *adequate* explanation of these and other facts of the natural and moral order.

Now, one's attitude towards the arguments as we have stated them will be determined at least as much by one's acceptance or rejection of the *presuppositions* behind them as by one's agreement or disagreement with the reasoning in them. What are these presuppositions and how do they differ from those of the naturalistic philosophers who reject them?

One of the main differences between the presuppositions of theists and those of naturalists is to be found in their conceptions of *explanation.*

(1) In the cosmological argument the theist maintains that the principle of sufficient reason is applicable to the contingent world as a whole, while the naturalist believes that it should be applied only to contingent events within the world. This is due to the fact that the theist is content with nothing less than an ultimate explanation of the world, in accordance with what H. J. Paton calls "the demand of reason for wholeness and completeness" in thought,[113] and therefore cannot be satisfied with an explanation of contingent events by other equally contingent events. On the other hand, the naturalist holds

---

[113] Paton, H. J.: *The Modern Predicament,* New York, Macmillan, 1955, p. 327.

that such an ultimate explanation is impossible and is content with the scientific explanation of contingent events by other contingent events. Hence, the theist is convinced that reason requires a Necessary Being as the transcendent Cause of the world, whereas the naturalist regards this as an illegitimate extension of the causal principle as employed in science.

(2) Again, in the teleological argument the theist recognizes that the structure and function of an organism can be described in terms of mechanical causes, but he thinks that "wholeness and completeness" in thought require final causes or ends also. In contrast, the naturalist demands an explanation of natural order by efficient causes and if he admits final causes at all does so for heuristic reasons alone and denies that an adequate analysis of apparently purposive biological phenomena would find purpose operative at all.

(3) Finally, the theist in the teleological and moral arguments interprets the purpose of nature in the light of the evolution of conscious persons and the realization of values by them. Hence, he sees intelligent will and the attainment of good as the primary key to an ultimate explanation of the world. On the other hand, naturalistic philosophers tend to regard conscious persons as only one species of living beings among others and values as purely subjective means to pleasure or personal and social well-being. Hence, they dismiss interpretations of the world in terms of personality and value as unscientific, arbitrary, and anthropocentric.

These differences between the conceptions of explanation presupposed by theists and naturalists result from differences between them with respect to the *primary categories* they employ in interpreting the world. In brief, the primary categories used by the naturalistic philosopher in explaining the world are those of modern science, especially natural science, e.g. space, time, number, energy, and motion. They are the categories required by science for the description of natural phenomena in space and time. Although the basic categories are those of mathematics, physics, and chemistry, additional categories have been found by biologists to be required for the description of living beings, e.g., "organism," and by psychologists for the description of human behavior, e.g., "stimulus and response." The theist also employs these categories of science, of course, when he speaks about natural phenomena, but his primary categories are those required for the ultimate explanation of the world as a whole and the meaning and purpose of human existence. They are categories such as "mind" or "spirit," "purpose," and "good."

What is the *origin* of these radical differences between the theist and the naturalist with respect to their conceptions of explanation and the primary categories they employ? The answer is to be found in a fundamental difference between the *visions* or *intuitions* of reality which lie behind all their thinking. In an earlier chapter[114] we pointed out that a metaphysical world view is based upon an intuition of a certain aspect of reality as being of primary importance for an understanding of reality as a whole. This aspect of reality provides a key which is applied by analogy to other aspects of reality in order to test its capacity to explain them. The metaphysician seeks to show by argument that the aspect of reality he has chosen as his key can serve as the basis for a consistent and comprehensive interpretation of reality as a whole and that this interpretation is more adequate than the interpretations offered by alternative world views. The conception of explanation and the primary categories he employs are determined by the aspect of reality he has selected as his key and hence by the intuition or vision which is his starting-point.

This accounts for the radical differences between the theist and the naturalist of which we have been speaking. The key used by the *naturalist* in his interpretation of reality is the primary importance of natural objects in space and time and the changes they undergo as a result of their causal interaction. Therefore, he seeks to interpret every aspect of reality by means of categories such as number, energy, motion, and efficient cause, applying them not only to the lower levels of nature described by the physical sciences but also to the higher levels of life and mind. Thus, he attempts to show that living organisms are material systems and can ultimately be described in physical and chemical terms. Since they are more complex in their organization than inanimate objects, he may use special categories to describe the remarkable way they function as wholes in which each part is both a means and an end. But he will refuse to supplement explanation by efficient causes with teleological explanation. There is, of course, a considerable difference between the "lower naturalism" of materialists and the "higher naturalism" of philosophers such as Samuel Alexander who acknowledge the fact that new qualities have "emerged" from the fundamental stuff or matrix of space-time at the higher levels of life and mind. But the emergence of these new qualities is not believed to have been brought about, as in theism, by the creative activity of mind seeking to realize purposes.

In contrast, the key used by the *theist* to interpret the world is derived from man's experience of his own intelligent will creating order and realizing good in accordance with its purposes. As a result of his religious experience, he seeks to explain the world as a product

[114] Ch. 1.

of the creative activity of a transcendent Will analogous to his own. Hence, the primary categories he employs are mind, purpose, and value, together with categories such as infinity, eternity and perfection which are necessary to describe the transcendent character of the divine Will. By means of these categories he also interprets the lower levels of nature, i.e., matter and life. This does not mean that he must regard material objects and living organisms as conscious, purposive, personal beings like himself. But it does mean that he interprets the natural order, inorganic and organic, as a teleological system which can be adequately understood only when account is taken of the fact that it has produced persons capable of envisaging purposes and realizing values. Thus, as naturalism interprets the higher levels of reality as far as possible by categories derived from the lower, theism interprets the lower levels by categories derived from the highest. For he views them as instrumental to the realization of good by persons and other living beings.

This explains why one who has committed himself to the naturalistic method of explanation and its primary categories for the interpretation of reality will probably find every argument for the existence of God unconvincing. His presuppositions will not permit him to make use of a method of explanation and primary categories derived from the highest level of reality, intelligent will and purpose, in interpreting reality as a whole. Also, even if he is a "higher naturalist" who acknowledges that new qualities in nature have emerged at the higher levels of life and mind, he will not be able to believe that a transcendent Will analogous to that of a person is the ultimate explanation of the existence and order of nature. Since he has accepted the naturalistic view that nature, the totality of things and events in space and time, is the whole of reality, it does not need to be explained by a cause beyond itself.

On the other hand, if the intuition that intelligent will governed by purpose and seeking to create value is accepted as the key to an understanding of the world, as it was by the Biblical writers and by Plato, a theistic world view which subordinates categories used in describing the lower levels of nature to categories derived from the highest level of mind and purpose will be convincing. Therefore, the fundamental decision which must be made by anyone considering the arguments for God's existence is whether the intuition of the world which has given rise to them and the categories in which that intuition has been expressed are in accord with what seems to him of supreme importance in the world. If they are, he will find the arguments to be valuable not as demonstrations but as supports of belief in the God of theism.

The fact that naturalism and theism are based upon two different visions of reality does not mean that one's decision in favor of one of them depends entirely upon its being in accord with his own previous vision of reality. Undoubtedly, decisions between world views in most cases *are* made on that basis. That is why we have recognized that one who has hitherto based his world view on the naturalistic vision of reality is not likely to be persuaded by rational arguments for the existence of the God of theism. However, the vision of reality which has in the past been the source of one's world view can be—and sometimes is—modified by further experience and reflection, and, if the modification is sufficiently radical, it can give way to a different vision and hence to a change of world views. As a person can pass from one religious faith to another, a person can pass from theism to naturalism and many have done so under the influence of modern skepticism. But also one can pass from naturalism to theism if one is led by a religious experience towards belief in God and finds that evidence from other forms of experience supports this belief, as we have maintained. Can anything further be said to anyone who may wish to consider the possibility of making such a change?

In an earlier chapter, we pointed out that a metaphysical theory may be evaluated in comparison with other metaphysical theories by applying the criteria of consistency, comprehensiveness, and adequacy to them. If one compares theism with naturalism by reference to these criteria, we would argue, one will find that it is more *comprehensive* since it accounts for aspects of experience which naturalism either neglects or fails to take seriously. The most important of these is religious experience of the Holy which the naturalist is forced to explain away as an illusion, a product of pre-scientific ignorance of the causes of things and/or a projection of human desire upon an indifferent nature. It is also unable to account for the existence of the world of contingent beings, as the cosmological argument does, and hence must assert that nature requires no explanation but is self-explanatory. Yet the question continues to arise: "Why is there being rather than nothing?"

Theism is also more nearly *adequate* than naturalism in the account it gives of other aspects of experience. For example, we have shown that naturalism cannot explain the striking fact that the structure of the human mind is such that it is able to know the structure of nature. John Macmurray asserts that the strength of the teleological argument does not lie in the mere "existence of orderly structure, however fine," but in the fact that "the order of nature is adapted to our modes of knowing and so comprehensible to us." "How does it come about," he asks, "that at times the scientist, by purely theoretical calculation can define in advance an unknown aspect of the order of nature which is then looked for and found? . . . Is it not something of a miracle . . . unless, perhaps, something like the capacity for thought which enables us to order our activities is at work in the ordering of the world?" [115]

Also, naturalism cannot do justice to the unique nature and capacities of *mind* and tends to identify it with physiological processes in the brain or with publicly observable behavior.[116] More generally, the emergence of *man* as a personal being with qualities which set him apart from and above physical objects and lower animals and enable him to transcend nature is unintelligible if "nature is all there is." The most striking thing about a person is that he is not an object in a world of objects, but a subject who is able to experience objects and even to make himself an object in self-consciousness. He is also free, a center of activity capable of initiating his acts from within and governing them by principles instead of allowing himself to be determined from without. Moreover, he is a rational and spiritual being, acknowledging the claim of spiritual values such as truth and justice upon him and devoting himself to the realization of them. Although he is an individual distinct from others, he is related to other persons in a community by bonds of sympathy and love. Finally, he is able to transcend nature and subordinate her to his spiritual purposes and to transcend the flux of time by binding the past to the present in memory and projecting purposes into the future by imagination.[117]

It is difficult to believe that a blind and purposeless nature could have produced rational, free, and creative persons capable of devoting themselves to spiritual values such as truth and goodness, serving the needs of others in love, and seeking to unite themselves by faith to the eternal Ground of their being. Therefore, the attempt of naturalistic scientists and philosophers to explain man with his mind, purpose, and values as an accidental by-product of natural forces seems less reasonable than the view that he has developed in the evolutionary process through the creative activity of a purposive Mind with personal attributes analogous to his own.

If so, we must next attempt to analyze the *nature* of the God of theism. After all, it may be more important, as Karl Rahner has said, to "stammer about God" than to "speak exactly about the world."

[115] Macmurray, John: *Persons in Relation,* New York, Harper, 1961, pp. 207, 208.
[116] Cf. the analysis of naturalistic and behavioristic views of mind in ch. 10.
[117] See the analysis of the nature of man, his mind and spirit, and his freedom in chs. 10, 11.

7

The Nature of God

It is possible to believe that God exists without believing *in* Him. To give an intellectual assent to the proposition that asserts His existence is not to have faith in Him as the source of meaning and value in one's life. "The devils believe and tremble," says the *Letter of James*; but it is not said anywhere that they worship and serve Him. And many men have professed belief in Him without either trembling in fear of Him or worshipping and serving Him with the love that casts out fear. One of the reasons for this is that, if there is to be faith in God in the religious sense of the term, the will and the affections as well as the intellect must be engaged. But there are also intellectual difficulties which stand in the way for many. Perhaps the most important of these are the problem of evil, on the one hand, and unworthy conceptions of God and His relation to the world, on the other; and sometimes the former is made worse by the latter. It is necessary, therefore, for the philosopher of religion who believes in the existence of God to go further and inquire what can be known or reasonably believed concerning the nature of God.

It must be admitted that some philosophers of religion and theologians have tended in recent years to assume that it is impossible to know anything about God's *nature* and *attributes* and that we must be content to speak about His *acts*. But, difficult as it is, the problem of the nature and attributes of God cannot be avoided in this way. Any statement a philosopher makes about the "effects" of God in nature or any statement a theologian makes about the "mighty acts" of God in history implies a belief about His nature, and without such a belief one is not likely to discern either His causal activity in natural or His redemptive activity in historical events. Moreover, as Frederick Sontag says, "we are not always clear or in agreement as to how God acts." [1]

[1] Sontag, Frederick: *Divine Perfection*, London, SCM Press, 1962, p. 17.

"Disagreements at this level, as classical theology knew full well, often rest upon a fundamental diversity in the ways in which we conceive God's nature and His attributes." [2] Hence, the view that we can speak about God's acts but remain silent about His nature is illusory.

This is not to claim in rationalistic fashion that we can know with certainty the innermost secrets of the divine life. We can only infer from the evidence available to us certain reasonable beliefs concerning His nature and relation to His creatures, revising our thinking about Him again and again in the light of further experience and reflection in order that it may be less unworthy of Him. In this life, as St. Paul says, we see Him "as in a glass, darkly." [3] But this does not relieve us of the responsibility of trying to understand what we see as best we can.

The necessity of making this attempt is shown by the fact that false or vicious conceptions of God have always been disastrous for religion and morality. Plato criticized the popular Greek polytheism on the ground that it represented the gods as capable of changing their form to accomplish their arbitrary purposes and that it regarded them as sources of evil as well as good. Even the Christian conception of God has been distorted again and again with evil consequences in the lives of men. One does not know which has been more disastrous, the view of God as primarily concerned with orthodoxy of belief, a view which led to the burning of heretics, or the modern view of Him as so indulgent and sentimental in His benevolence that His justice disappears, a view which has led in some circles to a religion incapable of making any moral demands and concerned only to make men happy by giving them peace of mind. As these examples show, it is not true to say "All that counts is belief in something beyond oneself." For belief can be a force for evil rather than good in life if its object is unworthy of devotion. If it is directed towards a vague and indeterminate object rather than an evil one, its consequences are also dubious since it fosters an amorphous religiosity consisting of subjective feelings and aspirations without objective content. Thus, the way one conceives of the nature of God and His relation to man determines whether his religion will be good, evil, or only innocuous.

Is God's Nature Unknowable?

Nevertheless, there have been philosophers and theologians who have been agnostic with respect to the nature of God on the ground that we may know *that* God is but cannot know *what* He is. We do not

[2] *Ibid.*, p. 17.
[3] I Corinthians 13:12.

have in mind here philosophers like Kant who have denied the possibility of metaphysical knowledge of *all* supersensible realities. We refer to those who have thought that there is some characteristic of God which puts Him beyond man's knowledge or some limitation of man which prevents him from apprehending God. It is necessary to examine briefly several forms of this agnostic view.

(1) Sometimes it has taken the form that God is "inexpressible" or "ineffable." This view has been influenced by mysticism which seeks a union with the divine by abandoning all images and ideas derived from finite things. To mystics of a certain kind, God is completely ineffable. Consequently, they prefer a negative theology which says that God is *not* "this" and *not* "that" rather than positive assertions as to what He *is*. Rudolf Otto was undoubtedly affected by mysticism when he asserted in *The Idea of the Holy* that there is a nonrational element in the holy which he called the "numinous," and he emphasized this element to such an extent that he has sometimes been appealed to by philosophers who maintain that God is "inexpressible."

A recent example is Thomas McPherson who argues that the "worry" of some philosophers as to whether religious statements are "absurd or nonsensical" can be avoided if we regard them as inexpressible. "There are some things that just cannot be said. . . . The way out of the worry is retreat into silence." [4] Referring to Otto's view that the meaning of the "numinous" cannot be expressed or communicated in words but must be immediately experienced or felt, he claims Otto as a religious authority who supports his view. Actually it is not the religious experience as described by Otto but his own empirical theory of knowledge which is the basis of his position. He cites the early statement of Wittgenstein, "Not *how* the world is, is the mystical, but *that* it is," and Wittgenstein's view that questions concerning "the problem of life" cannot be sensibly asked or answered.[5] "Religion belongs," McPherson concludes, "to the sphere of the unsayable, so it is not to be wondered at that in theology there is much nonsense (i.e., many absurdities); this is the natural result of trying to put into words— and to discuss—various kinds of inexpressible 'experiences,' and of trying to say things about God." [6] He admits that his conclusion may exclude not only theological but "first-order" religious assertions, but does not regard it as antireligious.[7]

Now, there is an important element of truth in the mystical view

[4] Flew, A., and MacIntyre, A.: *New Essays in Philosophical Theology*, London, SCM Press, 1955, pp. 132, 133.

[5] *Ibid.*, pp. 138, 139.

[6] *Ibid.*, p. 142.

[7] *Ibid.*, p. 142.

that God is ineffable. It arises from a vivid awareness of the transcendence of God and provides a salutary warning that finite man can never
fully know the essence of God and must never expect to comprehend
Him in clear and distinct ideas. But to infer from this that He is
wholly ineffable is to overlook the fact that He is immanent as well as
transcendent and may be known in a measure through His effects in
nature and experience. Moreover, religious persons, including mystics,
have in fact always found ways to express that which they have experienced of the divine. Even the negations of the mystics imply some
positive knowledge, and they have made use of images of various kinds
to express their relationship to God. Hence, the theory of McPherson
bears no relation to the religious experience of mystics, and those who
do not accept the principle of logical positivism that statements are not
meaningful unless they admit of verification by sense experience may
dismiss the claim that God is "inexpressible" as without grounds. The
importance of this conclusion for religion has been recently pointed
out by Frederick Ferré. To lose the possibility of speaking about God
"would be equivalent to the loss of all cognitive claims for religion";
public worship, which "requires at the very least the focusing of attention on common concepts, would have to be given up"; and even
private religion, including prayer, could express no belief and "would
become no more than vague and amorphous feeling-states." [8] In actuality, prophets and founders of religions and their many followers have
never thought that the object of their worship was inexpressible. They
have communicated their insights to others and religious communities
have transmitted them to later generations.

(2) A less extreme form of agnosticism concerning the nature of
God is that of Maimonides, the greatest Jewish philosopher of the
Middle Ages. Maimonides held that, since attributes are distinct from
the essence of a thing and since God's essence is absolutely simple, the
addition of attributes to His essence would introduce plurality into it
and thus negate its simplicity.[9] Thus, we can avoid polytheism only
by denying all positive attributes to God. The only attributes which
are appropriate to Him are those describing His actions,[10] since they
do not refer to His essence. In consequence, only negative attributes
can be predicated of Him with respect to His essence, and "our knowledge consists in knowing that we are unable truly to comprehend
Him." [11] However, he qualifies this conclusion by asserting that a

[8] Ferré, Frederick: *Language, Logic and God*, New York, Harper, 1961, pp. 36, 37.
[9] Maimonides, Moses: *The Guide for the Perplexed*, Dover Publications, 1956,
ch. 51.
[10] *Ibid.*, ch. 52.
[11] *Ibid.*, ch. 59.

name such as "wise" may be attributed to God as a relation between Him and His creatures.[12]

Maimonides' position is worthy of respect because it results from his strong insistence upon the transcendence of God. But it is open to several criticisms. (a) It is not true that the attribution of qualities to God destroys His simplicity by introducing plurality into His nature. Maimonides' belief that it does so is due to the fact that he holds an abstract view of God's simplicity or indivisibility which rules out every kind of differentiation. But if God's indivisibility is interpreted as analogous to that of a spiritual being, it is not composed of parts like those of a body but may possess qualities and relations which are distinguishable from each other.[13] (b) Maimonides also assumes that names such as "wise" and "good" cannot be predicated of God and creatures with the same meaning, "univocally," but only with a wholly different meaning, "equivocally." Since the transcendence of God makes it impossible to apply them with the *same* meaning, he was driven to the conclusion that they could only be applied to God in an *equivocal* sense. But this overlooks a third possibility, i.e., that the *thing signified* by the name can be applied to God but that its *mode of signification* is different. As we shall see, this distinction underlies the view that positive attributes can be predicated of God in an *analogical* manner. (c) The view of Maimonides that "wise" and "good" may be predicated of God with respect to His *actions* and His *relations* to men qualifies his agnosticism but it is an untenable compromise. As Aquinas says, God could not be the cause of goodness if He were not Himself good, i.e., He could not cause a pure "perfection" in His creatures unless He possessed it Himself. To deny this is to deny the fundamental assumption which makes positive knowledge of God possible, i.e., that we can infer the nature of a cause from its effects.[14] Moreover, the statement "God is wise" must mean more than "God acts as a wise man would act," because there is a connection between a person's acts and his character and the former disclose the latter.

(3) According to Karl Barth, every attempt of natural or rational theology to attain to a knowledge of God's nature is bound to fail and man must depend for knowledge of Him solely upon His revelation of Himself in the Scriptures. Hence, Barth is critical of the attempt of philosophers to attain knowledge of God through reason. Every concept or image of God man constructs is arbitrary, a product of his own imagination. While God is holy, man is a sinner; while God is in

[12] *Ibid.*, chs. 54, 57.
[13] Cf. the criticism of Aquinas' similar view of God's simplicity in Thomas, G. F.: *op. cit.*, ch. 5.
[14] Aquinas, Thomas: *Summa Theologica*, Q. 13, a. 2.

light, man is in darkness.[15] Therefore, man cannot possibly know God by reflection upon his own experience, even his religious experience. Indeed, he does not even possess analogies derived from his experience by which he can conceive God's nature. God can be made known to us "not in an already existent analogy, but only in an analogy to be created by God's grace, the analogy of grace and faith to which we say yes as to the inaccessible which is made accessible to us in incomprehensible reality." [16]

Now, it is true that natural theology has sometimes proposed views of the nature of God and His relation to the world which have been completely inadequate from the point of view of theism, e.g., Spinoza's pantheism or Hegel's immanentism. But natural theology, like other branches of philosophy, must develop by the criticism of errors and partial truths, and philosophers from the time of Plato have contributed important religious insights. However, this consideration is secondary to the main issue. For Barth's attack on natural theology rests upon his theological position, i.e., his exaltation of God's grace as the sole source of salvation for man. This leads Barth to a view of man that automatically rules out every possibility of a natural knowledge of God through human experience and reason, condemning every claim to such knowledge as evidence of man's pride as a sinful being, and it does so in the face of many passages of the Bible which seem to express the opposite view.[17] It is difficult to see why man, who is said in the Bible to be made in the image of God and capable of understanding His will, should be regarded as proud when he uses his reason to inquire concerning the nature of God. If so, we must reject the claim of Barth that philosophical thinking about God's nature must always result in error since it is the work of man, while the Biblical revelation can contain nothing but truth since it is the work of God. Both are fallible because human reason and experience have been at work in both. And the thinking of theologians as well as that of philosophers may be infected with pride!

Ways of Knowing God

We have critically examined three forms of agnosticism concerning the nature of God and have offered reasons for rejecting all of them. The value of these and other forms of such agnosticism lies in their warning to us that our knowledge of the nature of God is and always will be limited because of His infinity and the finiteness and distortion

[15] Barth, Karl: *Church Dogmatics*, Edinburgh, T. and T. Clark, II-I, 1957, p. 103.
[16] *Ibid.*, p. 85.
[17] Romans 1:18–20.

of our reason. But they should not dissuade us from attempting to think as clearly as we can about the problem so that we may attain beliefs about Him which are as reasonable as possible. In doing so, we should note that the problem of God's nature is closely related to the problem of His existence. For any argument for the *existence* of God concludes from evidence of a certain kind to the existence of a God with a certain *nature* and *relation* to the world. Hence, reasoning about His nature must depend, at least in part, upon the same kinds of evidence as have been used in reasoning about His existence. In a sense, it simply carries further the process of reasoning that leads to His existence by inquiring what can be inferred about His nature from the conclusions which have been arrived at concerning His existence.

To illustrate this point, the conclusion of the *cosmological* argument is of great importance because the Necessary Being to which it leads cannot belong to the world of contingent beings but must be transcendent to it. This can provide the basis for an inference that there is a gulf or "ontological distance" between God and all contingent beings and hence for a negative theology which safeguards His transcendence by denying of Him all qualities of contingent beings that are essentially imperfect. Thus, negative predicates such as immutability and eternity can be inferred from the fact that God is a Necessary Being who transcends the world. Again, although we have admitted that the *teleological* argument points to a Designer rather than a Creator, it provides a basis for the belief that God possesses intelligent mind and purpose and therefore that He is personal. Moreover, the evidence it offers that His purposive will has been active throughout the evolutionary process indicates that He is not merely the original source of the natural order like the God of deism but also has a concern for the development of His creatures. Finally, the *moral* argument specifies further the nature of His will, insofar as His purpose is concerned with persons. It indicates that He is good and that He requires goodness of men. It also suggests that, since the highest morality has its source in love, the ultimate ground of moral imperatives is God's love for all men. Thus, the conclusions arrived at in the arguments provide a foundation for both a negative theology which expresses the transcendence of God and an affirmative theology which expresses His immanence in nature as a personal being with a purpose for all finite beings and a will characterized by goodness.

For this reason, it is misleading, to say the least, to contrast "the God of Abraham, Isaac and Jacob" with "the God of the philosophers," unless one has in mind only pantheistic philosophers such as Spinoza and monistic idealists such as Hegel. The God of theistic religion cannot be different from the Necessary Being on whom all contingent beings depend, the Intelligent Mind who is the source of the order of nature and the evolution of living things, and the Moral Will who demands goodness of persons because He loves them and seeks their highest good. For the God of religion upon whom men depend for their salvation must also be the Being who can be known by philosophers as the creator and sustainer of the natural order and the governor of the moral order. God is the Lord of *nature* as well as the Savior of *men*.

However, we must also appeal to religious experience and prophetic insight, if we are to attain a knowledge of God which is religiously adequate. In the past, many philosophers have depended exclusively upon rational inference from natural phenomena, moral experience, and other evidence available to all men, and consequently have not considered insights derived from religious experience and recorded in the scriptures of the great religions. Because they assumed that "natural" or "rational" theology must be separated completely from "revealed" theology, they cut themselves off from one of the most valuable sources of the knowledge of God's nature. This is an artificial separation which must be overcome.[18] The philosopher of religion must use evidence concerning the nature of God which is drawn *both* from general experience of nature and man *and* from the insights of historic religions. If he has become convinced that Western theism is superior to its major rivals, pantheism and monism, as we have argued,[19] this means that he should pay special attention to the insights expressed by the Biblical writers.

For although the God of religion cannot be different from the God of philosophy, theists believe that He possesses characteristics and manifests attitudes which cannot be inferred by reason from evidence accessible to all men alike. Hence, He can provide an answer not merely to the theoretical question concerning the explanation of the world but also (and primarily) to the existential question concerning the ultimate source of good and of deliverance from evil. Religious men are interested in God's relation to nature, but they are concerned above all with His attitude towards themselves and other men. They ask whether God cares for them, whether He has a purpose for them, and whether He helps them to realize that purpose and to overcome the evils that threaten to frustrate it. The answers to religious questions such as these have come not from philosophical reasoning but from encounters with God in concrete historical situations as interpreted by prophetic minds. Above all, from the interpretation of His activity in history by Hebrew prophets and Christian apostles,

[18] Cf. Temple, *op. cit.*, Lecture I.
[19] Ch. 4.

beliefs concerning His nature and His attitude towards men have arisen which have enriched men's understanding of Him.

An interesting example of this is the way in which the experience of God's *holiness* by ancient Hebrews such as Isaiah[20] has given a deeper and more positive meaning to His transcendence in relation to nature and man. As Jean Danielou has said, the Hebraic experience of the Holy awakened a sense of awe and dread, but this had nothing to do with ordinary fear. "It belongs to the metaphysical order, and expresses the total disproportion between the greatness of God and the capacity of the human mind. This grandeur, this immensity, which overflows man in every dimension, is called majesty. . . . It comes to undermine man's claim to be enclosed within his own limits, to be sufficient to himself." [21] But holiness means not only this "strangeness" and "apartness" of God's being; it means also His perfect goodness. "But holiness expresses also transcendence within the order of value; it is a sign of the infinite excellence of God, which He lays upon man not only as an overwhelming fullness of existence but also as sovereign perfection, from which man cannot withhold unconditional respect, and which arouses in him the fundamental religious attitude, which is that of adoring worship." [22] This led to a radical change in the Hebraic conception of religion, for "if His transcendence is not only of the order of being, but also of that of goodness, what He asks from man is, first and foremost, that he should be holy, even as He is holy . . . by fulfilling His commandments and observing His law." [23] Moreover, there was a development in the Hebraic understanding of God's attitude towards those who have *not* fulfilled His commandments. Although he continued to be regarded as the heavenly Judge who rewards those who obey and punishes those who disobey Him, He was interpreted by some of the greatest Biblical writers as above all the divine Husband who forgives His faithless wife or the compassionate Father who pities His children.[24] Thus, the Holy One before whom men feel awe and dread becomes the Heavenly Father whose mercy transcends His justice.

Thus, the philosopher of religion who seeks to determine the nature of God should not confine himself to conclusions derived by reason from evidence accessible to all, but should also take into account beliefs that have arisen from religious experiences as interpreted by

[20] Isaiah 6.
[21] Danielou, Jean: *God and the Ways of Knowing*, New York, Meridian Books, 1957, p. 129.
[22] *Ibid.*, pp. 130, 131.
[23] *Ibid.*, p. 132.
[24] Hosea; Psalm 103.

prophetic minds. Although these beliefs cannot be verified by everyone, they can be confirmed by religious experiences of men today, and
in some cases, as we shall see, they can be supported by evidence of
other kinds.

We shall now consider the dominant conception of the nature of
God in traditional theism and the reformulations of it by a few recent
philosophers.

Traditional Theism:
The Doctrine of Analogy

Medieval theologians such as Aquinas were influenced by both the
Biblical revelation and Greek philosophy in their descriptions of the
transcendence of God. They could draw upon concrete terms from the
Bible, e.g., "almighty" and "everlasting," as well as abstract concepts
of philosophers, e.g., "omnipotent," "eternal," "immutable," and "infinite." They were also affected in their thinking by Neo-Platonic and
Christian mystics who had exalted "the Good" or "the Godhead"
above everything finite by denying all positive qualities and relations
to it. The result was the *negative theology* which played such an important part in Aquinas' doctrine of God.

As we have said elsewhere,[25] the negative "way" of Aquinas had as its
main aim the safeguarding of the transcendence and otherness of God
from the tendency of polytheism or pantheism to reduce Him to the
level of natural beings or being, as well as to prevent theists from picturing Him in crude anthropomorphic terms. It sought to elevate Him
above all His creatures by denying that terms derived from their imperfections could be applied to Him. Thus, He must be said to be
"infinite," not finite or limited; "eternal," not involved in time; "immutable," not changing; "simple" or indivisible, not composed of
parts; and "perfect," without potentiality but fully actual in His
being. Aquinas was not content simply to accept this negative way of
speaking from earlier theologians; he sought to demonstrate that the
God whose existence he had proved must be spoken of in this way.
For example, the Unmoved Mover, First Cause, and Necessary Being
whose existence had been proved in the first three of his arguments
must be completely actual without any potentiality whatever, *actus
purus,* since He is the ultimate cause of the changes, the efficient
causes, and the contingent beings we experience. Hence, He must be
perfect. This implies that there can be no change of any kind in Him,
so that He is *immutable,* and no succession of before and after in
Him, so that He is *eternal.*

[25] Thomas, *op. cit.,* ch. 5.

Clearly, negative theology in some form is indispensable for an understanding of God since it emphasizes the "ontological distance" that separates Him from the finite beings which are His creatures and prevents men from falling into idolatry or anthropomorphism. Unfortunately, the way in which negative terms such as eternity and immutability were understood by medieval thinkers was largely determined by Greek philosophy and the use of them led to a distortion of the theistic conception of God expressed by the Biblical writers. "Perfection" was conceived as pure actuality which lacks nothing and hence admits of no increase of any kind.[26] "Immutability" was opposed to all change whatever, since change involves passing from potentiality to actuality and there is no potentiality in God.[27] "Eternity" was contrasted with time and conceived not only as having no beginning or end but also as containing no succession, so that God's eternity was viewed as the simultaneous possession of past, present, and future in one "eternal now." [28] As a result, God was described in the negative theology as a static being unaffected by changes in time. Thus, Christian theists such as Aquinas protected the transcendence and "ontological distance" of God by the negative theology, but at the cost of seeming to remove Him completely from the world and making Him so independent of it as to be unconcerned with the fortunes of His creatures involved in time and change.

This not only distorted the nature of God's transcendence of the world; it also profoundly affected men's understanding of His personal attributes which are of vital importance for religion. These attributes are the concern of *affirmative theology* which considers the "names" or terms that may be predicated in a positive sense of God because they have no essential imperfections in them. In Aquinas' doctrine of God, these names include the "most proper" or appropriate name of "being" but consist mainly of names of attributes and acts derived from our knowledge of human persons, i.e., "knowledge," "life," "will," "love," "justice and mercy," "providence," "power," and "beatitude." [29] While Aquinas makes it clear that these names are to be predicated of God "properly" rather than metaphorically, and "substantially" as signifying the divine substance itself, they "fall short of representing Him." [30] Also, while they belong properly to Him as regards "what is signified," as regards their "mode of signification" they do not properly and strictly apply to God but to creatures.[31]

[26] Aquinas, Thomas: *Summa Theologica,* Q 4, a 1.
[27] *Ibid.,* Q 9, a 1.
[28] *Ibid.,* Q 10, a 1.
[29] *Ibid.,* Qs. 13–26.
[30] *Ibid.,* Q 13, a 2.
[31] *Ibid.,* Q 13, a 3.

The principle which is to guide men in predicating these names is expressed in the doctrine of *analogy*. They are to be predicated of God and creatures not "univocally," i.e. in the same sense, or "equivocally," i.e. in a wholly different sense, but "analogically," i.e. in a sense that is "a mean between pure univocation and simple equivocation." [32] In this way we can avoid the opposite extremes of anthropomorphism, which results from the application of them in a univocal sense to God and persons, and agnosticism, which results from applying them in a purely equivocal sense. If we predicate them in an analogical sense, we can make positive statements about the attributes of God but at the same time avoid pretending that we know *how* they belong to Him and hence know His *essence* by our own natural powers. For we must ascribe them to Him "in a more eminent way." [33]

The doctrine of analogy has been interpreted in different ways and there has been a long debate in Catholic circles as to which is the proper interpretation. The "analogy of proportion" is based upon the fact that God is the cause of all the perfections of His creatures,[34] or, as Aquinas expresses it, "according as there is some relation of the creature to God as to its principle and cause, wherein all the perfections pre-exist excellently." [35] The "analogy of proportionality," on the other hand, involves the possession of the attribute by both God and man, but each of them possesses it in a mode proportionate to his nature. For example, the wisdom of God belongs to Him in a way proportionate to His nature as the wisdom of man belongs to him in a way proportionate to his nature. The latter kind of analogy allows us to predicate the "analogue" or attribute of both God and man but makes clear the fact that it is present in them in different ways which are determined by their different natures.

There has been considerable controversy over the question whether the "analogy of proportion" or the "analogy of proportionality" represents Aquinas' own view of analogy or whether he accepted both. We cannot deal with this historical question, and an answer to it is not necessary for our purposes. Some contemporary interpreters of the doctrine such as Eric Mascall and Frederick Copleston maintain that the two kinds of analogy should be combined. The "analogy of proportion" affirms that the relation between God and creatures on which analogy is based is that of creative causality. But since a cause is not necessarily similar to its effect "formally," i.e., in its form, the "analogy of proportionality" explicitly affirms that, while the attribute being

[32] *Ibid.*, Q 13, a 5.
[33] *Ibid.*, Q 13, a 3.
[34] *Ibid.*, Q 13, a 5.
[35] *Ibid.*

predicated belongs to Him as well as to the creature "formally," it is present in different ways in them as determined by their different natures.

There are difficulties in the doctrine of analogy which have led some contemporary philosophers to reject it as useless. The "analogy of proportion" affirms the analogue in a formal sense of only *one* of the "analogates" or terms between which the analogy holds, affirming it of the other merely in a derivative sense, e.g., in Aquinas' example "healthy" is predicated "formally" of the body but of "medicine" only "virtually" as it is the cause of health in the body. As Mascall says, "we are, so far as analogy of attribution [proportion] is concerned, saying no more than that God has goodness or being in whatever way is necessary if he is to be able to produce goodness or being in his creatures . . . it does not seem to necessitate that God possesses them formally himself." [36] The "analogy of proportionality" suffers from a quite different limitation. It affirms, for example, that

$$\frac{\text{The wisdom of God}}{\text{The nature of God}} \quad . \quad . \quad \frac{\text{The wisdom of man}}{\text{The nature of man.}}$$

This seems on the surface to be similar to a mathematical ratio, e.g., $2:4 :: 64:x$, in which the value for x can easily be determined since it is the only unknown. But the case is quite different with the analogy between the wisdom of God and that of man, because there are two unknowns. Although we have some knowledge of *both* the wisdom *and* the nature of man, we know *neither* the wisdom of God *nor* the nature of God. Another difficulty in the doctrine has been pointed out by Frederick Ferré. Although its purpose is to "mediate between univocality and equivocality," it seems in reality to be "a combination of—or a running back and forth between—the two unacceptable extremes." [37] Thus, it oscillates between anthropomorphism and agnosticism as it tends towards one or the other of the extremes. For example, two distinguished Catholic interpreters of Aquinas, Jacques Maritain and Etienne Gilson, differ in that the former believes the use of analogy gives us some, however modest, positive knowledge of God, while the latter argues that it enables us to make judgments about Him but gives us no knowledge of His essence, what He is.[38]

Do these difficulties render the doctrine of analogy useless? Fred-

---

[36] Mascall, E.: *Existence and Analogy*, London, Longman's, 1949, p. 102. Brackets added.

[37] Ferré, *op. cit.*, p. 75.

[38] Maritain, Jacques: *The Degrees of Knowledge*, New York, Charles Scribner's, 1959, Appendix III. Gilson, E.: *The Christian Philosophy of St. Thomas Aquinas*, New York, Random House, 1956, pp. 103–110.

erick Ferré maintains that the "logic of analogy" as usually interpreted is not "cogent," since it cannot provide us with information about supernatural entities.[39] Hence, it is of value only "as one means of providing criteria for the disciplined use of ordinary language in theological contexts." [40] If it is interpreted in this linguistic manner, "its function is not to inform but, rather, to limit the proper employment of language within the framework of theistic systematic assumptions." [41] There is much truth in this view because the use of analogy cannot give us precise "information" as to the way in which God's attributes belong to Him, as was said above; and the doctrine of analogy is presented by Aquinas as a way of determining whether and how "names" can and should be "applied" to or "predicated" of God. However, the doctrine cannot tell us how to "limit the employment of language" about God without presupposing some knowledge of Him, so that its linguistic function is dependent upon the metaphysical claim that we have knowledge of Him. This is why Aquinas says that "everything is named by us according to our knowledge of it" or that "we can give a name to anything in as far as we can understand it." [42]

Therefore, we would maintain that the doctrine of analogy is of great value, although the knowledge of God it presupposes and seeks to express is modest. Farrer points out that it can help us in the "task of purifying or elevating the ideas of human spirit," e.g., of will and intellect, when we use them in speaking of God. For it demands that we ask ourselves whether we must eliminate certain aspects of them as "unworthy of God" before predicating them of Him. This is necessary because the "mode of signification" of names is not the same for God as it is for creatures. But when names such as "will" and "knowledge" have been "purified" of aspects that are "unworthy of God," they can express for us our conviction that the attributes or acts signified by them, "what is signified," belong to God not metaphorically but properly and essentially. As Farrer puts it, they define "an area or a direction in which the truth lies" by indicating perfections of creatures, which it is appropriate to predicate of God.[43] At the same time, the doctrine warns us that we must not predicate them of Him until we have removed from them any imperfections which are associated with them in creatures.

Of course, the use of analogy does not provide us with precise information about God, what Descartes calls "clear and distinct ideas" of

---

[39] Ferré, *op. cit.*, p. 76.
[40] *Ibid.*, p. 76.
[41] *Ibid.*, p. 77.
[42] Aquinas, *op. cit.*, Q 13, a 1.
[43] Farrer, *op. cit.*, pp. 53, 54.

Him. But only those who insist that we should not speak of knowledge at all where we do not have such ideas will conclude from this limitation that the doctrine of analogy is useless. In reality, "clear and distinct ideas" which enable us to comprehend the essences of objects completely are attainable only in very limited areas such as logic and mathematics. It is unrealistic and presumptuous to demand that we think and speak of God only in terms of such ideas and to dismiss as useless ideas which cannot comprehend God's essence as the idea of a circle or a triangle comprehends its essence. Obviously, the transcendence and otherness of God make it impossible for our finite and earthbound minds to comprehend His essence. Nor is it necessary that we do so before we are permitted to speak in positive terms about Him.

Moreover, the predication of names by analogy is unavoidable if we are to speak of God at all. There is no alternative. The only terms we have are those which we have derived from our experience of the qualities, actions, and relations of things and persons. At the same time, we are aware of the transcendence of God and hence of the "ontological distance" between Him and all things or persons. Therefore, the only way of speaking about Him which is open to us is to use terms derived from the highest and least imperfect qualities and acts we have experienced, i.e., those of spiritual persons, to purify them of imperfections, and then to predicate them of God by analogy. If we do this, fully recognizing that we do not know the mode in which the attributes and acts signified by these terms are possessed "in a more eminent way" by God, we shall not be tempted to think that we comprehend His essence but we shall at least have the assurance that we are thinking and speaking of Him in the most worthy terms of which we are capable.

Our general conclusion is that both the negative theology which safeguards the transcendence of God and the affirmative theology which offers us positive knowledge of Him are valuable and indeed indispensable. However, there is a fundamental weakness in the traditional doctrine, and it is a serious one. As we have indicated, medieval theologians developed their negative theology under the influence of Greek philosophical conceptions of attributes such as "perfection," "immutability," and "eternity," and this resulted in an interpretation of the transcendence of God in relation to the world which was very different from that of Biblical theism.

Equally serious was the distortion of the attributes of God in the affirmative theology, under the influence of this misinterpretation of the negative theology. This may be illustrated by a reference to Aquinas' analysis of God's *knowledge,* which is affected at almost every point by his understanding of God's perfection, eternity, and immutability.[44] Since He is immutable, Aquinas argues, His knowledge must be unchanging despite the fact that the things He knows are always changing. Since He is eternal as well as immutable, His knowledge must not be discursive but must include "all things together at once" in a single act of intuition and must extend even to "future contingent things" such as the acts of men. In addition, His knowledge, "insofar as his will is joined to it," is the cause of all things. In all of these respects, God's knowledge seems to be completely different from that of man and hence to be virtually evacuated of any meaning we can grasp. Moreover, the fact that the "future contingent things" He knows in His eternal intuitive vision will infallibly occur would seem to be incompatible with the freedom of man's will. This is borne out by Aquinas' analysis of the *will* of God which parallels that of God's knowledge. He wills from eternity whatever He wills; His will is always fulfilled since it is "the universal cause of all things"; it is unchangeable because His substance is immutable; and it is the cause not only of the things that are done but also of the manner in which they are done, e.g., of the fact that contingent events are due to contingent causes.[45] Thus, His will, like His knowledge, is utterly different from ours; and the fact that it is eternal, unchanging, and always fulfilled makes any real contingency impossible. Moreover, His *providence* is simply the unfolding in time of an eternal pattern in His mind, involves no change whatever in His will, and all things are subject to it and "happen as they have been foreseen." [46]

Finally, God in His transcendence is *independent* of the world. "Since, therefore, God is outside the whole order of creation, and all creatures are ordered to Him, and not conversely, it is manifest that creatures are *really related* to God Himself, whereas in God there is no *real relation* to creatures, but a relation only in idea, inasmuch as creatures are related to Him." [47] Aquinas illustrates this absence in Him of a "real relation" to creatures by the relation of a column to an animal which has moved: "a column is on the right of an animal without change in itself, but because the animal has moved." [48] In other words, God stands outside the world eternally unmoved and His creatures move and change in time below Him without affecting Him because He is completely independent of them. In fairness it should be added that this is not Aquinas' last word about God's relation to the world. In a later question in the *Summa* on God's *love*, he asserts,

---

[44] Aquinas, *op. cit.*, Q 14.
[45] *Ibid.*, Q 19, aa 6, 7, 8.
[46] *Ibid.*, Q 22, aa 2, 4.
[47] *Ibid.*, Q 13, a 7, italics mine.
[48] *Ibid.*

"A lover is placed outside himself, and made to pass into the object of his love, inasmuch as he wills good to the beloved, and works for that good by his providence as he works for his own." [49] Thus, he combines with the Aristotelian concept of God as the self-sufficient unmoved mover who is wholly independent of the world the Christian view of Him as moved by His love to communicate His perfection to the world. However, it can hardly be denied that the picture of Him as "outside the whole order of creation" and having in Him no "real relation" to it exaggerates His transcendence and suggests His complete detachment from the world. It is easy to see why many modern theists have seen in this view the triumph of Greek philosophy over the Jewish and Christian belief that He is immanent in the world, is affected by the fortunes of His children, and deals with them according to their changing needs instead of imposing upon them an eternal and unchanging pattern by His sovereign will.

Process Philosophy: Charles Hartshorne

Recent philosophers have reacted sharply against this traditional doctrine. One of the most interesting of them is Charles Hartshorne who has made some radical criticisms of Aquinas' doctrine from the point of view of Whiteheadian "process" philosophy. A consideration of these criticisms and of the constructive proposals offered by Hartshorne will be of value to us in approaching the problem of reinterpretation.

Hartshorne writes as a theist who has been deeply influenced by the Christian idea of God but whose method is that of a metaphysician rather than a theologian. He sees a contradiction between the personal nature of God as a being who is affected by relations with other persons and the traditional view of Aquinas that He is "absolute," "perfect," "immutable," "impassive," "simple." [50] In contrast, Hartshorne conceives of God as "social." Like Whitehead, he regards all beings, God, men, plants and animals, and even "inanimate" things, as psychical in various degrees and as capable of experiencing other beings and feeling their feelings with sympathy. Reality is composed of a society of living, sentient, creative individuals which are in relation with one another. God is the supreme member of this society who dominates the other members by His influence and coordinates their

[49] *Ibid.*, Q 20, a 2.
[50] Hartshorne, Charles: *The Divine Relativity*, New Haven, Conn., Yale University Press, 1948, p. 25.

activities in such a way that they form a world order.[51] He is sensitive to all the other members and sympathetically feels their feelings.

Now, there is a contradiction, says Hartshorne, between this Whiteheadian and Christian view of God as "social" and the Thomistic view of Him as "absolute," "perfect," and "immutable." As we have seen, His absoluteness was interpreted by Aquinas to mean His "independence" of all other beings. In His knowledge, for example, God was held not to be dependent upon and affected by His objects, although they depend upon and are affected by Him. In contrast, Hartshorne maintains that the mind is "the most relational or relative of all things"[52] and that God's certain and completely adequate knowledge is in the highest degree relative to its objects. Hartshorne seeks to overcome this contradiction and thus to make the theistic conception of God philosophically acceptable. His way of doing so is to deny that God is identical with the "absolute" and that His excellence consists in His absoluteness and to assert that His absoluteness or independence is only a "constituent" or aspect of His nature which is abstracted from His concrete reality.[53] As a concrete individual, He is "superrelative," i.e., relative to and affected by all other beings. In His *abstract* character He is *independent* in the sense of neutral as to which possible other beings are actualized, and so His essence is unaffected by them. On the other hand, in His *concrete* individuality as a subject of knowing, willing, and loving He is *dependent* upon and affected by all other beings.[54]

This emphasis upon the personal or social nature of God and upon His relations with all other beings leads Hartshorne to make sharp criticisms of the traditional *negative theology* which seems to him to contradict the positive attributes of God as a personal being. (1) He insists that the traditional conception of God's *perfection* must be reinterpreted. The Thomistic definition of perfection as completeness of being or pure actuality without any potentiality implies that God cannot be greater than He is and hence that there can be no addition of any kind to His being. On the contrary, Hartshorne defines a perfect

[51] Hartshorne, C.: *Reality as Social Process*, Glencoe, Ill., Free Press, 1953, pp. 132–133.

[52] Hartshorne: *The Divine Relativity*, p. 8.

[53] *Ibid.*, p. 18.

[54] The similarity of Hartshorne's "abstract character" or "essence" to Whitehead's "primordial nature" of God and of his "concrete individuality" to Whitehead's "consequent nature" of God will be obvious to those who know Whitehead's *Process and Reality*. Also, Hartshorne's conception of God as "relative" to and "dependent" on other beings presupposes Whitehead's "principle of relativity," i.e., that every "actual entity" including God is related to every other.

being as one "than which no *other individual* being could *conceivably* be greater, but which *itself,* in another 'state,' could become greater (perhaps by the creation within itself of new constituents)." [55]

(2) Obviously, this definition of God's perfection, which permits an "increase" and "enrichment" of His being, requires a reinterpretation of His *immutability.* According to the Thomistic view, it is necessary to negate change of every kind in God, since any change would imply that He previously lacked something. On the contrary, Hartshorne denies that "the possibility of an enrichment in total value" would detract from the "admirableness" of God. Therefore, we must interpret the immutability of God to mean the reliability and endurance of His character, e.g. of His compassion towards all. For this is entirely compatible with change in Him as He sympathetically responds to the good and evil, the joy and sorrow, of other beings.

(3) This reformulation of divine perfection and immutability presupposes a radically different conception of *eternity* from that of Aquinas' view of it as without beginning and end and without succession of before and after. Hartshorne rejects this view because it does not take time seriously and because it makes a "real relation" of God to the lives of His creatures in time impossible. Like Whitehead, he maintains that there is a temporal aspect of God's nature and that His eternity is identical with "everlastingness." This implies, of course, that there is succession in His experience. But Hartshorne denies that this involves "perishing," and hence loss of value. It is the reality of the new *as added to that of the old,* rather than the unreality of the old, that constitutes process.[56] This view of eternity as everlastingness and as including succession in time without loss of the past is the basis of Whitehead's concept of the "objective immortality" of all values achieved in the past within the "consequent nature" of God.

How does Hartshorne conceive of the positive attributes of God in the *affirmative theology,* e.g., knowledge, holiness of will, and power? Clearly, he regards them as primary in any attempt to understand God as a personal or social being. Indeed, he maintains that positive attributes such as "wisdom," "love," and "person" should be applied "literally" to God. Although he approves of the use of "analogy" or the "way of eminence," he holds that we do not rise from the finite to the infinite, starting from the personal attributes of man and elevating them by a process of idealization. Rather, we have an *a priori* knowledge by intuition of personality and its attributes as belonging primarily to God and as participated in only imperfectly by men. Therefore, he

[55] *Ibid.,* p. 20.
[56] Schilpp, P. A.: *The Philosophy of Alfred North Whitehead,* Evanston, Ill., Northwestern University Press, 1941, essay by Hartshorne, p. 542.

interprets analogical predication as much closer to univocal than to equivocal predication, as shown by his remark that personal attributes should be applied "literally" to God. "Love, defined as social awareness, taken literally, is God." "Thus God is wise—period." [57] These positive attributes are, however, to be conceived in terms appropriate to the personal or social nature of God. They are "types of social relationship" between Himself and other beings, ways in which His relationships with them are completely adequate and appropriate.

(1) For example, when we speak of God's *knowledge,* we characterize it as "omniscience." This means that it is fully "adequate" or "equal" to its objects in its apprehension of them. Thus, omniscience is absolute "cognitive adequacy" to all objects, possible and actual. It includes not only the highest degree of clearness but also the complete comprehensiveness of God's knowledge.[58] However, it does not imply "foreknowledge" of all future contingent events, e.g., the acts of men's free wills, and it does not imply *providence* in the sense of "an absolute contriving of all events." [59] This would make God responsible for all acts of sin and all tragedies of life, as well as destroy human responsibility and choice. Rather, "providence" means "the faith that God is to be relied upon to do for the world all that ought to be done for it— leaving for the members of the world community to do for themselves and each other all that they ought to be left to do." [60]

(2) The *will* of God is characterized by the attribute of *holiness* or *righteousness.* This consists in "the single aim at the one primary good, which is that the creatures should enjoy rich harmonies of living and pour this richness into the one ultimate receptacle of all achievement, the life of God." [61] The unique feature in this view of the aim of God's holy will is the idea that the intrinsic value of the universe must be in the divine consciousness, so that God is "the ultimate or inclusive beneficiary of achievement" and hence is an effect as well as a cause of creativity.[62] At the same time, it conserves all human values in the life of God.

(3) God possesses *power* which is "adequate for cosmic need." [63] It is power to do for the cosmos "all desirable things that could be done and need to be done by one universal or cosmic agent." [64] But Hartshorne qualifies God's omnipotence radically by saying that there

[57] Hartshorne: *The Divine Relativity,* pp. 36, 37.
[58] *Ibid.,* p. 122.
[59] *Ibid.,* p. 23.
[60] *Ibid.,* p. 24.
[61] *Ibid.,* pp. 127, 128.
[62] *Ibid.,* p. 131.
[63] *Ibid.,* p. 134.
[64] *Ibid.,* p. 134.

are things which can be done only by other agents, e.g., the free acts of men, and that these cannot also be caused by the divine will. God can set conditions favorable to a certain choice by a man, but the choice itself is not inevitable and may not occur.[65] To assert the contrary, as Aquinas does, is to imply that God causes the most wicked acts and the most tragic events and sufferings.[66] Thus, there is chance as well as teleology in events, and the details of human life such as a man's sufferings are not divinely planned. In short, God's power "is absolutely maximal, the greatest possible, but even the greatest possible power is still one power among others, is not the only power." [67]

(4) The divine power is brought to bear upon other beings through *persuasion* or "social influence." Hartshorne accepts Whitehead's view that each agent or "actual entity" is free in the sense of self-determining. Within limits set by its relation to other "actual entities," it creates itself. Hence, God is only a partial creator of other beings. He controls them not by forcing them to choose as He wills but by influencing them through the objects of their knowledge. Thus, He controls us "by inspiring us with novel ideas for novel occasions." [68] This implies a unique view of the *creation*. God did not create the world out of nothing at the beginning. The creation is essential to Him as a social being and He is a primary factor in the creation of all things. But things are only partially dependent upon Him, since they actualize themselves by their own creativity with the aid of the "subjective aim" they derive from Him.

The general view of the relation of God to the world in which Hartshorne's doctrine of God culminates is that of *panentheism*. The traditional view of Catholic and Protestant theology is that God is transcendent to His creatures and that His immanence or omnipresence must be interpreted in terms of His operation *upon* them rather than their presence *in* Him. Hartshorne rejects this view as involving a dualism between God and the world which is inconsistent with his own view that the world is essential to God and contributes to the enrichment of His life. Instead, he maintains that God *includes* the world in Himself. In a significant passage on the relativity of the divine knowledge to its objects, he explains the nature of this inclusion of the world in God. "To include relations," he says, "is to include their terms. Thus we agree with modern absolutism and orthodox Hinduism that the supreme being must be all-inclusive." [69] To the objection that God

[65] *Ibid.*, p. 135.
[66] *Ibid.*, p. 135.
[67] *Ibid.*, p. 138.
[68] *Ibid.*, p. 142.
[69] *Ibid.*, p. 76.

is good and wise and hence cannot include the predicates bad and foolish, Hartshorne replies that predicates which are "outside" a thing as not being applicable to it as a whole may be "inside" it as properties of its constituents.[70] "In this way, God is really all-inclusive, and yet is not wicked or foolish." [71]

But while God "includes" the world, he also *"transcends"* it. In His "superrelative" aspect as a concrete individual, He contains the actual universe and in this sense is the All; but in His "absolute" aspect or "essence," He infinitely transcends it, since different totalities than the actual one are possible and new ones are continually coming into being. This transcendence of the world by God's essence gives "freedom" to both men and God, to men because they are allowed the power of decision between possibilities and to God because alternative experiences or states are compatible with His essence.[72] Hartshorne maintains that panentheism of this kind is superior to both pantheism and traditional theism. Panentheism agrees with pantheism in holding that God in His concrete actuality (i.e., as "superrelative") is all-inclusive, with theism in insisting that God in his essence (i.e., as "absolute") is independent of any particular world. Thus, God both includes the world and is transcendent to it.[73]

It cannot be doubted that Hartshorne's reformulation of the theistic conception of the attributes of God and His relation to the world is one of the most important contributions of recent philosophy of religion to the doctrine of God. It rests upon a view of the perfection of God which is radically different from that of traditional theology. Whereas the traditional theology of Aquinas regarded perfection in a static fashion as completeness of being and therefore conceived it as immutable, Hartshorne views it as dynamic, admits potentiality in it, and therefore pictures it as involving change. This dynamic conception of perfection is expressed in terms of a philosophy of process which takes time so seriously that it is willing to introduce unrealized potentiality, change and "increase" into the being of God Himself. As we have seen, it also necessitates a definition of the immutability of God as the reliability and endurance of His character, e.g., of His compassion for other beings, for only immutability in this sense is compatible with change in Him as He responds to and is affected by other beings. Moreover, it involves a complete rejection of the traditional conception of divine "impassibility," since this is obviously incompatible with God's compassion for all other beings. Above all,

[70] *Ibid.*, p. 145.
[71] *Ibid.*, p. 145.
[72] *Ibid.*, p. 89.
[73] *Ibid.*, p. 90.

Hartshorne's emphasis upon the immanence of God, at a time when many feel the "absence" and some speak of the "death" of God, is a valuable reminder that Western theism (when it has not been perverted by false conceptions of transcendence) has always affirmed the nearness and accessibility of God to His children and the depth of His concern for them. His strong reaffirmation of the personal attributes of God in an age of impersonal thinking has been equally important. These emphases, together with his use of process philosophy, have made it possible once more to give full weight to the theistic view of God as wise and good personal will actively engaged in nature and history and affected by all that occurs in the world of time and change.

However, it may be questioned whether he has not gone so far in his reinterpretation as to jeopardize the transcendence and otherness of God which have traditionally been safeguarded by the negative theology. This may be shown in several ways.

(1) In the first place, Hartshorne is highly critical of *negative theology* in general. He refers to "the metaphysical false modesty of seeking to honor deity by refusing to apply any of our positive conceptions to Him," and asks, "what is the difference between refraining from applying any concept to a thing and just not thinking at all?" [74] This indicates not only a lack of sympathy with but also a misunderstanding of the negative theology. Negative statements about God not only have the function of safeguarding God's transcendent otherness; they also usually rest upon positive knowledge of some kind, e.g., the negative predicate "simplicity" which denies composition to God rests upon the positive insight that He is a spiritual, not a corporeal being. In contrast, Hartshorne exalts the *affirmative theology* in an uncritical manner when he asserts that love and wisdom are affirmed of God "literally." Although he seems to qualify this by saying that they are affirmed "analogically and eminently," we have seen that he interprets analogical as close to univocal predication.

(2) His inadequate appreciation of the value of negative predicates has the effect of weakening his view of the *transcendence* of God and exaggerating the immanence of God. He does insist that God not only "includes" but also "transcends" the world. But He transcends it only in the sense that in His absolute aspect or essence He is independent with respect to which particular beings are actualized. This is not an adequate interpretation of what theism has always meant by God's transcendence of the world, i.e., that the world is distinct from Him as Creator and that His creatures are therefore "over against" Him. Is it not possible to conceive of Him as responding to and affected by

[74] *Ibid.,* p. 35.

all other beings, as Hartshorne rightly does, and at the same time to maintain His distinctness from them? Certainly, the Biblical view of Him insists that He is both the Holy One, exalted above all His creatures, and the Heavenly Father who loves His children and is very near to them.

(3) The effect of this minimizing of the negative theology and consequent weakening of the divine transcendence is evident in Hartshorne's tendency to stress man's dependence on God less and God's dependence on man more than theists have usually done. This is most clearly illustrated by his view of the *Creation*. Hartshorne's view that creation is essential to God and had no beginning is widely held today and may be justified in the sense that one cannot conceive of God as existing at any time without communicating His perfections to other beings. But he regards God as only a partial Creator, since the creatures by their own free decision in considerable measure create themselves. The radical distinction between God as a Necessary Being depending on nothing beyond Himself for His being and man as a contingent being depending absolutely upon God for his existence and nature is, to say the least, blurred. Hartshorne's *panentheism* carries his tendency to exaggerate God's relativity to and dependence on the world to its logical conclusion by asserting that the world is "included" in God. Although this extreme emphasis upon the divine immanence is qualified by the statement that God in His abstract character also transcends the world, it comes perilously close to pantheism.

(4) From all of this it seems clear that the major weakness of Hartshorne's doctrine of God is his one-sided emphasis upon its strongest point, the *"relativity"* of God. This is the strongest point in his doctrine because it expresses so clearly the theistic belief in the immanence of God and His love for His creatures and leads to a modification of the traditional negative theology which tended to obscure this relationship. On the other hand, his extreme emphasis upon God's "relativity" weakens his doctrine, for he does not do full justice to God's majesty, His radical difference from His creatures, His transcendent otherness. The only way this weakness can be overcome is to accept Hartshorne's criticisms of the traditional *formulation* of the negative theology and then to attempt a constructive *reformulation* of the negative attributes which will safeguard the transcendence of God but in such a way as to be compatible with His positive attributes.

Perfection, Infinity, Immutability, Eternity

An interesting attempt at such a constructive reformulation of one of these attributes, *perfection,* has been made by Frederick Sontag. He traces the historical development of this concept from Plato to Hegel and shows how concepts such as infinity, actuality, and self-sufficiency have been used to explicate its meaning. The perfect was identified by Plato with the complete, that which has attained its end, and by Aristotle with that which has actuality without any potentiality.[75] Thus, the foundations were laid in Greek philosophy for the medieval idea of divine perfection.

The medieval thinkers regarded *self-sufficiency*, "dependence upon nothing other than itself for its own existence and activity," as indispensable for God's perfection, since they assumed that without it He could not fulfill the functions ascribed to Him. "If He is to create and to be responsible for creative sustenance, His own ability to control and sustain Himself cannot itself be in question." [76] For the same reason, Aquinas attributed to Him *actuality* as Aristotle had conceived it and therefore excluded from Him motion and change as involving potentiality. Similarly, self-sufficiency was thought to require *necessity* in His activity and to exclude all contingency from it. For the same reason, patristic thinkers asserted that God was *"impassible."* "It is clear," says G. L. Prestige, "that impassibility means not that God is inactive or uninterested, not that He surveys existence with Epicurean impassivity from the shelter of a metaphysical insulation, but that His will is determined from within instead of being swayed from without. It safeguards the truth that the impulse alike in providential order and in redemption and sanctification comes from the will of God." [77]

But the divine self-sufficiency or independence does not require, as Sontag points out, to be expressed in terms of actuality without potentiality, or of necessity in His acts, or, we may add, of impassibility. It does not exclude potentiality, because certain kinds of change in God do not imply His dependence upon anything outside Himself; it does not require necessity in His activity, because freedom can be ascribed to His activity in creating the world by selecting between different possibilities; and it does not require impassibility, because God can feel sympathy for and respond to the needs of His creatures without His will to help them being "swayed from without." Thus, God's self-sufficiency, the independence of His being and activity, is indispensable, if He is to fulfill His functions as Creator and Preserver of the world, but it can be expressed in such a way as to include change and free activity in Him. Of course, the kind of change which is uncontrolled and which involves passing away, as in finite beings, should not be attributed to God. Similarly, free, creative activity of the will

[75] Sontag, Frederick, *op. cit.*, ch. 1.
[76] *Ibid.*, p. 109.
[77] Prestige, G. L.: *God in Patristic Thought*, London, S.P.C.K., 1952, p. 7.

can be attributed to God without threatening His self-sufficiency, provided it does not involve contingency in the divine nature itself. "Contingency may characterize Divine *action,* but not the *substance* of the Divine attributes themselves." [78]

Thus, while the divine perfection involves self-sufficiency or independence, this does not require that God be conceived as having actuality without potentiality (which would exclude change) or necessity in His will (which would exclude free, creative activity). If the change in Him and the freedom with which He acts are under the control of His power and do not threaten the unchanging identity of His nature and attributes, they are quite compatible with His perfection. For example, changes in the objects of God's knowledge are compatible with the unchanging character of the knowledge which is part of His nature. This makes it possible to say, with Hartshorne, that God's knowledge of future acts of free will arises only when they occur. In a similar fashion, God's acts can change in response to the changing situations and needs of His creatures, while the nature of His will and its purposes never changes. In this way, His intimate relationship with His creatures as a personal or "social" being can be maintained but without threatening His perfection by making Him dependent upon them.

The perfection of God involves not only His self-sufficiency or independence but also His *infinity.* This predicate of the negative theology in its traditional form raises great difficulties, and most modern religious thinkers agree that it must be reformulated. Indeed, F. R. Tennant is so impressed with the difficulties in the traditional view that he proposes to drop the term from philosophical theology altogether. We cannot say that God is infinite in the sense of "indeterminate," he says, for this is to say nothing in particular about Him. We cannot speak of Him as "limitless" in size or number, for quantitative conceptions are unsuitable to Him. We cannot apply "infinity" to Him in the more positive sense of the *"omnitudo realitatis,"* for "an *omnitudo* of all qualities however mutually incompatible" is everything in general and nothing in particular. "Philosophical theology, however, should confine itself to definite ideas and appropriate terminology; and inasmuch as the one definite and distinctive sense that 'infinite' can now bear is mathematical, it should be surrendered to the mathematician." [79]

Is it really necessary to eliminate the concept of infinity altogether, or is it indispensable for our thinking about God? If it were true that the only appropriate sense of the term is mathematical, the answer would clearly have to be in the affirmative, but theologians have seldom

[78] Sontag, *op. cit.,* p. 134, italics added.
[79] Tennant, F. R.: *Philosophical Theology,* Vol. II, p. 143.

used it in that sense. Nor have they used it merely in the sense of
"indeterminate." Rather, they have used it to express the fact that
there is a qualitative difference between God and everything in the
natural order and that we should apply to God in an infinite mode the
qualities or attributes He is said to share with limited beings.[80] Sontag
points out that infinity as a Divine perfection really means that whatever primary qualities are assigned to God (e.g., power, will, love) must
be ascribed to Him in an unlimited way in contrast with the limited
extent of similar qualities in man.[81] "One attribute of the Divine nature
may limit another, but each attribute in its own right is infinite. There
are always the traditional considerations of 'what God cannot do,' but
these do not, as they do in man, spring originally from a state of inherent weakness." [82]

If the concept of infinity is interpreted along these lines, it is indispensable as a way of expressing the radical difference between the
attributes of God and those of the creatures. It is also a necessary condition of the effectiveness of God's creative, sustaining, providential,
and redemptive activity in nature and history. But it is important to
stress the fact that, while limitations are excluded from God which are
due to deficiencies in His nature, there are limitations due to factors
outside of Him which in some measure prevent His attributes from
having the effect they might have otherwise. For example, God's power
is limited by the fact that finite beings, especially men, also possess
power and that God cannot force them to do His will without destroying their freedom. It is also limited by those factors in the Creation
which are the causes of natural evil, i.e., evil which is not due to acts
of free will.

There has been much discussion of the infinity of God in relation to
natural evil in recent philosophy of religion. Edgar Brightman argued
that "surd" evils such as the "waste" of life in some species and the
"futility" of the existence of species which have not survived in the
evolutionary process make it impossible to believe that the God who
created the world is infinite as well as good. Since the goodness of God
is more essential than His power from the religious point of view,
Brightman maintained that He should be regarded as perfectly good
but not infinite in power. More specifically, He is limited by a part of
His own nature which Brightman called "The Given." This factor
within Himself, consisting of nonvoluntary impulses and other forces,
is the source of evil in the world. God as intelligent and purposive will

[80] Sontag, *op. cit.*, p. 89.
[81] *Ibid.*, p. 91.
[82] *Ibid.*, p. 91.

struggles to control and master it, and man is called upon to cooperate with Him in doing so. This theory of a finite God Brightman traced back to Plato who regarded the divine "Demiurge" as limited in creating the cosmos not only by the "Pattern" of eternal "Forms" which he imitated but also by "Necessity." But he differed from Plato in putting both the rational and the nonrational factors *within* rather than outside God.[83]

This is an appealing theory because of the seriousness and honesty with which it deals with the problem of natural evil, and it has the merit of not compromising the goodness of God by making His will the source of evil. But it solves the problem at the cost of including natural evil within the being of God as "The Given." For this reason, it is incompatible with His perfection and implies a dualism in His nature which cannot be accepted. Moreover, it does not rid God of the responsibility for natural evil. According to Brightman, while natural evil is not caused *by* His rational will, it arises from "The Given" *in* Him. For these reasons, the worthy purpose he had in mind, i.e., to free God from responsibility for actively willing natural evils, can be accomplished better by attributing them to a limitation of another kind. As we shall see, the limitation seems to consist in the fact that the creation of the world with its opportunities for the attainment of good incidentally made natural evil possible.[84] This is superior to Brightman's solution, since it acknowledges a limitation on God's power but regards it as a freely accepted necessary condition for the creation of good. Thus, it is an external limitation of His infinity rather than an internal one.

Since God's perfection includes the infinity of His attributes, it is contrasted with the limited reality and value of all finite beings. Hence, it is the foundation of the negative theology which safeguards His transcendence by contrasting Him with the finite world. At the same time, it has a more positive meaning, for it accounts for the "perfections" which exist in different degrees in finite beings. As Aquinas says, the "perfections" we experience in the world pre-exist in a more eminent way in God the Perfect Being.[85] Thus, the religious significance of the divine perfection is not only that it expresses His transcendence and makes Him worthy of worship, but also that it explains the apparently inexhaustible fecundity with which He brings forth as Creator goods of different kinds and in different degrees in finite

[83] Brightman, Edgar: *A Philosophy of Religion,* New York, Prentice-Hall, 1940, ch. X.

[84] Ch. 8.

[85] Aquinas, Thomas: *Summa Theologica,* Q 4, a 2.

beings. In the words of *The Letter of James,* "Every good endowment and every perfect gift is from above, coming down from the Father of lights with whom there is no variation or shadow due to change." [86]

If the divine perfection is reinterpreted in such a way as to be compatible with change in God, His *immutability* also must be interpreted in a way that is quite different from that of Aquinas. In brief, it must be defined as the identity and continuity of His nature or essence through changes in the objects of His knowledge and the acts of His will. He must be immutable in this sense if He is to fulfill His functions as Creator and Sustainer of nature and Redeemer of men, since the natural order could not be maintained or enduring purposes realized in history without continuity in His activity. One of the great insights of the ancient Hebrews was that God does not act from caprice or on impulse like the gods of Greek polytheism, but that His acts in nature and history are expressions of a steadfast will. Because of this men could depend upon Him, have faith in His promises, and hence face the future with hope. They could be sure that He would be faithful to the covenant He had established with His people and could hope that He would not abandon them even when they were unfaithful to their covenant with Him. Although His acts in history change as He adapts them to the changing circumstances and needs of life, His will is unchanging and His purpose for His people remains the same. Immutability in this sense is not merely a metaphysical attribute which distinguishes God in His transcendence from His creatures; it is, above all, an expression of faith in the faithfulness of God towards men.

Obviously, His immutability is bound up with His *eternity.* As the Necessary Being upon whom contingent beings depend, He is self-existent and without beginning or end. Thus, His eternity, like His immutability, safeguards His transcendence by contrasting Him with finite beings that come into being and pass away. But this does not imply that He is timeless, i.e., above time and unaffected by it. If His immutability is conceived as identity through change, as we have argued, there must be a succession of before and after in His experience. However, that which was of value in the past need not be lost from His experience, as it is from the experience of man. As Whitehead has said, we can conceive of the past as being conserved in His everlasting life. The religious meaning of His eternity in this sense is bound up with that of His immutability. As His will is "steadfast" or unchanging, His love and care for His people "endures" through all time, so that they can look forward to the future with faith and hope for themselves and their descendants. Since He "abides" with them through all the "change and decay" of their existence in time, they

[86] James 1:17.

can face anxiety and insecurity without despair. Thus, the author of Psalm 100 urges men to give thanks to God and praise Him:

> For the Lord is good;
> his steadfast love endures for ever,
> and his faithfulness to all generations.[87]

The author of Psalm 103 contrasts His steadfast love and righteousness with the transitoriness of man's life:

> As for man, his days are like grass . . .
> But the steadfast love of the Lord is
> from everlasting to everlasting
> upon those who fear him,
> and his righteousness to children's children, etc.[88]

Understood in this way, God's eternity and immutability exalt Him above the limitations of time and change, but at the same time provide grounds of hope and courage for men who are subject to them.

An Ontological-Existentialist View: Paul Tillich

Whereas Hartshorne has emphasized the personal attributes of God, Paul Tillich has rejected "supranaturalism" and radically reformulated the theistic conception. Like Schleiermacher, he emphasizes the immanence of God; indeed, he asserts that God includes the world in Himself. Although he also affirms God's transcendence, he does not interpret it to mean that He is distinct from the world as its Creator but only that finite being is free to turn away from its essential unity with Him as its creative ground. Again, Tillich rejects the theistic view that God is "a being" and asserts that He is "being-itself," the "ground of being" and the "power of being." To call God "a being," he insists, is to imply that He is only one being among others, and this is inconsistent with His ultimate and unconditioned nature. Furthermore, Tillich maintains that "God is being-itself" is the only non-symbolic statement we can make about Him and that every statement that goes beyond this is symbolic. Since a religious symbol is derived from a finite reality, it participates in the infinite reality of God and thus can express Him in some measure. But it is inadequate to express His infinite reality and hence it must be denied as well as affirmed of Him. This is a crucial point for Tillich's conception of God. Since man symbolizes God, the object of his "ultimate concern," in terms derived from his own being as a self, he represents Him as

[87] Psalm 100:5.
[88] Psalm 103:15, 17.

personal, dynamic, and free. But inasmuch as being-itself transcends the structure of being from which these symbols are drawn, their capacity to express knowledge of God is very limited.

This may be illustrated by reference to Tillich's view of the symbol "personal." He holds that this symbol for God is "absolutely fundamental," because "man cannot be ultimately concerned about anything that is less than personal." [89] But he sees a difficulty in the use of the term "personal God," because it seems to imply that God is simply an individual being whereas He also participates in everything.[90] His solution of this difficulty is a drastic one. " 'Personal God' does not mean that God is *a* person. It means that God is the ground of everything personal and that he carries within himself the ontological power of personality. He is not a person, but he is not less than personal." [91] Since the term "personal God" is a "confusing symbol," it is not surprising that Tillich says very little about the divine attributes of "will" and "intellect" which have had such great importance in traditional theism. "Will," he says, symbolizes the "dynamics" of the divine, while "intellect" symbolizes its "form." Beyond this, the only thing he has to say about them is that they "express infinitely more than the mental acts of willing and understanding." [92]

In contrast to Tillich's reserve about these personal symbols for God is his unqualified approval of the symbol "spirit." "God *is* spirit. This is the most embracing, direct, and unrestricted symbol for the divine life." [93] The influence of German idealism, for which "spirit" was the ultimate reality, shows itself here as well as elsewhere[94] in Tillich's thought. Perhaps it helps to explain why he seems to prefer impersonal categories for God such as "being" to personal ones such as "will" and "intellect." This suggests that in the last analysis his world view is that of monistic idealism, which regards ultimate reality as an infinite Spiritual Life that manifests itself in finite spirits and reunites them to itself when they become estranged from it.

This raises the fundamental question whether Tillich's view of God is that of Christian theism or that of idealism. This question has been provoked not only by his reserved attitude towards personal symbols for God in the *Systematic Theology* but also by some statements in *The Courage to Be*. Speaking of the anxiety of contemporary men aroused by their sense of meaninglessness, Tillich suggests that faith

[89] Tillich, Paul: *Systematic Theology*, Vol. I, p. 244.
[90] *Ibid.*, p. 245.
[91] *Ibid.*
[92] *Ibid.*, p. 247.
[93] *Ibid.*, p. 249.
[94] *Ibid.*, Vol. III.

in the God of theism cannot give them the "courage to be," but that they can be saved from despair by embracing an "absolute faith" in an undefined God beyond the God of theism.[95] Some readers of the book have interpreted these statements to mean that Tillich himself abandoned faith in the God of theism and accepted this "absolute faith." However, he asserted that his statements about this "absolute faith" had been misunderstood as implying a pantheistic view and denied that this was his view.[96] Therefore, it is probably best to assume that he continued to the end to accept a broadly theistic view, but was deeply influenced by impersonal categories of monism such as "being." The result was a tendency to agnosticism about the cognitive value of personal symbols for God.

This tendency was strengthened by the mystical element in Tillich's thinking which is attributed to the influence of Eckhart and other mystics upon him. When he speaks about the "God beyond the God of theism," for example, one is reminded of Eckhart's distinction between *Deus,* the personal God of Christian theism, and *Deitas,* the Godhead which is above God as the heaven is above the earth.[97] The result of these monistic and mystical influences upon Tillich is that his conception of God puts in question the theistic view of Him as personal.

How should his conception of God as "being-itself" rather than "a being" be evaluated? Theists have always thought of Him as "a being," but competent theologians have never regarded Him simply as one being among other beings. Indeed, they have sought to safeguard His transcendence and otherness by negative theology, as we have seen. Therefore, although Tillich's criticism of theism at this point is useful as a corrective to the natural tendency of men to reduce God to the level of finite beings, it does not apply to the theistic conception when it is properly interpreted. Moreover, the term "being-itself," which is associated by Tillich with the term "ground of being," inevitably suggests an impersonal, if not wholly pantheistic, view, and it is an abstract metaphysical term which has no definite meaning. Since Tillich holds that all other terms applied to God are symbolic and that they are to be denied as well as affirmed, the result is that God becomes virtually unknowable. Finally, Tillich's insistence that God is not "a being" is bound up with his reluctance to use the symbol "personal God" because this seems to emphasize the individuality of God rather than His immanence and participation in all beings. But while human personality belongs to individuals, that which distinguishes it from in-

---

[95] Tillich, Paul: *The Courage to Be,* ch. 6.
[96] Tillich, Paul: *Systematic Theology,* Vol. II, p. 12.
[97] Otto, Rudolf: *Mysticism East and West,* New York, Macmillan, 1932, pp. 7, 8.

dividuality is that a person has a vast capacity to participate in other beings and values. If so, there is no reason why God's personality should be denied a capacity for universal participation. As we shall see, He can and must be conceived as a personal center of knowing and willing, but also as present and active everywhere in the world.

God as Spiritual and Personal Being

When we consider the personal attributes of the *affirmative theology*, we must bear in mind that qualities belonging to finite beings should be predicated of God only by analogy. As we have said, there are difficulties with the doctrine of analogy. But the only way to avoid the extremes of agnosticism and anthropomorphism with respect to God is to ascribe to Him by analogy the highest positive attributes known to us.

(1) Although we would reject the view of Aquinas that *"being"* is the "most proper" name for God, it is clearly the *most fundamental* name since "being" is that to which all attributes and acts are ascribed and which is therefore presupposed by them. To the theist, God is not "Being-itself," as Tillich maintains, but the Supreme Being. Of course, when we conceive of Him as a being, even the Supreme Being, there is a danger that we shall imagine Him as like other beings, especially ourselves, and hence fall into idolatry. As Matthew Arnold said, men often picture God as a "magnified non-natural man." However, it is possible to guard against this danger by the negative theology and the doctrine of analogy, as we have said, and it is probably not as serious a danger for the religious life as the Tillichian concept of God as "Being-itself," which identifies Him with the indeterminate ground of being and makes it difficult to ascribe any definite attributes to Him.

Although the assertion that God is a being is fundamental, we can determine His nature or essence only by distinguishing Him from other beings. "Being," when it is not qualified, is the most abstract and poorest of the categories, as Hegel said. Therefore, we must add that God is the *Supreme Being* and the *Highest Good*, or, as Anselm expressed it, "supremely great and supremely good." It is because He unites the greatest reality and the highest value that He is worthy of the worship and obedience of men. If He were the Supreme Being alone, He might be regarded with awe as the greatest and most powerful of all beings; it is because He is also the Highest Good that He is worthy of reverence and love. On the other hand, if He were the Highest Good alone, He might be admired and even loved; it is because He is also the Supreme Being who possesses the power to realize good and overcome evil in the lives of His creatures that He is able to fulfill His creative and redemptive functions in the world. As W. P. Montague expressed it, religion is based on the belief that "what is highest in spirit is also deepest in nature, that the ideal and the real are at least to some extent identified, not merely evanescently in our own lives but enduringly in the universe itself." [98]

(2) God is also a *Spiritual Being*. He is a Subject, a conscious being who experiences objects and can never be reduced to an object. Only by conceiving Him in this way can we avoid picturing Him as one being among other beings, located at one point in space and separate from other beings. For if He is spiritual rather than corporeal, He can be immanent in all things, creating, sustaining, and directing them to their ends. Therefore, we must conceive Him as analogous to the human spirit, i.e., as a conscious, self-determining, active being who works within the material world of space and time and uses it as a medium for the fulfillment of His purposes.

It was the greatest contribution of nineteenth-century philosophical idealists such as Hegel that they analyzed the nature of spirit, affirmed its primacy in the world, and interpreted both God and man as spiritual. Unfortunately, their insights have been almost completely lost in our time, mainly because of the dominance of naturalism and positivism, and the category of spirit is hardly mentioned in contemporary Anglo-Saxon philosophy. This is due partly to reaction against the dualistic conception of man's spirit as opposed to his body, a conception which originated with Plato and had an unfortunate influence on medieval asceticism. But it is also due to Hegel's virtual identification of God the Absolute Spirit with the human spirit, which emphasized the immanence of God at the cost of minimizing His transcendence and the gulf that separates Him from man. Therefore, although we must recover the insight of the idealists that God is spiritual and akin to the spiritual aspect of man, we must recognize the limitations of the analogy between Him and the human spirit. For man is not a pure but an embodied spirit, and spirit is only an aspect of his nature which is intimately related to biological and psychical aspects.[99] Moreover, he is a finite and imperfect being in the spiritual as well as in every other aspect of his nature. As Niebuhr says, he stands "at the juncture of nature and spirit," and the union of finiteness and freedom in him is the source of the tragedy as well as the greatness of his existence. If this is clearly understood, we can affirm once more, without falling into Platonic dualism or Hegelian monism, that "God is spirit" [100]

[98] Montague, William P.: *Belief Unbound*, New Haven, Conn., Yale University Press, 1930, p. 6.
[99] Cf. Tillich, Paul: *Systematic Theology*. Vol. III, Part IV: I, A.
[100] John 4: 24.

and as such is everywhere present and active in nature and human life.

(3) God is also a *Personal Being*. Since this has often been a source of criticism and even ridicule of the theistic conception, we must insist that it does not mean anthropomorphism. Obviously, God's personality must be different from personality as we know it in ourselves. One thing that is involved in personality is being an individual, concrete reality, and we have implied that God is an individual center of experience and activity in speaking of Him as "a Being" rather than "Being-itself." But man as an individual expresses himself through a body, is separated from other individuals by his position in space and time, and is limited in his experience by his natural and social environment. If God is perfect, He must possess the concreteness of individuality without these limitations of human individuals, but we cannot know how this is possible. Again, if God is immutable in His nature, as we have said, His character cannot admit of growth and development based upon decision and effort, although we have argued that there is change in the objects of His knowledge and the acts of His will. Above all, if God is infinite, He cannot be limited in His personal being. Whereas man is limited in all of his personal attributes and activities, God's personal attributes of knowledge, will, and love must be without internal limitations. For example, whereas man does moral evil, God is not subject to temptation or moral evil of any kind.

In these and other ways, we can see that God's personal being must *differ* substantially from our own. But we cannot know how it is *like* our own for the simple reason that we can never know God directly as we know a human person. We know each person as a concrete whole, whose aspects are integrated into greater or less unity. His body is visible to us and reveals by movements and acts something of his mind and character. We know how he thinks and feels, at least in part, from his behavior and his speech. Thus, although a person is complex and will always remain in part unknown to us, we can grasp in some measure his nature as a whole and can know many aspects of his personality and their relations to each other. This is impossible in the case of God. Since He is a spiritual being, He cannot make Himself visible to us. Hence, we can know Him only indirectly, through His effects. We can feel His presence and power as a living reality in religious experience, can be conscious of the demands of His will upon us in moral experience, and can infer something of His wisdom and purpose from our experience of natural order and historical events. But although we can know aspects of His nature in these and other ways, we cannot know directly His attributes or His personal character as a whole.

Considerations such as these have led many persons to deny that

God is personal in any meaningful sense of the term and to accept the pantheistic view that He is "impersonal." Others have affirmed that there must be something in Him which is the cause of the existence of human persons but have preferred to say that He is neither personal nor impersonal but "suprapersonal." In a previous chapter we have indicated some of the difficulties in the pantheistic view of God [101] and need not speak further of them. The view that God is "suprapersonal" is somewhat different from that view, since it is offered as a compromise between the affirmation and the negation of personality in God. But its meaning is far from clear. The idea behind it seems to be that God is not "less" but "more" than personal. If this means that He *is* personal but in a way far *superior* to human personality, it is not incompatible with the theistic view that God is personal. For theism, properly understood, affirms the personal nature of God only in an analogous sense, removing the imperfections of human personality before applying the name "personal" to Him and recognizing that attributes which are not personal, e.g., infinity, eternity, and immutability, must also be ascribed to Him. But if "God is suprapersonal" means that He is wholly *above* personality and that we must *deny* that He has personal attributes, it is virtually identical with "God is impersonal." Therefore, while the term "suprapersonal" may be useful in reminding us that all personal attributes are analogies and must be applied to God only after the imperfections of human persons have been removed from its meaning, it should never be substituted for the term "personal" in speaking of God.

What, then, does the theist mean when he calls God "personal"? He means that God manifests Himself in effects which can be explained most nearly adequately as products of intelligence and will seeking to realize purposes. Therefore, since intelligence, will, and purpose are known to us only as functions of persons, it is appropriate to ascribe personal character to God. We cannot know or even imagine *how* any of these personal attributes are present in God or *how* they are related to one another in Him. We can only ascribe them to Him after removing the imperfections that limit them in human persons and acknowledging that the wisdom and will of God the Perfect Being must be very different from those of man. When we do this, the real danger is not so much that we shall think of Him in anthropomorphic terms but that we shall evacuate these personal attributes of their usual meaning and thus destroy their value for faith and worship.

Why, it may be asked, if we cannot know precisely *how* God is personal, should we insist upon calling Him personal? The first reason

[101] Ch. 4.

is that religious experience, at least for most persons in the more advanced religions, has found impersonal conceptions of God inadequate for religious needs. It is not only the three great religions of the Middle East and West, Judaism, Christianity, and Islam, which have affirmed a personal conception of God. Although Hindu monism and certain sects of Mahayana Buddhism do not conceive the divine in personal terms, the gods of the popular Bhakti religion of Hinduism and the Buddha of an important sect of Mahayana Buddhism are worshipped as personal beings who care for and bestow grace upon their devotees. God is regarded as personal in all of these great religions because men have experienced Him not only as holy or transcendent, but also as gracious toward those who put their trust in Him. For man depends upon the aid of a Personal Being who is akin in some measure to himself, who cares for him, and whom he can trust to assist him in his quest for fullness of life. The belief that God is personal is also demanded by the logic of worship. Since worship may appropriately be directed only to a being of absolute worth, a Perfect Being, it is essential to ascribe to God the attributes which are the highest known to men, those of personality.

If the religious experience of the great theistic religions were not supported by evidence derived from other sources, its validity might be questioned on the ground that belief in a personal God is only a product of human need. But in the preceding chapter we have shown that belief in the existence of the personal God of theism is supported by independent evidence of many kinds. The intelligibility of the order of nature to human minds and the culmination of evolution in conscious persons capable of realizing values point to the existence of an intelligent and purposive Will. The unconditional demand of moral imperatives is an evidence that this Will is good and demands goodness from men. Since intelligence and will, purpose and goodness are attributes of personality, they must belong to a Being who is personal, although He must also possess nonpersonal attributes, as we have seen.

We shall not attempt to speculate on the form of the divine *intelligence* and *will* or that of the *acts* in which they manifest themselves. As we have said, we can infer the nature of God's attributes only from their effects and we cannot know how they are present in God Himself. When we try to imagine them, we inevitably picture His intelligence and will as acting from a particular position in space, even if we do not conceive of them as associated with a particular body and acting through it. If we succeed in thinking of Him as a spiritual being without such a localized body, we tend to imagine His intelligence as an impersonal ocean of consciousness that includes everything in it and His will as an impersonal stream of energy flowing into and through everything. For the limitations of our mind prevent us from conceiving how the intelligence and will of a *concrete* and *individual* being can be *universal* either in its scope or in its effects. The reason for this is not only that we associate intelligence and will with a body which limits them in both of these respects but also that we inevitably picture individual persons as separated from and excluding each other. This is a false view of the relationship between persons even at the human level, as John Macmurray has pointed out. "The more universal a person becomes in his self-transcendence, the more unique does he become in his individuality. . . . Absolute personality, in terms of our analysis, must involve absolute universality and absolute individuality at once, each of these qualities being the condition of the other. . . . The transcendence of God is His unique individuality; His immanence is His absolute universality; and these are therefore not peculiar characteristics of Deity, but the fundamental characteristics of all personality carried to their infinite limit. What is human love but the immanence of one human personality in another? Yet it does no violence to the unique individuality, the transcendence, of either." [102]

But although we know that the intelligence and will of an infinite Being must be *universal* in their scope and effects, we cannot imagine how this is possible. Aquinas seeks to explain it by asserting that God's knowledge is not discursive but grasps all things in a single intuition and that His will realizes its purpose for all things in a single act. But this is a speculative inference based upon assumptions we have questioned, e.g. that there can be no movement or change in God's knowledge or will. Again, we know that God's will must have adequate power to fulfill His purposes, but can we say with Aquinas that His will is *always* fulfilled in view of the pervasiveness of evil in the world? Must we not admit that the time and manner of their fulfillment are beyond our understanding and that even their ultimate fulfillment is a matter of faith? Thus, while the theist has adequate grounds for applying personal attributes to God if he removes imperfections from them which are incompatible with God's infinity and perfection, he cannot deduce either the form of these attributes or the mode of their expression in acts.

The Goodness and Love of God

Western theism has attributed to God not only intelligence and will but also *goodness*. Indeed, we have indicated that the God of Western theism has been conceived not only as the Supreme Reality but also as

[102] Macmurray, John, in Streeter, B. H. (ed.): *Adventure*, New York, Macmillan, 1928, pp. 193–94.

the Highest Good and the source of all the perfections or values of finite beings. The most obvious evidence for this belief is men's experience of all the good things of life, of what the Book of Common Prayer calls "the blessings of this life." In our examination of the moral argument, we pointed out that there is also evidence in men's experience of moral imperatives that God is the ultimate source of moral goodness and must possess goodness Himself. How are we to conceive of His goodness?

The difficulty of interpreting the divine goodness is illustrated by the development of Biblical conceptions of it. In the eighth century B.C., Amos asserted that God is righteous and demands righteousness of His people. Stressing the sterner side of God's goodness, he warned the Israelites that God required social justice from men and would punish those who were callous to the needs and indifferent to the rights of others.[103] In contrast, Hosea emphasized God's mercy towards His people and His willingness to forgive those who repented and turned back to Him.[104] The basis of these conceptions of God's goodness was an insight into His holiness, which the prophets interpreted as involving not only His transcendence but also His moral perfection. This insight was expressed most vividly in Isaiah's vision of God's holiness, in the presence of which he shrank back because he knew himself to be a man of unclean lips who dwelt among a people of unclean lips.[105]

Ever since these ancient prophets, Western theists have affirmed that God's goodness includes both *justice* and *mercy* and that He requires justice and mercy from His people. But the nature of the relation between His justice and His mercy has been a problem for Jewish and Christian thinkers, and the different solutions of the problem offered by them have had important implications for the related ethical problem of the relation between human justice and mercy. On the one hand, since the ancient Hebrews believed that God had entered into a covenant with them and that they had promised to obey His commandments, His justice seemed to them to require that He reward those who obeyed and punish those who disobeyed Him. Doubtless, this assumption reflected the influence of human justice, which has always sought to secure conformity to laws by sanctions of reward and punishment. But it may also have had a deeper root in men's experience that those who flaunt the moral law suffer evil consequences, whether legal punishments are inflicted upon them or not. Experience of this kind may lie behind the Hindu belief in the law of Karma, which asserts that the

[103] Amos 5:21–24.
[104] Hosea 6:6.
[105] Isaiah 6:5.

good or evil condition of a person in this life is the inevitable consequence of his acts in this and previous lives. Whatever its sources may have been, this conception of God's justice led to the view that He is a strict Judge and that men's happiness in this life and/or their salvation in the next depend upon their obedience to His will as defined in an elaborate code of laws.

On the other hand, many profoundly religious men have been dissatisfied with the view that God's goodness is primarily that of a Lawgiver and Judge and that His will can be adequately expressed in a code of laws. The ancient Hebrews believed that God had chosen them to be His people by a free decision of His will and not because they merited it. Hence, the prophets viewed His commandments as expressions of His love for His people and desire for their welfare, not as mere demands of His sovereign will. This led the greatest of them to interpret His goodness not in terms primarily of strict justice but of mercy. Thus, Hosea pictured Him as moved by compassion for His sinful people to forgive them, as a wronged husband forgives his faithless wife, on condition that they repent and turn back to Him. Jesus carries this emphasis upon God's mercy even further, picturing Him as a father who goes out to meet His prodigal son on his return home or a man who seeks a lost sheep and rejoices when he finds it.[106] He also represents God in the parable of the laborers in the vineyard as not being bound by human ideas of justice in His relations with men but as dealing with those who come late to work for Him more generously than they deserve.[107] Thus, the ancient Hebraic view that He metes out strict justice as a Judge gives way in the great prophets and in the New Testament to the view that He is above all a merciful Father who forgives His children and desires to save them from their sins rather than punish them. However, the relation between the justice and the mercy of God has continued to be a problem for Jewish and Christian thinkers. While they have usually held that His mercy transcends His justice as mercy should temper justice among men, they have also been convinced that the claims of His justice are not set aside. But they do not know and cannot know how the tension men feel between the demands of justice and mercy is overcome, as it must be, in God.

God's moral Will must not be identified with a particular code of moral rules or laws, for no code can adequately express His Will for all people and all times. Hence, it must be distinguished from man's interpretations of it in the past and the present, if His name is not to be used to sanction and support outworn moral codes of the past or

[106] Luke 15.
[107] Matthew 20:1–16.

unworthy ones of the present. Goodness as a quality of the will must be attributed to Him by analogy with man's goodness, but the imperfect moral rules and values of men must never be ascribed to Him without qualification. As transcendent and perfect in His goodness, He stands in judgment on man's good as well as his evil deeds.

Finally, since the purest form of moral goodness is that which is motivated by love and since unselfish love is the highest value known to man, theists affirm that *love* is an attribute, indeed, the highest attribute, of God. In the prophets of the Old Testament and the Gospels and Letters of the New Testament, God's love is even more fundamental than His mercy and is the motive behind it. However, like all attributes of the affirmative theology, it can be applied to God only by analogy with the highest form of love known to man. This is why the Bible speaks of God's love to man as like the love of a father for his children. "Like as a father pitieth his children, so the Lord pitieth them that fear Him." [108] The heavenly Father is perfect in His love, for "he maketh his sun to rise on the evil and on the good, and sendeth rain on the just and on the unjust." [109] However, a love like that of a father may be attributed to God only when the imperfections of human fatherhood are removed. "If ye, then, *being evil* know how to give good gifts unto your children, *how much more* shall your Father which is in heaven give good things to them that ask him?" [110]

This Biblical view of God's love is the highest and purest which has ever been conceived, and the philosopher of religion should take it seriously when he seeks to interpret the nature of God. It is true that there is much in human experience that appears to contradict the belief that God, the Supreme Reality who is the source of all things, is characterized by love. There are many things in nature which suggest that it is either indifferent or hostile to the happiness of man and the attainment of his ideals. And man's inhumanity to man and other living things, his cruelty and his callousness even toward those of his own kind, is proof to many that the ultimate reality which has produced him is heartless. In brief, the problem of natural and moral evil makes it difficult for men to believe that God loves His creatures. The theist, therefore, must face squarely the problem of evil, which has always been the greatest stumbling-block to his faith.

However, there are also many evidences, as we have shown, that the Supreme Reality is good, e.g., the natural blessings of life and the unconditional demand for moral goodness. Above all, there is the power

[108] Psalms 103:13.
[109] Matthew 5:45.
[110] Matthew 7:11, italics mine.

of love that binds men together in families and communities, seeks to break down the barriers that separate races and nations, and reconciles men to each other when they have become estranged. At the highest level, there have been men who in their relations to others have manifested unselfish love in its purest and highest form, men such as the Buddha, Jesus, St. Francis, Schweitzer, and Gandhi, men who have embodied in their lives and exemplified for others a love that has seemed human but also more than human. For whenever men have manifested an all-inclusive, unconditional, and self-giving love, it has seemed to others a channel through which a divine love was flowing toward mankind. Hence, we can ascribe no more worthy attribute to God, if we are to conceive Him as a Personal Being by analogy with the highest and best in human personality.

8

The Problem of Evil

"If God is God He is not good
If God is good He is not God,
Take the even, take the odd. . . ." [1]

What is evil? Is it real or only an appearance? If it is only an appearance, what causes it to appear and why do men regard it as a reality? If it is real, what is its nature and how is it related to good? Is there a greater quantity of good than evil or of evil than good in the world, or, if no answer can be given to that question, which is primary and which is secondary? In brief, what is the nature of evil, what is its ontological status, and what is its relation to good? Questions such as these constitute the problem of evil for the metaphysician. They are not practical questions concerning what man should *do* about evil but theoretical questions concerning what he should *think* about it.

In contrast, the engineer, the doctor, or the social reformer is concerned not with these theoretical questions but with practical questions which have to do with the causes and the prevention or elimination of particular kinds of evil. For example, since the doctor is interested in knowing the cause of a disease such as cancer and the way to deal with it, he appropriates and uses the theoretical knowledge provided by the sciences. But his aim is practical, the prevention or the removal of it.

Like the metaphysician, the philosopher of religion is concerned with the problem of evil in the theoretical sense. Although he may be interested as a man in practical problems such as the attainment of social justice, his interest as a philosopher is in the problem of the nature and status of evil in general. However, if he is also a religious believer, his interest in this problem is bound to be an existential one,

[1] MacLeish, Archibald: *J.B.*

since his concern is the attainment of fullness of life or salvation and this purpose requires the conquest of evil and not merely the explanation of it. Thus, the philosopher of religion may combine a theoretical interest in the solution of the problem of evil with a practical concern for the overcoming of evil by good.

The usual way of defining the problem of evil in Western philosophy has been to ask whether the existence of a God who is omnipotent, omniscient, and perfect is compatible with the existence of the evils we experience in nature and human life. "If God is perfect," men have said, "we would expect a world created by Him to be perfect and hence free from evil. If He possesses unlimited power and knowledge, we would expect Him to be able and to know how to create such a world. But the world as we actually experience it is burdened by many evils. Therefore, either God is not perfect and does not will to create a world without evil, or He desires such a world but lacks the power and/or the knowledge to carry out His desire." Both of these alternatives are incompatible with theism in its orthodox form, although the second is not necessarily incompatible with certain modern forms of it.

Theories of Evil: Monism, Dualism, and Theism

The problem of evil is especially acute for theism. Indeed, many would say that the pervasiveness of evil in the world rather than doubts raised by science or philosophy is the major cause of atheism and skepticism. Paradoxical as it may seem, however, one of the main sources of the appeal of theism to men has been that it has taken evil so seriously and has offered a way of deliverance from it. A comparison of the attitudes of non-theistic and theistic religious philosophies will serve to illustrate this point.

(1) *Hindu monism* is well aware, as we have noted,[2] of the existence of evil in the form of suffering, but the problem of evil as it is defined in Western religious thought does not exist in this religious philosophy. For Brahman is not conceived as a personal God who demands goodness, and good and evil alike emanate from Him (or It). How, then, could evil raise a doubt about His possession of a goodness which is not claimed for Him? The *pantheism* of Spinoza also seeks to avoid the difficulties raised by the existence of evil, as we have seen.[3] God or Nature is perfect, and, since the many things of nature are only "modes" of the divine "substance," they are all perfect. True, there are different degrees of perfection, e.g., the mouse is less perfect than the

[2] Ch. 4.
[3] Ch. 4.

angel and the murderer than the saint. But the perfection of God requires many degrees to express its fullness.

The *idealistic monism* of Hegel is closer to Spinoza's pantheism than to Hindu monism. While the "Absolute Spirit" or God is the ultimate reality, it comes to self-consciousness and realizes itself by going out of itself and into its other, thereby manifesting itself in nature and man. Thus, the ideal is the real and the real is the ideal, i.e., the ideal is realized in space and time through nature and history. But Hegel is not willing to say, with Spinoza, that everything *actual* is ideal and perfect as it is, for the Absolute is not static Substance but dynamic Spirit and manifests its perfection only as it realizes its potentialities in time. Rather, there *is* evil but it is a necessary stage in the development of the Absolute Spirit. For the finite spirit of man is estranged from the Absolute Spirit and must be reconciled to it by coming to a knowledge of its unity with the Absolute. In this way, Hegel's view avoids Spinoza's denial of the reality of evil by treating it as a stage or "moment" in the life of the Absolute Spirit which is overcoming it in time. To this extent He is influenced by the theistic view and takes evil seriously. However, he affirms in an optimistic spirit that evil is a necessary stage and is progressively overcome. The inevitable result is a complacent and conservative acceptance of the rightness of things, since they can be regarded as necessary for the self-realization of the Absolute.

We have seen that all three of these forms of monism in different ways minimize the evil in the world. In doing so, they contradict man's experience of evil as evil and accept it as necessary. If the monist says that evil is only an illusion due to the ignorance of the empirical self, we must reply that judgments of good and evil can be made only by the empirical self, that the validity of these judgments can logically be denied only if one also denies the validity of all judgments, and that this involves one in an all-engulfing skepticism. Moreover, it is fatuous to say that evil is only an appearance, since it is experienced as evil and the experience of it is real.

The practical consequence of monistic views which deny man's experience of evil as real and opposed to good is the complacent acceptance of things as they are and the refusal to struggle against them. It is notorious that Hindu monism tolerated moral and social evils such as the caste system for centuries until they were challenged by modern religious and political leaders. Paradoxically, Spinoza recommends an ethical ideal of freedom from bondage to the passions and implies that an individual can freely choose to follow that ideal and thereby attains blessedness. But the logical conclusion to be derived from his monism and determinism would be the acceptance of everything, good and evil alike, as necessary and perfect. Hegel is more consistent with his monistic theory of evil in the conservatism of his ethical and political theory. For he maintains that the individual should determine his duties not by his own conscience but according to his "station" in society and regards the state as "the Divine Idea on earth." Thus, monism logically leads to a conservative acceptance of things as they are and tends to paralyze the moral will in its struggle against evil.

(2) At the opposite extreme from monism in its attitude toward evil is *dualism*. The most striking example of this in religious history has been Zoroastrianism, the ancient Persian religion founded by the prophet Zarathustra. According to Zoroastrianism, the world is a battleground on which opposing forces of good and evil are struggling with one another. Ahura Mazda, or God, is the spiritual principle of good and is associated with light; Ahriman is the principle of evil and is associated with darkness. In the struggle, men take sides. Those who strive for truth and justice on the side of Ahura Mazda will be rewarded while those who choose evil on the side of Ahriman will be punished at the end when the dead will be resurrected and will face a last judgment. This dualism is obviously an attempt to account for the evil in the world, physical as well as moral, by attributing it to evil spiritual powers rather than to God who cannot be the author of any kind of evil. But since God is powerful as well as perfectly good, evil is not a permanent factor in the universe. The outcome of the struggle is certain: the devil will be banished, hell purged with fire, the earth renewed, and evil men after receiving punishment will be purified and restored to an eternal life of holiness.[4]

This dualistic religion had a profound influence upon the development of Jewish eschatology after the Jews came under the domination of the Persian empire, and Christianity later inherited from Judaism belief in the resurrection of the dead, the last judgment, and eternal rewards and punishments. It is easy to see why it had so much appeal. Since it does not minimize the power of evil but faces it squarely and seeks to overcome it by moral striving, it appealed especially to morally earnest men. At the same time, it gave them courage by its promise that in the end Ahura Mazda and the forces of good would triumph and Ahriman and the forces of evil would be overcome.

However, Zoroastrianism was philosophically and religiously inadequate. Men cannot be philosophically satisfied with a dualistic world view, since it asserts that there is a basic incoherence in reality, evil being an independent cosmic principle over against good. Moreover,

---

[4] Moore, G. F.: *History of Religions*, Vol. I, New York, Charles Scribner's Sons, 1948, pp. 404, 405.

the belief that Ahura Mazda is opposed throughout history by Ahriman who is independent of Him limits Him too much to be religiously satisfactory. Above all, such a dualistic conception can lead to a pessimistic idea of the world. Thus, Jewish apocalyptic literature before and during the time of Jesus pictured the world as in the power of Satan and the demons; and Manichaeanism, combining Persian dualism with Greek dualism of soul and body, viewed the material world as in bondage to the powers of darkness. In Christianity, the dualistic element which was taken over from Judaism served a religious purpose in emphasizing the power of sin and guilt in the lives of men and the necessity of divine aid to redeem them from it. But in orthodox theology it has led to serious difficulties. It has never been possible for orthodox Christian thinkers to interpret Satan and the demons in a consistent way. As monotheists they have affirmed the dependence of Satan upon God for his existence and have pictured God as consenting to his activity in tempting men to sin. On the other hand, they have had to account for the existence of an essentially evil being in God's good creation by a myth representing him as originally an angel who fell into sin through pride. Hence, he has appeared to act in complete independence of God and to challenge His sovereignty. It is not surprising, therefore, that so many Christian theologians today regard the devil and other demonic beings not as spiritual beings but as symbols of the power of evil in the personal and social life of men.

(3) The *theistic* view of evil differs from both the monistic and dualistic views. First, it acknowledges and even emphasizes the reality and gravity of evil in both its physical and its moral forms. In this respect it is strongly opposed to monism and is akin to dualism, regarding evil as a destructive power which God seeks to overcome. Indeed, orthodox Christian theism has often taken such a dark view of human sin and wickedness that many modern men have condemned it for its "pessimistic" conception of the "natural" or "unregenerate" man. But, second, it also holds that the Creation in its essence is good and that the moral evil under the burden of which man groans is not a necessity of his nature but a distortion of it due to his fall into sin. So strongly does the Book of Genesis emphasize the goodness of the Creation in the beginning that it explains even physical evils such as death, hard labor, and the pains of childbirth as a result of man's fall rather than as a part of the original nature of things. Thus, theism is as opposed to the dualistic tendency to pessimism about the world as it is to monistic optimism. It also stands in sharp contrast to early Buddhism, for the Buddha held that all existence is suffering and that the only escape from suffering is to cut the root of it in desire or craving.

Third, Biblical theism offers no philosophical *explanation* of evil and no general theological *vindication* of God's way of dealing with the world. Although it is deeply concerned with human sin, it does not usually consider God responsible for sin but puts the blame for it squarely upon man himself.[5] It is also preoccupied with the problem of suffering. Although the prophetic and historical writers of the Old Testament believed that suffering is a punishment for sin, it was difficult to square this theory with the suffering of innocent persons. When Job protests his innocence and demands an explanation of his suffering, he receives none and is rebuked by God for thinking that he has a right to demand one. Thus, although certain beliefs were expressed in the Bible with respect to the cause of sin and suffering, there was no consistent and comprehensive theory about it.

For the dominant attitude of the Biblical writers toward evil is *practical* rather than theoretical. Their concern with evil is not so much to explain it or to justify it but to be delivered from it. They are poignantly aware of the brevity of life and the certainty of death. The psalmists beseech God in times of illness to save them from death, and later the hope for a resurrection from the dead and a blessed life for the righteous is expressed.[6] But it is sin and guilt rather than death which is usually regarded as the greatest evil in the Bible. Since sin alienates man from God and invites punishment at His hands, one of the major themes of the prophets is the judgment of God upon sin and the necessity of repentance if man is to obtain mercy from Him. Thus, the Old Testament is dominated by the thought that evil is real but that God can save men from it. And the Gospel or "Good News" of the New Testament is that men suffer under the burden of sin and death, but that God has sent His own Son to redeem them from sin and to conquer death.

Theodicy: Augustine, Leibniz, Milton

Unlike the Biblical writers, many Christian theologians and philosophers have not been content to treat the existence of evil as a practical problem but have sought for a theoretical solution of it which would justify God for permitting it to exist. One of the main reasons for this has been the philosophical demand for consistency of belief. Since the pervasiveness of evil in the world seems *prima facie* to be incompatible with either the omnipotence or the goodness of God, it was inevitable

---

[5] However, there are a number of passages in both the Old and the New Testament which represent God as the cause of the sin of particular individuals and of evil in general. For example, He is said to harden Pharaoh's heart (Exodus 7:3) and to create good and evil (Isaiah 45:7).

[6] Daniel 12:1–3.

that Christian thinkers should interpret it in such a way as to show that it has a function in relation to His purpose for the world. Another reason for the development of theodicies was that belief in the goodness and even the existence of God seemed to be threatened by the suffering men have to bear and by the sin which estranges them from God and each other, so that religious faith seemed to demand some kind of solution. Finally, although the dominant attitude of the Biblical writers was a practical one, as we have pointed out, some of them had expressed beliefs which could be made the starting-point for comprehensive theories about the role of evil in the world. These philosophical and religious motives have had a strong influence upon Christian thought, especially in times when men's confidence in the power of reason has been great. Let us consider briefly a few of the theodicies which have resulted.

(1) One of the most influential is that of Augustine. After his conversion, Augustine wrote several treatises in which he refuted the errors of the Manichaeans. In *The Nature of The Good* he argued that the natures or essences of all things which God has created are good. Although men may regard as evil such creatures as spiders because they receive injuries from them, the nature of every kind of creature is good in itself and has its place, however low, in the order of creation. Evil is not a substance or thing with a reality of its own, but a privation or lack of good, *privatio boni*. For example, blindness is not a being but only the absence of sight in a being. Therefore, evil presupposes the existence of the substances to which it belongs and is parasitic upon them; and these substances have a measure of good in them as long as they exist, e.g., a disease is an evil which preys upon the body and can last only as long as the body endures and the good of life remains in it.

This conception of evil as a privation of good seems at first sight to be inconsistent with the conception of sin in Augustine's later treatises such as *The City of God*. In these treatises he asserts that sin has its origin in the pride, *superbia*, by which man turns away from love of God, *amor Dei*, to love of self, *amor sui*. Thus, sin seems to be an act which is a positive evil rather than a privation of good. But there is only a difference of emphasis rather than an inconsistency between the two views. For man's turning away from love of God to love of self involves the abandonment and loss of a higher good so that sin is a kind of privation of good. The main difference between the two views is that in the earlier treatises he is contending against the Manichaeans that the creation is good in its essence and that evil is only a distortion of it, while in the later ones he is analyzing the act by which the distortion we call sin arises in man, i.e., the defection of his will from a superior to an inferior good. As Augustine says, "the defection of the will is evil, because it is contrary to the order of nature, and an abandonment of that which has supreme being for that which has less," e.g., avarice is sinful because it involves loving gold more than justice which is incomparably better. "Consequently he who inordinately loves the good which any nature possesses, even though he obtain it, himself becomes evil in the good, and wretched because deprived of a greater good." [7]

Augustine also maintains that the opposition of contraries, including good and evil, adds to the perfection of the world, as antitheses lend beauty to a poem. This aesthetic principle requires not only that there should be smaller as well as greater bodies but also that there should be miserable as well as blessed souls. "The fact that there are souls which ought to be miserable because they willed to be sinful contributes to the perfection of the universe. . . . Because there are souls whose sins are followed by misery and souls whose righteous conduct is followed by happiness—because it contains all kinds of natures—the universe is always complete and perfect." [8]

Augustine's conception of evil as a privation of good has value as a criticism of Manichaean dualism with its pessimistic view of the creation and as an affirmation of the Biblical view that the creation in its essence is good. His assertion that natures which belong to lower levels in the scale of creation are not evil merely because they are not good in the same degree as those at higher levels is useful for the same reason. The common criticism of the "privative" view that it denies the existence of evil is not valid, since the absence of a good from a being which normally possesses it, e.g., of health from a diseased body, is itself an evil. Nevertheless, the "privative" view is misleading. It is easy to suppose that that which is not a substance or thing but only the absence of a good is not really evil. But while a physical evil such as a disease or a moral evil such as cruelty may be from the *ontological* point of view only a privation of the good of life or kindness, it is from the *valuational* point of view a positive evil, since the negation of a value is a disvalue. For this reason, the "privative" view is dangerously misleading, since it can easily be interpreted in such a way as to suggest a too optimistic view.

Indeed, when combined with the aesthetic principle that the opposition of good and evil contributes to the beauty of the world as a whole, the "privative" view led Augustine himself to attribute a perfection to the universe which seems closer to Neo-Platonism than to Christian

[7] Augustine: *City of God*, tr. by Marcus Dods, Edinburgh, T. and T. Clark, 1871, Book XII, ch. 8.

[8] Augustine: *On Free Will*, tr. by J. H. S. Burleigh in *Augustine: Earlier Writings*, Philadelphia, Westminster Press, 1953, Bk III, ch. 3, 25, 26.

theism. "You have not made the world any better," writes Austin Farrer, "in saying it is spoilt by its own anarchy and decay, rather than by adulteration with a dark element, foreign to its nature. If the milkman brings us curdled milk, we may not greatly care whether he has dropped acid into it, or simply let it turn bad; either way it is undrinkable. St. Augustine has not eased the problem of evil, or exculpated God. He has merely defended the single origin of the world. A good God created good sorts. The problem remains, why he should let them go so rotten." [9]

(2) Leibniz' *Theodicy* is the most comprehensive philosophical attempt to justify God's relation to the evil of the world which has ever been written. Although Leibniz was separated from Augustine by many centuries, he was deeply influenced by him and the effect of Augustine's privative view of evil and his aesthetic principle is apparent at many points. However, he differs from Augustine and reflects his own age in that he uses the method of philosophical rationalism in dealing with the problem. This is evident even in the syllogistic form he adopts in his "Summary" where he states and answers a number of objections to his argument. We shall consider only a few of these objections and his answers to them.

"Objection I.

"Whoever does not choose the best course is lacking either in power, or knowledge, or goodness.

"God did not choose the best course in creating the world.

"Therefore God was lacking in power, or knowledge or goodness." [10]

His answer to this objection is based upon his denial of the minor premise. In attacking this premise, Leibniz admits that there is evil in the world and that it was possible for God to have made a world without evil or not to have created a world at all. But he denies that whoever makes things in which there is evil does not choose the best, since "it is possible that the evil may be accompanied by a greater good," that "an imperfection in the part may be required for a greater perfection in the whole." [11] However, Leibniz is not content to show that "a world with evil *may* be better than a world without evil"; he attempts to prove that "this universe *must* be indeed better than every other possible universe." [12] God's perfection requires this: "it is a re-

[9] Farrer, A.: *Love Almighty and Ills Unlimited*, Garden City, N.Y., Doubleday & Co., 1961, p. 31.
[10] Leibniz, G. W.: *Theodicy*, tr. by E. M. Huggard, London, Routledge and Kegan Paul, 1952, "Summary of the Controversy Reduced to Formal Arguments," Obj. I., p. 577.
[11] *Ibid.*, p. 378.
[12] *Ibid.*, italics mine.

sult of the supreme perfection of the Sovereign of the Universe that the kingdom of God should be the most perfect of all states or governments possible, and that in consequence what little evil there is should be required to provide the full measure of the vast good existing there." [13] From this statement it is clear that Leibniz' extremely optimistic view, which is well expressed by his reference to "what little evil there is," does not depend upon empirical evidence; it depends upon reasoning from what he takes to be self-evident premises such as the *perfection* of God.

The details of his elaborate proof that this must be the best of all possible worlds and therefore that the evil in it must be accompanied by a greater good we need not consider. We shall only illustrate his rationalistic method by reference to a few of his answers to objections.

"Objection II.

"If there is more evil than good in intelligent creatures, there is more evil than good in all God's work.

"Now there is more evil than good in intelligent creatures.

"Therefore there is more evil than good in all God's work." [14]

Leibniz denies both the major and the minor premises of this syllogism concerning intelligent creatures. He denies the major on the ground that, even if there were a surplus of evil over good in *intelligent* creatures, the surplus of good over evil in *nonintelligent* ones might compensate for and even exceed it.[15] He denies the minor, i.e., that there is more evil than good in intelligent creatures, on the ground that "the glory and perfection of the blessed may be incomparably greater than the misery and imperfection of the damned," although the blessed are smaller in number than the damned.[16] Finally, even if it should be admitted that there is more evil than good in *mankind,* it would not follow that there is more evil than good in *all* intelligent creatures, since there is "an inconceivable number of Spirits of many different kinds in the whole City of God." [17] In this answer to the objection, Leibniz offers no empirical evidence whatever to show that there actually *is* a surplus of good over evil in nonintelligent creatures or that, if there is such a surplus, it exceeds the surplus of evil over good there may be in intelligent ones; he only says that it "may" be so. Moreover, he simply *assumes* the orthodox Christian belief in an eternal life for the blessed in heaven and for the damned in hell as well as the existence of many different kinds of angelic Spirits

[13] *Ibid.,* Obj. II., p. 380.
[14] *Ibid.,* p. 379.
[15] *Ibid.*
[16] *Ibid.*
[17] *Ibid.,* p. 380.

in heaven. Finally, his argument that there is a surplus of good over evil even among mankind when one compares the good of the blessed with the misery of the damned in the after life is nothing but an unsupported speculation.

Objection IV asserts that, since God could prevent the sin of intelligent creatures but does not do so and rather contributes to it, He is an "accessory" to it, i.e., partially responsible for it.[18] Leibniz answers that God could not prevent sin without acting unreasonably. Making use of a distinction by Aquinas, he argues that, although God wills by His "antecedent" will that men sin not, He permits them to sin by His "consequent" or "final" will for "superior reasons."[19] The "consequent" will, he says, "tends towards the production of as many goods as can be put together, whose combination thereby becomes determined and involves also the permission of some evils and the exclusion of some goods, as the best possible plan of the universe demands."[20] There are two related difficulties with this answer. The first is based upon the fact that, according to Leibniz, God predetermined the whole future career of every substance when He created it, which implies that He predetermined the acts of every human being. If so, those who sin were predetermined to do so when they were created, so that it is misleading to speak only of God's "permission" of sin. Hence, He cannot be absolved from responsibility for their sin, or, as Leibniz expresses it, from being "accessory" to it. The second difficulty is that, although Leibniz asserts that God willed to create sinners for "superior reasons," he gives no indication whatever of the nature of the reasons. It is probable that he has in mind the aesthetic principle asserted by Augustine, i.e., that the presence of evil as the contrary of good enhances the perfection of the world. But whatever his reasons, it is difficult to see how they could justify God in creating men predetermined by Him to sin and therefore doomed to eternal damnation. For Him to do so would be to treat persons not as ends in themselves but as means to the beauty or perfection of the universe, which would be incompatible with their intrinsic worth and the love of God for them.

In his answer to Objection V, Leibniz makes use of the Augustinian principle that evil is only a privation of good and requires no "efficient" cause but only a "deficient" one. Augustine had written that the cause of an evil will "is not efficient, but deficient, as the [evil] will itself is not an effecting of something, but a defect," "a defection from that

---

[18] Obj. IV, p. 382.
[19] *Ibid.*, p. 383.
[20] *Ibid.*

which supremely is, to that which has less of being." [21] With this principle in mind, Leibniz answers the objection that "God is the cause of sin." While God is the cause of all perfections, he asserts, "limitations or privations result from the original imperfection of creatures which restricts their receptivity." [22] The implication is that the original imperfection of men, not God, is the cause of their sin. "It is as with a laden boat, which the river carries along more slowly or less slowly in proportion to the weight that it bears: thus the speed comes from the river, but the retardation which restricts this speed comes from the load." [23] This seems a plausible answer to the objection that God is the cause of sin until one remembers that God created all creatures including their imperfections. Therefore, He is responsible not only for the good they possess (corresponding to the "speed" from the river) but also for the privation of good in them (corresponding to the "retardation" from the load). This is clear from Leibniz' admission that God "does not give it [the soul] all the good that would overcome its evil," because to do so He would have had to produce new natures in His creatures or miraculously change their natures and "this the best plan did not allow." [24] Apparently, the reason the best plan did not allow it was an aesthetic one: "There are some disorders in the parts which wonderfully enhance the beauty of the whole, just as certain dissonances, appropriately used, render harmony more beautiful." [25] Thus, Leibniz' answer to the objection that God is the cause of sin is similar to his answer to the preceding objection, i.e. that God created men with the imperfection or privation of good which is the source of their sin but that He was justified in doing so because "the best plan" for the world required it. The idea that sin is only an imperfection or privation of good and requires no efficient cause as perfections do offers an escape from the charge that God is its cause, but it is only a verbal escape. For Leibniz admits that God could have created men without the imperfection or privation which constitutes their sin if "the best plan" had allowed it.

Perhaps this critical examination of a few of Leibniz' arguments is sufficient to illustrate his rationalistic method and to uncover some of the fatal weaknesses in his reasoning: (i) We have shown that his arguments are not based primarily upon empirical evidence but upon logical reasoning from premises which are far from self-evident and

[21] Augustine: *The City of God*, Bk. XII, ch. 7.
[22] Leibniz, G. W.: *Theodicy*, Obj. V, p. 384.
[23] *Ibid.*
[24] *Ibid.*
[25] *Ibid.*, p. 385.

are often arbitrary. This completely vitiates his attempt to prove that there is a surplus of good over evil in intelligent beings and in the world as a whole. (ii) We have also pointed out that his attempt to answer the objections that God is an "accessory" to and even the "cause" of sin in men is based upon an uncritical acceptance of Augustine's aesthetic principle that evil contributes to the harmony of the world by its opposition to good and therefore is required by "the best plan" for the whole. This results in the reduction of the man who sins to nothing more than a part of the whole whose good is sacrificed to the beauty of perfection of the whole. (iii) Finally, we have brought to light the basic assumption of determinism which underlies his arguments, i.e., that God created each substance in the world with its imperfections and predetermined its whole future development. This implies that God is responsible for man's sin, and Leibniz' attempt to escape from this objection by asserting that sin has no "efficient" cause is only verbal.

These weaknesses do not necessarily invalidate Leibniz' main thesis that the evil in the world may be accompanied by a greater good, but they do show that his attempt to demonstrate rationally that this *must* be the case is a failure. It is not surprising, therefore, that Voltaire in his *Candide* poured scorn upon the *Theodicy* as a product of blind optimism which was contradicted by the many evils in the world.

(3) Finally, we shall consider briefly a theodicy which differs radically from the theodicies of Augustine and Leibniz and which was written by one who was neither a theologian nor a philosopher but a poet: John Milton's *Paradise Lost*. Milton's justification of God's ways to man is concerned almost exclusively with the moral evils resulting from disobedience to God's will and with the terrible consequence of that disobedience in suffering. Natural evils such as death and the discord between animal species are explained as effects of man's sin, as in the account of the fall of man in the Book of Genesis. One of the main limitations of Milton's theodicy is his failure to consider the problem of natural evil apart from moral evil, for it is impossible for a modern theist to explain it as only a consequence of sin. Despite this limitation, *Paradise Lost* is one of the greatest theodicies produced in the West and is free from some of the errors we have noted in Augustine and Leibniz.

Milton's treatment of moral evil centers upon three closely related questions: What was the *origin of sin* and the suffering that follows it in a world which was created good? What was the *response of God* to sin? What are the *possibilities* which are open to man after his sin and in the light of God's response to it? A clear and unambiguous answer to the first of these questions was important, Milton thought, because a vindication of God's ways with man required that the responsibility for man's sin should be placed squarely upon man himself. Although Milton was a Puritan, he agreed with Plato that God is the cause of good but not of evil and with the New Testament that God loves all men and desires their salvation. Consequently, he affirms unequivocally that God did not will that man should sin but created him free and able to stand or fall by his own choice. Satan fell, self-tempted; Eve fell, tempted by Satan; Adam fell, tempted by Eve; but all three fell by their own free choice and were without excuse. Therefore, God was in no way responsible for their sin or for the long train of natural and moral evils which followed it.

What was God's response to man's fall? Milton represents God as foreknowing that Adam and Eve would fall into disobedience when tempted by Satan and would thereby deserve eternal punishment at His hands. But because of His love for man His mercy triumphs over His justice and He takes counsel in His heavenly court as to how He can save men from their sin and its terrible consequences. Christ, His Son, offers to descend to the earth as His Messiah at the appointed time and suffer death to atone for men's sin. The Father gladly consents to this plan for the salvation of men because it fully accords with His own desire. Thus, the response of God to man's disobedience even before it occurred was a determination to redeem him from his sin and misery. The significance of this for Milton's theodicy is obvious: not only is God not responsible for sin and should not be blamed for it, but also His attitude towards it is characterized by mercy and His purpose from the beginning has been to deliver men from its power and the punishment it deserves. It has often been pointed out that Milton does not succeed as a poet in expressing vividly and movingly the love of God and Christ toward man. But there is no doubt that he meant to emphasize it.

The third question concerning man's possibilities after the fall is closely related to the second, since the possibilities which are open to man depend upon God's response of mercy and His purpose to redeem men from their sin. After a period of self-pity and mutual recrimination following their disobedience, Adam and Eve repent and beg God for forgiveness. They are shown in a vision the evil consequences of their sin in the lives of their descendants, but are also told of God's plan to redeem men from it. If men repent, they will receive God's grace, be able to obey His will with His help, and be saved. When Adam and Eve see both the consequences of evil and the possibilities of good which will result from their sin, they are filled with remorse and sorrow for the evil their sin will bring into the world, but they are struck with wonder and gratitude at God's love in offering redemption to their posterity. When they contemplate first the greatness of their offense and then the immensity of God's love and grace, the belief arises within them that perhaps their fall was a fortunate one, since it was to issue in such happy consequences for those who would repent and be restored to obedience.

> O goodness infinite, goodness immense!
> That all this good of evil shall produce,
> And evil turn to good; more wonderful
> Then that which by creation first brought forth
> Light out of darkness! full of doubt I stand,
> Whether I should repent me now of sin
> By me done and occasioned, or rejoyce
> Much more, that much more good thereof shall spring,
> To God more glory, much more good will to Men
> From God, and over wrauth grace shall abound.[26]

The paradox that is expressed in these lines has perplexed the minds of theologians, and Milton scholars are not in agreement on Milton's own solution of it. If so much good has come from evil that there is more glory to God and more good will toward men than before, it would seem that the fall was in the end good. "The Adam who has sinned and through effort risen again," writes Allan Gilbert, "is 'happier far' than the sinless Adam of the garden. The nature of man was, it is true, originally good and pure, but the wisdom of human experience, and the excellence gained through suffering are still better." [27] In any case, when Adam and Eve are expelled from the Paradise they have lost, they can face their future and the future of their posterity with sorrow but also with hope. For God in His mercy has set before them the possibility of attaining a "Paradise within" which is "happier far" than the Paradise they have lost.

In evaluating Milton's theodicy, it is important to bear in mind that he was not a philosopher but a poet and that he expressed his intuitions in Biblical terms which are mythological in character. Clearly, one of his greatest contributions is his complete repudiation of the theological determinism which seemed to make God responsible for moral evil. In his insistence that man is responsible for his own sin, he was deeply influenced by the emphasis of Renaissance Humanism upon the dignity of man which is bound up with his freedom, but he was also in accord with the dominant Biblical view. It must be said that God permits moral evil, since He must have foreseen that man would fall when He created him free to stand or fall. But to give him freedom to

[26] Milton, John: *Paradise Lost*, XII, 469–478.
[27] Gilbert, Allan: "The Problem of Evil in Paradise Lost," J.E.G.P., XXII, 1923, pp. 186, 187.

fall and thus to permit him to sin is not the same as to predetermine
that he would sin because the divine plan for the best of all possible
worlds required it (Leibniz) or to will that, when he had sinned, saving
grace would be given to some but denied to others (Augustine and
Calvin). Moreover, Milton never attempts to justify the moral evils
which actually exist on the ground that they are a necessary condition
of moral goodness; he simply asserts that God created men free and
capable of choosing between moral good and evil because a forced
obedience to His will would have had no worth.

> Freely they stood who stood, and fell who fell
> Not free, what proof could they have given sincere
> Of true allegiance, constant Faith or Love,
> Where only what they needs must do appeared,
> Not what they would? What praise could they receive?
> What pleasure I from such obedience paid,
> When Will and Reason (Reason is also choice)
> Useless and vain, of freedom both despoil'd,
> Made passive both, had served necessitie,
> Not me.[28]

The other contribution of Milton's theodicy is implicit in his
answers to the second and third questions concerning God's response
to man's sin and the possibilities open to man after his sin. Despite
the fact that man is responsible for his own sin and that God's justice
in punishing him cannot be impugned, God's attitude is not that of
the stern Judge who is determined to exact punishment from him in
accordance with strict justice but that of the merciful Father who
sends His own Son to atone for man's sin by suffering on his behalf
and who forgives him on condition of repentance. Thus, God does not
stand apart and aloof from man's sin and suffering. He has not only
shown Himself ready to forgive him, He has also acted in history
through His Son to redeem mankind from sin and has bestowed His
grace on men to help them break its power and restore them to
obedience. Thus, God overrules the evil of man and brings good out
of it, so that in his struggle with sin and suffering he has the possibility
of attaining a higher moral and spiritual state than that which he
enjoyed in the innocence of his lost Paradise. The importance of this,
of course, is that any "solution" of the problem of evil which is to be
adequate must not only vindicate God's justice in permitting evil in
the world, but also show that man need not be overwhelmed by it but
can face it with courage since God is with him in the struggle to overcome it.

[28] *Ibid.*, III, 101 ff.

Natural Evil

Any modern attempt to deal with the problem of evil must begin by distinguishing natural and moral evils. *Natural* evils are those which do not belong to the acts and dispositions of human wills. Many of them result from natural causes which operate according to general laws, e.g., earthquake, famine, flood, pestilence, and death. These evils bring pain and suffering upon both animals and men, so that the problem of natural evil is one of the major forms of the problem of evil. In contrast, *moral* evils are those which arise from men's free choices and are expressions of their evil wills.

Although the distinction between these two kinds of evil is clear enough, confusion often arises because of their relations to one another. Although natural evils usually result from natural causes, some of them are also partly caused by human acts or failures to act and moral factors are involved in them. For example, floods are caused by heavy rains and rapidly melting snow, but in some cases they could have been avoided by building higher and stronger dikes or by diverting the water in rivers from their usual courses. A stomach ailment is the effect of physiological causes, but these may have been affected by overeating. And a famine of grain is due to the failure of fields to produce an adequate supply, but a change in methods of farming might have avoided it. In ways such as these, human acts which have a moral aspect are partial causes of many natural evils. On the other hand, natural causes are often among the conditions, even if they are not the sufficient causes, of moral evils, e.g., a chemical deficiency or brain injury may be one of the conditions of moral irresponsibility and acute hunger may tempt a man to steal.

Although these relations between natural and moral evils make the problem of evil more complex, it is highly important to distinguish them from one another because they raise different problems which must be dealt with in different ways. When the distinction has not been clearly made, serious errors have resulted. Perhaps the most serious of these errors has been the attempt to explain all adversity and suffering as a *punishment* for sin and wickedness. The retributive theory of suffering was rejected explicitly in the Book of Job and implicitly in the Gospel of Luke. Although it is true that moral evil is sometimes one of the causes of natural evil, as we have just said, there is no evidence that there is always a causal connection between them. Despite this, the tendency to explain natural calamities as divine punishments for sin has been strong. The most famous case was the Lisbon earthquake which killed thousands of people and provoked

Voltaire in *Candide* to satirize the assertion of Leibniz that this is the best of possible worlds. In Camus' *The Plague* a priest preaches a sermon in which he explains the frightful plague that is striking down the inhabitants of the city as a punishment for their wickedness. Apart from the fact that usually no causal connection can be shown between such natural calamities and moral evils, the fallacy in the retributive theory is that a calamity such as an earthquake or plague does not discriminate between the wicked and the innocent among its victims. It also assumes that God deliberately wills natural calamities and the sufferings they bring with them, an assumption we shall have occasion to question.

(1) Other thinkers have attempted to explain human pain and suffering as a *means* to higher good. There is obviously much truth in this view. It is well known that pain and suffering often give rise to moral virtues such as fortitude, patience, sympathy, and kindness. "One reason, plainly, why God permits suffering," writes Fr. G. H. Joyce, "is that man may rise to a height of heroism which would otherwise have been altogether beyond his scope. Nor are these the only benefits which it confers. That sympathy for others which is one of the most precious parts of our experience, and one of the most fruitful sources of well-doing, has its origin in the fellow-feeling engendered by the endurance of similar trials." [29] Also, pain has value as a stimulus to the activities which have made civilization and cultural achievements possible. "The advance of scientific discovery, the gradual improvement of the organization of the community, the growth of material civilization—all these are due in no small degree to the stimulus afforded by pain." [30]

However, recent philosophers have emphasized the limitations of this attempt to justify pain and suffering. Distinguishing between the "first order evil" of suffering or pain, on the one hand, and "second order evil" such as moral evil and "second order good" such as moral virtue, on the other, J. L. Mackie criticizes the view that "first order evil" is a necessary condition of "second order good" and that its value in this respect outweighs the suffering it involves.[31] One of the difficulties in this view, he says, is that it seems to imply that God is not sympathetic with human suffering, since He does not minimize it but uses it to promote "second order good." [32] Yet there is an immense

[29] Joyce, G. H.: *Principles of Natural Theology*, London, Longman's Green, 1923, p. 595.

[30] *Ibid.*, 597.

[31] Mackie, J. L.: "Evil and Omnipotence" in *God and Evil*, ed. by Nelson Pike, Englewood Cliffs, N.J., Prentice-Hall, 1964, pp. 53, 54.

[32] *Ibid.*, p. 54.

amount of suffering in the world, and we regard the relief of suffering by men as a duty and indifference to it as an evidence of moral callousness. Another difficulty is that, while suffering sometimes leads to "second order good," it sometimes leads to "second order evil," e.g., painful and prolonged disease may lead to self-pity and resentment or physical punishment to hatred.[33]

H. J. McCloskey also points out that it is not certain that the physical evil of pain plus the "higher order good" it produces is better than the natural good of pleasure plus the "second order good" it produces. "The theist's argument" he says, "is seen to imply that war plus courage plus the many other moral virtues war brings into play are better than peace and its virtues; that famine and its moral virtues are better than plenty; that disease and its moral virtues are better than health." [34] But "first order goods" such as those of peace, plenty, and health also bring into play "second order goods," and "first order evils" such as war and disease lead to "second order evils" or moral vices in others. "No one can be sure beforehand," says Farrer, "how a man's character will be affected by the trials he undergoes. Tom's business disappointments may not make him gentle, they may make him morose. So Tom, in turn, becomes a trial to his mother and his wife. These women, perhaps, rise to the level of their opportunities and edify the old ladies by an exemplary cheerfulness. But then, again, they may not. The whole family, a prey to ill-temper and mutual irritation, becomes a trial to the neighborhood. It will be admirable if it brings out the best in the neighbors; but very likely it brings out the worst. . . . Good, even animal good, such as physical health or a moderate plenty, is a more fertile breeder of good on the whole—yes, even of moral good —than distress of any kind can be. Were it otherwise, we should be faced with an intolerable dilemma. We should be bound to fear that in consulting our friends' natural happiness, we should be imperiling their spiritual salvation." [35]

The conclusion we must draw is that, while some natural evils do enrich the world by the "second order goods" such as moral virtues they stimulate, others give rise to "second order evils." Also, it cannot be shown that the sum of natural evils plus "second order goods" stimulated by them is greater than the sum of natural goods plus "second order goods" stimulated by them would have been. Hence, it is far from certain that the immense amount of natural evil in human life is outweighed by the amount of "second order good" it produces.

(2) This conclusion is supported by the fact that there is much suf-

[33] *Ibid.*, p. 54.
[34] McCloskey, H. J.: in *God and Evil, op. cit.*, p. 75.
[35] Farrer, *op. cit.*, pp. 147, 148.

fering in the world which has no relation to "second order goods" such as moral virtues and cultural values. Above all, this is the case with *animal pain*. According to Aquinas, God wills that the lion's prey should die in order that the lion may survive. However, there are difficulties with this view. It seems to rest upon the assumption that the life of the lion is a higher good than that of its victim, whereas all that is certain to us is that the lion is stronger than its victim. Moreover, it raises the question why it was necessary, if God is omnipotent, for Him to create animal species which must depend upon killing other animals in order to survive. In this struggle for existence man is involved no less than lower animals. One of the most unforgettable passages in Melville's *Moby Dick* is the "sermon" rebuking the sharks which were feeding off the carcass of a whale attached to the ship. Coming from a member of the crew of a whaling ship, it is an ironical reminder that man preys upon the fishes as they prey upon each other. When one considers this preying of animal species upon each other, one must admit that the "first order evil" of human suffering which can be justified as a means to "second order goods" such as moral virtue is only a part of the total amount of "first order evil" in the world.

It has often been pointed out that the suffering of animals has an important *biological function,* as a warning against danger and a stimulus to effort, and therefore is not an unmitigated evil. "To cut the matter short," says Farrer, "we may boldly say that pain, and the remedial action which normally springs from it, are as vital as any functions of animal consciousness. Without them no living species above the most elementary would have the slightest chance of survival. . . . Pain, being the grip of a harm the creature has failed to shun, *enforces the heed* that was lacking, or *evokes the effort* that was unexerted." [36] Another function of animal pain, at least in some species, is to *awaken compassion* for the sufferer in others of its kind. "The suffering is felt to be a common evil; and as it moves the sufferer to get rid of the cause in himself, so it moves the kindred to get rid of it for him. . . . If there were no pain, no compassion would be excited, and the creature would lose a valuable source of succor in harm or danger." [37] However, animal pain serves these useful biological functions only on the whole, since pain that does not stop when it is ineffective is useless. "If the animal body is injured, it hurts, and the hurt animal fights. It does not know that the fight will be vain. . . . Yet the pain the animal feels in being mauled, when it is destined to be devoured, is just as useless as the pain of disease, under which it is

[36] Farrer, *op. cit.,* p. 80, italics mine.
[37] *Ibid.,* pp. 92, 93.

destined to succumb." [38] Thus, while we can discern the biological usefulness of animal pain in general, much of it seems useless and the amount of it excessive.

We cannot even prove with certainty that there is a *surplus of pleasure* over pain in animal life as a whole. Even if a man could experience all of the pleasures and pains experienced by an animal throughout its life, he could not determine by a hedonistic calculus whether its pleasures outweighed its pains, since there is no fixed unit of pleasure by which he could measure the different kinds and degrees of pleasure it experienced. Despite this lack of mathematical proof, Farrer maintains that the goods must exceed the evils experienced by an animal while it lives, for "while the animal survives, it is successful rather than the reverse" and "survival normally carries certain satisfactions such as opportunities of mating and palatable food to eat." [39] To the objection that animals do not survive for long, he replies that "the hand of death falls for the most part with merciful swiftness on the animal creation." [40] And although most animals do not reach maturity, they enjoy life while they have it and do not know it will be short.[41] William Temple also points out that it is possible for sensitive persons to exaggerate the evil involved in animal pain, for there is no evidence that animals remember pains they have suffered or anticipate with dread the pains and death that are to come.[42]

While this may be true, it *mitigates* rather than *removes* the problem of animal pain. If God's omnipotence is interpreted as meaning that He is the direct cause of everything that happens, including all the particular evils from which animals suffer, it is difficult to justify the vast amount of pain, conflict, and waste in animal life. This leads us to raise the question whether God's relation to natural evils may be interpreted by theists in a different way.

(3) One of the most striking features of recent philosophy of religion is that a number of philosophers such as F. R. Tennant have developed a theory of God's relation to natural evils which differs radically from the orthodox one. According to Tennant, animal suffering is an essential and unavoidable condition of organic evolution. It not only is a warning against danger, as we have seen, but also "renders unnecessary a large amount of inheritance of specialized structure and function and so prevents the suppression of plasticity." [43] Human suffering is

[38] *Ibid.*, p. 82.
[39] *Ibid.*, pp. 74, 76.
[40] *Ibid.*, p. 76.
[41] *Ibid.*, p. 77.
[42] Temple, William: *Nature, Man and God*, London, Macmillan, 1951, pp. 359–360.
[43] Tennant, F. R.: *Philosophical Theology*, Cambridge, University Press, Vol. II, p. 199.

also essential because a physical order characterized by law or regularity is a necessary condition of the moral order. "Without such regularity in physical phenomena," says Tennant, "there could be no probability to guide us: no prediction, no prudence, no accumulation of ordered experience, no pursuit of premeditated ends, no formation of habits, no possibility of character or culture. Our intellectual faculties would not have developed . . . while our nobler feelings would have been unable to prevent the ascendancy of the lower instincts, and our active powers would have abandoned themselves to purposeless agitation." [44]

Now, we cannot have the advantages of a determinate order of things characterized by uniformity or constancy without the disadvantages accompanying it. But we do not need to think that these disadvantages are directly willed by God as particular means to particular ends. Rather, the law-abidingness of nature, which is a necessary condition of the moral order, gives rise to natural evils by virtue of the inherent properties of things, e.g., the properties which enable water to bestow benefits upon the world of living organisms, including men, also give it the capacity to drown us.[45] "Mere determinateness and fixity of nature," says Tennant, "involve such and such concatenations of qualities, and rule out others. Thus physical ills follow with the same necessity as physical goods from the determinate 'world-plan' which secures that the world be a suitable stage of intelligent and ethical life." [46]

It might be objected against this view that the general regularity of nature could normally be maintained by God but overriden by His omnipotence when harm would result from it. But this would overlook the fact that God's exercise of His power is limited by the determinateness of His nature and purpose which requires constancy and consistency in His activity. If God intervened with miracles to save men whenever they were threatened by an earthquake or pestilence, He would do so at the cost of renouncing the natural order which is the basis of the moral order. "But the general suspension of painful events, requisite on the vast scale presupposed in the elimination of physical ills, would abolish order and convert a cosmos into an unintelligible chaos in which anything might succeed anything." [47]

According to this view, God should not be regarded as the direct cause of natural evils which affect animal and human life. Therefore, it is unnecessary to suppose that every form of suffering such as cancer is willed by God as a means to some particular end, or that the birth

[44] *Ibid.*, pp. 199, 200.
[45] *Ibid.*, p. 201.
[46] *Ibid.*, p. 201.
[47] *Ibid.*, p. 202.

of an imbecile or insane person is an act of particular providence, or, worst of all, that the distribution of human ills is due to a divine plan by which particular sufferings are adjusted to the needs and circumstances of particular sufferers.[48] If God has bestowed upon the world a sort of "delegated autonomy," as Tennant holds, we do not have to believe that God has willed these and other afflictions as such or for any purpose. "They are rather inevitable, if incidental, accompaniments or by-products of the world-order, which, as a whole, and by means of its uniformity, is a pre-requisite of the actualisation of the highest good that we can conceive a world as embodying." [49]

The great advantage of this interpretation of natural evils is that it is consistent, as the orthodox interpretation of them as directly willed by God is not, with the *goodness* of God. As we have seen, deterministic theodicies which assume that God's will is the cause of everything that happens must maintain that every particular evil is necessary for the divine plan and contributes to the perfection of the world. In contrast, Tennant's interpretation makes God responsible for the regularity of the natural order as a necessary basis of the moral order but does not require us to affirm that particular natural evils are a part of the divine plan or that the world that contains them is the best of possible worlds. The crucial question is whether such an interpretation saves God's goodness at the cost of His *omnipotence* and the efficacy of His will. The answer one gives to this question will depend upon what he takes "omnipotence" to mean when attributed to God. If one takes it to mean that God's power is limited in its exercise by nothing, not even by His own nature and unchanging purpose for the world, one will doubtless think that it is denied. But if one takes it to mean that God has adequate power to do whatever is required by and consistent with His nature and purpose for the world, one may think that it is affirmed. For Him to create natural beings with definite properties and to give them the power to act constantly in accordance with these properties in order to carry out His purpose is to limit His exercise of His power but only in order to give effect to His will.

Perhaps the main difficulty with Tennant's view is not that it involves a limitation of God's power by His purpose but that it seems to reduce the function of the natural order to that of a means to the moral development of man. If this is really his view, it implies an *anthropocentric* conception of God's purpose for nature which is too narrow. Although man may well be the culmination of the evolutionary process up to the present time and moral goodness may well be the highest value it has attained, there is no reason to suppose that

[48] *Ibid.*, p. 203.
[49] *Ibid.*, p. 204.

God has no other purpose for the natural order than to provide a suitable environment for the realization of moral personality by man. It is much more probable that the existence of every species of creatures, especially living organisms, has an intrinsic worth and a place of its own in the divine purpose. This does not mean that it may not also exist for the sake of man and his moral development, for the many species of creatures are interrelated and serve each other's needs. But it does mean that the meaning and value of every species is partly to be found in its own life and that it is never a mere means to human ends. Indeed, Tennant himself seems to assert a similar view when he inquires into the purpose of the world-process as a whole, for he does not claim that man is "the highest being under God, or the final stage of progressive cosmic evolution, or the end and the whole end of the cosmic design," or that "lower creatures evolved in the world-process are necessarily of but instrumental value as stages or means to ends" and "mere by-products in the making of humanity." [50]

We have pointed out that (a) *animal* pain has a necessary biological function and that animals seem to realize value in their lives. On the other hand, (b) much of their pain seems to be biologically useless, we cannot know whether pleasures outweigh pains in their experience, and the lives of most of them are short. We have also argued that (c) while the natural ("first order") evils suffered by *men* often give rise to moral ("second order") goods, it is impossible to justify all of them in this way. Hence, (d) if God is assumed to be omnipotent in the traditional sense and to be the direct cause of all natural evils, it is possible at best to mitigate the problem of natural evil but not to solve it. However, (e) natural evils may be viewed not as directly willed by God but as *incidental effects* of the regular working of the natural order which is necessary for the evolution of life and the moral development of man. Although this view involves a reinterpretation of the orthodox idea of God's omnipotence, it is more consistent with His goodness.

Moral Evil

The problem of moral evil is related to the problem of natural evil, as we have seen, but it raises difficulties of its own which must be dealt with separately. The problem may be stated as follows: if God is good, why did He create men who have been guilty of so much moral evil and as a result have brought so much misery upon themselves and others? We have pointed out that orthodox theodicies failed to give an adequate answer to this question because of their deterministic concep-

[50] *Ibid.*, pp. 113, 114.

tion of God's relation to men. For example, the Augustinian view that
God's eternal punishment of the reprobate is a manifestation of His
justice cannot be defended when one remembers Augustine's view that
God could have saved them by His irresistible grace; and the Leibnizian
view that God's choice of the best of possible worlds required the creation of men predetermined by Him to sin is inconsistent with His
goodness. For this reason, many modern theists have rejected such
orthodox theodicies as incompatible with the Biblical view that man
rather than God is responsible for moral evil. They have agreed with
Milton's view that God endowed men with freedom of will so that they
were free to stand or fall. When the question has been raised why He
created them with a freedom which could be used to produce moral
evil, modern theists have usually replied that such a freedom was
necessary if men were to obey God without being determined to do so.
For only a goodness which was freely chosen when one *could* choose
to do evil instead would be truly moral goodness. What are we to
think of this modern view of moral evil?

That it is not without its difficulties is shown by the fact that a
number of recent philosophers have attacked it vigorously.

(1) J. L. Mackie has questioned the assumption that freedom of will
must be accompanied by the possibility of moral evils. Why could not
God have made men who would act freely but always choose the good?
To the objection that the possibility of making wrong choices is logically necessary if there is to be freedom, he replies that this is the case
only if freedom means "complete randomness or indeterminacy" with
regard to the choice between good and evil. God, he says, could have
made men's characters such that they would always have chosen the
good. Their choices would then have been free in the only acceptable
sense of "free," since they would have arisen from their characters.[51]

In our opinion, this argument is not valid. If God had created men
with characters such that they would always have chosen the good,
their acts would have been determined by Him and they would have
had no freedom of choice. Mackie's view that human acts could have
been determined by God and still be free seems to rest on the assumption that freedom would be compatible with determinism if our acts
were determined by our own characters as created by God. But if God
had made creatures such that they would always have chosen the good,
they would not have been men and they would not have been free;
they would have been puppets. The alternative to this deterministic
view is not freedom in the sense of "randomness" or "indeterminacy,"
as Mackie asserts. Freedom does not mean indeterminism, for human
acts as well as natural events have causes. It means the capacity of the

[51] Mackie, *op. cit.*, p. 56.

self to determine its acts in accordance with its own ideals and purposes and at times to transcend its present character in doing so.[52]

(2) Mackie also sees a difficulty in the idea that God can control men's wills, i.e., determine them to choose good, but *refrains* from doing so. "But why, we may ask, should God refrain from controlling evil wills? Why should he not have men free to will rightly, but intervene when he sees them beginning to choose wrongly? If God could do this but does not, and if he is wholly good, the only explanation could be that even a wrong free act of will is not wholly evil, that its freedom is a value which outweighs its wrongness, so that there would be a loss of value if God took away the wrongness and the freedom together." [53] But we must assert that freedom which was limited in this way would not be freedom at all, since for God to "leave men free to will rightly but to intervene when he sees them beginning to act wrongly" would have the same effect as for Him to "make men such that they always freely choose the good." Moreover, Mackie misunderstands the reason for God's refusal to prevent a wrong choice. It is not that "its freedom is a value that outweighs its wrongness," but that God's prevention of wrong choices would take away the possibility of both moral goodness and moral wrongness.

(3) Antony Flew has developed a view similar to that of Mackie but has worked out its implications in more detail. He argues that "there is no contradiction involved in saying that God might have made people so that they always in fact *freely* choose the right," basing his argument on the principle that "acting freely" or "being free to choose" does not necessarily involve action that is unpredictable or uncaused.[54] He takes as a "paradigm case" of acting freely the decision of a man to marry a certain girl "when there was no question of the parties 'having to get married,' and no social or parental pressure on either of them." [55] To say that he was free to marry her is not to say that his choice was unpredictable or uncaused, but only that "being of an age to know his mind, he did what he did and rejected possible alternative courses of action, without being under any pressure to act in this way." [56] Again, to say that a person "could have helped doing something" does not mean that his act was in principle unpredictable and uncaused, but only that "*if* he had chosen to do otherwise he would have been able to do so." [57] If so, there is no contradiction in saying that an action was *both* free

[52] Cf. ch. 11.

[53] *Ibid.*, p. 57.

[54] Flew, A.: in *New Essays in Philosophical Theology*, ed. by A. Flew and A. MacIntyre, p. 149.

[55] *Ibid.*, p. 149.

[56] *Ibid.*, pp. 149, 150.

[57] *Ibid.*, p. 150.

and could have been helped *and* predictable and even foreknown. On the basis of this view of freedom, Flew concludes that "Omnipotence might have, could without contradiction be said to have, created people who would always as a matter of fact freely have chosen to do the right thing," [58] so that "there is no need for any vale of soul-making." [59] However, Flew is inclined to think that "the whole notion of an omnipotent creator God is logically vicious" and that "the problem of evil cannot arise, since the notions of God as either all-powerful, or all-good, or as even existing at all will all be equally vicious." [60] Thus, the arguments he has advanced in favor of "an omnipotent creator God" being able to make men such that they would always freely choose the right are only "reductions to absurdity" of that notion.[61]

It is not necessary to deal with this position in detail. It is based upon the kind of "soft determinism" which has been so popular with empiricists since Hume defended it. According to this view, all men's acts are determined and their freedom consists only in the fact that their acts flow from their own volitions rather than being caused by external forces acting upon them.[62] Thus, Flew's argument involves a contradiction, since it asserts that men could have been completely determined by God and yet free in their choices. His essay is interesting chiefly as an example of the tendency of skeptics and atheists to attack the theodicy of orthodox theism by adopting its assumptions, e.g., that God is omnipotent and good, and then showing that they lead to consequences which are unacceptable. Thus, since God has *not* in fact created men such that they always choose rightly He must lack either omnipotence or goodness. From this Flew concludes that the very idea of an "omnipotent creator God" is "logically vicious" and that God does not exist. At no point does he take into account the view of modern theists like Tennant that divine omnipotence is limited by that which is impossible. If he had done so, he might have seen that it would have been impossible for God to have created man free and capable of choosing between good and evil and yet to have made him such that he would always choose the good, for this would have involved a contradiction.

(4) H. J. McCloskey has argued that free will would have been compatible with *less* moral evil than actually occurs. "Clearly God could have created man with a strong bias to good," he says, "whilst still leaving scope for a decision to act evilly," or he "could so have ordered

[58] *Ibid.*, p. 152.
[59] *Ibid.*, p. 155.
[60] *Ibid.*, p. 165.
[61] *Ibid.*, p. 165.
[62] Cf. ch. 10.

the world that it was less conducive to the practice of evil." [63] Thus, it would have been possible for God to have reduced the amount of moral evil resulting from its exercise.

There is a certain plausibility in this argument and it chimes in with the natural tendency of men to blame the defects of their *nature* —in this case a weak "bias to good"—or in their *environment*—in this case the fact that it is "conducive to the practice of evil"—rather than their own wills. Doubtless every man has at times of moral weakness and temptation longed for a strengthening of his inclination to goodness and a weakening of the temptation assailing him. Moreover, the theistic view of man, as we shall see,[64] recognizes his moral imperfection and his need for grace to empower his will and deliver him from evil. But the argument of McCloskey assumes that God deliberately withheld from man a strong tendency to good and an environment favorable to it. This assumption is justified only if God's omnipotence is interpreted in a deterministic manner to mean that His will is the cause of all things as they actually are. But Biblical theism affirms that God created the nature of man good and that the present weakness of his tendency to good and the strength of his temptations are due primarily to men's wrong choices in the past which have corrupted both their wills and their environment. If this view is correct, there is every reason for them to pray for a renewal of their original "bias" toward good but not to complain that they were created with a weak "bias" toward it.

(5) McCloskey also maintains that freedom of will can be justified as a necessary condition of moral goodness only if the number of people who practice moral virtue and attain happiness thereby is "sufficient to outweigh the evilness of moral evil, the evilness of their eternal damnation, and the physical evil they cause to others." [65] Since it is impossible to prove conclusively that this is the case, we can only say that moral evil *may have* but not that it *does have* a justification.[66] This objection has merit because there is no way of proving that the number of those who attain moral goodness is sufficient to outweigh the immense amount of moral and physical evil which results from the exercise of freedom. It is quite impossible to make a comparison of the goods with the evils, moral and physical, which are experienced by all men. Indeed, it is not even possible to determine with certainty the number of those who attain moral goodness or the number of

[63] McCloskey, H. J.: in *God and Evil,* ed. by Nelson Pike, Englewood Cliffs, N.J., Prentice-Hall, p. 80.

[64] Ch. 12.

[65] *Ibid.,* p. 81.

[66] *Ibid.,* p. 81.

those who choose moral evil on the whole, since to do so we would have to know the motives of men as well as observe their acts. But the justification of freedom of will as a condition of moral goodness does not depend upon the possibility of a quantitative comparison of the goods and evils which have resulted from its exercise. It is primarily the *purpose* of God in giving freedom to man rather than the *use* man has actually made of it which determines whether the gift was compatible with God's goodness. Whether it was "immoral" for God to create men with freedom, knowing that moral evil as well as moral good would result from it, depends upon one's estimate of the worth of moral goodness and other goods of which freedom is a necessary condition.

(6) The final objection raised by McCloskey is based upon his comparative valuation of moral and other goods. "Are free will and its goods," he asks, "so much more valuable than the next best alternatives that their superior value can really justify the immense amount of evil that is introduced into the world by free will?" [67] What is the "next best" alternative he has in mind? Not "automata, machine-like creatures, who never make mistakes because they never make decisions," but " 'rational' agents predestined always 'to choose' the right things for the right reasons—that is, if the language of automata must be used, rational automata." [68] This is illuminating because it makes clear once more that determinism is the only alternative to God's creation of men with freedom of will despite His knowledge that moral and natural evils as well as moral and natural goods would result. For beings who were "predestined always 'to choose' the right things for the right reasons" would be "automata," even if they were "rational" rather than "machine-like" ones. "God, were He omnipotent," says McCloskey, "could preordain the decisions and the reasons upon which they were based; and such a mode of existence would seem to be in itself a worthy mode of existence, and one preferable to an existence with free will, irrationality and evil." [69]

Would it be? Or are the moral and other goods which free will makes possible of such worth that human existence blessed by them but also darkened by moral evils is superior to the existence of "rational automata" prevented from falling into moral evil and always choosing goods they are predetermined to choose by their Creator?

The Crucial Question

This is the crucial question, and it should not be answered lightly. For while we have argued that the skeptic cannot prove that the moral

[67] McCloskey, *ibid.,* p. 83

[68] *Ibid.,* p. 83.

[69] *Ibid.,* p. 83.

and natural evils outweigh the moral and natural goods resulting from the exercise of freedom, it cannot be denied that the evils are very great. When one considers the depth of degradation to which men often fall and the amount of suffering they inflict upon others, one is tempted to question the wisdom and goodness of God in bestowing the dangerous gift of freedom upon them.

The question becomes more acute when one reflects upon the *distribution of evils* which results from the misuse of freedom. For it often seems as if the sufferings which follow wickedness fall more heavily upon the innocent than upon the guilty themselves. Dostoievsky was haunted especially by the suffering of innocent children and in *The Brothers Karamazov* Ivan's "rebellion" is provoked by his compassion for them. "Men are themselves to blame, I suppose; they were given paradise, they wanted freedom, and stole fire from heaven, though they knew they would become unhappy, so there is no need to pity them. . . . But there are the children, and what am I to do about them? That's a question I can't answer. . . . Listen! If all must suffer to pay for the eternal harmony, what have children to do with it, tell me, please? . . . I understand solidarity in sin among men. I understand solidarity in retribution too; but there can be no such solidarity with children. And if it is really true that they must share responsibility for all their fathers' crimes, such a truth is not of this world and is beyond my comprehension. . . . While there is yet time, I hasten to protect myself and so I renounce the higher harmony altogether." When his brother Alyosha says, "That's rebellion," Ivan challenges him to say whether if he were "creating a fabric of human destiny with the object of making men happy in the end, giving them peace and rest at last, but that it was essential and inevitable to torture to death only one tiny creature," he would "consent to be the architect on those conditions," Alyosha says, "No, I wouldn't consent." [70] This modern version of the problem faced by Job is made more harrowing by the fact that the examples of undeserved suffering are innocent children and the cause of their suffering is not natural calamity but the wickedness of men.

The problem is deepened further by the fact that men's wickedness causes not only the suffering but also the *moral corruption* of others. For the susceptibility of men to temptation by others raises the question whether their freedom to choose the good may not be so limited under certain circumstances as to be almost wholly lacking. In many cases this can be explained by the Aristotelian principle that a man may be unable to resist a temptation now but that he would have

[70] Dostoievsky, Fyodor: *The Brothers Karamazov*, New York, Grosset and Dunlap, pp. 267, 269.

been able to resist it if he had not in the past yielded to it. But in other cases the environment by which a person is surrounded from the beginning, first in his family and then in society as a whole, is such as to present him with few incentives to good and with almost insuperable temptations to evil. "Our humanity itself," says Farrer, "is a cultural heritage; the talking animal is talked into talk by those who talk at him; and how if they talk crooked? His mind is not at first his own, but the echo of his elders. . . . And if the inculcated attitudes were warped, or the suggested ideas corrupt, we shall never be rid of the influence, and we may be incurably vitiated by it . . . . How many persons, how many conditions, have made us what we are; and in making us so, may have undone us." [71] This inescapable fact of solidarity in sin helps to explain the universality of sin among men and is doubtless one of the main sources of the doctrine of original sin. Its relevance here is that it seems to cast doubt on the explanation of moral evil as due to a misuse of freedom of choice for which the individual is responsible.

Thus, the vast amount of moral evil, the undeserved suffering it inflicts upon the innocent, and the corruption of men's wills by the evil influence of others are bound to raise questions about the wisdom and goodness of God in creating men with freedom of choice. Nor are these questions fully answered by Milton's conviction that through a man's repentance for his sin and with the aid of divine grace he can attain a happier condition than that of the paradise of innocent bliss which, according to the myth of the Fall, he has lost. There is a profound truth in the doctrine of the "fortunate fall," *felix culpa,* since it is a fact that men who have sinned and repented are often more mature in wisdom and stronger in character than before. But many of those who sin do not repent, are not restored to obedience by grace, and therefore do *not* attain the spiritual and moral maturity Milton describes.

Thus, although the objections to theism raised by skeptics from Hume to Flew and others of our time are not convincing, it is also clear that there is no way of *proving* that the moral good and other values made possible by freedom of choice justify the moral evil of men and the suffering they inflict upon others. Therefore, the modern theist should not claim, as earlier thinkers such as Leibniz have done, that he can rationally demonstrate that God's ways with men in moral evil are justified. The day of elaborate theodicies which attempted to show that evil as the contrary of good contributes to the perfection and beauty of the world and that this is the best of possible worlds is over.

Nevertheless, it is a striking fact that men of different religions and philosophical types have been convinced that the highest values and

[71] Farrer, *op. cit.,* p. 102.

achievements of men could not have been attained without struggle against evil. This conviction has usually arisen as an intuition based upon experience but it has also been strongly supported by argument. For example, Josiah Royce points out that we deceive ourselves in our thinking about good and evil when we conceive the meaning of these terms in an abstract way by considering them apart from one another. Such an abstract view of good and evil leads us to suppose that life with any evil at all in it is not as good as it would be if there were no evil and that in estimating the worth of life on the whole we must set the good over against the evil and compare the amount of the one with the amount of the other. In reality, when we look at them more concretely as we actually experience them, we find good and evil interrelated in complex ways so that a "secondary" good is often realized through the experience of a "primary" evil. "But I insist," writes Royce, "that, in general, the only harmony that can exist in the realm of the spirit is the harmony that we possess when we thwart the present but more elemental impulse for the sake of the higher unity of experience, as when we rejoice in the endurance of the tragedies of life, because they show us the depth of life, or when we know that it is better to have loved and lost than never to have loved at all, or as when we possess a virtue in the moment of victory over the tempter. And the reason why this is true lies in the fact that the more one's experience fulfills ideals, the more that experience presents to one, not of ignorance, but of triumphantly wealthy acquaintance with the facts of manifold, varied, and tragic life, full of tension and thereby of unity." [72]

As an absolute idealist, Royce combines this view of man's struggle against evil with a monistic conception of man's unity with God, so that his evil and suffering are a logically necessary and eternal constituent of the divine life. However, Royce's analysis of the relation between good and evil in human experience does not depend upon this dubious monistic view of man's life as included in the life of the Absolute or God. What is essential and valuable in it is his insight that spiritual and moral good can be attained only through the overcoming of evil, on the one hand, and his conviction that God works with man in overcoming it, on the other.

A somewhat similar conception of evil and its relation to good has been expressed by the Russian existentialist philosopher Berdyaev. Affirming the existence of "an uncreated freedom which precedes being and is submerged in the irrational sphere," he holds that recognition of this freedom "sets before man the creative task of continuing the

[72] Royce, Josiah: *Studies in Good and Evil*, D. Appleton and Co., 1898, p. 23.

creation of the world, and makes evil itself a path, a grievous experience, but not an ontological principle which passes over into eternity (hell)." [73] "Evil is but a pathway, a testing, a disruption; to fall into sin is above all a testing of freedom. Man moves towards the light through the darkness." Berdyaev defines the good in man as the subordination of the life of both the soul and the body to a spiritual principle, evil as the loss of this inner unity and wholeness by the breaking away of passions as parts of the self from its spiritual center. Thus, his view of both good and evil rests upon the centrality of man's spiritual nature and the necessity of subordinating both the soul and the body to it through creative activity springing from freedom. "It is not evil itself which has been an upward path, but the spiritual strength of the resistance aroused by it and the knowledge which was born of it. . . . Man must go through the testing of all possibilities, he must pass through the experience of the knowledge of good and evil, and evil itself may become a dialectic moment of good." [74]

In this view, also, there are questionable ideas. For example, Berdyaev's assertion of the existence of an irrational freedom before the creation shows the influence of Boehme's mysticism. But the essential point is similar to that of Royce: man is a spiritual being who can realize his spiritual possibilities only in a dialectical process through the struggle with evil, so that evil is a "pathway" over which man passes and on which he undergoes a testing of all his possibilities.

In a recent book on the problem of evil, John Hick takes a similar view and makes clear the presupposition underlying it. Raising the question whether the existence of evil is compatible with belief in a God of love, he rejects the Augustinian view that God created man perfect in his original state and that evil is a result of a fall of the first man into sin. Rather, he accepts the explanation of evil by Irenaeus, that "man was created as an imperfect, immature creature who was to undergo moral development and growth" and that the world is characterized by "mingled good and evil as a divinely appointed environment for man's development towards the perfection that represents the fulfillment of God's good purpose for him." [75] This purpose for man could be realized not through a divine fiat but only through man's willing cooperation and hence required his freedom, since "one who has attained to goodness by meeting and eventually mastering temptations, and thus by rightly making responsible choices

[73] Berdyaev, Nicolas: *The Divine and the Human,* tr. by R. M. French, London, Geoffrey Bles, 1949, pp. 90, 91.

[74] *Ibid.,* p. 91.

[75] Hick, John: *Evil and the God of Love,* London, Macmillan, 1966, pp. 220, 221.

in concrete situations, is good in a richer and more valuable sense than would be one created *ab initio* in a state either of innocence or of virtue." [76] Hence, God created a world which would challenge man by its difficulties and trials to realize the highest potentialities of his personality, or, in John Keats' phrase, "a vale of soul-making."

This involved creating man with a relative autonomy or independence and placing him in a natural environment in which God was not immediately and continuously evident to him. As a result of this "epistemic distance" of man from God, it was natural that he should become immersed in nature and alienated from God.[77] Thus, God was ultimately responsible for the existence of evil, since He created the world and placed man at a distance from Himself although He was aware that this would make sin and suffering virtually inevitable.[78] But this was justified as a necessary condition for the development of the moral and spiritual personality of man by his own free decisions and it does not take away man's own responsibility for the decisions he makes. Therefore, the view of Hume and others that it would have been better for God to have created a "hedonistic paradise," a house for man "as comfortable and convenient as possible," must be rejected by all who believe that the moral and spiritual perfection of man is a more worthy goal for him than the enjoyment of a maximum of pleasure, although the attainment of the goal is impossible without suffering.

One of the merits of Hick's "Irenaean" explanation of evil is that, while it stresses the freedom of man and his responsibility for moral evil, it recognizes the ultimate responsibility of God for creating him imperfect and placing him in an environment which veils from him his true Good so that he inevitably tends to seek his good in inferior things. This helps to explain why all men fall into sin and why the realization of their moral and spiritual potentialities involves moral struggle and suffering. However, we would maintain that man's "epistemic distance" from God is only one aspect of the situation which leads him to moral evil. As we shall see, there are also biological and social factors which foster self-centeredness and self-assertiveness.

Another merit of Hick's view is his realistic recognition of the fact that God's purpose for man is so often frustrated by the moral failure of men to make the right choices, as well as the fact that so much human suffering seems excessive and tends to disintegrate the personality. For this reason, Hick believes that a theodicy is incomplete

[76] *Ibid.*, p. 291.
[77] *Ibid.*, pp. 321, 322.
[78] *Ibid.*, p. 326.

without faith in the ultimate redemption of all men from sin and suffering in an afterlife.[79] Obviously, this eschatological solution of the problem of evil is logically necessary if one believes that God's omnipotence requires the ultimate fulfillment of His purpose for every person in creating the world as a "vale of soul-making," and it will have a deep appeal to one who has a firm belief in the after life. But even those who do not share Hick's conception of God's absolute sovereignty or his firm eschatological faith can accept his main thesis that the natural and moral evil in the world are not incompatible with the existence of a God of love. For the purpose to develop men as spiritual and moral persons is of such transcendent importance that it justifies the risk of moral failure with many and the necessity of struggle and suffering for all.

If the insights of such thinkers as these are true, the gift of freedom was the indispensable condition not merely for the attainment of moral goodness by man but also for the development of all his spiritual possibilities as a being made in the image of God and called by Him to participate in the creative process of the world.

Why do so many *not* use their freedom for this purpose but bring moral evil into the world and inflict suffering upon themselves and others? We have seen that part of the cause of this, which is a tragic frustration of God's purpose for man, lies in the solidarity of every person with others from childhood and the consequent corruption of his thoughts and acts by their wickedness. If we push the question still farther back and seek an explanation of the wickedness of those who corrupt him, we can also see that there are certain aspects of their existence which have provided occasions or temptations to moral evil. As William Temple points out, an inescapable aspect of the life of every finite self is its self-centeredness. Since its perspective is determined by the particular body which is associated with it and by the particular place and time in which it lives, it is limited in its appreciation of good and evil. "The mind by a necessary tendency of its own nature attaches more importance to values which find their actualisation in itself than to those which find it elsewhere; or to put it crudely, each man cares more about what seems to be good for him than about goods which he does not expect personally to enjoy. . . . So he becomes not only the subject of his own value judgments, which he can never cease to be, but also the centre and criterion of his own system of values, which he is quite unfit to be." [80]

Man shares this natural self-centeredness of finite being with the animals. But unlike the animals man is also self-conscious, distin-

[79] *Ibid.,* ch. XVII.
[80] Temple, *op. cit.,* p. 365.

guishing himself from his environment and from other selves and choosing the ends he shall pursue.[81] In consequence, he is self-assertive as they are not. Moreover, his imagination enlarges the ends with which he identifies himself, so that his will becomes unlimited in its desires and can never be fully satisfied. As Niebuhr says, man's imagination transmutes the "will to live" which he shares with the animals into a "will to self-realization" and this becomes a "will to power" when he seeks to escape from the anxiety into which his insecurity drives him.[82] The influence of other self-centered selves, as Temple points out, strengthens this tendency to self-assertiveness and will to power. "We are, in part, reciprocally determining beings. We make each other what we are. Therefore, the existence of one self-centred soul would spread an evil infection through all who come within its range of influence. This happens both positively and negatively. If A is self-centred, B tends to become so by imitation; but also B becomes so in self-defence. The instincts of gregariousness and of fear combine to produce the same result." [83] As a result, human society is to a large extent a "network of competing selfishnesses, all kept in check by each one's selfish fear of others." [84]

Skeptics such as Hume who have attacked the theistic view have usually done so because they have not believed that the spiritual and moral good made possible by freedom is greater than its cost in moral evil and innocent suffering. In contrast, theists have believed that the moral and spiritual values made possible by freedom are of such supreme worth that they justify the risk of moral evil and suffering involved in freedom.

It is not possible to demonstrate rationally that one of these views is true and the other false. As we have indicated, a comparative valuation of moral goods and moral evils, together with the pleasures and pains accompanying each, cannot be made. Therefore, one's decision between the two views must be made on the basis of his conception of the nature of man and of the values which enable him to realize his potentialities. One who accepts a hedonistic conception of man as an animal who seeks the satisfaction of his appetites and a social being whose interests are determined by his culture will usually tend to a view of his good which subordinates moral and spiritual development to the attainment of maximum happiness along with minimum pain. Therefore, he will be likely to adopt the skeptical view that a good God

[81] *Ibid.,* p. 366.

[82] Niebuhr, R.: *The Children of Light and the Children of Darkness,* New York, Charles Scribner's Sons, 1944, pp. 18–20.

[83] Temple, *op. cit.,* p. 367.

[84] *Ibid.*

would have created man such that he would always choose the good in order to make himself and others happy, although this would mean the absence of moral goodness and other spiritual values insofar as they depend upon freedom of choice. On the other hand, one who accepts a spiritual conception of man will tend to accept the theistic view that God was justified in creating him free in order that he might realize his spiritual possibilities, although this might entail less pleasure and more pain. Thus, a man's decision between the skeptic's rejection and the theist's justification of God in the presence of moral evil rests, in the last analysis, on his understanding of the nature of man and of the good suitable to man.[85]

We have attempted to show that a comprehensive theodicy like that of orthodox theologians and rationalistic philosophers of the past is unconvincing. It is possible for the philosopher of religion to throw some light upon the problem of natural and moral evil, and we have attempted to do so. But difficulties remain and the mystery is not dispelled. In the end, each of us must make a *decision* between rebelling like Ivan Karamasov against every justification of God's relation to the evil of the world and accepting like Job the goodness of God despite the evils in nature and human life.

But the decision to accept rather than rebel need not be merely a matter of blind faith. As we have seen, the believer can see some meaning in natural evil or suffering, not only because of its biological function in the life of animals, but also because it is incidental to the operation of a uniform natural order which is a necessary condition of the moral and spiritual development of man. He can also see that moral evil is the price that must be paid if he is to be endowed with the freedom which is required for attainment of moral and spiritual values and for participation in the creative and redemptive work of God. Thus, his affirmation of faith despite the evils in the world may be supported by at least a partial insight into the role of natural and moral evil; so that he will not need to regard it as an arbitrary imposition upon men by an unjust or indifferent God.

In conclusion, we would return to a point which we made earlier: the primary concern of the theist with evil is not theoretical but practical. As a rational being, he cannot avoid the problem raised by evil or the task of seeking an answer to it; but as a religious being he seeks above all to be delivered from it with *God's help,* and as a moral being he struggles to overcome moral evil in himself and to relieve suffering in others. When he groans under the heavy burden of evil, he can gain

[85] Cf. ch. 10.

courage and confidence from the faith that he is not alone but that God will help him to bear it. For whatever the explanation of evil may be, he believes that God is good and that His face is always and everywhere set against it. Although His use of His power is limited to that which is consistent with His purpose and with the nature of the creatures He has made, His providence is at work in every situation to direct men to their good and to deliver them from evil. Moreover if the theist believes that God suffers with men in their suffering, he does not need to feel that his struggle with moral evil and adversity has been imposed upon him by One who stands above and outside it and calls him to account as a judge. In this faith he can find the courage to commit himself to the struggle against evil despite his inability to find a certain and complete explanation of it.

Obviously, the belief that God is actively involved in the struggle against evil and identifies Himself with man's suffering can only arise from a living experience of Him. The philosophy of religion cannot produce such a belief, as it cannot demonstrate the belief in providence which is bound up with it. Its role is the more modest one of testing such beliefs to see whether they are compatible with experience and of formulating them in concepts which are clear and consistent with each other. It is because philosophy of religion can do no more than this that William Temple sees it as pointing beyond itself to a revelation which will make God's activity in overcoming evil a living reality to men. "God has so made the world," he says, "that evil has occurred in it; then either He must subordinate that evil to a good enhanced by its occurrence, or else He is not God as we have learnt to understand that Name." [86] "Natural theology" can "describe" God but cannot "confront" man with Him and show man that evil is actually "being transmuted into good" by Him. Hence, it "ends in a hunger which it cannot satisfy," "a hunger for that Divine Revelation which it began by excluding from its purview." [87]

Whatever one may think about the answer of revelation to the problem of evil, the decision one makes between the acceptance and the denial of God when one is confronted with evil is a vital one and its practical consequences are great. "An overmastering sense of human ills," says Farrer, "can be taken as the world's invitation to deny her Maker, or it may be taken as God's invitation to succor his world. Which is it to be? Those who take the practical alternative [the latter] become more closely and more widely acquainted with misery than the

[86] Temple, *op. cit.*, p. 511.
[87] *Ibid.*, p. 519.

onlookers; but they feel the grain of existence, and the movement of the purposes of God. They do not argue, they love; and what is loved is always known as good. The more we love, the more we feel the evils besetting or corrupting the object of our love. But the more we feel the force of the besetting harms, the more certain we are of the value residing in what they attack; and in resisting them are identified with the action of God, whose mercy is over all flesh." [88]

[88] Farrer, *op. cit.*, pp. 164, 165. Brackets added.

9

Man: a Problem to Himself

In our time man has become a problem to himself. During the nine-teenth century he seemed supremely sure of himself, at least in the West, and looked forward with unclouded confidence toward the future. Although it was an age of increasing skepticism concerning God, men were buoyed up by a profound faith, questioned by only a few hardy thinkers, in man. It is quite different in our century. Beginning with the First World War, man's optimism has been rudely shaken and has been giving way to a growing pessimism concerning his future. For he has lost faith in himself and in his ability to extricate himself from the threatening situation in which he has become involved. Moreover, he knows, at least in his more lucid moments, that he is responsible himself for the dangers confronting him. He may try to put all the blame for them upon some menacing force outside himself, e.g., Com-munism or the Bomb, but he knows that totalitarian movements and weapons of mass destruction are products of human minds and are dangerous primarily because they serve evil human purposes. Man begins to suspect that the enemy that threatens him is not outside the gates but within the inner citadel, himself.

This loss of confidence in himself has been accompanied by a loss of certainty about his own nature. This is ironical in a century which has witnessed an unparalleled development of the sciences of man. An immense amount of knowledge about man as an individual and as a social being has been acquired and made available to everyone. Anthro-pologists have patiently accumulated detailed information about many cultures hitherto unknown; sociologists have collected masses of data concerning social institutions, relationships, and changes; and psy-chologists have investigated behavior and probed the unconscious. Yet the secret of man, the clue to his nature and destiny, eludes us. The title of a book by a French doctor expresses our ignorance and our perplexity: *Man the Unknown*.[1]

That we are not exaggerating the extent to which man has become a problem to himself is shown by the preoccupation of existentialist philosophers with human existence, almost to the exclusion of nature and other problems. The existentialists are concerned above all with the failure of men to attain "authentic" existence as they flee from their true selves and passively reflect what "they" (others) do and say (Heidegger) or become mere "functionaries" in a mass society (Marcel). Similarly, psychoanalysts describe man as suffering from anxiety concerning himself, seeking for his "identity," needing to discover his "real" self. Theologians influenced by them describe the anxieties which threaten man with despair and lead him to seek for a ground for the "courage to be" (Tillich). And countless novels and plays picture him as haunted by loneliness and seeking desperately to find a meaning in his life.

How are we to explain this questioning of contemporary man about himself? Martin Buber offers at least a partial answer. He points out that when man feels himself solitary he becomes a question to himself, and that we are living in an age which fosters a sense of solitariness. He distinguishes between "epochs of habitation" in which "man lives in the world as in a house, as in a home," and "epochs of homelessness" in which "man lives in the world as in an open field and does not even have four pegs with which to set up a tent." [2] In "epochs of homelessness" thought about man ceases to be only a part of thought about the cosmos.[3] Modern man entered such an epoch after Copernicus had disclosed to him the infinity of the universe. "Once the concept of infinity has been taken seriously a human dwelling can no longer be made of the universe," says Buber;[4] and Pascal cried out, "The eternal silence of these infinite spaces frightens me."

But it is only in our time that man's feeling of homelessness and solitariness in the world has become so acute as to produce a crisis. This has resulted from two recent developments. The first is sociological, the rapid decay of the old organic forms of the life of man with man, e.g., the family and the village community.[5] These communities were not too large to bring men together in a direct relation with each other and give them a sense of security and a feeling of being at home in the world. But they have decayed in our industrial society, and the

---

[1] Carrell, Alexis: *Man the Unknown*, New York, Harper, 1935.
[2] Buber, Martin: *Between Man and Man*, Edinburgh, R. and R. Clark, 1945, p. 126.
[3] *Ibid.*, p. 126.
[4] *Ibid.*, p. 133.
[5] *Ibid.*, p. 157.

new community forms which have replaced them in the cities, e.g., clubs and trade unions, have not re-established the sense of security.[6] The second development is spiritual. "Man is no longer able to master the world which he himself brought about: it is becoming stronger than he is, it is running free of him, it confronts him in an almost elemental independence." [7] In the realm of technology, machines which were invented to serve men are forcing him to serve them. In the economic realm, production has greatly increased but has not been properly coordinated and has gone beyond man's control. In the political realm, man feels that he is in the grip of impersonal destructive powers. Buber speaks of man's simultaneous power and powerlessness, as he has been confronted by these impersonal products of his technological, economic, and political activity.[8] They have put immense power into his hands and have been the source of great pride to him. But they have brought forth vast changes which he does not know how to cope with and dangers which threaten his very survival. In short, he is powerless to control the power he has created. He also knows, we might add, that he is powerless to control himself and to use his power for good ends. He fears that, while he has the physical strength of a giant, he has the moral wisdom of a child.

It is not surprising, therefore, that contemporary man has become a problem to himself, has lost confidence in his ability to overcome the dangers confronting him and has become confused about his nature and destiny. This attitude towards himself differs radically from that of man in the medieval and early modern periods. Up to the latter part of the nineteenth century, Western man generally accepted the view of himself and his place in the world which had been formed by the synthesis of classical humanism and the Biblical conception of man. According to this view, the "great chain of being" extended from inanimate nature through plants and animals to man, the highest of terrestrial beings, and above him to the angels and God. Thus, man occupied a middle position in the scale of being, exalted above all earthly creatures as a rational being made in the image of God and destined for eternal life, but subordinated to God as a creature wholly dependent upon his Creator. Hence, he had a sense of his worth and dignity as the only terrestrial creature made in God's image and sustained by the hope of eternal life in His presence, and at the same time he was humbled by his inferiority to the angels and his dependence upon God for his being and his destiny. His earthly life might be brief and subject to many evils, but it had meaning as a time of

[6] *Ibid.,* pp. 157, 158.

[7] *Ibid.,* p. 158.

[8] *Ibid.,* p. 159.

discipline and of preparation for eternity and his earthly achievements, however imperfect, yielded a measure of happiness which could be accepted with gratitude. Moreover, he had a definite conception of his nature and his needs, of the duties which were expected of him, of the values which he should seek, and of the principles of natural law which should guide him in his social conduct.

This vision of man, his place in the world, his good, and his destiny has virtually disappeared from the horizon of contemporary man. As a result, he has been left without any settled and sure convictions about his nature, his place in the world, and his destiny. It is imperative, therefore, that he should attain a clear understanding of himself, one which will do justice to all sides of his nature and enable him to overcome his estrangement from the world and from his authentic self.

10

The Nature of Man

Although the philosophy of religion has always been primarily concerned with the problem of God and His relation to the world, it has also been profoundly interested in the problem of man and his relation to God. Religious philosophers since the time of Plato have analyzed the soul and inquired into its relation to the body, and philosophical theologians such as Augustine have wrestled with the problem of man's freedom and its relation to God's grace.

The reasons for this preoccupation of religious thinkers with the problem of man are clear. The first is that although it is centered in God as the object of faith and devotion, *religion* arises in human persons and communities. Since it involves all the functions of man's personality and affects all the aspects of his life, an understanding of it requires an understanding of man himself. The second reason is less obvious. The interpretation of *God's nature* largely depends, as we have indicated, on the use of analogies derived from the attributes and acts of human persons. Hence, it will be adequate only if man's understanding of himself is sufficiently profound. In the history of religions the knowledge of God and the knowledge of man have advanced together, e.g., the attribution to God of a spiritual nature and a concern for moral goodness became possible for the Hebrew prophets only as they came to respect the worth of persons and their pre-eminence in nature. On the other hand, men have been ridiculed since the time of Xenophanes for picturing their gods as like themselves, and the dangers of anthropomorphism can be avoided only if they have a clear understanding of man's limitations as well as his capacities. Thirdly, religion requires a sound view of man's *relation to nature* no less than his relation to God. Otherwise, he may be persuaded to think of himself as merely a part of nature, one animal species among others, and thus to dehumanize himself. Or he may be tempted to think of himself more highly than he ought and thus to deceive himself with romantic dreams and hopes. Only a person's true view of himself can enable him to see himself as a finite and imperfect creature and at the same time to affirm his dignity as a person.

There are good reasons, therefore, for the philosopher of religion to concern himself with the nature of man, especially with his mind and spirit, and to inquire into the reality and limitations of his freedom.

Three Conceptions of Man

There are three conceptions of man's nature which are competing for his acceptance in the Western world: the classical humanistic, the naturalistic and the theistic. If he is to choose intelligently between them, he must be clear about the nature of each and the differences between them. When we analyze them, we find that each contains insights which must be included in an adequate view of man.

The classical *humanistic* conception of man originated in ancient Greece, and was revived and modified during the Renaissance. Renaissance Platonists like Pico della Mirandola exalted the "dignity" of man, superior to the animals by virtue of his reason and able by the exercise of his freedom to raise himself to the highest possible level in the scale of being. Turning away from the otherworldliness of medieval asceticism, they were fired with enthusiasm for spiritual values such as truth and beauty. They developed a humanistic conception of education, the aim of which was to realize the potentialities of the individual that he might enjoy a rich and creative life, and this conception has provided the basic principles of modern liberal education. Humanism has also fostered democratic government by its affirmation of the dignity, rationality, and freedom of the individual, and its ethical ideal, self-realization in a well-rounded and harmonious personality, continues to have great influence.

But despite these and other contributions, the classical humanistic conception of man has shown itself to be inadequate. One of its limitations is that it concentrates almost exclusively upon the qualities and capacities of man which distinguish him from other animals and from the rest of nature. This is justified insofar as it calls attention to what is unique in man and prevents him from accepting views of himself which would reduce him to the subhuman level. But it overlooks or at least minimizes the characteristics he shares with other animal species and the limitations these impose upon him. In consequence, it fosters the tendency to identify man's nature with the rational or spiritual aspect of it and thus enhances his pride.

Another limitation of the classical humanistic conception is that it underestimates the power, for good as well as for evil, of the emotional and other non-rational forces in man. As a result, it overemphasizes the formal elements of human life and represses or unduly subordinates the dynamic elements. A reaction inevitably occurs, as in the revolt of spontaneity and feeling in Romanticism against the emphasis on reason and form in Classicism. By its exaggeration of the power of reason, humanism also fosters political Utopianism, encouraging too optimistic a view of human nature and its possibilities when liberated from unjust political or economic institutions.

Finally, although some of the greatest ancient and modern humanists such as Plato and Milton have been deeply religious men, the primary interest of humanism has been in man, his dignity and his achievements. As a result, it has become increasingly secular in the modern period. As Maritain has pointed out, it gradually lost the feeling of the greatest classical and Renaissance humanists for the religious dimension of man and exalted man in and for himself apart from his relationship to God.[1] As late as Milton's *Paradise Lost* it was possible for a great humanist to affirm that subordination to God's will is a necessary condition of man's virtue and happiness, while proud rebellion against Him is the ultimate source of his fall and misery. But after the seventeenth century the mainstream of humanism became separated from the religious tradition. Man was exalted no longer because he was created in the image of God, but because of the uniqueness of his nature and capacities as a rational, free, and creative being. His pre-eminence among living beings and his mastery over nature were glorified, while his dependence upon God and responsibility to Him for the use of his talents were forgotten. As a result, the humanistic conception of man, which is so close in many respects to the religious conception and has so often been a strong ally of it, has become its chief rival in many intellectual circles.

The *naturalistic* theory asserts that man is simply a part of nature and denies that he is dependent upon any being or power beyond nature. It pictures him as an unintended product of the evolutionary process who has come into existence like other animal species by natural selection. Hence, he is continuous with the animal species from which he descended, and his intelligence and other characteristics that constitute his uniqueness differ in degree but not in kind from theirs. This is interpreted somewhat differently by "reductionist" and "non-reductionist" naturalists. The former accept the materialistic and mechanistic view of nature which was dominant in the latter half

---

[1] Maritain, Jacques: *True Humanism*, New York, Charles Scribner's Sons, 1938.

of the nineteenth century. They maintain, therefore, that human thought and behavior can in principle be explained by means of the same general laws that govern physical and chemical events. In contrast, "non-reductionist" naturalists such as Samuel Alexander use such terms as "emergent evolution" to indicate their belief that, while man is a product of nature, he possesses certain unique qualities which are irreducible to those found in lower animals.[2] Thus, while naturalists of both types agree in describing man as part of nature, the "non-reductionists" put greater emphasis upon his uniqueness.[3] However, both types reject the humanists' tendency to exalt man as a spiritual being above the rest of nature and to affirm the objective reality and universal validity of his values. And both types repudiate the theistic conception of man as a creature who is dependent upon and responsible to God and capable of transcending nature through his moral and spiritual activity.

The appeal of the naturalistic conception lies partly in its claim to be the only view of man consistent with modern science. It stresses an important truth about man, i.e., that he is a natural being subject to the conditions and limitations of all natural beings. Whatever else must be said about man, he belongs to an animal species which has evolved like other animal species. As such, his physiological structures and processes are similar to theirs, and some of his psychological functions such as sensation and appetite he has in common with them. He is also subject to the natural evils that afflict them, e.g., pain, disease, and death. Moreover, his participation in the limitations of animal existence often weakens or distorts his rational and spiritual activity. Thus, the naturalistic conception is strong precisely where the humanistic one is weak, emphasizing the earthly and animal aspects of man's existence which provide the basic conditions of his life but also limit his higher achievements.

But while man is certainly a natural being, he is also a spiritual and moral being who is capable of transcending nature. It is impossible to explain him as only a biological organism moved by psychological drives and shaped in his behavior by social causes. In brief, as the humanistic conception is too high, the naturalistic view is too low, in its understanding of the human condition. It cannot do justice to the mind, the freedom, and the creativity of man. Man is a natural being, but he is far more than a complex animal.

[2] Alexander, Samuel: *Space, Time and Deity,* London, Macmillan, 1926.

[3] For this reason, there are *naturalistic* as well as *classical* humanists. We are describing three *ideal* types, and a thinker may belong to more than one of them, e.g., Julian Huxley is a naturalist *and* a humanist and Milton was a theist *and* a humanist.

We have pointed out that there are important insights in both the humanistic and the naturalistic conceptions of man which must be included in any view which is to be adequate. But we have also shown that each of them concentrates upon one side of human nature to the neglect of another side which is also important. In short, both of them are inadequate not so much because they are false as because they are too simple.

It is one of the great advantages of the Western *theistic* view of man that it recognizes the complexity of man. This can readily be seen by considering briefly the major affirmations of the Bible about him. First, man is a being created "in the *image of God*." [4] In this simple statement the Bible expresses a view of man which is even higher than that of the humanists, since it asserts that his uniqueness consists not merely in his superiority to other natural beings but in his likeness to God. This exalted position of man is beautifully described in Psalm 8:

> When I look at thy heavens, the work of thy fingers,
> the moon and the stars which thou hast established;
> What is man that thou are mindful of him,
> and the son of man that thou dost care for him?
> Yet thou hast made him little less than God,
> and dost crown him with dignity and honor. [5]

Although the exact meaning of "image of God" in the story of creation is not certain, it is clear that it does not refer to a physical likeness. Some theologians have held that it is man's reason which constitutes him a being in the image of God, others that it is his capacity to respond to God's Word and obey God's will in his conduct. In any case, it clearly refers to a special relationship to God through which he has the capacity to transcend himself by serving higher purposes than his own.

On the other hand, man is a *creature*, one of the many kinds of creatures on the earth. As such, he is finite and subject to all the limitations of finite beings. He is limited in physical size and strength, in intelligence and virtue. He is moved by animal appetites and passions. He suffers from natural calamities. His life is brief. Above all, he is of the earth, earthy; created from dust, to dust he must return. Thus, the theistic conception emphasizes the duality, although not the dualism, of man's nature: he "stands at the juncture of nature and spirit." [6] In consequence, it includes the elements of truth in both the

[4] Genesis I:27.

[5] Psalm 8:3–5.

[6] Niebuhr, R.: *The Nature and Destiny of Man*, New York, Charles Scribner's Sons, 1941–43, Vol. I, p. 181.

humanistic and the naturalistic conceptions, complementing and quali-
fying each by the other.

This duality of spirit and nature is not all that characterizes man,
according to the theistic view. There is a third aspect of that view
which separates it sharply from both humanistic and naturalistic views:
man is a *sinner*. From the Biblical point of view, man is able to fulfill
the high destiny for which God created him if he acknowledges his
dependence upon God and centers his actions upon obedience to God's
will. But in actuality all men have turned away from God and centered
their lives on themselves. As Augustine expressed it, they have turned
from love of God, *amor Dei*, to love of self, *amor sui*. The myth of
the Fall of Adam in the Garden symbolically describes the disobedience
not simply of the *first* man but of *every* man. As a result, man is
estranged from God, from his fellows, and from himself. Western
theists have differed at certain points in their interpretation of man's
sin, e.g., some have taken a more pessimistic view of its nature and
consequences than others, but they have agreed that all men have
sinned and brought guilt and misery upon themselves and others.
They have also agreed that men cannot break the power of sin in
their lives by their own unaided efforts but must be redeemed from
bondage to it by the power of God. Although this doctrine of sin
is the aspect of the theistic conception of man against which modern
humanists have most strongly rebelled because it seems to contradict
their idealistic view, it is an integral part of the theistic perspective.

This theistic conception of man, like the theistic conception of God,
was derived not from rational argument but from religious experience
by man of his absolute dependence upon, his kinship with, and his
alienation from the divine Ground of his being. However, it is possible
to examine it critically by reason to see whether it is in accord with
our general experience of man and whether it explains more adequately
than other conceptions the different aspects of his nature. In making
such an examination, we shall concentrate upon two affirmations about
man which have usually been considered by theistic philosophers to be
implied in the Biblical conception we have outlined: the uniqueness
of *mind* and its spiritual activity, on the one hand, and the reality and
limitations of *freedom,* on the other. It is true that these affirmations
are never stated explicitly in the Bible, that the formulation of them by
theistic philosophers in conceptual terms has been made under the
influence of philosophical thought, and that the interpretation of them
has not always been agreed upon by all theists, e.g., some theologians
have denied human freedom and asserted divine determinism. Nevertheless, the uniqueness of mind, its capacity for spiritual activity, and
its freedom are implied, we would maintain, in the Biblical belief

that man has been created in the "image of God" and is pre-eminent among the creatures; and the limitations of his freedom are implied in the Biblical belief that he has fallen into bondage through his sin.

Mind: The Traditional View

The traditional view of mind which dominated Western thought until the eighteenth century, although often challenged, was a synthesis of Biblical and Greek ideas. According to the Bible, man is a living being, whose soul and body constitute a unity. The closeness of the relation between soul and body in the Old Testament is shown by the fact that his soul, *nephesh,* is regarded as the animating principle of his body and his various psychical functions are attributed to particular bodily organs, e.g., thinking to the heart. But since the body is never considered as a mere physical machine but always as animated by the soul, there is no materialism. Moreover, in certain cases, the soul of man is invaded by the Spirit, *ruach,* of God. When the Spirit takes possession of a national leader or a prophet, for example, he receives an access of extraordinary power or insight which enables him to do or say things beyond the capacity of ordinary men. Thus, the Bible views man as a psychophysiological unity whose soul and body are not opposed to one another. But it also affirms that some men are laid hold of by the Spirit of God, brought into special relationship with Him, and made instruments of His purpose.

The other major source of the traditional view of mind is Greek philosophy during the classical period. Early Greek thought had regarded the soul, *psyche,* as the principle of motion and life in all living beings, plants and animals as well as men. Socrates added a new dimension by conceiving the soul as also the conscious seat of knowledge and virtue and by insisting that it was the duty of each man to care for his soul above all else. Adopting this view, Plato maintained that the highest "part" or function of the soul is the intellect, *nous,* which is capable of knowing the eternal and unchanging Forms and above all the Form of the Good. He distinguished sharply this spiritual or intellectual "part" from the inferior "parts" of the soul and from the body. If the soul was to attain wisdom and virtue, he asserted, the intellectual "part" must control the other "parts" and bring them into subjection. This led him in the *Phaedo* to a dualism between soul and body. Although he modified substantially this dualistic view in other dialogues such as the *Phaedrus* and the *Republic,* it has had a powerful influence upon later thought. In contrast, Aristotle rejected dualism and maintained that the soul is united with the body as its "form" which actualizes its potentialities as a living human organism.

But while the lower functions of the soul such as sensation and appetite are dependent upon the body, its noblest part, the "active intellect," is independent of the body, coming into it "from without" at birth and surviving its death.

The theories of Plato and Aristotle profoundly affected early and medieval Christian thought concerning the soul. St. Augustine accepted the dualistic Platonic view that the soul and the body are related only in an external manner and are in conflict with one another. On the other hand, St. Thomas Aquinas rejected dualism and adopted Aristotle's view of man as a composite substance consisting of soul and body in intimate relation with one another. The soul is the "form" of a particular body and depends upon the sense organs of the body for the impressions of objects from which it derives its ideas. "There is nothing in the intellect which was not before in sense." At the same time, Aquinas agreed with Augustine that the soul is in its essence a spiritual principle and held that its *activity* in thinking is independent of the organs of the body, despite its dependence upon the sense organs for the impressions which furnish it with the raw *materials* of its thought. In consequence, the soul is not "corruptible" like its body and can survive the dissolution of the body at death.

In this brief sketch of Biblical, Greek, and medieval ideas concerning the soul, its intellectual "part" and its relation to the body, we have indicated the nature of the traditional view of man's mind in its two major forms, the Platonic-Augustinian and the Aristotelian-Thomistic. This traditional view in its Platonic-Augustinian form was the source of Descartes' view of the mind as a *spiritual "substance,"* but he made radical changes in it. He defined the essence of the mind narrowly as "thinking substance," *res cogitans,* thus identifying it with the intellectual principle but not as also the animating principle of the body. At the same time, he defined the essence of matter as "extended substance," *res extensa,* and conceived the body as a mere machine which is governed in a mechanical fashion by physical laws. Thus, the mind became an intellectual or thinking substance which was externally related to a bodily machine. It was able causally to interact with the body at one point in the brain, affecting the body and being affected by it, but the interaction was between two completely different kinds of substances. The result was a *dualism* between mind and body more extreme than that of Plato, for whom the soul was the animating principle of the body as well as an intellectual principle.

Although Descartes thus preserved the traditional view of the mind as a spiritual being irreducible to the body, his acceptance of a purely mechanical view of nature, including the body, and his confinement of the action of the mind to one small part of the body alienated the mind from the natural world. E. A. Burtt has pointed out that, as the scientific view of Galileo and others became dominant in modern thought, the mind tended to become a passive spectator of things and changes in the world around it.[7] Descartes' dualism was an early expression of this view, and it helped to foster the cosmic homelessness and loneliness of modern man in a world governed by natural laws and indifferent to his purposes and values.

Modern Criticisms: Hume and Kant

The traditional view, in both its dualistic and its non-dualistic forms, was subjected to sharp criticism by David Hume who denied that we have any knowledge of a spiritual substance. Assuming that an idea can be known to correspond to a real object only if it has been derived from an immediate "impression," he examined critically the idea of a *"self"* which possesses "personal identity." When he looked within for such an "impression," he said, he could find nothing but a succession of ideas, volitions, feelings, and other conscious states following each other in time. Nowhere did he come upon an "impression" of a "self," a substance to which these psychical states belong and which remains identical with itself during the succession of them. From this he drew the conclusion that there is no ground in experience for affirming the existence of such a self and that the term "self" is only a name for the ever-changing series of psychical states. Since all of our perceptions are "separate" and "distinct" from each other, there is no real unity between them. The idea of a self with a personal identity, therefore, corresponds to nothing real and arises only from the causal relations of our perceptions with each other and a confusion between the *resemblance* of many of them and their *identity*. Thus, Hume dissolved the self or mind into a succession of conscious states, separate and distinct from one another and related only by means of the association of ideas.[8]

With such a skeptical view of the self, it is not surprising that Hume also denied any knowledge of an activity of the *will*. He argued, for example, that we do not normally have any awareness of the physiological changes that occur between an act of volition and a bodily movement that follows it, so that we cannot directly experience the power

[7] Burtt, Edwin A.: *The Metaphysical Foundations of Modern Physical Science*, New York, Harcourt, Brace and Co., 1925.

[8] Hume, David: *A Treatise of Human Nature*, Oxford, Clarendon Press, 1949, pp. 251 ff.

of our will to produce the movement.[9] He also reduced the "liberty" of the will in its volitions to the fact that they are determined not by external causes but by internal ones, i.e., by antecedent psychical states.[10] Moreover, if the mind consists of nothing more substantial than transitory psychical states, it is natural to regard the apparent continuity of these states as dependent upon the body with which it is associated. Therefore, it was only a step from Hume's denial of the "personal identity" of the "self" to the reduction of mind by Thomas Huxley to "epiphenomena" which accompany physiological processes in the brain and possess no causal efficacy of their own. Thus, Hume's skepticism prepared the way for the reductionist naturalism of the nineteenth century.

Any critical evaluation of Hume's attack upon the traditional view of mind must answer two different questions: (1) Why did his skeptical conclusions seem plausible to Hume despite the fact that they seem to contradict not only the view dominant among philosophers before him but also the view of ordinary people? and (2) is his own view of self or mind superior to the traditional one?

(1) It is sometimes said by defenders of Hume that he simply reported what he saw when he looked within and that anyone can confirm by introspection that his skeptical conclusion is correct. The obvious answer to this is that neither Hume nor anyone else could ever come upon the self or mind by the method he employed. He seems to assume that if a mind with personal identity exists, it must be an object which can cause "impressions" like an external object. Since he failed when he looked within to receive any impression from a mind existing as an *object* alongside or behind the succession of conscious states, he concluded that we have no knowledge of such a mind. He overlooked the fact that, if the mind does exist, it exists as a conscious *subject* of experiences, and that we can have no impression of such a subject comparable to an impression of a physical object.

But why did Hume assume that if the self is real, it must be capable of being experienced by an impression of an object? The answer is to be found in the influence upon him of the scientific method which had been employed with such success in describing the objects of the physical world. Since scientists like Newton had analyzed physical objects into their atomic elements and had explained their changes by means of the force exerted by them upon each other, it was natural for eighteenth-century thinkers like Hume to regard the mind as an object and to use the same method in dealing with it. Thus, Hume

[9] Hume, David: *Inquiry Concerning Human Understanding*, Oxford, Clarendon Press, 1894, p. 68.

[10] *Ibid.*, pp. 80–103.

analyzed the mind into atomic elements of experience ("separate and distinct" "perceptions") and explained the relations between them by laws of the association of ideas comparable to the law of gravitation in the physical world. This method proved to be fruitful, at least to some extent, in the development of psychology, since it made possible the careful description of the *contents* of mind which the psychologist treats as objects of scientific investigation. But the cost was great, for it eliminated the *subject* to which these contents belong.

Hume's skeptical conclusion also resulted from his empirical theory of knowledge. According to this theory knowledge arises from impressions passively received and from the combination of ideas by a process of what has been called "mental chemistry." Since our knowledge of the self or mind (as distinguished from its states or contents) arises in part from our experience of its activity in knowing and since Hume denied knowledge of such an activity, it was inevitable that he should deny a mind or self which is the subject of knowledge.

(2) Although the influence of Newtonian physics and British empiricism may help us to understand why Hume's skeptical view of mind seemed plausible to him, it is clearly inadequate. The method developed by the physical sciences to describe the objects and events of the external world cannot be applied without substantial modification to the inner world of the mind, and the empirical theory of the origin of all knowledge in "simple ideas" or "impressions" is too narrow. Two simple facts are sufficient to prove this.

In the first place, Hume's assertion that introspection discovers only a succession of conscious states is not in accord with the view of most philosophers before his time and is in flat contradiction to the view of ordinary men. It is significant that he himself found it difficult to maintain his skepticism when he left the philosopher's study and that he denied it by his own language in passages where he describes *himself* as looking for an impression of the "self." For only a self or mind identical with itself through its changing experiences could look within to seek for an impression of a self. The fact is that every person is intuitively aware of a distinction between himself as a subject of experiences and the objects which constitute the world around and within him. What Tillich calls the "split" or duality of subject and object belongs to the very structure of experience and cannot be denied without absurdity.

In the second place, every person is conscious of himself as actively adopting purposes and carrying them out in time. Hume's view of a volition as merely a particular psychical state determined by antecedent psychical states is incompatible with our experience of ourselves as striving in the present to attain certain ends in the future. This is clear especially in moral activity in which continuous effort over a period of time is necessary. Such purposeful conduct can arise only from a center of activity which is continuous and identical with itself through time.

A criticism of the traditional theory was also offered by Kant, although it was less radical and more constructive than that of Hume. The "empirical" ego or self, according to the first *Critique*, is simply the totality of psychical phenomena which are to be described by psychology in the same manner as the physical sciences describe external phenomena. However, Kant maintained that knowledge requires not only the passive reception of impressions through "sensibility" but also the active synthesis or organization of the multiplicity of impressions by means of categories and principles of the "understanding." This is possible only if we presuppose a logical subject, an "I think" or "transcendental unity of apperception," which accompanies all experiences and binds them together in a unity. This subject can synthesize a plurality of impressions into an object of knowledge only if it is the same subject which experiences all of them in succession, remembers the earlier ones, and combines all of them together in the unity of its consciousness. However, Kant rejected the claim of the rational psychology of his time that this presupposition of a *logical subject* of knowledge enables us to assert the existence of a *spiritual substance* or soul which is identical with itself, independent of the body, and immortal. For we may assert the existence of an object only if it can be presented to our minds by means of a sensuous intuition, and it is obviously impossible to have a sensuous intuition of a spiritual being.[11]

In his second *Critique*,[12] Kant also maintains that the practical reason requires us to presuppose the reality of a rational and free will which lays down moral laws to govern conduct. Like the logical subject presupposed in knowing, this *transcendental self* presupposed in moral action cannot be apprehended by sensuous intuition and hence cannot be known by our categories. Despite these negative elements in Kant's view of the mind, however, his positive insight into its nature is very important: although we cannot speak of the mind as a *substance*, it is presupposed as a principle of *subjective activity* in all our knowing and moral willing. We shall return later to this *dynamic* conception.

[11] Kant, Immanuel: *Critique of Pure Reason*, New York, Humanities Press, 1950, "The Paralogisms of Pure Reason."

[12] Kant, Immanuel: *Critique of Practical Reason*, tr. by T. K. Abbott, London, Longmans, Green and Co., 1909.

Naturalism and Behaviorism: Ryle

During the nineteenth century naturalistic philosophers repudiated the traditional view of mind as a spiritual substance and reduced it to a succession of psychical phenomena dependent upon physiological processes. As we pointed out, Hume prepared the way for this reductionist view of mind by dissolving the self into a succession of conscious states. However, the new scientific developments during the century also favored the reductionist view. For example, the Darwinian theory of evolution by natural selection seemed to many scientists to imply that there is no discontinuity between man and other animal species, that his intelligence and moral sentiments differ in degree rather than in kind from those of other species, and that therefore his claim to uniqueness because of his possession of mind is exaggerated. As a result, they drew the conclusion that mind is only an accompaniment of the physiological processes of the brain and nervous system and has no causal power to effect changes.

Why did naturalistic scientists like Thomas Huxley reduce the mind to an "epiphenomenon" of the brain and nervous system? [13] Part of the answer is to be found in the monistic tendency of reason to explain everything in terms of one kind of being. In the modern period the remarkable success of the physical sciences in describing the material world and of biology in describing the physical and chemical aspects of living organisms has increasingly led to naturalistic monism. To minds trained in the methods and concepts of Newtonian physics matter extended in space and endowed with energy seems more intelligible than mind, so that it is natural for them to seek to explain mental activity by means of bodily processes. For mind as it is known from within differs radically from matter in its properties and functions and therefore appears utterly mysterious to those who conceive of explanation in terms of physical causes rather than reasons or purposes. Unlike the objects of the physical world, it is neither visible nor tangible, and it can be observed by others only indirectly through its objective expression in behavior.

Closely related to this is another reason. From the beginning modern physical science has sought to describe in mathematically exact terms the quantitative aspects of nature. This is why it has concerned itself since the time of Galileo with the measurable "primary qualities" such as size, shape, and motion, relegating "secondary qualities" such as color and sound to the status of subjective effects of these. Since mind is not a physical object subject to this kind of mathematical descrip-

---

[13] Huxley, Thomas: *Hume*, New York, Harper's, 1879, pp. 76, 78.

tion, physical science has excluded it from the world it has sought to describe. As a result, it has come to appear as a strange and shadowy thing, less real than the objects of the physical world and wholly dependent on them. It is not surprising, therefore, that naturalistic biologists have tended to reduce it to a powerless by-product of physiological processes. Moreover, the principle of the continuity of nature, which is closely allied to the monistic tendency in science, seems to naturalistic scientists to require that higher kinds of beings should be regarded as different from lower ones not in kind but only in degree. The fact that the apparent gap between inanimate matter and living organisms seems to be bridged by intermediate forms and the fact that intelligence and moral sentiment exist in more elementary forms below the level of man have strengthened this belief.

Thus, the monistic tendency to seek for unity in all things, the apparent intelligibility of matter in contrast to the mysteriousness of mind, and the scientific demand for continuity between the higher and the lower levels of nature have combined to produce the naturalistic conception of mind. It is not our purpose here to offer arguments against this conception. It stands or falls with naturalism as a whole and with the scientism on which that philosophy largely rests. In the last analysis, however, the naturalistic conception of mind can be most effectively refuted not by arguments against it but by showing that another conception is more adequate, and it is the purpose of this and the following chapter to do this.

However, it may be pointed out that the attempt of many nineteenth century scientists to reduce mind to matter and energy does not find favor with recent distinguished physiologists such as Sir Charles Sherrington who have done extensive research on the brain and its mechanisms. Sherrington asserts that the natural sciences, including physiology, have been able to bring within the "energy-scheme" of science the most diverse phenomena but that they cannot explain even a simple mental act such as perception. "The energy-scheme deals with the star as one of the objects observable by us; as to the perceiving of it by the mind the scheme puts its finger to its lip and is silent. . . . So with the whole of mental experience, the energy-scheme leaves it aside and does not touch it. Our mental experience is not open to observation through any sense organ. . . . The mental act of 'knowing' we are aware of, but we cannot sensually observe it. It is experienced, not observed." [14] Sherrington also points out that, although there is a correlation between mental processes and brain processes, knowledge of the latter does not explain the former. "For myself, what little I

[14] Sherrington, Sir Charles: *Man on His Nature*, Garden City, N.Y., Doubleday and Co., 1953, pp. 244, 245.

know of the how of the one does not, speaking personally, even begin to help me toward the how of the other. The two for all I can do remain refractorily apart. They seem to me disparate; not mutually convertible; untranslatable the one into the other." [15] It is difficult to see how there could be a more emphatic repudiation of the naturalistic reduction of mind to bodily processes or a clearer affirmation of its distinctive character.

The most interesting *behavioristic* theory of mind which has been proposed by a philosopher is that of Gilbert Ryle.[16] It is a sustained and uncompromising polemic against the traditional view of mind as a spiritual substance associated with but distinct from the body. Ryle regards this view as a product of the "two worlds" theory of Descartes, according to which man is composed of two different substances, one material and the other spiritual. He refers to this theory as the dogma or myth of "the ghost in the machine," and his purpose is to exorcise this "ghost" and to offer an alternative theory which will provide a better account of mental facts. He argues that it results from a "category-mistake," since it uses the category of substance to describe the mind and the category of causality to describe its operations.

To this dualistic view, Ryle opposes his own theory that the mind is not a spiritual substance but consists of enduring "dispositions" or "tendencies," on the one hand, and episodic "occurrences," on the other. Although he does not deny the existence of subjective states such as feelings, he rejects again and again the traditional view that they are causes of men's actions and seems to think of them as merely accompanying publicly observable behavior and being of quite secondary importance. For example, virtue and knowledge can be analyzed as "dispositions" to behave in certain ways under certain conditions. A "disposition" is described by hypothetical propositions which state that if A occurs, B will occur. Just as the meaning of "Glass is brittle" can be expressed in propositions such as "If a hard blow strikes a glass object, it will break into pieces," so the meaning of "Smith is kind" can be stated in propositions such as "If someone known to Smith suffers and is in need, Smith will help him." On this view, mind is not a spiritual substance or theatre where ideas and feelings take place behind the scenes but a name for "dispositions" to do certain things and "episodes" of publicly observable behavior in which these are from time to time actualized.[17]

In order to test the adequacy of this behavioristic view, we shall

[15] *Ibid.*, p. 252.

[16] Ryle, Gilbert: *The Concept of Mind*, London, Hutchinson's University Library, 1951.

[17] *Ibid.*, Ch. V.

examine critically Ryle's application of it to several mental functions.

(1) *Motives* for actions, he asserts, can be described in terms of dispositions without reference to "thrills" of feeling, e.g., vanity in terms of behavior such as talking a lot about oneself. Ryle does not deny that feelings may accompany the behavior, but he does not regard them as causes of it. Even if a person reported that he experienced a feeling of vanity before doing a vain act, we could not trust his report and know it to be true, whereas we can verify the existence of a vain disposition in him by observing whether he talks a lot about himself and is impatient when others are praised rather than himself. This argument is significant, because it suggests that one reason for Ryle's exclusive interest in behavior is that it is publicly observable and can be known more certainly by others than private experiences hidden from them. By identifying the mind with its outward expression, "turning it inside out," it is possible to attain a more accurate picture of it.[18]

Now, the identification of motives with feelings alone is obviously an abstraction, since a kind feeling or a feeling of vanity cannot be separated from the disposition to act with which it is associated. But this does not prove that the feeling has nothing to do with the motive, but only that it is not the whole of the motive. In fact, the denial that feelings have an effect upon conduct involves a rejection of the common conviction, expressed in ordinary language, that they have a powerful influence on man's actions. The fact that a person may not describe his feelings correctly to others or may deceive himself in thinking that a certain feeling was not his motive for a particular act does not require that we give up this conviction, although it shows that we do not know our own motives or those of others as clearly as we may think we do and that we should supplement our knowledge of motives through feelings by the knowledge of them we can gain through behavior.

(2) One of the most interesting of Ryle's behavioristic descriptions is his account of "knowing how." Knowing how to do something, he says, involves the correct performance of an action and thinking what one is doing while doing it.[19] According to the traditional view, he says, the performance of the action must be preceded by an intellectual acknowledgment of the rules for performing it correctly. But " 'thinking what I am doing' does not connote 'both thinking what I am doing and doing it,' " for it is "doing one thing and not two." [20] An example is the cleverness exhibited by a clown in tripping and tumbling. "The

[18] *Ibid.*, pp. 86–93.
[19] *Ibid.*, p. 28.
[20] *Ibid.*, p. 32.

spectators applaud his skill as seeming clumsy, but what they applaud is not some extra hidden performance executed 'in his head.' It is his visible performance that they admire, but they admire it not for being an effect of any hidden internal causes but for being an exercise of skill." [21] And this skill is not "an occult or ghostly happening" but a "disposition, or complex of dispositions." [22]

Is this an adequate description of "knowing how" to do something? It is true, as Ryle says, that the spectators applaud the skill of the clown as exhibited in his behavior and do not consciously think about the mental events "in his head." But it is *not* true that the skill of his performance can be described without any reference to the thought he had to exercise in the past in order to attain his skill and the attention he has to pay to his exhibition of it in the present. Moreover, spectators are well aware that these mental processes, past and present, lie behind and make possible the skill of the performance.

Ryle's arguments against this non-behavioristic view of "knowing how" are unconvincing. Intelligence, he says, is sometimes displayed in performances by people who have not previously formulated rules for doing them correctly, e.g., in fishing without benefit of a book on the art, and even if one has learned the rules or principles for a correct performance, one must be able to apply them in concrete cases before one can be said to "know how." Both of these statements are obviously true, but the conclusion Ryle draws from them, i.e., that no "specific antecedents" in the form of mental processes are required for "knowing how," is completely false. It derives whatever plausibility it has from its caricature of the non-behavioristic view. The mental processes which are necessary conditions of "knowing how" to do something correctly do not have to be *formulated* in propositions and then *applied* to concrete actions. For actions involving "knowing how" are directed by practical intelligence rather than by rules formulated by theoretical reason, so that they do not have to be preceded by the thought of such rules and the application of them to the concrete action. Again, the fact that calculations in mental arithmetic go on in the mind and are not publicly observable is irrelevant, says Ryle, because they can equally well be done out loud and thus be observed. This is true, but it does not prove that "knowing how" to calculate would be possible without mental acts that are unobservable; it proves that "knowing how" may *express* itself in overt behavior but not that it *consists* of such behavior.

(3) Ryle's description of *intellect* is especially interesting in view of

[21] *Ibid.,* p. 33.
[22] *Ibid.,* p. 33.

the fact that intellectual activity has usually been regarded as the highest function of the mind and as a proof of its spiritual character. He defines "intellect" in terms of "those capacities which are originally inculcated and developed predominantly by didactic discourse, and are themselves exercised, inter alia, in teaching the same lessons or adaptations or expansions of them in further allocutions." [23] This definition rightly emphasizes the fact that intellectual powers are originally developed partly by teaching and may manifest themselves in the capacity to teach others. But it describes the *process* in which they arise and are exercised rather than the *essence* of them. It also implies that thinking can be identified with talking, either silently or aloud, in a certain frame of mind. "Saying something in this specific frame of mind, whether aloud or in one's head *is* thinking the thought. It is not an after-effect of thinking the thought, such that the author might conceivably have thought the thought, but shirked saying the thing to himself, or to the world." [24] The difficulty with this is that, although there is a close connection between thinking and talking, the essential thing about intellect is the capacity to make judgments and inferences and this involves inner *mental activity*. Without it, the *behavior* of talking, to oneself or to another, would consist of nothing more than meaningless noises.

(4) Finally, Ryle's view of *self-consciousness* and *self-control* is wholly inadequate. The apparent division of the mind into a part that knows or acts and a part that is known or acted upon, he asserts, is due simply to the fact that "higher-order" actions can operate upon "lower-order" ones in oneself as well as in relation to others.[25] Therefore, "self-consciousness" is only "a special case of an ordinary more or less efficient handling of a less or more honest and intelligent witness," i.e., oneself, while "self-control" is "simply a special case of the management of an ordinary person by an ordinary person, namely where John Doe, say, is taking both parts." [26] These "higher-order" acts are not mysterious; they are the same in kind as "higher-order" acts of persons shown in their dealings with one another.[27]

It is misleading, to say the least, to compare self-consciousness or self-control to the "handling" or "management" of one person by another. The mystery of the self's transcendence of itself, its turning back upon itself, cannot be dispelled by treating it as similar to the action of one person upon another. It is a manifestation of the capacity

[23] *Ibid.*, p. 309.
[24] *Ibid.*, p. 296.
[25] *Ibid.*, p. 191.
[26] *Ibid.*, p. 195.
[27] *Ibid.*, p. 198.

of the self to make itself, not another self, an object for itself, a subject. This capacity is wholly unintelligible on the basis of the behavioristic conception of mind. For self-consciousness or self-control does not involve bodily behaviour of any kind, it consists of the direction of attention or effort by the self inward upon itself. At the same time, it does not divide itself into two selves but remains one. This is one of the mysteries of mind, and it is possible only because the mind is more than a behaving organism.

We have critically examined some of the activities and capacities of mind as described by Ryle—feeling, "knowing how," intellect, and self-consciousness—and have argued that his behavioristic account of them is unsatisfactory because it does not do justice to their distinctive nature. We know them in a measure through their overt expression in behavior but also through consciousness and introspection, although our knowledge of them is fallible. However, there is value in Ryle's attempt to give a behavioristic account of mind. It serves as a corrective of the dualistic concept of mind and its relation to the body. It shows that the relation between mental states and bodily behavior is far closer than Descartes realized. Because of their close relation, observation of our behavior supplements and corrects in a valuable way the knowledge of our minds we attain through introspection. It is even more indispensable for our knowledge of the character and capacities of others, to whose inner experience we have no direct access. Therefore, it is essential that the study of human behavior should be carried as far as possible and that knowledge of it should be correlated with knowledge gained from introspection. It is true that "from within out of the heart" [28] come men's thoughts and deeds; but it is also true that "each tree is known by its own fruit." [29]

Furthermore, the examination of behavior shows us that the mind is not a thing existing apart in a separate world of its own but that it lives and acts in the ordinary world. Thus, it can deliver us from a false spirituality which exalts the inner life by divorcing it from its expression of itself through the body in the objective world.

The Substantival View

At the opposite extreme from the naturalistic and behavioristic theories we have been considering is the *substantival* view of mind as a spiritual substance. This view, which has been deeply influenced by the traditional view of Plato and Descartes, has recently been defended

[28] Mark 7:21.
[29] Luke 6:44.

by C. A. Campbell. He is critical not only of the behaviorism of Ryle[30] but also of the empiricist view of Hume that the self is only a succession of psychical states without personal identity.[31] Against the latter view he uses Kant's argument that a plurality of impressions must be present to a subject which is the same or identical with itself, if knowledge of an object is to be possible. Campbell has restated this argument very clearly, taking as an example our experience of succession in time. If I hear a clock striking, I can apprehend the second stroke as the second only if I remember having heard the first, and I cannot remember this unless I am conscious that it was I, the same subject, who heard the first stroke and am now hearing the second.[32] Campbell contends that the self's consciousness of its identity in and through these different experiences implies that it is an enduring substance. He also points out that the capacity to learn and the development of character show that past experiences survive and influence the present through tendencies or dispositions to think and to act in definite ways, despite the fact that such experiences do not continue to exist in the intervening period as conscious states. The theory that these past experiences persist as unconscious "traces" which are passed on successively from one mental state to another until they produce their effects in the present seems absurd; and the alternative theory that a past experience without the aid of such "traces" somehow leaps across the temporal gap and produces a present effect is unintelligible.[33] Campbell concludes that only the existence of a substantival self or mind can account for the "dispositions" brought about by past experiences.[34]

These are persuasive arguments for the irreducibility of mental activity to bodily processes and they have not been taken seriously enough by Ryle and others who have ridiculed the substantival theory. In addition, there is a profound insight in Plato's substantival view, expressed in the *Phaedo* and the *Phaedrus* in somewhat different terms, that the rational soul—or what we would prefer to call "the mind in its spiritual activity"—aspires to higher values such as wisdom and virtue, is often in conflict with the desires associated with the body, and should subordinate the latter to the realization of these spiritual values. We shall analyze later the nature of spiritual activity and its values. The essential point to note here is that the mind at its highest

[30] Campbell, C. A.: essay "Ryle on the Intellect" in Lewis, H. D. (ed.): *Clarity Is Not Enough.*

[31] Campbell, C. A.: *Selfhood and Godhood,* London, George Allen and Unwin, 1957.

[32] *Ibid.,* pp. 76, 77.

[33] *Ibid.,* pp. 124, 125.

[34] *Ibid.,* pp. 125, 126.

level seeks values which require that it gain control over the body in order to regulate its appetites and use its energies to serve spiritual as well as biological ends. In doing so, it becomes in some measure the organizing principle, the principle of unity of the person as a whole. This insight must never be forgotten, despite the fact that many men seem to use the mind merely as an instrument for the satisfaction of bodily desires.

But the difficulty with the substantival view of Plato, Descartes, and Campbell is that it requires us to think of a person as composed of two different substances, mind and body, which have little or nothing in common. This destroys the unity of the person and is incompatible with the intimate association of the mind with the body. The other form of the traditional view, which was developed by Aquinas, attempts to avoid this dualism by affirming with Aristotle that the soul is the "form" of the body and the soul and body together compose one substance, but that the soul is a spiritual substance which depends upon the sense organs for its ideas but is independent of the body in its essence. But is there not a contradiction between these two sides of Aquinas' view? How can it be true *both* that the soul and body together compose one substance *and* that the soul is itself a spiritual substance? Aquinas is able to avoid the appearance of a contradiction only by using "substance" in two different senses, *both* as what exists only as a part of a whole *and* as what can exist by itself.[35]

Thus, despite the important insights expressed in it, it is necessary to reject the substantival theory of mind in both its Platonic-Cartesian and its Thomistic forms. The intimate relationship of the soul to the body is incompatible with the dualism to which the theory inevitably leads. In addition, William Kneale has pointed out that the experiences of a person happen to his body in the sense of being "compresent with inner perceptions of a living body." [36] For example, experiences of perception such as seeing and hearing are closely connected with processes in the body, i.e., a person sees with his eyes and hears with his ears. Again, experiences of volition such as walking or speaking involve processes in the legs or vocal organs. This does not mean that perceptions and volitions are *identical* with the bodily processes with which they are connected, for seeing is an inner *perception* that occurs *through* the eyes and speaking involves the *will* to communicate *through* the vocal organs. Hence, Kneale insists that "we must retain the Platonic notion of mental events which are distinct from anything

[35] Gilson, E.: *The Christian Philosophy of St. Thomas Aquinas*, New York, Random House, 1956, p. 196.

[36] Kneale, William: *On Having a Mind*, Cambridge, Cambridge University Press, 1962, p. 51.

in the physical world and manifest a certain kind of connectedness." [37]
But the "close connection" or "compresence" of inner experiences of
perception and volition with "happenings" in the body, he thinks, is
fatal to the substantival theory of Plato.

These philosophical arguments against the substantival theory are
supported not only by modern psychology but also by the Biblical
view of man. Old Testament scholars, as we noted, have often emphasized the fact that there is no suggestion of a dualistic view of soul and
body in the Old Testament.[38] The ancient Hebraic view was that man
is a psychophysiological unity. There is no tendency to disparage the
body as evil—like the material world as a whole, it is good because it
is part of a good creation—and to set the soul or mind in opposition
to it.

Most New Testament scholars agree that the conception of man in
the New Testament is similar to that of the Old Testament. There are
passages which may show the influence of Platonic terminology, but a
careful examination of them shows that their meaning is not dualistic
in the Platonic sense, e.g., the contrast in St. Paul between the "flesh"
and the "Spirit." There is a passage in which St. Paul lists seventeen
"works of the flesh" but of these only six are connected with the body,
e.g., adultery and drunkenness, while the other eleven have nothing
to do with physical impulses and desires, e.g., idolatry, envying, strife,
and sedition.[39] This indicates that "the flesh" does not stand for one
part of man, his body, which is bad, and "the Spirit" for another part,
his "soul," which is good. Rather, "the flesh" stands for the kind of
man in whom the whole person, the psychical as well as the physical
aspects, is corrupted by self-centeredness, while "the Spirit" represents
the kind of man in whom the whole person, the physical as well as the
psychical aspects, is characterized by love for God and his neighbor.[40]
Thus, the dominance in Christian theology of the substantival view
of the mind and of dualism between mind and body, especially in the
Middle Ages, must be attributed to the influence of Greek philosophy,
especially Platonism, rather than the Bible.

A Dynamic View

The conclusion we would draw from our critical examination of
major theories of mind from Plato to the present is that neither the

[37] *Ibid.*, p. 56.
[38] Wheeler Robinson, H.: *The Religious Ideas of the Old Testament*, London,
Duckworth, 1913, ch. IV.
[39] Gal. 5.
[40] Owen, D. R. G.: *Body and Soul*, Philadelphia, Westminster Press, 1956, ch. IX.

traditional "substantival" view nor the modern skeptical, naturalistic, or behavioristic view is adequate. Rather, mind is the subjective knowing, willing, and feeling activity of a person and is intimately associated with his body. We may call this a *dynamic* view of mind to emphasize that it is neither a substance nor a kind of behavior but a unique and irreducible form of subjective activity.

The most fundamental characteristic of mind, conceived as the subjective activity of a person, is what existentialists call its "*intentionality.*" It is not pure subjectivity turned inward upon itself but openness towards what is other than itself. From the beginning it is involved in encounter with objects beyond itself which are present to it as having meaning and value. Thus, its original relationship to the world is that of participation. Its knowledge of objects is based upon its experience of their presence in relation to its intentions. Another way of expressing the point is to speak of the mind's capacity to "refer" to objects. As Peter Bertocci puts it, "in knowing there is an event which exists as psychic but whose very being consists in its being referred beyond itself by the knowing being. This reference beyond itself makes error (and truth) possible, and it distinguishes the being who can 'refer' from every other being we know." [41] It is not confined to external objects which are perceived in the present; it also extends through memory to past events, through purpose to future ones, and through thought to ideal objects such as justice and God. Thus, the mind is capable of presenting all kinds of objects before itself, and thus "becoming" all things in the sense of participating in them.[42] It is false, therefore, to picture consciousness as consisting of a succession of ideas, images, and other inner states which it contemplates and from which it then infers the existence of external objects corresponding to them. For we are conscious of *objects,* not of ideas, and of the *meaning* of objects in relation to our intentions.

As the concepts of "intentionality," "reference," and "meaning" imply, the mind is not usually passive in receiving impressions of objects but *actively responds* to them in knowing them. By distinguishing particular elements of its experience in selective acts of attention and relating them to each other, it makes judgments about them and builds up its knowledge of objects and of the world as a whole. "It is not a kind of lambent illumination which reveals ready-made objects to some mysterious passive spectator (called 'the mind'), but the activity of selecting, distinguishing, and relating elements within a felt

[41] Scher, Jordan M.: *Theories of the Mind,* New York, The Free Press of Glencoe, 1962, pp. 400, 402.
[42] *Ibid.,* Veatch, H. B.: "*Minds: What and Where in the World are They?*", p. 318.

manifold which it transforms by continuous stages of elaboration into a world of related objects." [43]

This activity of knowing is *purposive* in its character and practical as well as theoretical in its motivation. "For as rational beings," says Veatch, "we consider that we are able not merely to know what's what, but also to choose and to act freely in the light of that knowledge," and mind is simply "that characteristic power or ability which human beings have of intending objects both cognitively and purposefully." [44] Indeed, mind should be conceived as primarily practical rather than theoretical in its activity. This does not mean that knowledge is merely instrumental, for the truth which it seeks is an intrinsic value of a high order. It means only that knowing is a form of activity arising from the purpose to attain truth and that this purpose, like all purposes, must be adopted and carried out by the will. It means also that the purpose to attain truth is intimately related to the other purposes of a person and to the whole pattern of values he seeks to realize.

This view was first stated by St. Augustine in terms of the *primacy of will* over intellect. Greek philosophers such as Aristotle had maintained the primacy of intellect in the soul, on the ground that knowledge is the source not only of truth but also of moral goodness. In contrast, St. Augustine asserted that the will, motivated by love of the good, has primacy over the intellect and that even the intellect's search for knowledge depends upon the will's direction of attention to the truth. Modern psychology and psychoanalysis have strongly supported this "voluntaristic" view against the "intellectualistic" view of Greek philosophers. Indeed, it has sometimes been carried to the extreme of irrationalism, as in Nietzsche's glorification of the will to power, or instrumentalism, as in Dewey's view of thinking as a means of adjusting the organism to its environment. However, the acceptance of the primacy of the will, i.e., of the conative function as a whole and the emotional aspect which is closely associated with it, does not require any such subordination or disparagement of the intellect. It involves only the recognition that mind should never be viewed as merely observing the world and mirroring it in consciousness for the sake of knowing it, but as always engaging in purposive activity even when seeking knowledge of the world.

If we conceive of mind as subjective activity which is primarily will rather than intellect in its essence, its *unity* and *continuity* can be interpreted in dynamic terms. Austin Farrer defines the will as "the self-actualizing potency of a project," since it actualizes in particular

[43] *Ibid.*, Harris, E.: *"Mind and Mechanical Models,"* p. 486.
[44] Veatch, *op. cit.*, p. 320.

actions the potentialities it has adopted as its projects or goals.[45] Each particular action has a unity of its own binding its different stages together, from the entertainment of a project to the actualization of it.[46] But there is also a unity of the self as a whole, "the total complex of acts both higher and lower, in its extension through time." [47] This unity has a physical basis in the pattern of instincts of the body, a basis which both limits it and provides it with concrete materials.[48] From this starting-point a further unity is attained by means of the unity of the projects or aims of the rational will as it develops through time, and continuity results from its tendency to follow purposes adopted in the past.[49] Unity and continuity of another kind are also achieved by the focusing or concentration of all the past acts of the will as ingredients in the present act.[50] Thus, the self is "a continuous intellective and creative activity which proceeds by concentration into successive particular acts." [51]

The value of this description is not in its psychological details but in its general account of the *mind as a subjective activity of will which manifests its unity and continuity by constructing a higher pattern of rational aims upon the foundation of a lower pattern of bodily instincts.* As it moves by successive concentrations of its activity into the future, it brings its past to bear upon each present act and grounds its future upon its past by continuing the aims it has previously adopted. *Thus, while it depends upon and is limited by the body, it is essentially creative, purposive activity.*

Such a dynamic conception of the mind enables us to avoid the temptation to picture it as similar to a physical thing and thus to reduce it to one object among others in the world. As language about minds is largely derived from language about physical things and events, it is all too easy to assimilate them to objects, especially since psychology seeks to describe them with scientific precision as natural phenomena. Therefore, it is necessary to emphasize the distinctive character of the mind by saying that it is primarily not an object but a *subject of experience.* This implies that it can never be adequately described by the scientific method which was designed to describe the world of objects, although it is possible to apprehend (by introspection) its actions and the contents of its experience and (by observation) the behavior in which it manifests itself.

[45] Farrer, Austin: *Finite and Infinite,* Westminister, Dacre Press, 1943, pp. 115, 119.
[46] *Ibid.,* Ch. XI.
[47] *Ibid.,* p. 171.
[48] *Ibid.,* Ch. XV.
[49] *Ibid.,* Ch. XVI.
[50] *Ibid.,* p. 229.
[51] *Ibid.,* p. 229.

The dynamic conception of mind as purposive activity actualizing potentialities in successive particular actions also enables us to avoid the error of thinking of the mind as an essence which is complete from the beginning and only unfolds itself through its actions and experiences. In reality, the essence of the mind develops only in the course of time and it is shaped largely by its own decisions, as existentialists such as Kierkegaard have pointed out. Thus, the being of the mind is fully manifested only through its *becoming*. This also implies that the mind as purposive activity does not exist *apart from* its particular actions but *in* and *through* them. One of the dangers involved in the substantival view is that it seems to conceive of the mind as something beneath its activities as a kind of unknowable substratum, whereas it appears and expresses itself in them.

Spirit and Its Activity

The synthesis of the Biblical concept of "spirit" (*ruach* or *pneuma*) and the Platonic concept of "reason" (*nous*) in Western theism led to the idea that man's soul or mind at its highest level of activity is spiritual. What is the meaning of "spirit"? How is man's spirit related to other aspects of his personality?

When we speak of a person as "spiritual," we do not mean that he is *pure* spirit, since his body is obviously an essential part of him. Nor do we mean that there dwells within him *a* spirit which is active as a distinct being within him. We mean that his mind is capable of spiritual activity, that he is distinguished from the lower animals by his ability to conceive of ideal realities and values which transcend the world of the senses, and that he can determine his thinking and action, at least in some measure, by reference to them. We mean, also, that by virtue of this capacity he can attain a higher level of life than that of ordinary human existence. Classical humanists and theists alike accept this conception of the human spirit and the spiritual life. However, theists differ from classical humanists in believing that spiritual life, in its purest form and at the highest level, must be based upon faith in and love for God and is impossible without the aid of the Spirit of God.

The human spirit can best be understood by analyzing several forms of activity in which it expresses itself. In the first place, it is capable of devotion to *spiritual values* such as truth and goodness which have no necessary relation to biological needs. It is one of the great insights of Plato that the activity of the soul is teleologically rather than mechanically determined, i.e., that it acts in accordance with ends approved by reason rather than from necessity. This is quite compatible, as Socrates explains in the *Phaedo,* with the use of bodily mechanisms by the soul as means to its ends. But it is not compatible with a purely mechanical explanation of the soul's actions, e.g., with an explanation of Socrates' refusal to flee from prison by reference to the state of his bones and muscles without taking account of his reasons. Rather, it implies that the soul is free to determine its acts in accordance with its own purposes.[52] We shall analyze the nature of this freedom in the next chapter, and it is necessary here only to point out that it presupposes the spiritual capacity of mind.

Spiritual activity directed towards spiritual values is governed by *spiritual laws* which are quite distinct from natural laws. For example, the laws which govern the mind in its thinking—when its aim is to attain truth—are logical rather than physical or biological laws. Whereas natural laws merely describe phenomena and their relationships, logical laws such as the law of contradiction prescribe the principles which are to be followed in correct thinking. Of course, the mind often fails to follow logical laws when it thinks; but this is due to the fact that men are ignorant of them, are careless in their thinking, or seek other ends than truth when they think. For reason can be used as an instrument for the attainment of worldly ends such as wealth and power rather than for the discovery of truth. Similarly, moral conduct is governed, not by biological, psychological or anthropological laws describing the ways men *usually* act, but by moral laws prescribing the way they *should* act. In their actual conduct they can and often do refuse to obey these laws, but when they do they are not acting morally.

Moreover, the mind has the capacity to deny or subordinate the natural desires of the psychophysical organism to the purposes of the divine will as it understands them. In this *religious activity,* according to the theistic view, the spiritual capacity of the mind manifests itself most clearly. For man transcends ordinary worldly existence when he apprehends the reality of God by faith and seeks to fulfill the destiny for which He has created him instead of merely satisfying his desires as a biological and a social being. When he does so, he devotes his energies, not merely to specific spiritual values such as truth and goodness which enable him to realize his potentialities, but also to the service of the ultimate Ground of these and all other values.[53] He serves God from love and thereby attains perfect freedom and fulfillment.

In describing the spiritual activity of the mind in terms of spiritual values such as these, we must not forget that functions of the mind

[52] Plato: *Phaedo,* 96–99.

[53] This is the main point at which *theistic* differs from most *classical* humanism.

which are more closely related to the body, e.g., sensation, desire, and natural affection also have spiritual significance. The philosopher of religion should never fall into the spiritualistic error of supposing that the spiritual life is opposed to the life of the body and the values of ordinary human existence. The dualistic conception of mind and body and the ascetic ideal of religion connected with it have often fostered this error. As we have seen, the mind is intimately related to the body and to the world around it. Hence, the spiritual capacity of the mind is manifested not only in devoting itself to spiritual values such as truth and moral goodness but also in transforming all the functions of the self and the life of society as a whole under the guidance of spiritual purposes. A few illustrations will serve to indicate the way in which this can occur.

Sensation in the life of animals below man is primarily, if not solely, a servant of biological needs and satisfactions. Stimuli received by the animal organism through its sense organs such as the eye, ear, and nose give rise to perceptions which enable it to satisfy its hunger, propagate offspring, and survive. Thus, sense perception brings the animal organism into contact with particular objects in its environment which are indispensable for its existence. However, it does not, as far as we know, stimulate in these animals a process of thinking with the purpose of attaining knowledge for its own sake nor does it inspire them to create new forms by imagination for the sake of contemplation and enjoyment unrelated to biological needs.[54] In the case of man, sensation can stimulate the intellect to conceive general ideas dissociated from the objects which originally suggested them—"free ideas"—and to construct systems of scientific knowledge and philosophy. Or it can stir up the imagination to create works of art and poetry. Or it can arouse feelings of awe and wonder before the mystery and sublimity of nature and become a window through which the religious man looks beyond nature to the eternal. Thus, while the basic function of sensation is the perception of objects which fulfill biological needs, it can also be for man the occasion of intellectual, artistic, or religious activities through which the spirit both transcends its natural environment and discovers a higher meaning and value through it. In this way, sensation plays an indispensable role in the spiritual life of the self by providing material

[54] There is some psychological and biological evidence that some animals continue to learn and to exercise skills beyond the point necessary to satisfy their immediate needs and that others enjoy beautiful colors and forms in connection with mating. But there seems to be a substantial difference between the practical intelligence and aesthetic feeling of animals and the intellectual and artistic creativity of man. Thorpe, William R.: *Biology and the Nature of Man*, London, Oxford University Press, 1962.

for it and by stimulating it to creative thought, imagination, and worship.

Again, *appetite* drives the animal to seek satisfaction of its needs through appropriate objects in its environment and thus to preserve itself and its species. Since an animal appetite such as hunger or sex is general, any object of a certain kind will normally satisfy it and it does not idealize the objects by which it satisfies itself. In the case of man, however, an appetite is affected by the context in which it arises, e.g., the society to which he belongs. The satisfaction of an appetite such as hunger or sex is modified by the customs of a particular society, e.g., the individual is expected to observe a code of manners at the table and conform to rules which regulate sexual intercourse. Moreover, he is capable of controlling his appetites by ethical principles and subordinating them to a general pattern of life he has adopted for himself. He can even deny satisfaction to an appetite altogether for the sake of a higher end, e.g., he can starve himself as a protest against injustice or take a vow of permanent celibacy. The spiritual capacity of the mind manifests itself not only in the modification and limitation of the appetites but also in the redirection and transformation of them. For example, the sexual appetite can be sublimated by the idealization of its object, as in romantic poetry and song, or transformed into an expression of personal love as in marriage. Thus, appetites which are biological in origin can be endowed with a higher significance and taken up into the spiritual life.

We have spoken of the spiritual capacity of the self to transform sensation and appetite into material and dynamic for the spiritual life. We must speak, finally, of the responsibility of the self to embody its purposes in *social* institutions and relationships. It is only by doing so that it can avoid the temptation to withdraw from society, its problems, and its evils into an otherworldly spirituality. William Temple warns Christians against an indifference to economic conditions which is based on the false assumption that it is only the inner spiritual life of the individual that is important. He calls Christianity the most "materialist" of all religions because it demands justice in economic and social institutions which profoundly affect the welfare of persons.[55] Thus, the spiritual life requires the transformation of social as well as personal life. In brief, mind at the spiritual level can struggle with all the forces in its social environment which are opposed to its purposes and seek to transform them into instruments of love and justice.

For although mind and spirit are functions of individual persons, a person is also a *social being* whose life is bound up with that of others.

[55] Temple, William: *Nature, Man and God,* London, Macmillan, 1951, p. 478.

One of the most serious errors of the modern period, especially in democratic societies that pride themselves on the dignity and freedom of the individual, is the view that the essence of personality is individuality in the sense of separate and independent existence. This has led to an aggressive assertion of rights without a corresponding concern for duties and to an exaggeration of the capacity of the individual to realize himself by his own efforts without the help of others. Self-centeredness is at the heart of this individualism and it is the major source of economic ruthlessness, social injustice, and lawlessness in our society.

In reality, a human person is born into a community and comes to self-fulfillment only as he transcends his separate existence and participates in the common interests and achievement of his community. The spiritual nature of a person is realized through his relations with other persons. Indeed, Buber maintains that the human spirit exists not so much *in* individual persons as *between* them, i.e., that it arises and develops only in personal encounters with other Thous.[56] In other terms, man learns to devote himself to spiritual values such as truth and goodness and to attain faith in and love for God only in community with other persons. In fact, the development of *every* function of the mind depends upon a person's relation with other persons and his participation in the culture of his society, e.g., he learns to think only with the help of the language he has been taught by and shares with others.

In brief, there are two quite different sides of human personality. On the one hand, each person is a unique individual and possesses worth in himself. As such, he should be treated, in Kant's terms, "as an end in himself and never as a mere means." Hence, the greatest evil of collectivism in all of its forms is that it submerges the individual in the group and thus reduces him to a mere part of an impersonal whole. On the other hand, a person's life is bound up with that of other persons in his community. His participation in the common life is the source of most of the values that give meaning to his own life. It is also the source of his responsibility to and for others. He is a moral being subject to unconditional imperatives because he is a social being upon whom others are dependent as he is dependent upon them. The freedom to obey these imperatives is one of the highest manifestations of his spiritual nature, especially when his acts are motivated by love for others.

Thus, mind, which at the lower stages of its development primarily serves the organism in its adjustment to its environment, can become

---

[56] Buber, Martin: *I and Thou*, Edinburgh, T. and T. Clark, 1937, p. 39.

when it is more fully developed the controlling factor in the life of a person.[57] It can then devote itself mainly to spiritual ends and use the body and its energies to serve these ends in ways such as we have described. It can also use the *material world* as a medium or vehicle for the realization of spiritual purposes, so that nature becomes what Temple calls "the sacramental universe." [58] The doctor uses medicines and instruments to care for the health of his patients; the artist works with canvas, brushes, and pigments to create a painting; the family makes a home the center of its shared life of love; and the religious man uses common elements like water, bread, and wine as symbols of his faith and worship. Thus, the spirit seeks not only to transform the lives of *persons* and the structures of *society* but also to make *nature* itself a means to the realization of its higher ends.

Conclusion

The conception of man we have developed in this chapter is mainly a product of the synthesis of classical humanism with Biblical theism. The classical *humanistic* elements in it are obvious. Although we have rejected the traditional view of the mind as a substance in both its Platonic and its Thomistic forms, we have defended a dynamic view of it which emphasizes its uniqueness as subjective activity and hence its irreducibility to the body. We have also affirmed that the highest function of the mind is spiritual activity and that the spirit is capable of becoming the controlling principle of the personality, a view which is similar in some respects to the view of Plato and Aristotle that the highest part of the soul is reason and that it can subordinate sensation and appetite to the attainment of wisdom and virtue.

However, our conception of man at crucial points is primarily *theistic* rather than humanistic, although it also owes much to criticisms of the traditional view by modern philosophers. In harmony with Biblical theism (as well as with much modern psychology) it describes the mind in dynamic terms as subjective activity rather than as a substance and as primarily will rather than intellect. It also rejects the dualism which resulted from the classical view of the mind as a substance. For it stresses the fact that the mental pattern of purposive activity presupposes and rests upon a bodily pattern of instinctive activity and emphasizes the close connection of mental states with bodily processes. Moreover, while our conception of the human spirit regards devotion to higher values such as truth and goodness as im-

[57] Temple, *op. cit.*, pp. 201, 202; 478, 479.
[58] *Ibid.*, ch. XIX.

portant, it stresses man's relationship to God as the basis for the fullest and purest spiritual life.

Thus, although our conception of man incorporates important elements from both classical humanism and modern thought, it is primarily theistic. This may explain why the decline of faith in the God of theism since the eighteenth century has been accompanied by a gradual loss of belief in the uniqueness of man in the world. Since the collapse of belief in the Absolute Spirit of philosophical idealism in the nineteenth century, the category of spirit has been abandoned by most philosophers; and since the triumph of naturalism in the twentieth century, belief in the irreducibility of the mind to its physiological basis or to publicly observable behavior has been greatly weakened among them.

This should surprise no one. As we pointed out at the outset, man's understanding of *himself* is affected by his understanding of *God,* and conversely. For many centuries Western man's belief in a spiritual and personal God supported and strengthened his belief in his own dignity as a creature made in the image of God. The loss of faith in God in the latter part of the nineteenth century was accompanied for a time by a naïve and exaggerated faith in man, but it has been associated in the twentieth century with a widespread denial by naturalistic philosophers of the irreducibility of man's mind and his pre-eminence as a spiritual being. This, in turn, has made it difficult, if not impossible, for many to maintain the theistic belief in a spiritual and personal God. For when man has ceased to see himself as made in the image of God, he finds it hard to believe in a personal God who is analogous to the highest in himself. If so, one may at least raise the question whether modern man can recover his belief in *himself* until and unless he comes to believe once more in *God.*

11

Freedom: Its Nature and Limitations

The perennial problem of freedom is one which is of special concern to men of our time. Man feels that his freedom is the necessary condition of his responsibility and creativity and that if he is deprived of it he loses his dignity. But since the Communist revolution of 1917 in Russia and the triumph of Fascism in Italy a few years later, the world has been engaged in a bitter struggle between those who believe in the freedom of the individual and those who are convinced of the necessity of totalitarian control over economic, political, and cultural life. Moreover, many have come to doubt, when they consider the vast impersonal social forces at work in our technological civilization, whether they have any real control over their lives.

But the problem of freedom is not only a political and social problem; it is also a *moral* and *religious* problem. Men have usually taken it for granted that moral judgments on conduct and character are justified because they are free and therefore responsible for what they are and do. If they ceased to believe this, would they still be justified in passing judgments of praise and blame upon the acts of others or in thinking that they can help to shape their own characters by choices that are free? Again, Biblical religion seems to affirm that God endowed man with the capacity to respond freely to His Word, holds him responsible for his sin, and calls upon him to repent. On the other hand, the Bible emphasizes the sovereignty of God over the lives of men, and Christian thinkers such as St. Augustine have insisted that freedom of choice has resulted since the fall of Adam in sinful disobedience to God's will and that only by God's grace can the ability not to sin be restored to him. This clearly implies that man's freedom of choice is limited in its value by his inability to use it well and that perfect freedom is possible only by God's grace. Thus, the problem of freedom assumes different forms in ethics and theology. For ethics is primarily concerned with the question whether man is free and responsible for his actions, while theology raises the question whether such freedom and responsibility are sufficient, apart from the transformation of man by divine grace, for him to attain his true good.

The Case for Determinism

Why have determinists denied man's freedom to determine his acts? The first reason is that men are continually being made aware by experience of the many *limitations* on their freedom. They know that circumstances have played an important part in making every person what he is and influencing what he does, e.g., the time and place of his birth, his relations to his parents, the institutions of his country, the values dominant in his culture. In addition, his biological heritage, e.g., his physical size, his strength, and his health, has had an effect upon him. When he considers that his social environment and his heredity have affected him from his infancy, and have helped to shape his attitudes and interests, it is natural for him to suppose that they have not only influenced but determined his character. This is why so many have been convinced that men's actions are determined by irrational drives such as sex (biological determinism), others by the Marxist view that men's attitudes and opinions are based upon their class (economic determinism).

Determinism of this kind has been strengthened by the development of *scientific psychology* since the latter part of the nineteenth century. Experimental psychologists have tended to assume that psychology cannot be fully scientific unless it employs the same method and makes the same assumptions as the natural sciences. Therefore, they think they must deal with men's acts in a strictly "objective" way, i.e., as publicly observable and precisely describable behavior, and must explain them by antecedent causes without reference to purposes. As a result, they have often regarded man as primarily if not exclusively a biological organism who reacts to stimuli from his environment and whose drives are expressed in ways determined by social conditioning. Psychical factors such as ideals and values are treated as products of social conditioning. Thus, psychological determinism is combined with biological and cultural determinism.

Doubtless, these forms of determinism would not have been so widely accepted if men's minds had not been prepared for them by the postulate of universal determinism in the modern *physical sciences*. Before the twentieth century revolution in physics, the assumption that every event in nature is determined by efficient causes which operate in accordance with natural laws was accepted without question in the physical sciences. Although it was rejected by a number of distinguished biologists, it was dominant in biology also. As man is an animal species who has emerged in the evolutionary process and whose life has a physical basis, it was assumed by many mechanistic biologists that his behavior must be determined ultimately by physical and chemical laws. Because of the dominance of Newtonian physics, this physical and biological determinism had a powerful influence in the latter part of the nineteenth century. Its influence still persists among scientists because of the dominance of naturalistic habits of thought inherited from the nineteenth century. These scientists and the naturalistic philosophers influenced by them take it for granted that man must be regarded as one object in a world of objects and that his acts must be explained as purely natural events by antecedent causes.

Thus, the main grounds for belief in determinism are (a) that men are conscious of the influence of their biological heredity and social environment upon their conduct and character, (b) that behavioristic psychology and sociology have emphasized the importance of social conditioning, and (c) that the physical and biological sciences until recently have assumed determinism in all natural events. It should be noted that although (a) and (b) advance empirical evidence that men's acts are *affected* by external and internal conditions, they do not prove that these conditions are sufficient to *determine* men's acts. It is clear, therefore, that modern determinism is primarily a *postulate* which has been made as a basis for investigation in the natural sciences, as indicated in (c), and has then been extended to the social sciences and psychology which deal with man. As Ernest Nagel says, the assumption of universal determinism is "capable neither of decisive proof nor disproof" but must be "regarded as a fruitful maxim or regulative principle for inquiry." [1] It is sometimes said that, although it is only a postulate, we have empirical evidence of the validity of determinism in the success with which it is possible to predict the behavior of men. We shall have to consider later whether this assertion is justified by the evidence. Determinists recognize, of course, that the prediction of human acts with certainty and precision is an ideal which is still far from being realized, but they hope that increasing knowledge of the external and internal factors which affect the conduct of each person will make possible its realization in the future.

The Case Against Determinism

Since the time of Spinoza the vision of nature as a system in which every event occurs by necessity has haunted the minds of scientists and

[1] Hook, Sidney (ed.): *Determinism and Freedom*, New York, Collier Books, 1961, p. 199.

philosophers. Even Kant was so completely under its spell that he could conceive of freedom only by attributing it to a transcendental self above the empirical self. But recent developments in the philosophy of science have made it clear that this vision rests upon the mistaken view that natural laws *prescribe* or legislate for events rather than merely *describe* the way they occur. It has also been recognized by philosophers of science, including eminent scientists, that the scientific method won its spectacular successes in the modern age by excluding from attention the mind and values of the scientist who applies the method. Yet the mind is as real as the physical objects and events it describes. Unless its acts can be reduced to the publicly observable events which make up behavior, they cannot be explained by the scientific method as determined by antecedent causes. Yet the scientist's decision to make science his vocation, his selection of his special field, his effort to discover new truth, his fidelity to fact in describing his conclusions, and his responsibility for maintaining the standards of truth of the scientific community—all of these presuppose his freedom of action. It is precisely for this reason that science is so often praised for the moral values it fosters.

However, the "physical determinism" we have been discussing is probably not as influential in our time as "psychological determinism." One reason is that, although the limitations of the scientific method are now recognized by leading physical scientists, many experimental psychologists still assume that if they are to be scientific they must employ that method alone. Behavioristic psychologists such as Clark Hull have been mechanists in their view of the motivation of human behavior.[2] In general, they have concentrated upon "drives" as the motivating forces behind human acts and have conceived these in biological terms.[3] According to Hull, apparently "purposive" behavior involving intelligence is to be regarded as a secondary phenomenon to be accounted for by deriving it from more elementary "objective" principles,[4] and the behaving organism is to be viewed as "a completely self-maintaining robot" [5] or mechanism, "a physical aggregate whose behavior occurs under ascertainable conditions according to definitely statable rules or laws." [6] Moreover, Hull holds that the principles discovered by behavioristic psychology should become the basis of the

[2] Peters, R. S., *The Concept of Motivation*, London, Routledge and Kegan Paul, 1958, ch. 4.
[3] *Ibid.*
[4] Hull, Clark, *Principles of Behavior*, New York, Appleton-Century, 1943, pp. 25, 26.
[5] *Ibid.*, p. 27.
[6] *Ibid.*, p. 384.

social or behavioral sciences and be applied to the task of "creating a new and better world." [7]

Psychological behaviorism is based upon the presupposition that psychology must be a natural science, using the same method and making the same assumptions as the physical sciences. This presupposition is not required by science. It is a product of what has been called the "methodological imperialism" of "scientism," which assumes that the only method of attaining truth is that of the physical sciences and therefore that that method must be extended to everything whatever. But although it may well be that psychology requires the postulate that human acts are determined, it does not follow from this that they must be determined, like physical events, by antecedent events according to general laws. It is, of course, true that biological "drives" and psychological "conditioning" are important *conditions* of human character and conduct, providing motives for many of man's acts and influencing his attitudes and purposes in many ways. But it does not follow that they *determine* his conduct, since he is not passive in relation to them but actively responds to them in a way we shall describe later. We conclude, therefore, that determinism in psychology is not required by science but is a product of reductionistic naturalism and scientism which assume that everything that occurs is part of a physical system and therefore is governed by necessity.

Modern psychoanalysis also has seemed to many, perhaps most, psychoanalysts to require determinism. "The sense of this principle," says Charles Brenner, "is that in the mind as in physical nature about us nothing happens by chance or in a random way. Each psychic event is determined by the ones that preceded it . . . In fact, mental phenomena are not more capable of such a lack of causal connection with what preceded them than are physical ones. Discontinuity in this sense does not exist in mental life." [8] But it should be noted that this view seems to rest on the assumption that the only alternative to determinism is absolute indeterminism, i.e., the view that things happen "by chance or in a random way." We shall argue later that this is not the case. Obviously, psychoanalysis would be incompatible with the complete "lack of causal connection (of mental phenomena) with what preceded them," since it views present mental states in the case of neurotic persons as causally related to past experiences. But it does not follow from this that *all* present mental states of *all* persons are completely determined by antecedent causes.

---

[7] *Ibid.*, pp. 400–401. Cf. Skinner, B. F., *Science and Human Behavior*, New York, Macmillan, 1953.

[8] Brenner, Charles, *An Elementary Textbook of Psychoanalysis*, New York, International Universities Press, 1955, p. 12.

Dr. Robert Waelder has recently pointed out that "complete determinism" in this sense is inconsistent with many things we believe
and do in ordinary life. "Moral judgments and moral appeals are a
constant feature of everyday life. . . . If all behavior is strictly and
completely determined by factors that do not include something like
a free-acting personality—for the inclusion of this factor brings in an
element of freedom through the back door—it is difficult to see why
some should be praised and others blamed." [9] Moral evaluations are
possible if influences which have shaped human life "are considered
only as *pressures*" to which resistance can be offered, but "if these
influences are seen as *causes,* there seems to be no room for praise or
condemnation." [10] Dr. Waelder adds that "psychoanalysts like other
people continue to bestow praise and blame and to treat in their daily
lives all but the sick as responsible individuals, capable within limits of
exercising choice and accountable for it." [11] Again, predictions of future
behavior can be made but "as probabilities rather than as inescapable
necessities." For the response of different persons to external pressures
may be different. "In the ultimate degradation and despair of the Nazi
concentration camp most people seem to have been reduced to the bare
struggle for survival; a few, however, became what another age would
have called saints—devoid of any concern for self, utterly devoted to
the service of others." [12] Moreover, certainty in prediction is impossible
because the relative strength of conflicting inner forces in a person may
be changed by a profound experience. "What was true this time need
not be true on another occasion, with a person changed by the very
experience. That is the story of Joseph Conrad's Lord Jim. He once
failed in a critical life situation and behaved as a coward. This memory
weighed heavily upon him throughout his later life; faced with a second
trial, he met it like a hero." [13] We conclude, therefore, that "psychic
determinism" is not required by the fact that the acts of neurotic persons are determined by unconscious forces. The distinction made by
psychoanalysts themselves between sick persons who need treatment and
others whom they regard as responsible for their acts and subject to
praise or blame for them must be maintained.

What are we to say about the argument for determinism from the
possibility of predicting the future behavior of persons on the basis of
observation of their past conduct? Although such predictions are prob-

[9] Waelder, Robert, "Psychic Determinism and the Possibility of Predictions," The
Psychoanalytic Quarterly, Vol. XXXII, 1963, p. 22.

[10] *Ibid.*

[11] *Ibid.*

[12] *Ibid.,* p. 32.

[13] *Ibid.,* p. 40.

able rather than certain, determinists hold that certàinty could be attained if our knowledge of all the factors involved were complete. Now, the *fact* of the successful prediction of much future conduct is undeniable. We can know with some assurance from observation of a person's behavior that he possesses a certain character, holds certain beliefs, and will probably act in accordance with his character and beliefs in the future. But the question is, what is the *ground* of this predictability? The answer is that we ordinarily assume that there is a continuity of character from the past to the future. We assume, for example, that if a person has adopted certain general principles and purposes, he will continue to act in the future in accordance with them. Many purposes require a long time to fulfill and some may involve most of one's life, e.g., the purpose to follow a particular vocation or to marry. Without such purposes, one could attain no unity in one's life and could accomplish nothing worth while.[14] But a successful prediction which is based upon a person's continuity of character or his consistency in maintaining his principles and purposes is not a proof of determinism. Of course, there are cases where the maintenance of a certain purpose has hardened into a rigid habit and acts flow from it in an almost automatic fashion. In cases of this kind, acts seem to be almost completely determined, e.g., in the case of a drug addict. But normally the adoption of a purpose leaves a person free to abandon or modify it. Even if a strong habit has been formed, it can generally with effort and some assistance be broken. For these reasons, it is impossible to predict with certainty the future acts of a person, and, although prediction of future conduct is often possible, it does not imply determinism but is quite compatible with the determination of acts by the self in a way consistent with its past decisions and present character.

Up to this point we have contended only that the arguments usually advanced in favor of determinism are not convincing. But we shall also present a positive argument against it which most people have regarded as fatal to its claims. In brief, it is the argument that determinism is incompatible with *moral responsibility* and would, if acted upon consistently, be destructive of morality. In developing this argument, however, it is necessary to distinguish between "hard" determinism which does "not shrink from such words as fatality, bondage of the will, necessitation and the like," and "soft" determinism, which "abhors harsh words" and is willing to speak of "freedom." [15]

According to those such as Spinoza and Jonathan Edwards who have

[14] Farrer, Austin: *The Freedom of the Will,* London, A. and C. Black, 1957, pp. 160, 161.

[15] James, William: *The Will to Believe,* etc., "The Dilemma of Determinism," New York, Longmans, Green, 1903, p. 149.

defended "hard" determinism, the desires and choices of a person as well as his character as a whole are completely determined by causes which have influenced him from the beginning of his life. In consequence, although he does what he chooses to do and therefore thinks he is free, that which he chooses is determined. His belief that his will is free in its choices is due, Spinoza asserts, to the simple fact that he is ignorant of the hidden causes which determine them. In contrast, "soft" determinists such as Hume and Mill have maintained that there is no contradiction between determinism and freedom. When we speak of an action as "free," they say, we do not mean that it was undetermined by causes but only that the agent was not compelled to perform it. He did it because he chose to do it, not because he was forced to do it. Therefore, he was free in doing it, although his choice to do it rather than some other act was determined. Moreover, he is morally responsible for doing it because he chose to do it and it is an expression of his character.

During the last generation *hard* determinism has had comparatively few advocates, and soft determinism has been more popular among English and American philosophers. The reason is obvious: soft determinism is in accord with the dominant view that science demands determinism, but at the same time it claims to "save" freedom and responsibility. However, certain philosophers have recently argued that soft determinism is a compromise whose conclusions are inconsistent with determinism. Among them are Paul Edwards and John Hospers.[16] Although they differ at certain points, they agree on the crucial point that determinism is incompatible with moral responsibility and therefore with moral judgments of praise and blame. According to Edwards, "human beings do not ultimately shape their own character," for it is a product of their heredity and environment. Therefore, we are forced to the conclusion that "they are never morally responsible." [17] Hospers expresses a similar view. Psychoanalysts have described many actions of "compulsive" behavior which have unconscious causes and are beyond conscious control,[18] and this raises the question whether men, "normal" or "abnormal," are responsible for their actions.[19] Hospers concludes that we have no right to praise or blame men for their character or to indulge in righteous indignation towards those less fortunate than ourselves.[20]

The appeal of hard determinism of this kind is due partly to the fact

[16] In Hook, *op. cit.*
[17] *Ibid.*, p. 125.
[18] *Ibid.*, p. 130.
[19] *Ibid.*, p. 135.
[20] *Ibid.*, p. 138.

that modern psychoanalysis has made us more aware of the unconscious and hidden factors behind the actions of criminals and others upon whom we all too easily pass judgments of blame. It is also due to the boldness with which hard determinists have carried through the logic of determinism to an extreme conclusion. Nevertheless, there are several defects of hard determinism which are fatal to its claims.

First, although it may seem to be more tolerant and charitable not to hold persons responsible than to pass moral judgments of blame upon them, it has serious consequences. "Sickness, accident, or incapacity aside," writes Sidney Hook, "one feels lessened as a human being if one's actions are always excused or explained away on the ground that despite appearances one is really not responsible for them. It means being treated like an object, or infant, or someone out of his mind." [21] Second, the denial of moral responsibility would lead to a paralysis of moral effort and consequently an increase in cruelty and suffering. "One of the commonest experiences," says Hook, "is to meet someone whose belief that he can't help doing what he is doing (or failing to do) is often an excuse for not doing as well as he can or at least better than he is at present doing. What often passes as irremediable evil in this world, or inevitable suffering, is a consequence of our own failure to act in time. We are responsible, whether we admit it or not, for what it is in our power to do and most of the time we can't be sure what it is in our power to do until we attempt it." [22] Third, the hard determinist seems to assume that the individual is wholly passive, an effect of causes, and is never active as a cause himself, so that he is powerless to bring about any change for the better in himself or the world. But the fact is that the choices I make and the acts I do today affect the desires I shall have tomorrow and thus alter the structure of my character. To deny this as impossible, as the hard determinist seems to do, is to make an unproved assumption without an empirical basis. "It has yet to be demonstrated, empirically and scientifically," as Howard Hintz says, "that acts of will, choices and decision, and *new* conditioning forces may not radically alter character structure itself." [23]

"Soft" determinists have sought to avoid these conclusions which would be destructive of moral obligation and effort by asserting that men are free and responsible for their actions if they are not *compelled* to do them by something external to themselves and are not *ignorant* of the nature and consequences of them. According to this view, when we say that a man is responsible for an act only on the condition that "he could have done otherwise," we mean by "could have" simply "would have—if." As P. H. Nowell-Smith expresses it, "could have" is a "hypothetical" rather than a "categorical" statement.[24] This means that under the *actual* conditions that existed when he acted, he did what he was determined to do, but under *other* conditions "he could have done otherwise." This is sufficient to make him responsible for his act, since he did what he chose to do without being compelled to do it.

Despite the acceptance of this view by many soft determinists as a way of "saving" moral responsibility, it is open to the same objections as hard determinism. If a person "could have done otherwise" is only a hypothetical statement, he could not *in fact* have done otherwise than he did under the conditions that actually existed and given the character he possessed at the time. As C. A. Campbell says, "It is totally irrelevant to X's moral responsibility that we should be able to say that some person differently constituted from X, or X in a different set of circumstances, could have done something different from what X did." [25] If so, soft determinism is as inconsistent with moral responsibility and with moral judgments of praise and blame as hard determinism.

The truth is that soft determinists such as Nowell-Smith are able to maintain that their position is compatible with moral responsibility only by a radical reinterpretation of basic moral terms which deprives them of their ordinary meanings. According to this reinterpretation, "responsibility" means simply accountability to the society of which one is a member. Words of "praise" or "blame" are applied to acts on the ground that they are approved or disapproved by that society. Moral traits which constitute "character" are called "virtues" or "vices" in accordance with the purpose of society to "strengthen or inhibit" dispositions which it approves or disapproves. Society achieves its purpose in using such moral terms because men dislike disapproval and fear punishment, long for approval and hope for reward.[26] As dogs can be trained to do tricks, men can be trained to behave in some ways and not in others. According to this view, morality seems to consist simply of conformity to rules or standards of conduct generally accepted by a society and imposed upon its members by training them through praise and blame, reward and punishment to develop those virtues which are likely to produce acts with desirable social consequences. The responsibility of the individual is only his accountability to society for what he chooses to do. But what he chooses to do is com-

[24] Nowell-Smith, P. H., *Ethics*, Baltimore, Penguin Books, 1956, p. 273.
[25] Campbell, C. A.: *Selfhood and Godhood*, London, George Allen and Unwin, 1959, p. 164.
[26] Nowell-Smith, *op. cit.*, pp. 301, 302.

pletely determined by his character as shaped by his heredity plus his social training.

This may be the meaning of moral terms such as "responsibility" in a purely *social* morality in which an individual's conduct is regulated by the moral rules of his society; for in social morality one is accountable to no one above or beyond society, and one's freedom is merely to do without resistance what one has been trained by it to do. But it is wholly inadequate as an analysis of the meaning of such terms either in a *rational* or a *religious* morality which is not based upon the conformity of the individual to social rules but upon the determination by the individual of his conduct by free decisions of his own. For example, the creative religious morality described by Bergson is not imposed by social "pressure" and does not consist in obedience to a set of social rules; it is the product of "aspiration" which springs from love and expresses itself in creative activity.[27] Moreover, those who live by such a religious morality regard themselves as members not merely of a limited "closed" society but also—and primarily—of a universal society which is to be realized, and their ultimate responsibility is not to their own society but to God. Obviously, the freedom required for such a creative morality is very different from that required for a social morality of conformity such as that described by Nowell-Smith, since it involves the determination of acts by each individual in creative decisions that are not themselves determined by antecedent causes. The nature of this freedom we shall now consider.

The Meaning of Freedom of Will

Since it has often been mistakenly supposed that the only alternative to determinism is indeterminism, it is necessary to begin our analysis of freedom of will by distinguishing it from indeterminism. For the term "indeterminism" is ambiguous, and, although in one meaning it is compatible, in another meaning it is incompatible, with free will. The first meaning is that there are some events, i.e., some human actions, which are contingent in the sense that they are not necessitated by antecedent events. In this meaning the believer in free will must embrace indeterminism, since he holds that some human actions are contingent in the sense that they are not necessitated by antecedent causes but are determined by present decisions of the self.

But "indeterminism" has meant to some thinkers something much more radical than this, i.e., that some human actions are completely

[27] Bergson, Henri, *The Two Sources of Morality and Religion*, New York, Henry Holt, 1935, Ch. 1.

undetermined. This interpretation is based upon the fact that "indeterminism" is thought to be the opposite of "determinism" and therefore to assert that some actions are not determined at all. If it is interpreted in this way, it is as incompatible with moral responsibility as determinism is. For moral responsibility for an action is ascribed to a person, not on the ground that it was undetermined, but on the ground that it was determined by him. Since the case for freedom of will is based partly upon the moral responsibility of persons for their actions, as we shall see, it is wholly inconsistent with indeterminism in this second meaning of the term. Although it maintains that some actions are *contingent* rather than necessitated by antecedent events, it does not hold that they are *undetermined* but that they are determined in a way different from events in the natural world below man.

Is it possible to formulate the nature of free will in such a way as to avoid both the denial of freedom by determinism and the assertion of an irresponsible freedom by indeterminism? In attempting to answer this question, we shall begin by analysing the position of C. A. Campbell, whose defense of free will has had a considerable influence. A basic presupposition of freedom of will, he points out, is that there are not only activities which occur *within* the self but also activities *of* the self.[28] In the case of the former, e.g., distracting impulses when the self is pursuing some end and feelings of pleasure or pain, the self is passive rather than active.[29] In the case of the latter, the self seeks to achieve ends it has adopted as its own, a common feature of our normal conscious life.[30] Now, some of these activities of the self are clearly determined by the self's congenital impulses and by the influence of the environment. These we do not regard as free. But there are others for which the self seems to be responsible and it is proper to praise or blame him. We judge these acts to be free. What warrants us in doing so?

Campbell's answer is simple. "Must we not recognize it as a condition of the morally free act," he asks, "that the agent 'could have done otherwise' than he in fact did? It is true, indeed, that we sometimes praise or blame a man for an act about which we are prepared to say, in the light of our knowledge of his established character, that he 'could do no other.' But I think that a little reflection shows that in such cases we are not praising or blaming the man for what he does *now* (or at any rate we ought not to be), but rather for those past acts of his which have generated the firm habit of mind from which his present act follows 'necessarily.' "[31] According to Campbell, then, a

[28] Campbell, C. A., *op. cit.*, p. 144.
[29] *Ibid.*, p. 144, 145.
[30] *Ibid.*, p. 147, 148.
[31] *Ibid.*, p. 162.

man can be morally praised or blamed for an act only if he could have done otherwise. Moreover, "could have done otherwise" is not a hypothetical statement, as Nowell-Smith asserts, but a categorical statement. It means that he was capable of putting forth the moral effort necessary to do otherwise and was responsible for doing so or failing to do so.[32] If he was, we praise or blame him for doing the act.

As we have said in our criticism of "soft" determinism, we agree with Campbell on this crucial point. However, his interpretation of free will at another point is open to serious question. Arguing in Kantian fashion that moral decision arises in a situation where there is a conflict between duty and desire, he asserts that the decision whether to do one's duty or not "does not issue from the self's *character* as so far formed." [33] His reason for this assertion is that character expresses itself in the strongest desire of the self and that this is in conflict with duty. In moral decision, therefore, "it is not the self merely *qua* formed character that acts, but the self as somehow *transcending* its own formed character." [34] Now, it is true that the self at any given time is not imprisoned within the limits of its character "as so far formed" but is capable of transcending it by creative moral decisions. But is it true that duty is always *opposed* to the formed character? Clearly, duty is opposed to the character of a person insofar as there are desires in him which run counter to the demands of duty, and it is probable that in every person, even the best, there are desires which are not in accord with duty. But is it not possible for a person at some point to attain a character which is at least not *dominated* by such desires, and may not his duty then be in line, on the whole, with his character rather than opposed to it?

Campbell's view of the opposition between duty and character would not be so serious if it did not imply that moral acts (and the free will manifested in them) are limited to those in which there is a conflict between duty and character. He assumes that every other act of a person is determined by his character and therefore by his strongest desire. We cannot accept this view because it involves an unjustified narrowing of moral action and freedom. Campbell goes so far as to say that there is no felt conflict between duty and desire in "perhaps 99 per cent of the choices in most men's lives," so that "over by far the greater part of the practical life, it is a man's character that determines his choices." [35] On the contrary, moral decisions are required in many, perhaps most, of men's acts. Of course, in many activities, such as play and

[32] *Ibid.,* p. 168.
[33] *Ibid.,* p. 149, 150.
[34] *Ibid.,* p. 150.
[35] *Ibid.,* p. 151.

artistic creation, a moral decision at every point is not required and would be out of place. But moral considerations are not irrelevant to such activities and moral decisions from time to time may be necessary. Although the motive behind them may be pleasure or the fulfillment of a personal interest rather than duty, moral decisions may be involved at several points, e.g., whether one ought to work rather than play on a particular afternoon, how long he should play, whether he should play fairly, and in what spirit he should accept defeat. However, the view that moral decision and free will are not limited to situations involving a conflict between duty and desire does not require an austere, moralistic attitude towards life and is quite compatible with spontaneous and "non-moral" activity.

How are we to interpret the assertion that the self can decide to act according to duty although this may require it to go against its character? Campbell replies that the self can do so because it is "something beyond its formed character." How can the self be "beyond" its character? To answer this question we would have to know the secret of the self's creativity. But creativity cannot be explained; it can only be experienced. "If an act is creative then nothing can determine it save the agent's doing it. Hence we ought not to expect to 'understand' it, in the sense of seeing how it follows from determinate elements of the self's character; for then it would just not be a 'creative' act. We can expect to 'understand' it only in the sense of being able to 'attach meaning' to it." [36] But we can attach meaning to it only if we approach it from the inside, i.e., from the standpoint of the agent when he is acting. "From the standpoint of the external observer," says Campbell, "the creative act is, inevitably, sheer mystery, or worse than mystery. But it is vital to bear in mind that only from the standpoint of living experience could anything of the nature of creative activity be grasped if it existed." [37]

The importance of this point for an understanding of freedom of will can hardly be overestimated. If we are to regard the self as free in an act, we must conceive it as creative in the sense of being capable of transcending its present character and initiating something new.[38] But to try to *explain* this capacity of the self to transcend its character by its present decision is to seek for *causes* of it; and this is to suppose that it is *determined* by these causes and thus to deny its freedom to initiate something new. It is possible to understand the self's capacity

---

[36] *Ibid.*, p. 153.

[37] *Ibid.*, p. 153.

[38] Even in cases where the self acts *in line* with its present character in making a moral decision, it *transcends* its character insofar as the decision to act in accordance with it is not *automatically* but *freely* made.

to transcend its character only from within, by living through or experiencing a creative act. To observe it as a spectator from without inevitably leads to the attempt to "explain" it as one event in a process or series of events, caused by the events antecedent to it. Even when one contemplates one's own act in retrospect, he is often tempted to view it in this way and to regard conditions which affected it as *causes* which necessitated it, although he was certain at the time that he was doing it freely.

Although we cannot "explain" a creative act of freedom by indicating causes for it, we can analyze it further by contrasting it with an event which is determined by natural causes. Austin Farrer has pointed out that many arguments used by determinists in discussing the problem of free will "trick us into stating personal-action themes in natural-event terms, and then force on us the consequences of our indiscretion." [39] For example, we accept "natural-event" language employed by determinists when we speak of will or volition as if it preceded an action and was something distinct from it. In reality, the volition and the action are not two things but aspects of the same thing.[40] The will or volition is not separate from the action, but embodies itself in it. Since "natural-event" language is scientific in character, it describes a decision of the will by retrospectively seeking for an explanation of it in terms of antecedent causes in the sequence of phenomena. In contrast, "personal-action" language speaks about the act of deciding as a way of determining something as yet undetermined.[41]

How, then, should we define decision or choice when we speak of it in the "personal-language" appropriate to it? Farrer defines it as "undetermined power to determine choice" [42] or "undetermined self-determination." [43] This means that it is not determined by external and/or internal antecedent causes, but by the self. Moreover, this "self-determination" is itself "undetermined," even by the character of the self, in its decision. Richard Taylor expresses a similar view by saying that we must "suppose that an act for which an agent is responsible is performed by him, but that he, in turn, is not causally necessitated to do it." [44] However, the fact that the self is undetermined by causes does not mean that it acts arbitrarily and without reasons. "We may further assume," says Taylor, "that for any act that is performed,

---

[39] Farrer, *op. cit.*, p. 114.

[40] *Ibid.*, p. 117.

[41] *Ibid.*, p. 138.

[42] *Ibid.*, p. 141.

[43] *Ibid.*, p. 173.

[44] Taylor, Richard: "Determinism and the Theory of Agency," in Hook, *op. cit.*, pp. 227, 228.

there are reasons why it is performed; but such reasons need not be causal conditions . . . To say, for instance, that an agent acted in a certain way in order to achieve a purpose is to give an explanation, but not a causal one, for his conduct." [45] Thus, the theory of freedom as "undetermined self-determination" differs from that of indeterminism, since it does not deny that human acts are determined but asserts that they are determined by persons in pursuit of their ends rather than by antecedent causes.

How, then, do we determine our acts? Perhaps the simplest and best answer is that we determine them by ends or purposes which are based upon what Farrer calls our "serious valuations." [46] Of course, many of our valuations are the result of social conditioning and psychological factors. That is the element of truth in cultural and psychological determinism. But the self also has the possibility of making creative valuations and adopting purposes based upon them. It is this which accounts for the transformation and development of valuations in the course of history.[47] Although moral valuation, for example, is often based upon mere conformity to the rules of social morality, as we have said, creative moral valuation arises from aspiration towards higher values than those acknowledged in that morality.[48] However, it must not be supposed that values determine our acts directly. Aesthetic, logical, and moral ideals or values can determine men's actions only if and insofar as men accept them. It is because men are not compelled to accept them that the determination of acts in accordance with them is compatible with freedom.[49]

To summarize, freedom of will is not indeterminism but the view that the self is free in its actions insofar as it could in a given situation have done otherwise. Freedom is not confined to moral actions performed from duty in opposition to the character of the self. However, it transcends or "goes beyond" the character of the self at any given time. It is not possible to "explain" such a free action in the sense of giving a cause for it, because to do so would be to deny what is distinctive of such an action and to treat it as a natural event determined by antecedent events. When it is grasped from within rather than observed from without, it is seen to arise from the self's "undetermined self-determination." But although the decision expressed in such an action is not determined by the motives which precede it, it is not with-

---

[45] *Ibid.*, p. 229.

[46] Farrer, *op. cit.*, p. 278.

[47] *Ibid.*, p. 285.

[48] *Ibid.*, p. 277.

[49] Hartmann, N.: *Ethics*, London, George Allen and Unwin, 1932, Vol. III, pp. 210, 211.

out reasons and hence arbitrary; it is made in accordance with the values and purposes of the self. Finally, the self is creative in its use of its freedom insofar as it bases its decisions upon values and purposes which it has not merely received passively from others but has actively adopted for itself.

The Case for Freedom of Will

We have set forth in some detail the concept of freedom of will. What grounds may be offered for accepting belief in it as true? (1) Some philosophers have held that the main ground for belief in it is the moral agent's *experience of freedom*, his intuition or feeling that he is free in making his moral decisions. "The appeal," says Campbell, "is throughout to one's own experience in the actual taking of the moral decision in the situation of moral temptation." [50] We must, he adds, also show that the supposed objections to the belief are not fatal to it, but no further positive evidence is necessary.[51]

Now, it is true that each person has an inner experience or consciousness of freedom. If he had not had such an experience, he probably could not be convinced of the reality of his freedom by arguments. But it is not true that no positive arguments are needed to support his belief in it. For many determinists such as Brand Blanshard admit that we have the feeling of being free to "do what we choose," but deny that this feeling proves that we are free to "choose our own choice." When we are making a choice, they say, we are looking toward the future rather than the past and consequently we may not be aware that we are under constraint.[52] Moreover, the interpretation of the consciousness of freedom in terms of free will clashes with what many still regard as the scientific demand for universal determinism according to general laws. Therefore, however strongly the defender of free will may be inclined to trust the evidence for freedom from the inner experience of it, he must also inquire whether there is other evidence for belief in it.

(2) One of the most familiar arguments for freedom of the will is that of Kant. Freedom, he argues, cannot be demonstrated by the theoretical reason, because reason falls into an antinomy or contradiction with itself when it deals with the problem. But the practical reason must postulate freedom as a *presupposition of morality*. For the fact that the will *ought* to obey the categorical moral imperative presupposes that it *can:* "I ought, therefore I can." Thus, freedom of the will

[50] Campbell, *op. cit.*, p. 169.
[51] *Ibid.*, pp. 169, 170.
[52] Blanshard, B., in Hook, *op. cit.*, p. 21.

is a "postulate" of the practical reason, i.e., a presupposition which is a necessary condition of obedience to the moral law. As such, it consists negatively of freedom from exclusive determination of the will's acts by natural laws and positively of its capacity to determine them by moral laws. This is not merely a sophisticated way of asserting that men will not try to obey the moral law unless they *believe* they are free to do so. This would be only a psychological assertion. Kant's meaning is that the reality of freedom is presupposed by the practical reason as a necessary condition of moral action. The practical reason confronts the will with a moral law which it "ought" unconditionally to obey. But this has no meaning unless the will "can" obey.

If one does not accept Kant's view that the moral imperative is "categorical" rather than "hypothetical," this argument will lose its force. For if moral laws are merely rules imposed by a society upon its members to attain certain social ends, or empirical generalizations concerning the kinds of acts most likely to result in happiness, the capacity of the will to obey them is not presupposed by the practical reason. The argument in its Kantian form will also fail to convince those who do not believe that morality consists of obedience to universal moral laws. However, it can be stated in other terms. Nicolai Hartmann, who advocates an ethic of values rather than an ethic of moral laws, regards the argument from responsibility as fundamental. "The originator (of an act)," he says, "finds himself involved in whatever occurs through his initiative, indeed even in what only might have occurred; he is aware that it is he himself upon whom rebounds everything, not merely what has actually been brought about." [53] In other words, the capacity to "take" or "assume" responsibility presupposes freedom, because one regards oneself as responsible for an act only if he was the "originator" of it and therefore was "involved" in its consequences. Moreover, a man "feels his human dignity to be violated, if his accountability for his deeds is denied," and he regards the denial of it "as a degradation and a kind of attack upon him in his capacity of self-directing agent." [54]

The argument that moral responsibility and accountability presuppose freedom is perhaps the strongest of all arguments for it. Of course, it is possible to deny such responsibility altogether, as the "hard" determinists are forced to do, or to contend that responsibility presupposes only the freedom to act as one chooses to act, as "soft" determinists do. But the denial of it by the former would undermine the foundations of morality, and the radical reinterpretation of responsibility by the latter

[53] Hartmann, *op. cit.*, p. 156. Parentheses added.
[54] *Ibid.*, p. 160.

would reduce morality to the level of mere social conformity, as we have seen.

However, the argument should not be used to justify the extreme view that the will is free in the sense that, at any given moment and merely by making an effort, it can do whatever it ought to do. "I ought, therefore I can" might seem logically to require this view, but the recognition of man's moral limitations will not permit it. For example, a person who has become addicted to narcotics may in principle be free not to surrender to his craving in a given situation, but in fact he may be so dominated by his craving that he will probably surrender to it unless a radical change in him is brought about in some way. We shall consider later the implications of this limitation of man's freedom in connection with the problem of grace. It is sufficient here to point out that he is not free in the sense of standing in each situation before alternative possibilities of action without being strongly influenced by his character to choose one rather than another, or in the sense that he is always able to resist that influence, however strong. As we shall see, this is one of the main facts which make it necessary to insist that man's freedom is finite and limited.

(3) Closely related to the argument from responsibility is the argument from consciousness of *guilt*. This differs from the consciousness of responsibility in that it arises only as a consequence of moral transgression, whereas the latter accompanies all moral acts. The burden of guilt is often so keenly felt and so heavy that the consciousness of it is inescapable. "It bursts in upon a man like a fate. He makes no mistake about the guilt. It is suddenly there, judging, contradicting, overpowering. But, nevertheless he feels that this bursting-in is not from outside. A power rises within himself, which brings evidence against him. . . . Everyone is acquainted with this phenomenon as the voice of conscience and with its peculiar moral character as 'remorse.' " [55] This consciousness of guilt is obviously connected with the consciousness of self-determination and the sense of guilt can be eliminated only at the cost of destroying moral personality. Of course, feelings of guilt in certain cases are abnormal and the patient must be relieved of them if he is to regain mental health, as psychoanalysts have pointed out. In other cases, they may be exaggerated as a result of an overscrupulous conscience, as priests and other counsellors have long known. But to take these perversions of the sense of guilt as evidence that it corresponds to nothing real in the condition of the guilty person is a superficial judgment. For the sense of guilt arises from man's consciousness of responsibility for his acts and consequently is a clear evidence of his freedom.

[55] Hartmann, *op. cit.*, p. 173.

(4) Another argument for freedom of will is that it is presupposed in moral judgments on the character and actions of persons. Unless a person is free in the sense that he could have done otherwise, it is not legitimate to *praise* him for doing his duty or *blame* him for failing to do it. For freedom is an indispensable condition of the moral virtues which constitute good character and of the acts in which they manifest themselves. Without it judgments of approval and disapproval passed upon character or conduct would be meaningless. That judgments of praise and blame presuppose freedom is shown by the fact that they have a quite different character from judgments in which admiration is expressed and respect is paid to those endowed with natural talents and abilities, except insofar as these have been further developed by self-discipline. For the development of the moral virtues which constitute character and the exercise of them in moral actions require an effort of the will, and a man is free to make or not to make that effort. Moreover, it is significant that a moral judgment of praise or blame is affected by our view of what is called the "degree of responsibility" of the agent. For example, we mitigate the severity of blame for an evil act when we are satisfied that there were "extenuating circumstances," e.g., that the agent acted under extreme provocation or when overcome by passion or after undergoing torture. And we praise a person less for doing a good act if it was not opposed by strong natural desire and was easily done than if it was done against the resistance of powerful inclinations or great obstacles.

(5) Although most of the arguments we have offered for freedom of will have been derived from different aspects of the moral consciousness and moral activity, it is important to realize that freedom in the sense of "undetermined self-determination" is the presupposition not only of *moral* but also of *all* creative activity. Free will is involved in every phase of the *creative life:* in the intellectual quest for truth, the artistic impulse to express meaning and create beauty, and the age-long effort to build social and political institutions on a foundation of justice and brotherhood. The explanation of this creativity, which has been the main root of all culture and progress, is to be found in the spiritual nature of man. Man as a spiritual being, we have said, is always seeking to transcend himself.[56] His being is realized only in the process of becoming as he continually seeks to develop his potentialities and to further the good of others. Thus, he is engaged, ceaselessly and to the end of his life, in making and remaking himself by a creative exercise of his energies. Existentialists such as Berdyaev have emphasized this truth about man and have shown clearly that man's existence

[56] Ch. 10.

is characterized by decisions arising from freedom.[57] Whitehead has argued that freedom in some degree is a factor in the creation of all actual entities, even those below the level of life. Whether creativity and freedom should be extended in this manner to beings at all levels of nature is problematic. That they are characteristic of man and belong to his essence as a spiritual being he cannot doubt without denying one of the most important capacities of his own nature.

The Limits of Freedom

Libertarians have sometimes made the mistake of affirming that the freedom of the self is unlimited. But man's freedom is that of a finite being, and it is presumptuous as well as irrational for him to claim that it is unconditioned. One of the major contributions of the study of psychology, history, and the social sciences is that they have made the individual more aware of the limits and conditions under which he must exercise his freedom. Psychology, especially the psychology of personality and psychoanalysis, shows him how his character has been shaped in the past and affects his decisions in the present, by the choices he has made, the habits he has formed, the interests he has developed. History describes the way his ends and the means necessary to realize them are profoundly influenced by the age in which he lives and the changing events of his generation. The social sciences analyze the social institutions and patterns which provide the framework for and limit the exercise of his freedom. Thus, his freedom must be expressed, in every situation in which he acts, under limiting conditions imposed by his own character, his historical situation, and his society. Furthermore, these external and internal conditions are seldom, if ever, ideal. The imperfect education he has received and the wrong choices he has made in the past have left him with attitudes and habits which in some measure narrow his outlook and distort his vision of the good. The age in which it is his lot to live is burdened with unsolved problems such as war that are inherited from the past, as well as with new difficulties of its own. And his society must struggle with entrenched evils such as racial discrimination and economic oppression.

To limiting conditions such as these must be added the tragic fact of the spiritual and moral weakness of most men. Kierkegaard remarks in his *Sickness unto Death* that most men are not even aware that they are spiritual beings and are content to live at the level of "sensuousness." [58]

[57] Berdyaev, N.: *The Destiny of Man*, London, Geoffrey Bles: Centenary Press, 1937, pt. II, Ch. III.

[58] Kierkegaard, S.: *The Sickness Unto Death*, Princeton, N.J., Princeton University Press, p. 67.

Heidegger has described in unforgettable terms the way all men sometimes and most men all of the time think and act as "They" do or
"One" does, and thus flee from "authentic" existence in which the self
faces towards its future possibilities.[59] The truth of the matter is that,
although freedom is part of the natural endowment of man, it must be
developed and exercised by effort. But many, perhaps most, men are
content to exercise their freedom not in creative activity for the sake of
higher ends but at the lower level of freedom to do as others do or as
one pleases. For the exercise of freedom in creative activity guided by
intellectual, aesthetic, moral, and religious ideals goes against the grain
of natural inclination and inertia, while the freedom to do as others do
or as one pleases is easy because it requires little effort. This helps to
account for the fact, which has been illustrated on a large scale in our
century, that men have often been willing to surrender their intellectual, political, or religious freedom into the hands of others in order
to avoid the burden of responsibility for the exercise of it. As Dostoievsky showed, men will give up their religious and moral freedom to
the leaders of an authoritarian church who will relieve them of their
conscience and assume the responsibility of telling them what to do.[60]
And the remarkable success of the totalitarian states of the left and the
right during the last two generations is further evidence for the human
—all-too-human—tendency to "escape from freedom" which has been
so vividly analyzed by Erich Fromm.[61] Thus, the effectiveness of man's
freedom is tragically limited by his own unwillingness to exercise it
creatively by assuming the burden of responsibility.

Up to this point we have spoken of conditions which narrow, weaken,
or negate the effective exercise of freedom. But freedom also *needs* to
be limited, in another sense of the term, if it is to be exercised creatively
at the spiritual level. For a man's freedom should be exercised under
the conditions imposed by his human nature and its capacities, by his
dependence upon other persons and his moral responsibility towards
them, and by the values which make demands upon him.

The necessity of limitations such as these may be shown by a critical
examination of Sartre's radical assertion that man's freedom is unlimited. It is not limited by his own nature or essence, says Sartre, for
his existence precedes his essence. He creates his essence by negating
his past and projecting himself towards his possibilities.[62] Also, his
freedom is not limited by the claims of objective values upon him. For
man's ends are projections of his freedom and are not based upon the

---

[59] Heidegger, Martin: *Being and Time*, New York, Harper, 1962, pp. 163–168.

[60] Dostoievsky, F.: *The Brothers Karamazov*, the "Legend of the Grand Inquisitor."

[61] Fromm, E., *Escape from Freedom*, New York, Farrar and Rinehart, 1941.

[62] Sartre, Jean-Paul: *Being and Nothingness*, tr. by Hazel E. Barnes, New York,
Philosophical Library, 1956, p. 440.

acknowledgement of an order of values independent of himself. By my choice of my ends I confer upon them a "transcendent existence" in relation to my "projects," but it is false to assume that I "encounter" them in the world as objective values, as if they come from God, from nature, from my own nature, or from society.[63] For I do not "receive" my ends from some objective source; they arise from my "original freedom," "the sudden thrust of the freedom which is mine." [64] Finally, each individual is essentially isolated and alone in his freedom and creates his values in his isolation. This does not mean that he chooses his values without reference to society, for in his choices he ideally legislates for other men also.[65] But since there are no objective values and each individual chooses his own values, the values of no individual are superior to those of any other and an atomic individualism of values results.[66] In short, man is limited in his freedom *neither* by his own essence or nature, *nor* by objective ends or values, *nor* by ends or values acknowledged by other members of society. *Nor* is he limited by his responsibility to God, for there is no God.

To this extreme view of freedom as unlimited Sartre joins an equally extreme view of responsibility. Man, he says, "carries the weight of the whole world on his shoulders." Since "he is the one by whom it happens that there is a world" and "the one who makes himself be," it follows that "whatever may be the situation in which he finds himself, the 'for-itself' (man) must wholly assume this situation with its peculiar coefficient of adversity, even though it be insupportable." [67] Even an "accident" such as mobilization in a war does not come from outside myself. I could avoid it by suicide or desertion, and if I do not avoid it in any such way, I have chosen it.[68] Therefore, I am "without excuse" and "it remains for me only to lay claim to this war." [69] Of course, since I did not ask to be born, "I am not the foundation of my being" and "everything takes place as if I were compelled to be responsible." [70] But I must assume this birth in responsibility and make it mine. "I am *abandoned* in the world . . . in the sense that I find myself suddenly alone and without help, engaged in a world for which I bear the whole responsibility without being able, whatever I do, to tear myself away from this responsibility for an instant." [71]

[63] *Ibid.*
[64] *Ibid.*, p. 443.
[65] Copleston, F.: *Contemporary Philosophy*, London, Burns and Oates, 1956, p. 194.
[66] *Ibid.*, p. 195.
[67] Sartre, *op. cit.*, pp. 553, 554. Parentheses added.
[68] *Ibid.*, p. 554.
[69] *Ibid.*, p. 555.
[70] *Ibid.*, p. 555.
[71] *Ibid.*, pp. 555, 556.

In an age which has found so many ways to deny the freedom of the individual and to justify him in escaping from responsibility, there is something stirring in this affirmation of a wholly unfettered freedom and a total responsibility. But it cannot withstand critical examination, and, when it is considered calmly, it seems fantastic. Having postulated with Nietzsche the premise that "God is dead," Sartre seems to draw the conclusion that each individual must attempt to be God to himself, creating himself out of nothing and assuming the burden of responsibility for himself and his world without help from any source.

It is true that in a measure each individual "makes" his own essence. As we have said, his being is realized only in becoming and he becomes in considerable measure by his own choices. But there is a common *human nature* or *essence* in which he participates and he possesses an individuality of his own. Does not Sartre himself make generalizations about man, *"le pour-soi,"* his freedom, and his reponsibility, and assume that they apply to all men? And does he not speak of an original "upsurge" or "thrust" of freedom by which each individual projects his ultimate ends, and do these not provide a framework which limits his proximate ends, a kind of "essence"? The freedom of every person is exercised under the limiting conditions of human nature, which has a definite structure of needs and capacities. Moreover, as he projects himself toward his future possibilities, his character as it has been developed in the past limits the possibilities which are open to him in the present.

It is equally true that if man's freedom is to be exercised creatively, it must be guided by *objective values* and *ideals* such as truth and justice which demand that he acknowledge them, and he can realize his potentialities as a spiritual being only by committing himself to them. For there is a correlation between man's spiritual potentialities and these higher values and ideals, since the former can be fulfilled only through commitment to the latter. If he refuses to accept this limitation and insists upon "creating" his own values arbitrarily, he will sacrifice spiritual and moral freedom for freedom to do as he pleases. Similarly, as a social being, he must exercise his freedom under conditions imposed by his responsibility to other persons who have special claims upon him and to society as a whole.

Finally, Sartre's view that man's unlimited freedom entails *total responsibility* since he creates himself and his world is utterly unrealistic. It is not true that man is responsible even for the calamities such as war that befall him. For he is dependent in every situation upon things and persons beyond himself for both good and evil. It is true that when he receives from them, he is not merely passive but responds in ways determined by himself. The attitude he takes towards calamities such as war depends largely upon himself, and the acceptance of adversity without self-pity and bitterness may enable him to win a kind of mastery over it. This is the most profound insight of ancient Stoicism and the heroic element in Sartre's view of responsibility may reflect its influence. But his proud assertion that man creates himself and arbitrarily chooses his own values leads him to claim for the individual an independence of everything outside himself and a total responsibility for his world which are appropriate to God alone.

12

Freedom and Grace

In our discussion of the nature of man and his freedom, we have hitherto been concerned with his *essence*. But religion, especially in its highest forms, is concerned primarily with his *existence* as he actually is. The great religions have recognized that there is a gulf between his essential nature and his existence, and in various ways they have sought to overcome it. For it is one of the main functions of religion to show man the way to salvation: deliverance from the evil that afflicts him and attainment of the good to which he aspires. One of the most interesting of the problems that confront the philosopher of religion is the nature and role of *divine grace* as a source of salvation or liberation. Theistic religions such as Bhakti Hinduism, Amida Buddhism, Judaism, and Christianity have affirmed that man cannot obtain salvation by his own efforts alone but must be aided by God's grace. Countless numbers of believers in these religions have been convinced that they have actually experienced grace in their lives and have been enabled by it to enter upon the way to salvation.

There are three tasks with respect to the problem of divine grace with which the philosopher of religion may properly concern himself. (1) He may analyze some of the different ways in which theists have conceived of the nature and operation of grace in human life. (2) Making use of the results of this analysis, he may attempt to formulate the general requirements for a conception of grace that would be consistent with the theistic view of God and the freedom and responsibility of man. (3) Finally, he may inquire into the nature of the evidence for belief in the reality in grace. We shall deal with these three tasks in order, starting with a critical analysis of several Eastern and Western conceptions of grace.

The Nature of Grace:
Bhakti Hinduism

Belief in divine grace has been at the heart of the great theistic sects of Hinduism. It is best illustrated by Vaisnavism in which *bhakti* or devotion to the god Vishnu has long been regarded as a way to salvation. In the *Bhagavad Gita*, devotion is centered on Krishna, one of the incarnations of Vishnu, and the promise is made that he will save by his grace those who trust and serve him. In the hymns and psalms of Vaisnavite poets, especially the Tamil *alvars*[1] and the Maratha psalmists,[2] Vishnu as manifested in his incarnations or in local gods is praised, and longing for union with him when absent and ecstatic joy in his presence are expressed in moving terms.

The conception of God and His relation to the soul which underlies this Bhakti theism is not that of Sankara's monism, which we considered in an earlier chapter, but that of Ramanuja's philosophy. According to Ramanuja, Brahman is "one without a second," as Sankara had maintained, but this does not mean that there is no world along with him but only that there is no second being equal to him. The world is real, for the testimony of our senses to the reality of the many things of space and time is reliable. Brahman is the personal God, Vishnu, who with conscious purpose and wisdom creates the world and maintains it from within. When the Upanishads affirm *Tat twam asi*, "That are Thou," they mean that Brahman permeates, supports, and controls the soul. Brahman is the "soul" and all of the souls form his "body," so that the unity of God and the soul is not that of identity, as Sankara had affirmed, but that of immanence or indwelling like the union of the human soul and its body. Even when liberation or redemption of the soul has been attained, this distinction between it and God is not lost.

This conception of God as personal and of the world as his creation which he indwells as the soul indwells its body is the basis of what Rudolf Otto calls "India's religion of grace."[3] When Brahman the ultimate reality is regarded as impersonal and as the sole reality, as in Sankara's monism, it is impossible to think of Him (or It) as having a gracious attitude towards men. But when He is identified with Vishnu, the personal God who creates and preserves the souls of men and supports and controls them from within, belief in His grace towards them becomes possible.

Now, the worldly life of man is opposed to the spiritual life that

---

[1] Hooper, J. S. M.: *Hymns of the Alvars*, London, Oxford University Press, 1929.

[2] Macnicol, Nicol: *Psalms of the Maratha Saints*, London, Oxford University Press, 1920.

[3] Otto, Rudolf: *India's Religion of Grace*, London, S.C.M. Press, 1930.

would bring him fulfillment. He is in a lost condition which involves separation from God and expresses itself by acts of wrongdoing. Hence, it is necessary that he should turn away from it, renouncing the evil ways of the world and committing himself to God. Otto quotes a dialogue between God and the soul brought before him for examination. God asks,

> "Why, dear one, wert thou not here long ago?
> Why didst thou tarry on the earth (in foreign parts)?"

The soul replies:

> "Because I had forsaken unity with thee,
> Because I, fool, had made my body me,
> Because I did not know thee who didst
>   dwell in me . . . .
> Because I threw away my very self, I therefore
>   was in chains." [4]

To men who are in this lost condition the appeal is made to give up their worldly life and commit themselves in faith and devotion to Vishnu. They must acknowledge Vishnu to be the only true God, but, more important, they must surrender themselves and all their powers to him and his service. The devotee must love and trust him above all things and be ruled by him alone as one who is absolutely trustworthy.[5] But such perfect trust, such single-minded devotion, is not possible to the man who is bound by the fetters of desire to his worldly life, and he cannot merit it by his own works. Therefore, divine grace must precede anything he can do to attain it.

> "And how does one attain? No act, no human
>   means procures it.
> It is the 'causeless act,' that has no cause
>   in work of man.
> No penitence can liberate thy heart and no
>   submersion.
> Only by grace of Hari [God] is it thine, without
>   cause." [6]

But he who receives God's grace realizes his true self in communion with the highest Self and attains bliss and peace.[7] He passes from darkness to light in this life and is liberated from the necessity of rebirth.

[4] Ibid., p. 49.
[5] Ibid., pp. 45–47.
[6] Ibid., p. 48.
[7] Ibid., p. 92.

One of the problems faced by the Vaisnavites was the relation of God's grace to man's work. The development of thought concerning it curiously parallels that of Christian theism in the West. Although Ramanuja had insisted that works prescribed by God are required along with grace, some of the later Vaisnavites, especially those in South India, affirmed that grace has no cause in the works of a man and precedes every work he can do to merit it. All that is needed from him is a simple "approach" to God, *prapatti*. He must surrender himself to God just as he is, in order that God may do with him what in His grace He wills. This insistence on the exclusiveness of grace as the sole source of salvation led to a prolonged controversy between two schools or parties. The Northern school maintained the "monkey-hold" theory of the relation of God's grace to man's effort. As the young monkey clings to its mother in times of danger and thus cooperates with her by its own action, so the self must cooperate with God for its salvation. In contrast, the Southern school defended the "cat-hold" theory. As the young kitten is carried by its mother in her mouth and remains completely passive, so the self can do nothing to help itself or please God but must surrender itself to Him and become passive in His hands.[8]

The similarities between this Indian religion of grace and Western theism are so striking that many students of religion have overlooked certain crucial differences. Otto has pointed out some of the differences between Vaisnavism and Christianity and has shown how they spring from more fundamental differences with respect to what is central in these religions. One difference is that, for the Vaisnavite as well as for the Hindu monist, salvation involves the rescue of the *individual* from the evils of the world but there is no necessary connection between his salvation and that of others. This is related to another important difference, the role of *moral conduct* in the two religions. As Otto says, the common assertion that Hindu theism is, if not "immoral," at least "non-moral" is false. It is taken for granted that one who has attained redemption is raised above passion and impurity, that he will not injure others, and that he will be benevolent towards them.[9] Moreover, virtues such as loyalty, chastity, and marital fidelity are praised, as in the story of Rama and Sita in the *Ramayana*. However, there is a difference between Hindu and Western theism with respect to morality. Whereas in Hinduism the service of one's fellows is not essential to the service that is rendered to God, in Western theism "the love of God is inseparably attached to the love of one's neighbor." [10] Perhaps

[8] *Ibid.*, pp. 56–58.
[9] *Ibid.*, p. 83.
[10] *Ibid.*, p. 84.

the most profound difference concerns the nature of the *evil* from which deliverance is sought in Bhakti Hinduism and Western theism. Whereas the Western theist conceives of salvation primarily as redemption from sin and guilt as he confronts the holiness of God, the Vaisnavite thinks of it as liberation from the bonds that attach him to *samsara,* the misery of this world and the necessity of rebirth.[11] Although the idea of sins is present, it refers mainly to disturbances to the soul caused by feelings of pleasure and pain, the troubles that burden existence in the world of *samsara.*

These differences are obviously due to the influence of fundamental beliefs of the two religions upon their conceptions of grace. For example, the fact that Western theism emphasizes the relation of the individual to his neighbors as essential to his relation to God and hence regards moral conduct as indispensable is due to the conviction of the Biblical writers that God was concerned with the good of the whole community of His people and that He was holy and demanded justice and mercy above all from them. Such differences are important and should not be minimized. But the similarities are even more important and they indicate that belief in grace springs from basic theistic beliefs and is an essential element in theism. It arises from the theistic conception of God as a personal being who has created men and who cares for them. It also presupposes a deep conviction on the part of men that they are estranged from their true being by their worldly existence and their consciousness of their own inability to free themselves from its evils and attain spiritual fulfillment for themselves. When these beliefs have been present in a religion, whether in the East or in the West, men have believed that God is willing and able to rescue them from the evils that burden them, have turned to Him with faith and devotion, and have experienced peace and joy in union with Him. Since the Hindu conception of God and of the evils of man's worldly existence differs at certain points from that of Jews and Christians, it is not strange that the Vaisnavite understanding of grace has differed in some respects from that of Western theism. What is more significant is the testimony it offers that the religious consciousness of men who believe in a personal God and have a realistic view of their own need for help seems to affirm that He will have compassion upon them and assist them by His grace when they put their faith in Him.

Grace and Freedom: Augustine and Pelagius

We have noted that there was a sharp division between two "schools"

[11] *Ibid.,* p. 87.

of Vaisnavites in India with respect to the relation of God's grace to man's effort and works. A somewhat similar controversy arose in Christian theism between Augustine and Pelagius in the fifth century, and it has broken out again and again in different forms since that time. According to Augustine, man's will is so completely dominated by sin that he is powerless to overcome it by his own effort. Therefore, his salvation, from its beginning with repentance and faith to its end in eternal life, is effected by God's grace. Even his acceptance of grace by faith is not the work of his own will but is a gift of God. For grace is "prevenient" in the sense that God does not wait for man to take the first step towards Him but precedes it and makes it possible. By "operating grace," *gratia operans,* God acts upon a person to plant the seeds of new life in him. Thereafter, through "cooperating grace," *gratia cooperans,* God enables him to overcome the temptations that assail him and fosters the new life of love that has sprung up in him. Thus, everything man does, including his faith and his later moral striving, depends upon God's grace. In the words of St. Paul, man is "justified" not by his own "works" but by God's grace which is received by faith.[12]

But this saving grace is bestowed only upon those who have been predestined by God from eternity to receive it, the "elect." These are enabled to remain steadfast to the end by "irresistible" grace. When asked whether irresistible grace is compatible with freedom of the will, Augustine's reply is that after grace has been given to a man, his acts continue to be determined by his own volitions but his will has been liberated from its bondage to sin and he is now able not to sin, *posse non peccare.* Since his will has been healed by grace and can choose his true good rather than some inferior good, he now has not only "formal" freedom of choice but "real" and effective freedom to choose rightly. In the life after death, he will enjoy a still higher freedom, the inability to sin, *non posse peccare,* so that he can continue in full security in the love of God and in eternal blessedness.[13]

Even from this brief summary of Augustine's doctrine of grace it is easy to understand why it has exerted such a great influence upon many profoundly religious men. It emphasizes the absolute dependence of man upon God rather than his own efforts for his salvation and thus ascribes all the glory to Him. At the same time, it seems to deliver man from the temptation to give credit to himself and thus to fall back into pride and self-love. Thus, the Augustinian doctrine has a double appeal: it acknowledges the sovereignty of God and it strikes at the root

[12] Romans 3:28; 4; 5:1.

[13] Hastings, James: *Encyclopedia of Religion and Ethics,* article on St. Augustine, Vol. II. *Catholic Encyclopedia,* article on St. Augustine, sec. IV.

of pride. In addition, his picture of man as in bondage to sin powerfully expresses the conviction of many that man should not deceive himself by trusting in his own reason and will but should recognize that all of his natural powers are distorted by self-love, so that he needs to be delivered from it by a power greater than himself. Thus, Augustine sharply defines the issue between classical and modern humanism with its trust in man's self-sufficiency and Biblical theism with its trust in God's grace.

On the other hand, if one demands of a theological doctrine that it shall do justice to all sides of the religious life and that it shall not contradict beliefs which are essential for the moral life, serious difficulties begin to appear. Does not Augustine's view of God's sovereignty and of man's absolute dependence rest upon a conception of God as sheer power and of his relation to man as that of a potter molding clay which is completely passive in His hands?

John Oman has pointed out that the Augustinian doctrine of grace makes the relation between God and man an impersonal one, since it conceives of God's will as overwhelming power which reduces persons to things by its way of dealing with them.[14] Is it not, he asks, inconsistent with God's love as a Father, who is patient and uses persuasion to win a free response from his children, to picture His will as an impersonal force which compels their obedience? Oman also insists that irresistible grace violates the moral personality of man. If the essence of moral personality is self-determination and moral independence, it is incompatible with a form of grace which does not call forth a free response from within. It is true that freedom of the will is not effective as long as the will is in bondage to self-love and that liberation from this bondage enables it to will the true good. But if the grace which brings about this change is irresistible, the will is determined by God to will its true good and is free only in name. Finally, the doctrine of predestination limits the universality of God's grace to the elect and is inconsistent with the Biblical conception of the divine love. Indeed, it seems to make God at least a partial cause of evil on a vast scale. Although Augustine maintains that sinners who do not receive saving grace damn themselves by their own guilt, is not God responsible insofar as He refuses to give them the irresistible grace that would save them, as a man is responsible for the drowning of another when he refuses to throw him a rope?

These criticisms make it clear that much of Augustine's conception of grace is unacceptable because it is inconsistent with the theistic view of God and His relation to man. However, this should not blind

[14] Oman, J.: *Grace and Personality*, Cambridge, Cambridge University Press, 1925, p. 13.

us to the truth of Augustine's insight into the nature of sin as love of self which expresses itself in pride and sensuality and into the power of sin to distort the freedom of man's will. Few Western theists today would accept Augustine's doctrine of "original sin," i.e., the hereditary transmission of sin from Adam to all his posterity, or his view that this has resulted in a "necessity of sinning" in all his descendants. But few would deny that all men in fact do sin or that there is a solidarity of mankind in sin, each generation being linked in its sins with preceding generations and each person being involved with the sins of his own society. In consequence, there is a widespread recognition in our time that freedom of choice does not guarantee that a person will choose his true good—or that of others—unless the power of self-love which leads him to center his desires on himself alone can be broken. There is also an increasing recognition that a person becomes prey to a sense of meaninglessness that leads to despair when his self-love destroys his capacity to enter into meaningful relationships with others and thereby to fulfill himself. To theists this suggests the profound need of man for help from a power beyond himself. That Augustine described this need so vividly and his own experience of divine grace transforming his life[15] is probably his greatest contribution to our understanding of grace.

The antithesis of the Augustinian theory of grace is that of Pelagius, a British monk. Pelagius developed his theory to counteract what he considered to be the morally enervating effects of St. Augustine's *Confessions,* which was being widely read in Rome and which seemed to him to encourage a passive attitude and lead to moral laxity. Hence, he preached that Christians should not depend upon special grace but should rely upon their own moral effort in obedience to the revealed Law. The Pelagian theory may be briefly summarized as follows: God has created man's nature essentially good and the idea of inherited sin and guilt is unthinkable; hence, every man at birth is in the same moral condition as Adam before he sinned, for he is endowed by grace with reason and free will; and these are sufficient to enable him to remain sinless. This implies that man's freedom of will is absolute in the sense that his determination of his act in each moment of choice is not impaired by his previous choices, so that he is always free to avoid choosing sin. Divine grace consists simply of the creation of man as rational and free, the revealed Law which tells him what to do, and the teaching and example of Christ.[16]

Since Pelagianism tends to reduce religion to moral obedience and rests upon an optimistic confidence in the sufficiency of moral effort

[15] Augustine: *Confessions.*
[16] Hastings, *op. cit.,* Vol. 9, pp. 703–711.

to attain salvation, it has never satisfied deeply religious men. Moreover, the psychology of the will which it assumes is shallow. It ignores the power of habit to affect the choices of the will and thus makes it impossible to account for the continuity of the personality or the persistence of sin in it. Also, in insisting that the individual is solely responsible for his own sin, it overlooks the solidarity of mankind in sin. As a result, it assumes that the individual can overcome the tendency to evil in him at every moment by moral effort, despite the influence of his own sinful choices in the past and of entrenched social evils upon him. As Augustine says, Pelagius pictures the will of man as it was when God created it, not as it actually is after it has fallen into sin; but this is as if one should attribute to a man whose legs are broken the power to walk because he once could walk.

Finally, Pelagius is led by his inadequate recognition of the power of sin to the conclusion that the only grace needed by man is his endowment by God at his creation with a rational and free will and the revelation to him through Christ of the moral law. This presupposes that all he requires in order to attain moral perfection is to know the moral rules that define his duties and to have an example of obedience to them before him. Thus, he defended the moral ability and independence of the human will against Augustine's disparagement of it, but he did so in a way which seems to cut men off from the assistance of the divine grace in their struggle to overcome sin.

Moral Autonomy vs. Grace: Maclagan

W. G. Maclagan has recently made a strong defense of the autonomy of the moral life. His discussion of the problem of grace is in the context of a general analysis of the "moral response" of man to the unconditional "moral demand" of duty upon him. Defining the moral response as "dutifulness" or "the willing acceptance, in the practical determination of action, of what duty requires," [17] he maintains that it must be free in the libertarian sense of the word.[18] The question of the relation of grace to man's freedom arises at the point where theologians make the claim that grace is operative *in* or *through* the will to enable it to make a moral response it could not otherwise make. Maclagan strongly rejects this claim and argues that it contradicts the very idea of a free will.[19] His reason for taking this view is that a man's act of will must be absolutely his own and cannot also be God's without

---

[17] Maclagan, W. G.: *The Theological Frontier of Ethics,* London, George Allen and Unwin, 1961, p. 95.

[18] *Ibid.,* p. 100.

[19] *Ibid.,* p. 111.

ceasing to be his own. To claim that it can be divine as well as human is to negate man's freedom.[20]

It should be noted that Maclagan does not reject grace in every form but only the form of it which involves divine immanence, i.e., grace working *in* the will. A man may be aided in various ways in doing something without its ceasing to be his own work, e.g., a boy's parents may encourage him to write an essay for a competition, provide pen and ink for him, and support him by their interest in his effort.[21] "All the help we can get remains as it were extraneous to the will: relative to the will it is all *environmental*, not *constitutive*, no matter how intimately environmental it may be." [22] What must be denied by the moralist is not dependence on divine grace in this "environmental" sense but dependence that enters into our willing "constitutively." A man's willing must be absolutely his own if his moral personality is not to be violated or reduced to a mode of the divine being.[23]

Moreover, the "environmental" action of God must not be supposed to be a necessary condition of our willing rightly. I can measure up to the moral demand of duty "simply of myself and altogether apart from God's help." [24] Moreover, I can do so not merely on a particular occasion but on every possible occasion,[25] so that "constitutive" grace is not necessary for the attainment of even the most complete dutifulness.[26] Maclagan realizes that this may seem like nonsense both to believers and to unbelievers who are aware of their moral failures, because there is a strong belief that moral imperfection is unavoidable and this seems to be confirmed by history.[27] But he thinks that this belief can be accounted for without supposing moral failure to be inevitable. Moral decisions vary in difficulty and we tend to suppose that a moral demand might be so exacting that it would be impossible for the will to meet it successfully.[28] This supposition combines with the sense of the universality of moral failure in history to convince us that perfect obedience to duty is beyond our capacity.[29] But while Maclagan admits that the possibility of attaining moral perfection is very small and that it is the rarest of achievements, he holds firmly

[20] *Ibid.*, p. 113.
[21] *Ibid.*, p. 114.
[22] *Ibid.*, p. 115.
[23] *Ibid.*, p. 118.
[24] *Ibid.*, p. 119.
[25] *Ibid.*, p. 119.
[26] *Ibid.*, p. 120.
[27] *Ibid.*, p. 121.
[28] *Ibid.*, p. 122.
[29] *Ibid.*, p. 123.

to the view that sin is not necessary in the sense of being inseparably connected with man's nature.

What is his reason for maintaining this thesis despite contrary indications of moral imperfection in personal experience and in history as a whole? The answer is to be found in his conception of a "bare will" which is a distinct part or aspect of the total self but seems to act in independence of other aspects such as impulse, appetition, and conative tendency.[30] The libertarian account of moral action requires that this "bare will" should be free to make the response demanded by duty, however difficult and costly it may be. The principle "I ought, therefore I can" implies that my "bare will" has the capacity to make a moral decision although my "whole self" cannot make it prevail over the other elements in itself. The paradoxical character of this view is illustrated by a passage in the concluding appendix in which Maclagan acknowledges that "human weakness" involves man's inability to attain the ideal by an effort of the will but affirms once more that we must retain "self-confidence" in the sense of a conviction that one has power over one's own act.[31]

Maclagan's defense of moral autonomy contains a salutary warning that the moral consciousness has presuppositions and makes demands which can be denied by theologians only at the cost of swallowing up morality in religion. It is important that the recent reaction of Neo-Orthodox theology against the humanistic tendency of much Protestant thought in the nineteenth century should not submerge the independent moral consciousness. There is also a danger that in reasserting the primacy of grace Neo-Orthodox theologians may minimize the freedom of man's will and his responsibility for cooperating with the divine grace as a mere assertion of pride on his part. The value of Maclagan's position lies in his insistence upon the demands of the moral consciousness and his protest against the disparagement of man's freedom and moral responsibility.

However, his view of grace cannot be accepted by anyone who approaches the problem from the point of view of Eastern or Western theism, on the one hand, and a realistic view of man, on the other. In the first place, his assertion that the unaided human will can make an adequate response to the absolute moral demand and can make it constantly and perfectly is wholly unrealistic. Without accepting the Augustinian view of the natural man's inability to avoid sinning, *non posse non peccare*, one must insist that Maclagan's supreme confidence in man's moral ability is inconsistent with human experience. It is true that impressive moral achievements have been won in human

[30] *Ibid.*, p. 126.
[31] *Ibid.*, p. 199.

history. But this does not justify extreme claims for the moral capacities of men in general. Indeed, such claims are refuted by Maclagan's own candid acknowledgment that moral perfection is very rare, that it is impossible to prove it in any particular case because of the hiddenness and impurity of motives, and that men have a "sense" of the universality of moral failure in history.

Indeed, his confidence does not seem to be based on experience but upon his view of what morality demands. His main argument is a logical one: the moral demand is unconditional; it requires a response of perfect dutifulness; and this implies the ability of the will to make such a response. Thus, it is based upon the Kantian principle "I ought, therefore I can," interpreted to mean that the "bare will" is free at every moment to obey the moral law whatever the moral condition of the "whole self" may be. On the contrary, we have pointed out that the Kantian principle does not justify the view that the self as it actually is and without undergoing any change can obey the moral law.[32] If so, the argument that man can by his own unaided will perfectly respond to the moral demand must be rejected. It is neither supported by experience nor required by the moral consciousness.

Maclagan's denial of "constitutive" grace and his restriction of grace to "environmental" influence are obviously related to his confidence in man's moral ability. This restriction of grace cannot be accepted by the theist for several reasons. First, it rests upon the assumption that the relation between God and man must be an external one if man's freedom is to be safeguarded. This overlooks the fact that man's freedom is not absolute but limited. He does not live and act as a separate being whose relations with other beings are only external. He exists in close and intimate relations with his fellows and is profoundly affected in his innermost thoughts and attitudes by his intercourse with them. Everything or every person one experiences helps to shape one's self. Similarly, the self is related to God in an intimate and personal way. God, as theists conceive Him, is not detached and aloof from man; He is concerned with man and actively intervenes in his life in order to help him fulfill his destiny. If this is true, grace cannot be confined to "environmental" influence, however broadly this is conceived. God cannot be kept at arm's length by the self, as if it had to preserve its integrity and independence by shutting Him out from its inner life. Second, man's need for help is too great for anything less than "constitutive" grace to be effective. He needs to be encouraged by beneficent influences from without; he needs also to be transformed and em-

---

[32] Ch. 11.

powered by the working of the divine Spirit within. Religious poems
and hymns of theists, Eastern and Western, have expressed this need
again and again. For men in their desperate need for deliverance from
evil cannot be content with external assistance which leaves them un-
changed; they cry out for the power and love of God to make them
new creatures, to endow them with a new spirit and a new heart.[33]

Finally, this "constitutive" grace working within the self does not
negate its freedom but makes it effective. It is not true that, if God
acts "in" or "within" our wills, our acts are His as well as our own
and therefore are not really our own. God acts in us, according to
Western theism, not to supersede our natural powers but to illuminate
our minds, purify our affections, and strengthen our wills. As Augustine pointed out, the will which is under the dominion of self-love
has freedom in the sense of freedom of choice, but its freedom is
weakened by the fact that its self-love prevents it from willing its true
good. Hence, "constitutive" grace is believed to be necessary to transform it, so that it may be unified and enabled to choose its true good,
love of God and love of neighbor as well as love of self. This does not
destroy the freedom of the will by making God the author of its acts;
it restores the will to its moral health and thus perfects its freedom.

Perhaps Maclagan fails to see this because of his abstract view of the
"bare will" as unlimited in its freedom. For it is only because of this
view that he is able to maintain his confidence in the absolute moral
ability of the "bare will" despite his frank recognition of the moral
failure of the "whole self." Although we have maintained that the will
is free in the sense of being able to transcend the present character
of the self in its decisions, we have also argued that its freedom is
limited by its present character because it does not function as a "bare
will" but as an aspect of the "whole self." Hence, it needs not only
"environmental" but also "constitutive" grace, theists affirm, to overcome the limitation imposed on it by self-love and thus to make its
freedom more effective.

The Nature of Grace:
Guiding Principles

In our critical analysis of theories of grace we have shown that
the Bhakti theism of the Vaisnavites bears eloquent testimony to the
tendency of men who have believed in a personal God and have felt
deeply the evils of worldly existence to trust in the divine grace to
save them. We have also examined two classical Western theories of

[33] Psalm 51:10. Cf. John Donne: "Holy Sonnets," XIV.

grace, that of Augustine and that of Pelagius, and have found that neither of them is acceptable although for quite different reasons. The Augustinian theory vividly describes the sin of man and his need for divine grace in his struggle to overcome it, but it conceives the operation of grace as irresistible power and attenuates (if it does not deny) man's freedom. The Pelagian view defends man's freedom and moral responsibility but fails to recognize the radical nature of his sin and his need for grace to restore his will to health. Finally, we have considered the recent criticism by Maclagan of "constitutive" grace and have argued that it rests upon an abstract view of man's freedom, an unrealistic estimate of his moral capacity, and a misunderstanding of the action of grace itself.

We shall now attempt to indicate briefly some of the requirements that must be met by a modern theory of grace, if it is to be consistent with the theistic conception of God and man which we have developed in the preceding chapters. Our purpose in making this attempt is primarily *analytical,* since the development of a new constructive theory of grace is beyond our competence and probably should be undertaken by a theologian rather than a philosopher of religion. Also, we shall state the requirements that must be met—or the guiding principles that must be followed—in developing a constructive theory in *general terms,* although it will be obvious that our formulation of them has been influenced mainly by Western theism. For a philosopher of religion can by his method determine only the general principles on which a theory of grace must be based if it is to be compatible with the form of theism he regards as most religiously adequate and philosophically acceptable. We shall defer to the next section consideration of the evidence for the *truth* of the belief in grace.

(1) A fundamental presupposition of the theistic conception of grace is that man stands in the *need* of God's grace. As we have said, this need is conceived differently in the various theistic religions. In Bhakti Hinduism, for example, it is seen primarily as the need for deliverance from the evils of life, especially from the necessity of rebirth. In Western theism, however, it arises primarily from the power of sin and meaninglessness over man and his inability to overcome it by his own effort alone. Augustine pointed out that all men by their love of self contradict their higher nature as beings made in the image of God, that this estranges them from God and from other men, and that it results in a sense of meaninglessness which often leads to despair. Reinhold Niebuhr has shown that self-love expresses itself in the form of pride, not only in the will to power of individuals but also in more subtle forms such as intellectual and moral pride.[34] He has also

[34] Niebuhr, *op. cit.,* Vol. I, pp. 186–203.

described the collective pride of classes, races, and nations which has been the greatest source of injustice in history.[35] All of this has become painfully clear to the men of our troubled century which has witnessed the tragic consequences of individual and collective pride on an unparalleled scale. The result has been widespread disillusionment with the optimistic and Utopian hopes of the nineteenth century which had been encouraged by idealistic views of man.

This does not mean that contemporary theists must accept Augustine's pessimistic conclusion that sin has destroyed man's ability not to sin, or the view that the condition of man apart from grace is one of total depravity. The condition of the "natural" man falsifies all extreme descriptions of him, whether naively optimistic or darkly pessimistic. On the one hand, the image of God is blurred but it is not effaced. Man's recognition of the claims of truth, justice, and love upon him, even if his response to them in his conduct is very imperfect, shows that he is not wholly self-centered and that spiritual aspiration is alive in him. Also, although he may not believe in the existence of God, his sense of the emptiness and meaninglessness of a self-centered life often testifies to his awareness of his alienation from the world, his fellows, and his true self. On the other hand, man's self-love, by centering his desires primarily upon himself, has greatly weakened his ability to choose the highest good for himself and for others. Although it has not destroyed his concern for truth, goodness and love, as we have said, it prevents him from being wholly disinterested in his devotion to them. As Temple says, man can broaden and elevate his interests by devoting himself to the search for truth and goodness, as humanists claim, but this leaves his own self still at the center of his concern.[36] The pursuit of truth often leads to intellectual pride and the effort to attain goodness can result in self-righteousness or moral pride. Even religious devotion can foster spiritual pride in the form of dogmatism and intolerance.

Thus, man's spiritual efforts may enrich his interests and refine his personality, but they cannot break the power of self-love over him. For the will which seeks to conquer self-love is itself in some measure possessed by it. Divided against itself, it cannot will with the whole of itself. Therefore, it needs to be transformed by a power beyond itself which can draw it out of itself and enable it to escape from its self-centeredness. Western theists believe that God has the power to bring about such a transformation by manifesting His love and mercy for men and awakening a response of love from them.

(2) The theological starting-point for a theory of grace is that God

[35] *Ibid.*, pp. 208–219.
[36] Temple, *op. cit.*, pp. 385–394.

is not only the Creator who is the ground of all being but also the *Redeemer* who has compassion upon men and in his love seeks to deliver them from the evil that prevents them from attaining fullness of life. It is at this point that the theist differs most radically from deism which views God as Creator but not as Redeemer. Hindu and Buddhist theists are at one with Jewish and Christian theists on this fundamental point. Thus, the main theological presupposition of the theistic conception of grace is clear; as the nature of *man* is such that he *needs* grace, the nature of *God* is such that He willingly *bestows* it. In brief, He is a personal God and one who is characterized not only by moral goodness but also by mercy and love.[37]

(3) If the conception of grace is to be consistent with this view of God, the offer of grace must be *universal* rather than limited to certain persons or a particular religion. If God is the Creator and Redeemer of *all* men, He cannot logically be regarded as interested in the salvation of some but not of others. This is the primary reason for rejecting the Augustinian (and Islamic) doctrine of the "predestination" of some to receive God's saving grace and the denial of it to others. The universality of grace is also incompatible with any conception which limits it to those who have accepted one particular religious faith and denies it to those of other faiths.

If this is the case, the fact that some have not responded to God's offer of grace by faith must be explained not by His refusal of it but by their *rejection* of it, while the fact that others have responded must be explained not by the irresistibility of His grace but by their *acceptance* of it. Of course, this raises difficulties for which there is no simple answer. If God wills the salvation of all men, why has He created some with physical or mental constitutions and others in social circumstances which are unfavorable to their acceptance of His grace? For some men seem to be born with such personal and social disadvantages that they are unlikely to respond to the proclamation of the divine grace, if they have the good fortune to hear it at all. We have argued [38] that men are conditioned rather than wholly determined by their heredity and environment, but their natural endowments and social circumstances are so unequal that it is easy for some and hard for others to accept the offer of grace. We cannot explain this, but the fact that we cannot should not lead us either to limit the scope of God's grace or to deny that man possesses the freedom, however circumscribed, to accept or reject it.

(4) However, the fact that men who accept grace do so freely does not imply that the divine grace has nothing to do with their acceptance

---

[37] See the discussion of the nature of God in ch. 7.
[38] Ch. 11.

of it. If God's grace is everywhere and always operative, it must be "prevenient" in the sense that it *precedes* or *anticipates* even the first step of faith man takes towards God. For if God seeks the salvation of every man, He does not wait for man to make the first movement but takes the initiative and seeks to turn him towards Himself. To suppose the opposite is to picture God as indifferent to those who do not know and love Him instead of seeking them out in His love. However, the prevenience of grace as a condition of faith is not incompatible with man's freedom to accept or reject it. Since God deals in a personal manner with man, His grace does not force faith upon him but illuminates his mind concerning his proper relationship towards God and his fellows and stimulates his will to turn away from love of himself to love of Him and them.

The *methods* through which this is done are doubtless many and complex. Augustine has analyzed one method in detail: the disappointment of foolish hopes and the frustration of worldly plans and desires which arise in a life governed by self-love. For example, he describes his increasing disillusionment with his life as a proud and ambitious teacher of rhetoric and his struggle to break the power of sexual desire. Thus, he interprets his experience before his conversion as a restless and fruitless search among finite goods for a happiness that always eluded him because his spiritual hunger could be satisfied with nothing less than the infinite and perfect Good which is God. As he expresses it, "Thou hast formed us for Thyself, and restless are our hearts until they find their rest in Thee." [39] This may be called a *negative* method by which the divine grace prepares men for faith. A more *positive* method is the influence of religious persons and communities, e.g., Augustine's mother Monica and Bishop Ambrose. For divine grace has normally been mediated to men above all through other individual persons, e.g., Moses and the prophets in Judaism or Christ and the apostles in Christianity. But it has also been mediated through the traditions, scriptures, worship, and life of a religious community, as well as through communities and institutions influenced by a religious attitude to life, e.g. educational and social service institutions.

(5) Since divine grace not only prepares a person for faith but also continues to act upon and in him to transform his whole self, the religious man regards grace as the *primary* source of his salvation and views his own effort as a response to it. However, it is misleading to speak, as Temple and others have done, of the "all-sufficiency" of grace for man's salvation,[40] or, as Luther has done, of salvation as due to

[39] Augustine: *Confessions*, Book I, ch. I.
[40] Temple, *op. cit.*, p. 402.

"grace alone," *sola gratia.* For man's response of faith and obedience, although secondary to grace, is indispensable. God does not will to bestow salvation upon man as a gift to be passively received but expects him to respond actively not only by faith but also by striving to overcome his love of self and by manifesting his faith through love and service to his neighbors.

Of course, men cannot attain the perfect obedience and goodness God requires. Therefore, they can never earn their salvation, so that salvation as a reward for merits is impossible. Rather, they are dependent upon God's grace for the love which enables them to obey His will and for forgiveness when they fail to do so. But the assertion of Temple that God's grace is "all-sufficient" for salvation is a misleading and dangerous way of expressing the necessity of grace. For, although moral effort in obedience to God's will is not a *condition* of grace, it is an indispensable *aspect* of the life that leads to salvation, and only man himself can make that effort. The power of the saint over the hearts and lives of ordinary religious people is due to the fact that he is not only a "man of God" who depends upon grace for what he is but also a man who manifests his godliness in a life which at least approximates perfect goodness.

(6) One of the *fruits* of grace is *communion with God.* This is accompanied by a conviction that one's sins have been forgiven and one has been reconciled to God, restored to a right relationship with Him. This leads to profound *gratitude* to Him. The literature of theistic religions abounds with moving expressions of gratitude for the "amazing grace" which God in His mercy has shown to unworthy and undeserving men. Those who have experienced it and the new life flowing from it offer their thanksgiving in prayers and sing their praises in hymns. The experience of forgiveness and reconciliation with God also gives rise to *joy* as men recognize that they have been delivered from despair. Joy is accompanied by *peace* since they are now in the right relationship with God and their fellows.[41] And *hope,* based upon faith in God's purpose to complete the work He has begun, enables them to look forward with confidence to the future. It is the task of the theologian rather than the philosopher to describe the fullness of life under grace which is expressed in such feelings and attitudes. But the philosopher of religion must take note of them and recognize their importance for an understanding of grace. For theists have believed that divine grace not only transforms the *will* so that it can respond

---

[41] This is not inconsistent with what we have said in ch. 3 about the fact that there is *suffering* and struggle in the life of the theist and that theism is a religion of *unrest* rather than rest or repose. Paradoxically, for the man of faith joy is possible despite suffering, peace in the midst of struggle.

to God's love with moral obedience but also releases powerful *emotions* and *energies* in the personality as a whole.

Grace and Truth

In the preceding section our aim has been a limited one. We have sought only to analyze the general requirements for a constructive theory of grace which would be consistent with the theistic view of God, the need of man for deliverance from sin and meaninglessness, and man's freedom and responsibility. However, the task of the philosopher of religion, we have argued, is not only to *analyze* religious beliefs but also to examine critically their claim to *truth*. Is there evidence that belief in the reality of grace is true? If so, what is its nature?

The belief in divine grace has arisen from *religious experiences* of theists in the East and the West which they have interpreted as evidence for God's favorable attitude towards them. For they have attributed these experiences to the activity of God in their lives, delivering them from evils they could not themselves have overcome, and have regarded this as a manifestation of His love and mercy towards them. These experiences, which have not been confined to the past but are enjoyed by many in our own time, provide the empirical evidence for belief in the reality of divine grace.

Now, it is possible to offer a naturalistic explanation of such experiences. One may assert that the experience of grace is a product of two natural elements, the experience of an influx of power from the subconscious mind and the humility of good men about their own resources.[42] For example, the explanation of St. Paul's conversion and subsequent achievement as due to divine grace does not admit of any decisive empirical test,[43] and it can be maintained that his ascription of it to God is really not a statement of fact but the expression of an attitude or a kind of praise.[44] But the crucial question here is whether we have any right to apply empirical tests of a scientific kind to religious assertions. As Basil Mitchell says, we must distinguish between two different requirements of the demand for a scientific test of an assertion. The first is the general "logical" requirement that "for a statement to count as an assertion (as distinct from, say, a command or a wish) it must be possible to conceive evidence which would tell against it." [45] The other is a "metaphysical" requirement that "all factual statements must 'in principle' be capable of being worked

[42] Mitchell, Basil: *Faith and Logic*, Boston, Beacon Press, 1957, essay on "The Grace of God," p. 153.
[43] *Ibid.*, p. 153.
[44] *Ibid.*, p. 154.
[45] *Ibid.*, p. 159.

into a scientific system governed by universal laws." [46] The first of these requirements is legitimate and can be satisfied by religious assertions; the second cannot be justified either on a priori or on empirical grounds.[47]

Thus, the empirical evidence for the truth of the belief in divine grace is the experience enjoyed by countless persons of being touched and laid hold of by a power beyond themselves and enabled by it to be and do what otherwise seemed impossible for them. Their interpretation of this experience as caused by divine grace or the divine Spirit within is not self-authenticating, and men can be and have often been deluded concerning the cause of an experience. But the question is whether their explanation of it, if it is confirmed by evidence of other kinds for the truth of theism, is the most adequate one.

It is especially the religious experience of the saints and its effect upon their lives which seems to point beyond them to God for its explanation. For while the saint attains human goodness, he also seems to manifest a quality and a power which transcend the human.[48] "The strength and graciousness of his personality," says Mitchell, "is somehow incommensurate with what we know of their natural antecedents." [49] It is not a sufficient explanation of the sense of the holy which the saint awakens in us to call him a religious "genius" who is "inspired" like the artistic genius. For the saint, unlike the genius, is essentially a man who is centered in God and utterly dependent on Him, and he has become a saint not by virtue of a special natural endowment but through a complete surrender to Him.[50]

However, the experience of grace has not been confined to those who have been recognized as saints, and ordinary men would not be so impressed by the great saints if they had not themselves enjoyed the experience in some measure. Most religious people have had the experience of being helped, strengthened, or inspired in their lives by a power which seemed to come from beyond themselves. This is true not only of those who have experienced conversion but also of those William James describes as the "once-born" who have never undergone an emotional crisis in their religious life.[51] Although with ordinary men the experience of grace is an "altogether slighter thing than the wind which blows through the saints," as Mitchell says, "it

[46] *Ibid.*, p. 160.

[47] *Ibid.*, p. 160.

[48] James, William: *The Varieties of Religious Experience*, Lectures XI–XIII on "Saintliness."

[49] Mitchell, *op. cit.*, p. 166.

[50] Steere, Douglas: *On Beginning from Within*, New York, Harper, 1943.

[51] James, *op. cit.*, Lectures IV, V.

serves as a clue to what the grace of God might mean, since it bears sufficient resemblance to the experience of the saints, in whom its characteristic fruits are found in their fulness." [52]

Belief in divine grace is supported not only by empirical evidence derived from religious experience, but also by the fact that it is *coherent* with other theistic beliefs and seems to be *required* by them. If God is conceived as a spiritual and personal Being who is the Ground of the natural order as Mind and of the moral order as purposive Will seeking the good of men, as we have argued,[53] it would be in accord with His nature that He should help men to overcome the evils that afflict them and to attain fullness of life in union with Himself. Moreover, if man suffers from the sin of self-love and cannot overcome it by his own will, as we have also argued, it is fitting that God should aid him by manifesting His mercy and love for him, awakening in him a response of love, and thus breaking the power of self-love over him.

Thus, belief in divine grace is based upon the religious experience of men in the great theistic religions and derives support from its coherence with the beliefs of both Eastern and Western theism concerning the nature of God and the need of man. However, it cannot be demonstrated with certainty and will always remain a matter of faith. All we have attempted to show is that faith in it is not arbitrary since it has arisen from and is confirmed by religious experience in the great theistic religions. Grace will always be a mystery, for the Spirit, like the wind, "blows where it wills, and you hear the sound of it, but you do not know whence it comes or whither it goes." [54] But a philosopher who knows that reason cannot dispel all mysteries will acknowledge that it is the heart of vital religion and the secret of its power, and he will take seriously its claim to truth. He will at least acknowledge that, although its truth cannot be demonstrated by reason, faith in it has sprung from the religious experience of many and is consistent with beliefs we have shown to be reasonable.

[52] Mitchell, *op. cit.,* p. 168.
[53] Ch. 6.
[54] John 3:8.

13

Faith and Reason

Throughout this book we have argued that religious belief originates with *religious experience,* but that the major beliefs of Western theism concerning God and man can be supported by *rational argument* based on evidence derived from other forms of experience. We have also assumed that the philosopher of religion must acknowledge no other authority than experience and rational argument.

But the religious life also involves *faith.* For religious experience which does not lead to faith in the divine Being who is its object may be nothing more than an occasional transitory feeling which has little effect on life. And rational argument may convince the mind that God exists and is worthy of devotion, but unless it issues in a commitment to Him it is important only for philosophy, not for the religious life.

Therefore, the philosopher of religion cannot avoid the task of inquiring into the nature and role of faith. Since faith makes affirmations which go *beyond* reason, the philosopher may assume that it is *contrary* to reason, irrational. But this would beg the question as to its relation to reason and would be denied by most men of faith. While faith obviously goes beyond reason in one sense, it claims, at least in some of its forms, to go beyond reason in a direction towards which reason itself points. It is imperative, therefore, that we analyze the nature of faith, especially in Western theism, and that we examine its relation to reason.

Faith Perfects Reason: Aquinas

According to Aquinas, faith is not contrary to reason, but "perfects" or completes it. While reason can demonstrate certain basic religious truths such as the existence of God and the immortality of the soul, revelation also makes available to man truths which are necessary for salvation but which reason cannot prove. These revealed truths must be accepted by faith.

Aquinas' analysis of faith is a classical expression of one of the most common conceptions of faith. The *object* of faith, he says, consists of propositions about things unseen. These propositions have been formulated by the Church and collected in a creed, since all believers need to know the truths which are required for salvation and to be guarded from errors in interpreting them, e.g., errors due to obscurities in the meaning of Scriptural passages and perversions by heretics.[1] With respect to the *interior act* of faith, Aquinas holds that belief has something in common with understanding but that it agrees with doubt and opinion in that "its knowledge does not attain the perfection of clear vision." [2] Since its knowledge is thus imperfect, the intellect is not coerced by the truth into assent but must be moved to assent by the will.[3] Although the knowledge gained through faith is less certain than science "for us" since it is above our human intellect, it is more certain "absolutely" since its cause, God, is more certain than human reason.[4] Moreover, it "contains virtually" the vision of God which is to come hereafter,[5] and Aquinas goes so far as to say that it is "a habit of the mind whereby eternal life is begun in us." [6]

As we have said, the *will* is involved in faith as well as the intellect, but in a different way. Faith "resides" in the intellect, since it prepares us for the vision of God hereafter and vision is in the intellect. But it proceeds from the will, since the will moves the intellect to assent. But the will does not by its own free choice alone move the intellect to assent, for faith is infused into man by God and hence is a gift. God not only "proposes" the things of faith to man by revealing them; He also "moves man inwardly to assent." [7]

The main value of Aquinas' conception of faith lies in his affirmation that it claims to provide us with knowledge, although this knowledge is imperfect, and that the will also is involved because it must move the intellect to assent in the absence of compelling evidence. Thus, he sees that intellectual and volitional elements are interrelated in faith. Moreover, faith is accompanied by hope since it looks forward to a more perfect knowledge of God hereafter. However, few modern

---

[1] Aquinas, Thomas: *Summa Theologica*, II-II, Q 1, a 9.
[2] *Ibid.*, Q 2, a 1.
[3] *Ibid.*
[4] *Ibid.*, Q 4, a 8.
[5] *Ibid.*, Q 4, a 1.
[6] *Ibid.*
[7] *Ibid.*, Q 6, a 1.

theists would agree with Aquinas that the object of faith consists of propositions directly communicated to men by God, defined for all by the Church, and accepted by all on its authority. For it has come to be realized that the Biblical revelation did not come to men in propositional form, that the interpretation of it in propositions has been the work of men, and that it can continue to awaken faith in men today only if it is in accord with their own religious experience and reflection.[8]

Faith Contrary to Understanding: Kierkegaard

Aquinas' view that faith goes beyond but is in harmony with reason was rejected by modern rationalists such as Spinoza who denied that revelation could provide men with religious truths inaccessible to reason. As a result, many philosophers of the Age of Reason dispensed with traditional religion based on revelation and sought to substitute a purely rational or "natural" religion for it. However, Hegel took a more positive view of revelation, maintaining that there were true insights in the great historic religions, and he attempted to reformulate the affirmations of Christian faith in philosophical terms and to demonstrate them by reason. But, as we have noted,[9] he succeeded only in transforming them into what he took to be universal philosophical truths, i.e., his own system. Thus, although he did not deny faith in revealed truths, as the Age of Reason had done, he distorted it by subordinating faith to reason, religion to philosophy.

This provoked a violent reaction from Kierkegaard. In his *Philosophical Fragments,* he contrasts the philosophical approach to religious knowledge represented in its purest form by Socrates with the Christian faith. Man, he suggests, cannot attain knowledge of God by reason but must depend upon God as Teacher to give him both the Truth and the condition necessary to receive it. Hence, He humbled Himself and took on the form of a man. But His revelation of Himself could not be perceived by the senses and cannot be demonstrated by reason; it must be accepted by faith.[10]

In accord with this view, Kierkegaard in his *Concluding Unscientific Postscript* attacked every attempt to prove the truth of Christianity by philosophical argument. The efforts of philosophers to discover the truth about God or immortality by "objective thinking" are bound to

[8] For a modern view of revelation, see Temple, William: *op. cit.,* ch. 12.

[9] Ch. 2.

[10] Kierkegaard, Soren: *Philosophical Fragments,* Princeton, N.J., Princeton University Press, 1936.

fail. Only if the mind of man were identical with the infinite mind of God would he be able to develop a "system" of thought which would comprehend all reality, as Hegel attempted to do. Moreover, the primary concern of the individual in his thinking should be with his own existence, and the attempt to develop a philosophical "system" distracts him from his true task of discovering the truth about his own existence.[11]

This criticism of the inability of "objective thinking" to provide the individual with religious truth sets the stage for Kierkegaard's strong affirmation of the superiority of "subjective thinking" in religion. Whereas objective thinking seeks truth in the sense of conformity of the subject to its object, subjective thinking is concerned with the true relationship of the subject to its object. The former is interested in the "what" of the object, the latter in "how" the subject is related to the object. This leads Kierkegaard to his famous definition of "subjective truth": "*An objective uncertainty held fast in an appropriation-process of the most passionate inwardness is the truth,* the highest truth attainable for an *existing* individual." It is in terms of this subjective kind of truth that Kierkegaard defines faith. "Faith," he says, "is precisely the contradiction between the infinite passion of the individual's inwardness and the objective uncertainty. If I am capable of grasping God objectively, I do not believe, but precisely because I cannot do this I must believe. If I wish to preserve myself in faith I must constantly be intent upon holding fast the objective uncertainty, so as to remain out upon the deep, over seventy thousand fathoms of water, still preserving my faith." [12] This implies that religious faith, unlike beliefs which arise from the interest of the intellect in objective truth, springs from the individual's deep concern about the meaning of his own existence, a concern which leads him to relate himself to God in a passionate commitment in order to attain fulfillment or "eternal happiness." That which distinguishes *Christian* faith from religious faith in *general,* e.g., from Socrates' belief in immortality, is that it affirms not merely the "objective uncertainty" but the "absurdity" of the Incarnation.[13] It is a "mystery" which was "never intended to be understood." For faith in the absurd, the paradox, is not "with the understanding," it is "against the understanding."

The contrast between this existentialist conception of faith as passionate commitment to a truth that is objectively uncertain or even absurd and the rationalistic conception of Hegel is great. But it is

[11] Kierkegaard, Soren: *Concluding Unscientific Postscript,* Princeton, N.J., Princeton University Press, 1941.
[12] *Ibid.,* p. 182.
[13] *Ibid.,* p. 188.

precisely at points where Kierkegaard differs from the latter conception that he makes his greatest contribution. In emphasizing the *subjective side* of faith, he makes it clear that faith is not merely the acceptance of beliefs or doctrines but is also a personal commitment and a total involvement of the individual. Therefore, an act of will is necessary, an act which God makes possible by His grace. Also, although the commitment of faith arises in response to a truth which is presented to the individual, e.g., the incarnation of God in Jesus, it is stimulated by an existential concern of the individual for the meaning and fulfillment of his own life. This is evident especially in his discussion of the Christian faith, where he maintains that the individual comes to faith in the "paradox" through his consciousness of guilt and his need for deliverance from despair.

However, Kierkegaard's view of the *objective side* of faith is far from satisfactory. It is true, of course, that there is "objective uncertainty" about the truth embraced by faith and therefore that a risk is involved in accepting it. It is also true that faith is a matter of such vital concern to the individual that he cannot afford to wait until the evidence is all in before making his decision, since new evidence on historical questions will continue to come in and new arguments on philosophical issues will continue to be put forward indefinitely. But it is not true that subjective concern is incompatible with objective thinking or that absurdity intensifies passion and strengthens faith. We have shown that objective thinking about the existence of God is not only compatible with but may support faith by arguments which indicate that theism offers the most adequate explanation of the world. Although we shall not attain objective certainty about the existence of God by such philosophical arguments, it does not follow that we should abandon objective thinking on that account. Indeed, it would be disastrous to reject objective thinking on religious questions. If there is no rational support for the existence of the object of faith, it is arbitrary to commit oneself to one object of faith rather than another. This is the case especially in our time, when rival faiths are competing for the allegiance of men.

Finally, Kierkegaard's claim that the passionate inwardness of faith is intensified when its object is not merely objectively uncertain but "absurd" and "against the understanding" is false. It is one thing to say that faith can be maintained despite difficulties and doubts; it is quite another thing to say that it is strengthened if reason sees nothing but absurdity in it. Even if this were psychologically possible, which is very doubtful, it would involve a radical split between the will and the understanding which would be a threat to mental health and fatal to religion itself.

The Will to Believe: William James

A philosopher who also emphasizes the volitional aspect of faith, although in a less extreme form, is William James in his famous essay *The Will to Believe*. James refers to it as "an essay in justification of faith, a defence of our right to adopt a believing attitude in religious matters, in spite of the fact that our merely logical intellect may not have been coerced." [14] He makes it clear that this "right to believe" does not apply to scientific questions, for on such questions we can wait until all the "objective evidence" has come in before making up our minds.[15] But the case of "speculative questions" such as those of religion is very different. Here the option between belief and unbelief is a "forced" one. We cannot escape decision by remaining neutral and waiting for more light for if we do so we shall lose the good that will result from belief if the belief is true. It is also "momentous," since the good we stand to gain by belief or to lose by unbelief is a vital one. Therefore, if the option is a "living" one, i.e., if the belief makes an "appeal" to us, we may and should exercise our right to believe.

In this argument James was obviously deeply influenced by his "empiricist" view that the certain truth available to us is very limited, so that most of the decisions we make on religious matters cannot be based upon purely intellectual grounds.[16] This is obviously the case with the propositions of theism. Since we cannot attain certainty concerning these propositions, it is not reasonable to suspend judgment indefinitely on them. Why, then, should we not allow our "passional nature" or our "willing nature" to decide?

One of the most valuable insights of James' essay is that the option between believing and not believing in God is a "forced" one. There is no middle ground of neutrality between these two alternatives, since the consequences of the agnostic's refusal to decide are virtually the same as those of the atheist's decision against belief. This is a salutary warning that decision cannot be indefinitely postponed without loss of the benefits which belief can bestow.

However, this does not throw any light on the question whether we are justified in deciding for a particular religious belief. For the practical *benefits* of believing, *e.g.*, a sense of meaning and direction in life, cannot take the place of *grounds* for believing if we are concerned about the truth of our beliefs. This is the most common objection to

---

[14] James, William: *Essays in Pragmatism,* essay "The Will to Believe," Introduction, New York, Hafner Pub. Co., 1948.

[15] *Ibid.,* VIII.

[16] *Ibid.,* VI.

James' argument. "For it authorizes us," says John Hick, "to believe ('by faith') any proposition, not demonstrably false, which it might be advantageous to us, in this world or another, to have accepted." [17] Is this not, he asks, merely "an impressive recommendation of 'wishful thinking' "? [18] To some extent, James might be defended against this objection. Since he asserts the right to believe only when there is "a genuine option that cannot be decided on intellectual grounds," he does not seem to mean that we may believe whatever would be advantageous to us even when there is *no* evidence for it. Rather, he seems to mean that we are justified in believing when the evidence is *not sufficient* to produce certainty or, as he puts it, "when our merely logical intellect has not been coerced." However, since he does not state explicitly that it is only strong evidence which should be the source of the "appeal" of a "living option," he has laid himself open to Hick's interpretation of his meaning and the criticism based upon it. Furthermore, his statement that it is our "passional nature" which must decide suggests that the role of reason in the decision is small. As a result, his critics have been quick to point out that his "will to believe" is open to the same objection that he himself made against Pascal's "wager," i.e., that it justifies us in believing merely because we have much to gain and little to lose. Thus, the real value in his essay does not lie in its assertion of the right of our "passional" or "willing nature" to believe, but in its emphasis upon the "forced" and "momentous" character of the decision to believe or not to believe and in its criticism of the rationalistic dogma that we have no right to believe what we cannot prove with certainty.

Faith as Ultimate Concern: Tillich

Perhaps the most influential recent analysis of faith is that of Paul Tillich in his *Dynamics of Faith*. Tillich begins with a *formal* definition of faith in the generic sense. "Faith is the state of being ultimately concerned." [19] Although man as a living and spiritual being is concerned with many things, each man also has an *ultimate concern* which demands that all other concerns be subordinated to it. As such, it demands "total surrender" and promises "total fulfillment." [20] This view of faith is obviously an existential one, since it emphasizes commitment of the individual to the object of his ultimate concern as a

[17] Hick, John: *Faith and Knowledge,* Ithaca, N.Y., Cornell University Press, 1957, p. 42.
[18] *Ibid.,* p. 44.
[19] Tillich, Paul: *Dynamics of Faith,* New York, Harper and Bros., 1956, p. 1.
[20] *Ibid.,* p. 1.

source of meaning for his existence. In this sense, everyone may be thought to have a faith. But a person's real faith may be different from his professed faith. For example, he may profess the Jewish or Christian faith, but his real faith may be in his race (the white supremacist) or in power (Napoleon or Hitler) or in money as a symbol of success (the "robber baron").

Faith is an act of the *total personality* which arises in the center of the self and includes all its elements, non-rational and unconscious as well as rational and conscious.[21] Hence, one-sided, partial views are "distortions" of it. For example, to define it exclusively in terms of intellectual assent to the object of faith is an "intellectualistic distortion." To assert that an act of will is necessary to make up for lack of sufficient evidence is a "voluntaristic distortion," [22] for "No command to believe and no will to believe can create faith." [23] Finally, the view of it as "a matter of merely subjective emotions, without a content to be known and a demand to be obeyed" is an "emotionalistic distortion" of it.[24]

The *source* of faith for Tillich is an awareness of the finite self that it belongs to the infinite, the unconditional, the absolute.[25] In this experience of the ultimate, the ordinary subject-object distinction, in which the object stands over against the subject, disappears. The act of faith arises in this experience, in which the finite self is "grasped by and turned to the infinite." [26] Insofar as faith is this immediate awareness of the infinite and ultimate, it is *certain*. But insofar as a "concrete content" or nature is ascribed to the infinite and ultimate, it is *uncertain* and the acceptance of it involves a risk. Hence, doubt is a necessary element of faith,[27] for any finite thing in which the unconditional has manifested itself and which is therefore used as a symbol to express the object of ultimate concern is inadequate, since that object transcends all finite things. Therefore, creeds should not be regarded as infallible, because "their function is to point to the ultimate which is beyond all of them." [28]

What is the relation of faith to *knowledge?* It is not "an act of knowledge that has a low degree of evidence" and is only "more or less probable." [29] Knowledge of the world is a matter of inquiry, not

[21] *Ibid.*, p. 1.
[22] *Ibid.*, p. 37.
[23] *Ibid.*, p. 39.
[24] *Ibid.*
[25] *Ibid.*, p. 9.
[26] *Ibid.*, p. 11.
[27] *Ibid.*, p. 18.
[28] *Ibid.*, p. 29.
[29] *Ibid.*, p. 31.

of faith, and the certitude of faith is quite different from that provided by knowledge. We have complete certitude only in the case of sense perception and logical or mathematical propositions, and we have knowledge with a higher or lower degree of probability in natural science and history.[30] Faith is unlike both of these kinds of knowledge. Its certitude is existential, since the whole existence of a person is based upon it.

However, this does not mean that there is no *truth* in faith. The intellect, along with other functions of the self, is involved in it. But faith does not give us "knowledge of the world"; it offers us "truth" concerning a "dimension of reality" of a higher order. Therefore, there is no conflict between faith and reason. For reason has an immediate awareness of the presence of the infinite and ultimate, as we have seen, and hence is involved in faith. "Reason is the precondition of faith; faith is the act in which reason reaches ecstatically beyond itself." For reason is aware of its own finitude and thus rises above it.[31] Hence, the ecstatic experience of an ultimate concern fulfills rather than denies reason.

Since the truth of faith grasped by "ecstatic reason" gives us certitude concerning the infinite rather than "information" about the finite, it does not conflict with *scientific truth*. Science describes the structures and relations of the world in quantitative terms, verifying its hypotheses by experiment.[32] Hence, scientific truth does not belong to the same dimension of meaning as the truth of faith, and as long as science is content to be science and religion to be religion there can be no conflict.[33] The conflict that arose between Christian orthodoxy and the theory of evolution was not a struggle between science and faith but between a philosophical interpretation of the evolutionary theory which denied the qualitative difference between man and animal and a religious interpretation of the Biblical myth of creation as a scientific description of the origin of species.[34]

Similarly, *historical truth* is factual truth about the origins and relations of events, while faith interprets the meaning of facts from the point of view of an ultimate concern.[35] For this reason, faith cannot "guarantee" the factual truth of any historical assertion in the Bible. This must be decided in each case by historical research. Faith can affirm that something of ultimate concern has happened in history

[30] *Ibid.*, pp. 33, 34.
[31] *Ibid.*, p. 76.
[32] *Ibid.*, p. 81.
[33] *Ibid.*, pp. 81, 82.
[34] *Ibid.*, p. 83.
[35] *Ibid.*, p. 86.

which has become the foundation of a faith, e.g., the Mosaic law for Jews, Jesus as the Christ for Christians, and Mohammed as the Prophet for Muslims. "But faith cannot ascertain the historical conditions which made it possible for these men to become matters of ultimate concern for large sections of humanity." [36] From this Tillich draws an important conclusion concerning the relation of faith to historical truth: "The truth of faith cannot be made dependent on the historical truth of the stories and legends in which faith has expressed itself," and therefore faith "cannot be shaken by historical research even if its results are critical of the traditions in which the event is reported." [37]

A critical evaluation of Tillich's conception of faith and its relation to reason must start with his *formal definition* of faith as "the state of being ultimately concerned." This definition, as we have said, is an existential one which emphasizes the individual's commitment to and expectation of fulfillment from the object of his faith. Its strength lies in its recognition that faith is more than an intellectual assent or an emotion; it involves a surrender to the object of ultimate concern as a source of meaning for existence. Its weakness is its emphasis upon the *subjective aspect* of faith, for it focuses primarily upon the state of the subject rather than the nature of the object of faith. Moreover, Tillich's concentration in this formal definition upon what religious faith has in common with other forms of faith such as nationalism and truth does not express what is distinctive of it. The crucial question is whether the faith of a person whose object of ultimate concern is some finite reality such as his nation or some value such as truth is not so radically different from the faith of persons whose ultimate concern is a transcendent God that it is misleading to use the same term for both. One's nation is finite, and truth is a human value. But God, to the theist, is neither a finite reality nor a human value; He is the ultimate ground of all finite realities and values who transcends them all. Of course, Tillich recognizes that faith in anything finite is "idolatrous," but his definition of faith in generic terms tends to blur the distinction between such a faith and true religious faith.

In the second place, Tillich is correct in his assertion that faith is a state or act of the total personality, and his criticism of the distortions of it by one-sided views is valuable because such views have prevented many people from developing a fully mature religion. The question we would raise about this is whether he does not carry his criticism of the "intellectualistic distortion" too far in denying that faith is a kind of knowledge. As we have indicated, he holds that there is a "truth of faith" concerning another dimension of reality than the

[36] *Ibid.,* p. 88.
[37] *Ibid.,* p. 89.

finite world described by science and history. But Tillich asserts that the source of this "truth of faith" is an immediate awareness of the ultimate and seems to think that it is not supported by objective evidence of any kind. Natural theology can raise the "question" about God but can give no "answer" to it. The answer arises from the existential need for God to give the individual courage to overcome the threat of non-being.[38] Thus, Tillich seems to base the truth of faith upon an "ecstatic" experience of the infinite combined with an existential demand for a "ground of being" which can give man the "courage to be." This lays faith open to the charge that it is only a product of intuition, on the one hand, and wishful thinking, on the other. Faith must be supported by evidence acknowledged by reason if it is to meet this charge.

Finally, Tillich's view that faith is not contrary to reason or in conflict with scientific and historical truth is fully justified. Conflict arises only when scientists or philosophers develop a naturalistic view of the world based on the assumption that science is the sole source of truth, or when religious people regard statements in scriptures as answers to scientific and historical questions. However, the relation of the "truth of faith" to "historical truth" is subtle and Tillich's view of this is open to serious criticism. He is clearly justified in his assertion that historical facts must be determined not by faith but by historical inquiry, but this does not imply that "faith cannot be shaken by historical research even if its results are critical of the traditions in which the event is reported." [39] The statement is true insofar as it refers to legendary and mythological elements in the Biblical narratives. But surely the Jewish faith *would* be "shaken" if it should be proved by historical research that there is no basis for the belief that God chose Israel and entered into a covenant with them. And the Christian faith *would* be "shaken" if historians should prove that Jesus never existed or that he was not the kind of man who is described in the Gospels. Thus, whatever may be thought of Tillich's formal definition of faith in the generic sense, his conception of the relation of "truths of faith" to "historical truth" does not adequately describe the faith of Judaism and Christianity. For both are historical religions in which faith is deeply rooted in historical events, although the Biblical accounts of these events obviously include legendary and mythical elements.

---

[38] Tillich, Paul: *Systematic Theology,* Chicago, University of Chicago Press, 1951, Vol. I., pp. 192–198; 209, 210.

[39] Tillich, P.: *Dynamics of Faith,* p. 89.

Faith as Apprehension and Interpretation

What is the source of faith as it is understood in Western theism? Orthodox Catholics and Protestants have often replied that it arises from the acceptance of *authority*. Orthodox Catholics have asserted that beliefs concerning the object of faith are accepted by the believer on the authority of the testimony of prophets and apostles in the Scriptures, as formulated by the Church. Orthodox Protestants have maintained that the Scriptures are the sole authority in matters of faith. There is an important element of truth in this orthodox view. Man is a social animal and his religious beliefs and practices are normally developed in childhood and youth under the influence of his family and religious community. As he learns the use of language, the mastery of skills, and the rules of conduct from others, so he learns religious attitudes and beliefs from others. He is taught to pray, to worship with others, to understand the Scriptures, and to act in accordance with the way of life approved by his family and religious community.

Moreover, it is as desirable as it is natural that the religious faith of the individual should *begin* with participation in the life of a religious community, since it is only in this way that he can enter into the religious heritage of the race in general or his society in particular. Without such participation, religious experience may not become a reality or religious beliefs assume meaning for a person. Under the influence of modern rationalism and individualism, this is often overlooked. But it is as unrealistic to suppose that an individual can discover worthy religious beliefs without instruction in the religious beliefs attained in the past as to expect him to become a physicist without instruction by others in the methods and conclusions of physics. Thus, faith normally arises and develops in the individual through his acceptance of the tradition of a religious community and its scriptures which mediate traditional beliefs and practices to him. Even religiously creative men such as the Hebrew prophets and Jesus have begun by accepting and being nourished by the religious tradition of their community.

But if we inquire concerning the *original source* of the faith of the religious community itself, we must give a different answer. For the founder or founders of a religious community whose tradition is later accepted by its members have not derived what is distinctive in their faith from the authority of others but from their own religious experience. Hence, the *ultimate source* of faith is not authority but *religious experience*. Furthermore, the *development* of religious belief has come about largely through the religious experience of creative individuals who are responsive to those elements in a religious tradition which are of permanent value. In addition, while it is true that the faith of the individual normally begins with his acceptance of the witness of others, his *personal commitment* to it depends upon his finding it to be consistent with his own experience. For it will not continue to commend itself to him unless its own inherent truth commands his assent by being in accord with his experience.

It is not necessary to describe in detail the religious experience which gives rise to faith, as we have analyzed it in an earlier chapter[40] and are here concerned only with the relation of faith to it. Faith arises out of a concrete religious experience in which there is an apprehension of the divine and an interpretation of its nature or activity. First, then, faith is *apprehension* of the divine as present in man's experience. It is not an arbitrary and groundless product of wishful thinking, as Feuerbach and Freud have contended. Rather, it is awakened in the self when it experiences the presence and power of a transcendent Being in and through some finite object, event, or person. Thus, the divine or holy is normally mediated through the finite, although the mystic claims that his experience of the divine is immediate. Men may encounter Him not apart from but along with finite things or persons and temporal events. As we have seen, the beliefs about Him in each religion are deeply affected by the nature of the things mediating His presence.[41] As Tillich expresses it, men have been "grasped" by the infinite, the ultimate, the holy through finite realities; and their faith is a response to that which has "grasped" them.

Thus, faith begins with an *apprehension* or experience of the infinite as mediated by finite things and events of nature and, in the case of Western theism, history. But this apprehension is not merely a blind and dumb feeling, passively experienced and without content; it involves an *interpretation* of the nature of the divine and its relation to the world and man, an interpretation which comes to be expressed in specific beliefs about it. At this point, Rudolf Otto's phenomenological analysis of "the Holy" has been misunderstood and has consequently led to misunderstanding. As we have noted,[42] Otto described "the Holy" as containing both a non-rational element, the "numinous," and a rational and ethical element. However, since he accorded a prominent place in his analysis of "the Holy" to the numinous and incomprehensible aspect, his influence has led some philosophers to view faith as a vague feeling of a mystical kind which is without content. Against

[40] Ch. 3.
[41] Ch. 3.
[42] Ch. 2.

this view we would agree with Aquinas that faith is usually expressed in definite beliefs which are affirmed as true. However, we would disagree with his view that these beliefs were revealed by God in propositional form. Rather, we would contend that they were interpretations by prophetic minds of God's nature and purposes as revealed in the events of history and the order of nature.[43]

These interpretations of the divine were products of *insight and creative imagination* based upon experience and reflection. A striking example is the call of Isaiah in the temple at the beginning of his prophetic ministry. Clearly, it was preceded and prepared for by the prophet's experience of sin and guilt in himself and his people and his insight into their incompatibility with God's holiness. Seeing a vision of the Lord "sitting upon a throne, high and lifted up" and with seraphim above Him, symbols of the utter transcendence of God, he hears the seraphim praising God in His glory. In the presence of the holiness of God, his consciousness of his own uncleanness and that of his people is deepened and he cries, "Woe is me!" One of the seraphim purifies his lips by a burning coal from the altar, a symbol of God's forgiveness. Then he becomes conscious of a call from God to speak to the people as a prophet and replies, "Here am I! Send me." [44] In this case, the manifestation of God comes in a vision rich with visual and auditory images, and the experience of forgiveness is expressed in a symbolic act of purification. Thus, the creative imagination of the prophet interpreted his insight into the gulf between God's holiness and Israel's sin in concrete and pictorial terms.

Those who regard imagination as nothing but an irrational play of fancy unrelated to reality and uncontrolled by reason may find this view of the interpretation of a religious apprehension difficult to accept. Under the influence of a rationalism which disparages imagination, they are likely to consider all insights expressed in imaginative terms as merely subjective and arbitrary.[45] But this is to overlook the distinction between "fancy," which associates ideas and images arbitrarily, and "creative imagination," which combines them to express truths hidden from the casual eye but apprehended by intuition. Among others, Wordsworth and Coleridge recognized that imagination in this sense is not irrational but is a function of reason which is essential for the expression of spiritual truth.[46] Plato used myths constructed by the creative imagination to express religious and meta-

---

[43] Temple, *op. cit.*, p. 314.

[44] Isaiah 6:1–8.

[45] Willey, Basil: *The Seventeenth Century Background,* London, Chatto and Windus, 1942.

[46] Wordsworth, William: *The Prelude,* Book 14.

physical intuitions which could not be formulated precisely in concepts or demonstrated by reason. The myth of creation with which the Book of Genesis begins is the imaginative expression of a profound religious insight. And the parables of Jesus such as the Prodigal Son present his interpretation of God and man in vivid and striking form. Hence, to say that faith involves an interpretation of encounters with God by creative imagination is not to say that it is unrelated to reality and indifferent to truth. Indeed, if "reason" is understood in a broad sense as including the intuitive apprehension of invisible spiritual realities and the expression of them in suitable words and images, we can say that interpretation of these realities by creative imagination is a work of reason at its highest level.

To say that faith involves an interpretation of a religious apprehension or insight by the creative imagination is not to deny that it is a response to a *revelation* from God, as believers have thought. We have pointed out that revelation should not be opposed to the religious experience of men, as if the former has come from God but the latter is merely a subjective human event with which God has had nothing to do.[47] If God is conceived as a Being who is immanent everywhere in His creation and actively concerned with the salvation of men, an apprehension of Him in religious experience may be a *response* to His presence and activity in that experience. Similarly, the interpretation by a prophetic mind of such an apprehension may be a response to God revealing Himself through that apprehension. Of course, the method employed by the philosopher of religion, as we have described it, does not permit him to determine whether a revelation in fact occurred in a particular situation, e.g., when Isaiah saw his vision in the temple. If a revelation is to be accepted, it must be accepted by faith.

Faith as Trust and Obedience

Up to this point we have been dealing primarily with that aspect of faith which is called "belief," *fides,* rather than with that which is called "trust," *fiducia.* We have considered belief first because it is logically presupposed by trust. Although it is possible to believe in the existence of God without trusting Him, it is impossible to trust Him without at least believing that He exists and that His attitude towards man is merciful and gracious. However, the fact that belief *in* God presupposes belief *that* He exists does not mean that the latter is the primary element, while trust is only a secondary element, in faith. The assumption that it is the primary element is a natural one for philos-

[47] Ch. 3

ophers, since they are concerned above all with the claim of religious belief to truth and with its relation to truths derived from other sources. But it cannot be emphasized too strongly that a vital and mature faith must combine clear belief with whole-hearted trust.

The distinction between "belief" and "trust" is similar to that made by philosophers between "belief-that" and "belief-in." H. H. Price has recently discussed at length the question whether in all cases "belief-in" a thing or person can be "reduced" to a "belief-that" it or he exists and has certain properties. Obviously, certain "factual" kinds of "belief-in" such as belief in fairies (or in King Arthur) *can* be reduced to "belief-that" they exist (or he existed). Also, certain "evaluative" kinds of "belief-in" can be reduced to "belief-that" a certain proposition is true, provided that "suitable value concepts" are introduced into the proposition believed. For example, my "belief-in" my doctor is reducible to "I believe that my doctor is *good at* curing diseases (or a specific disease) and that it is a *good thing* he is." But Price maintains that another kind of evaluative "belief-in" involves not only approving a person because he is "good at" something and it is a "good thing" he is, but also "trusting" him. Since "trusting" is not merely a cognitive but an "affective" attitude and hence has a "warmth" or "heart-felt" character, "belief-in" in these cases cannot be reduced to "belief-that" a proposition is true. Belief in God, like belief in a friend, is clearly an attitude of this kind. Moreover, at its best it is disinterested as well as interested, i.e., one trusts God not only for the benefits He has in His mercy and grace bestowed on oneself or on other men but also for His own sake.[48]

Their understanding of the importance of *trust* is one of the greatest contributions of Judaism and Christianity. In trust the finite self acknowledges its absolute dependence upon God for its "creation, preservation, and all the blessings of this life." This acknowledgement is based upon an awareness of the weakness and insufficiency of the finite self and of its need for God's care and help. It is accompanied by gratitude for God's goodness and grace toward the self in the past and by a firm reliance upon Him for care and assistance in the future. Trust in God also arises from men's consciousness of sin and their need for forgiveness. Trust in God's forgiveness on the condition of man's repentance and return to Him has an important place in the teaching of the Hebrew prophets. Indeed, one can say that from beginning to end the religion of the Bible is based upon trust in God's love and mercy toward weak and sinful men.

From trust in God finite and imperfect man draws strength in

[48] Price, H. H.: "Belief in and Belief That," in *Religious Studies*, Cambridge, Cambridge University Press, 1966, Vol. I, pp. 5–27.

weakness, comfort in sorrow, fortitude in adversity, and moral power for the struggle against sin. It is not strange, therefore, that many theists have regarded it as the most essential element in faith. Nevertheless, unless it is based upon clearly defined beliefs and issues in commitment of the will, it can result in an emotional distortion of faith and an excessive concern for the subjective state of the believer. He can become so preoccupied with the state of his own feelings and with the anxious examination of his own spiritual condition as to center his attention upon himself rather than God. Also, an exclusive emphasis upon trust can lead to a kind of passivity which paralyzes moral striving. In ways like these, when trust becomes divorced from the intellectual and volitional aspects of faith, it produces subjectivism and quietism.

It is essential, therefore, that trust should be grounded in belief and issue in *commitment* to God and *obedience* to His will in moral conduct. This volitional aspect of faith has been stressed above all in Judaism. Ever since the Hebrew prophets such as Isaiah and Micah insisted that belief in God is hollow and insincere if it manifests itself only in ritual observances and neglects deeds of justice and mercy, obedience to the will of God has been regarded as essential. Contemporary Jewish thinkers such as Abraham Heschel have rightly insisted upon the fact that Judaism requires not only external conformity to the Law, "religious behaviorism," but also the spirit of sincere faith and love.[49] But one of the most distinctive things about Judaism, as Heschel also emphasizes, is that it has been a religion not of "dogmas" but of "deeds." [50] In Christianity also obedience to the will of God, as expressed especially in the law of love, has always been central. Although St. Paul emphasizes faith in God's grace, he also asserts that "love is the fulfilling of the law";[51] and while Luther stressed trust, Calvin and the Puritans demanded strict obedience to God's will as expressed in the commandments.

In the Western religious tradition of ethical monotheism, therefore, the volitional aspect of faith has always been prominent. Indeed, serious religious persons with practical minds have often virtually identified religion with moral conduct, and it has been necessary at times for religious thinkers such as Schleiermacher and Otto to protest against moralism in order to restore feeling to its rightful place.

But despite dangers such as these, commitment and obedience are absolutely essential to a vital faith. According to Western theism, a

[49] Heschel, A.: *God in Search of Man*, New York, Farrar, Straus and Cudahy, 1955, ch. 32.

[50] *Ibid.*

[51] Romans 13:10.

faith which does not lead to the transformation of life is a hollow shell. For God has created man as a social being, has endowed him with a sense of responsibility for others, and has called him to cooperate with Himself in fulfilling His purpose for history. He has revealed Himself to man not to give him theoretical knowledge which will satisfy his curiosity, but to show him the way in which he must walk if he is to realize God's purpose for him and fulfill his destiny. Hence, a faith that does not lead him to commit himself to God, to obey His will, and to remain faithful and steadfast when threatened by trials and dangers is not true faith.[52]

Faith and Knowledge

Our view that faith arises from men's apprehension or insight into God's nature and purpose and their interpretation of it by creative imagination as revealed truth raises the question whether faith gives us *knowledge* and, if so, what kind of knowledge it is. There can be no doubt that believers have thought that knowledge has come to them through divine revelation mediated through the religious experience of prophets and apostles. They have also been convinced that this knowledge is of a *different kind* and at a *higher level* than the knowledge men have acquired through their senses and their reason. They have usually been willing to admit, with Aquinas, that it is imperfect knowledge because men cannot fully comprehend its meaning or demonstrate its truth. Hence, they have seen in it, as he did, only a foretaste of the vision of God which is to come and to which they look forward with hope. But they have believed that, despite its imperfection, it is the most important knowledge men possess because its object is God, the supreme Reality and highest Truth.

However, theists have not agreed among themselves as to the *nature* of this knowledge and its *relation* to other kinds of knowledge. As we have indicated, Aquinas held that it consisted of a number of truths which had been revealed by God in the form of propositions and had then been formulated with finality by the Church. This view is now defended by few religious thinkers because the painstaking work of Biblical criticism has shown that God did *not* reveal Himself through propositions communicated to the passive minds of prophets and apostles and recorded without error by them. Also, the careful work that has recently been done on religious language has made it clear that men's apprehension of the transcendent and infinite God of theism does not enable them to comprehend Him fully and express His nature

[52] See the Book of Daniel and the description in the Letter to the Hebrews, ch. 11, of the "men of old" who "received divine approval" because of their faith.

clearly in propositions, so that many of the most fundamental truths about Him have been and must be expressed in myth, analogy, and symbol.

Tillich goes still further in rejecting the view that the knowledge men receive through faith consists of propositional truths. Faith, he says, does not give us knowledge in the sense of information about matters of fact, and in this respect it differs completely from science and history which describe patterns of order in nature and sequences of events in history. We would fully agree with this, since the divine Being with whom the truths of faith are mainly concerned is quite different from the objects of ordinary knowledge. However, Tillich also maintains that we can make no "literal" statement about the unconditioned Being except that it is "Being-itself" and every other statement about it is symbolic and must be asserted and negated at the same time.[53] This, together with some of his statements about the personal symbols of theism,[54] suggests that for Tillich faith in the Biblical revelation does not give us any *definite* knowledge of God. Faith seems to be an intuitive awareness of the *reality* of an infinite, unconditioned Ground of all finite being,[55] but provides us with no specific knowledge of its *nature* which can be affirmed with confidence.

Thus, neither Aquinas' view that faith provides us with clearly defined propositional truths nor Tillich's view that it gives us an awareness of an unconditioned Reality which can be expressed but not definitely known through the symbols of theism is satisfactory. But a third view is possible, one which claims less for the knowledge derived from faith than that of Aquinas but more for it than that of Tillich. It asserts that faith affirms as true certain insights of prophetic minds into the nature and purpose of God and His relation to man, that these insights can be stated although imperfectly in propositions, but that their meaning and implications have never been and can never be fully comprehended and expressed in human language. It also asserts that these insights provide the basis for a theistic philosophy which is more adequate than other philosophies. It does not claim that we can have certain knowledge that these insights and the philosophical interpretation of the world based upon them are true, but it maintains that belief in them is reasonable because they are not only confirmed by religious experience but also supported by evidence drawn from other kinds of experience.

It has been one of the chief aims of this book to show that a critical examination of certain of these insights of faith, i.e., those concerning

---

[53] *Systematic Theology,* Vol. I, p. 235; pp. 238, 239.
[54] *Ibid.* and *The Courage to Be,* pp. 178–190.
[55] *Dynamics of Faith.*

the existence and nature of God, the problem of evil, the nature of man, and the relation of his freedom to the divine grace, strongly supports the belief that they are true. We have not attempted to prove that they were in fact revealed by God, as Western theists have generally assumed. As we have said, the method employed by the philosopher of religion is not capable of determining whether or not they were revealed. Our aim has been a more limited one, to subject these insights to critical examination to see whether they can be shown to be in accord with experience and reason. If one affirms that they originated in a special revelation by God to men in the past, it must be by an act of faith.

But since the truths that faith affirms cannot be known with certainty, faith will involve a *venture* and a *risk*. It will even require from the believer a willingness to confront doubt and difficulties such as the pervasiveness of evil and to maintain his faith, like Job, in spite of them. From this uncertainty and the element of venture involved in it, it is clear that faith "goes beyond" reason. Hence, the philosopher of religion cannot by his method determine whether or not faith is justified. However, two things may be said about this, one negative and one positive. The first is that the assumption made by many modern philosophers that faith is irrational and hence that it is unworthy of rational men to commit themselves to it is *not* justified. In every sphere of human interest and activity, men have always been impelled to venture beyond the realm of certain knowledge. To refuse to do so would put an end to human discovery and creativity. This is as true of science and philosophy[56] as it is of religion. The second thing is that to "go beyond" reason is not the same as to "go against" reason. We have maintained that the assertion by Kierkegaard that faith is "contrary to understanding" is false. We have also tried to show that, while reason cannot demonstrate that the beliefs of Western theism were revealed by God, the most fundamental ones concerning God and man are not irrational but can be strongly supported by experience and reason. In this way, reason may point the way towards truths of faith which go beyond it but which are in harmony with beliefs it can show to be reasonable.

This view of faith's relation to knowledge agrees with that of John Hick in maintaining that faith in the sense of belief is an interpretation of an apprehension of God in religious experience. But it disagrees with his view that "we neither require nor can conceive any

---

[56] A striking example in philosophy is Kant who argued in the *Critique of Practical Reason* that the unconditional demands of the moral law require man to "postulate" God, freedom, and immortality, although the theoretical reason cannot demonstrate them.

further validation of its reality." However, faith is not certainty.[57] This is why faith longs for a more perfect knowledge and looks forward to it with hope. Its attitude, at least for the theist aware of the transcendence of God and the finitude of man's reason, is that of St. Paul. "For our knowledge is imperfect and our prophecy is imperfect; but when the perfect comes, the imperfect will pass away. . . . For now we see in a mirror dimly, but then face to face. Now I know in part; then I shall understand fully, even as I have been fully understood." [58]

Fruits of Faith

We have argued that a mature and vital faith in the theistic sense of the term combines belief, trust, and commitment and thus involves the whole self: reason, emotion, and will. When all three of these aspects are present in balance and in tension with each other, faith provides not only a firm foundation for the religious life but also a power capable of *transforming* the whole of life. We would conclude by indicating briefly some of the benefits or fruits it can bestow.

The first and most obvious is its *unification* of the personality. As psychologists of personality such as Gordon Allport[59] and psychoanalysts such as Erich Fromm[60] have shown, it is impossible for a person without faith to integrate his interests in a consistent pattern. Since faith is a state or attitude of the whole person, it can discipline the energies of the body, sublimate and fulfill the instincts, and unite both with the conscious purposes of the mind.[61] Above all, it can give direction to all the activities of a person by relating them to his dominant interest or object of ultimate concern.

Closely related to this is the capacity of faith to bestow *meaning* on life. The emptiness and meaninglessness which are so characteristic of many persons in our time and which have been described so vividly by T. S. Eliot in *The Waste Land,* are due in large part to a lack of the unity and sense of direction which faith provided for men of a less skeptical age. We have pointed out that the feeling of homelessness characteristic of man in our time has come upon him partly because he has lost the belief of medieval and early modern man that he had a place of dignity in the world as a rational being and one made in the image of God. He has also lost the conviction that there are

[57] Hick, John: *op. cit.,* p. 132.
[58] I Corinthians 13:9, 12.
[59] Allport, G.: *The Individual and His Religion,* New York, Macmillan, 1950.
[60] Fromm, E.: *Man for Himself,* New York, Rinehart, 1947.
[61] Tillich, Paul: *Dynamics of Faith,* pp. 106, 107.

objective values which are worthy of his devotion and that his life has
a purpose that transcends his limited personal interests and is connected with the wider purposes of God for mankind. It is not strange,
therefore, that he suffers from a sense of meaninglessness which often
drives him to despair, for a life without dignity, values, and purpose is
inevitably a life without meaning. Whether this meaninglessness expresses itself in the dull resignation of those who can see no connection
between one experience and another[62] or the defiant rebellion of
atheistic existentialists against the "absurdity" of life[63] is of secondary
importance, for both result from the same cause. Faith is the remedy
for both, a faith in man's worth as a creature made in the image of
God and in the possibility of fulfillment through devotion to values
and purposes that have their source in God's will.

Again, faith can provide a powerful motive and a wider context for
creative morality. It is often said that the moral problem is not that
men do not know what they ought to do, but that they lack the will
to do it. There is much truth in this because self-love corrupts man's
desires by centering them in himself. Faith in God's love and mercy
towards man, as mediated through the love of other men, can awaken
a response of gratitude and love towards Him which can overcome
man's self-love and open him to the needs of his neighbors. At the
same time, it can provide him with a higher motive for doing his duty
than desire for reward or fear of punishment, or natural sympathy and
affection for others, or respect for the moral law. For faith in the
theistic sense views morality as far more than a means to attain personal happiness, or an expression of good will, or obedience to impersonal moral laws. Rather, moral imperatives have their source in
God's love for His children and His will that they should love one
another and serve one another's needs.[64] Thus, while faith does not
determine our duties for us but leaves us free to determine them by
our own intelligence in situations as they arise, it puts them in a wider
context. For it enables us to see them as ways of serving God's purposes
as well as meeting the claims of other men upon us.

Moreover, faith is a source of *courage*. Tillich has pointed out that
contemporary man is a prey to anxiety because he is threatened by
death, sin, guilt and, above all, a sense of meaninglessness.[65] Although
he attempts to escape from this anxiety in many ways, the only ade-

---

[62] Eliot, T. S.: *The Waste Land*, lines 301, 302:
> "I can connect
> Nothing with nothing"

[63] Camus, Albert: *The Myth of Sisyphus*.
[64] Cf. ch. 6.
[65] Tillich, P.: *The Courage to Be*, ch. 2.

quate answer to it is the courage to accept it as an inevitable aspect of finite human existence. This courage can arise even from the depths of despair if faith in God as the ground of being is present, for only God can overcome the threat of non-being in all its forms.[66] Theistic faith, which includes both belief in the power of God and trust in His love and care, is a source of courage which is stronger than Stoic resignation or existentialist defiance of the absurdity of existence.

Finally, faith is the ground of *hope* that endures. The connection of hope with faith is not an accidental but an essential one. Of course, men entertain many hopes that are vain and foolish because they arise from nothing deeper than natural desire or wishful thinking and have no foundation or support in ultimate reality.[67] But when hope springs from belief in God's power and trust in His love and care, man can look forward with confidence to the fulfillment of God's purpose for him here or hereafter, although he cannot know when or how it will be fulfilled. Thus, hope which is rooted and grounded in faith can endure throughout life, surviving every disappointment of worldly hopes.

[66] *Ibid.*, p. 55.
[67] Marcel, Gabriel: *Homo Viator*, New York, Harper and Row, 1965.

Index

Absurdity, 123, 341–5
Agnosticism, 180–3, 190, 197, 347
Alexander, Samuel, 266
Allport, G., 361
Analogy (analogical), 26–7, in metaphysics; 104, 148, 182–3, 189–94, of proportion; of proportionality, 189–91; 213, 263, 359 cf. Aquinas
Analysis, Linguistic, 14, 24–5, 191, 309, 359 cf. Philosophy
Anselm, and ontological argument, 141–5, passim; 210
Anthropocentrism, 242
Anthropomorphism, 188, 189, 213
Anxiety, 123, 127, 133, 152, 208, 362
Apprehension, and faith, 353–4; of God, 138
Aquinas, Thomas, Saint, 10, 16, 104, 239, affirmative theology, 185–92; analogy, doctrine, 189–94; cosmological argument, 145–7; faith and reason, 341–3, 354, 358–9; "five proofs," 145; on God's attributes: 188–93, goodness, 182, knowledge, 193, perfection, 195, 205, intelligence, 153, 193; negative theology, 187–9; soul and body, 270; soul as substance, 283; teleological argument, 151–5, passim cf. Analogy, God
Aristotle, 15, 34, 153; and soul, 269–70, 283, 286; and "unmoved mover," 194, 286

Atheism, xvi, 221, 347
Augustine, Saint, on conversion, 72, 127; freedom, 295; grace, salvation and election, 325–7, 335; prevenient, 336; primacy of will, 286; soul and body, 270; theodicy, his, 226–228 cf. Evil, Freedom, Grace
Authority, 55, 56, 353
Ayer, A. J., 14, 17–8, 132

Bhagavadgita, 70
Barbour, Ian, 93, n. 1
Barth, Karl, on natural theology, 182–3; revelation and religious experience, 67; Schleiermacher, 31
Behaviorism, philosophical (Ryle), 275–81; psychological, 297, 298–9; "religious," 358
Being, Being Itself, 47, 207–9 (Tillich); being-unto-death, 133; God as: ground of, 51, 128, 209, necessary, 145–52, passim, 171, 184, 187, personal and moral, 124, 128, 212–5, spiritual, 211–2; and nonbeing, 123–7; power of, 126
Belief, crisis of, xvi, xvii; from religious intuition, 23, 175, 178–9, 257, 340–55, 356, 360–3
"Belief-in," "belief-that," 356
Belief-full realism, 356
Berdyaev, N., 251–2, 315
Bergson, H., 60, 106, 305
Berthold, F., 127